The
EVOLUTIONARY
OUTRIDER

Recent Titles in
Praeger Studies on the 21st Century

The
EVOLUTIONARY
OUTRIDER

The Impact of the
Human Agent on Evolution

Essays honouring Ervin Laszlo

Edited by David Loye

Praeger Studies on the 21st Century

Westport, Connecticut

Published in the United States and Canada by Praeger Publishers,
88 Post Road West, Westport, CT 06881.
An imprint of Greenwood Publishing Group, Inc.

Printed in the United States of America

♾™

The paper used in this book complies with the
Permanent Paper Standard issued by the National
Information Standards Organization (Z39.48–1984).

10 9 8 7 6 5 4 3 2 1

English language edition, except the United States and Canada,
published by Adamantine Press Limited, Richmond Bridge House,
417-419 Richmond Road, Twickenham TW1 2EX, England.

First published in 1998

Library of Congress Cataloging-in-Publication Data

Laszlo, Ervin, 1932–
    The evolutionary outrider : the impact of the human agent on
evolution : essays honouring Ervin Laszlo / edited by David Loye.
        p.   cm.—(Praeger studies on the 21st century, ISSN
1070–1850)
    Includes bibliographical references and index.
    ISBN 0–275–96408–6 (alk. paper)—ISBN 0–275–96409–4 (pbk. :
alk. paper)
    1. Evolution—Philosophy.   2. Science—Philosophy.   3. Evolution
(Biology)—Philosophy.   4. Laszlo, Ervin, 1932–   .   5. General
Evolution Research Group.   I. Loye, David.   II. Series.
Q175.32.E85L39   1998
304.2—dc21   98–18868

Library of Congress Catalog Card Number: 98–18868

ISBN: 0–275–96408–6 Cloth
        0–275–96409–4 Paperback

A great change in our stewardship of the Earth and the life on it is required, if vast human misery is to be avoided and our global home on this planet is not to be irretrievably mutilated ... A new ethic is required [to] motivate a great movement, convincing reluctant leaders and reluctant governments and reluctant peoples themselves to effect the needed changes.

The Union of Concerned Scientists,
from a statement in 1993 signed by over 1,670 scientists,
104 of them Nobel laureates, from 71 countries of this Earth.

Planetary consciousness is the knowing as well as the feeling of the vital interdependence and essential oneness of humankind, and the conscious adoption of the ethics and the ethos that this entails. Its evolution is the new imperative of human survival on this planet. The 21st century shall be a century of planetary consciousness, or it shall not be at all.

Ervin Laszlo, from the Manifesto of the Club of Budapest, 1996.

On the Cover

Our cover is based on the visual configuration for the findings of a large sample study revealing what seems to be the thrust for human-impacted evolution. The "three-cornered-hat" design element is the data configuration for the three major clusters for attitudes and beliefs discovered by sociologist Paul H. Ray in his seven-year study of American values. Visually from left to right, the first two clusters orient to the status quo, the first for the conservative Traditionalists or Heart-landers, and the second or middle cluster for what Ray terms the Modernists. The third cluster is for the one in every four Americans, or 44 million, whom Ray terms the Cultural Creatives, who are more attuned to idealism, the future, and social action. The areas of overlap indicate where segments of the Traditionalists and Modernists share values with Cultural Creatives. Interest in these findings is mounting rapidly in the American political community and in the European political and economic community, with the same approach and methodology currently being applied by Ray and associates to studies in Europe (see Chapter 16).

Dedicated to the Members of the
General Evolution Research Group

Ralph Abraham, mathematician and chaos theorist, United States; Peter Allen, thermodynamicist, England; Robert Artigiani, historian, United States; Bela Banathy, systems scientist, United States; Singa Benko, Sweden; Thomas Bernold, management theorist, Switzerland; Gianlucca Bocchi, philosopher, Italy; Miriam Campanella, political scientist, Italy; Mauro Ceruti, evolutionary philosopher, Italy; Eric Chaisson, astrophysicist, United States; Allan Combs, psychologist, United States; John Corliss, biologist, United States; Vilmos Csanyi, biologist, Hungary; Riane Eisler, cultural historian and evolutionary theorist, United States; Duane Elgin, social scientist, United States; Sally Goerner, evolutionary systems theorist, United States; Susantha Goonatilake, information theorist, United States; Gyorgy Kampis, computer scientist, Hungary; Jurgen Kurths, physicist, Germany; Ervin Laszlo, systems philosopher, Italy; David Loye, social psychologist and moral systems theorist, United States; Pentti Malaska, management scientist, Finland; Edward Markarian, ecologist and philosopher, Russia; Ignazio Masulli, historian, Italy; Federico Mayor, General Director, UNESCO, France; Min Jiayin, evolutionary philosopher, China; Alfonso Montuori, systems scientist, United States; Mika Pantzar, management scientist, Finland; Karl Pribram, neuroscientist, United States; Ilya Prigogine, thermodynamicist, Belgium; Gerlind Rurik, interdisciplinary educator, Germany; Mária Sági, social psychologist, Italy; Stanley Salthe, biologist, United States; Peter Saunders, mathematical biologist, England; Jonathan Schull, psychologist, United States; Rudolf Treumann, physicist, Germany; Francisco Varela, biologist, France.

Contents

Contributors

Ralph Abraham, former professor of mathematics at the University of California, Santa Cruz, is a pioneer in the development of modern chaos theory. Active on the research frontier of dynamics in mathematics since 1960, he has taught at Berkeley, Columbia, and Princeton Universities, and has held visiting positions in Amsterdam, Paris, Warwick, Barcelona, and Basel. Abraham's books range from *Dynamics: The Geometry of Behavior* (with C.D. Shaw, in four volumes), to a wide-ranging survey of history and evolution *Chaos, Gaia, and Eros*, to *The WEB Empowerment Book* dealing with the nature and potential for human advancement offered by the World Wide Web. He is a co-founding member of the General Evolution Research Group.

Raymond Trevor Bradley is a pioneer in the application of brain research, physics, and modern consciousness research to the traditional concerns of the field of sociology. His book *Charisma and Social Structure: A Study of Love and Power, Wholeness and Transformation* moved beyond the classic study of Max Weber and current sociological studies to take the field into what are destined to be major areas for the sociology of the 21st century. A native of New Zealand, Bradley has taught at Columbia University, the University of Minnesota, the University of California at Santa Cruz, and Victoria University of Wellington, New Zealand. He is co-founder and director of the Institute for Whole Social Science in Carmel, California. Currently, with brain scientist Karl Pribram, he is exploring the implications of the work of Gabor, Piaget, Laszlo, and Pribram's holonomic brain theory for a new understanding of subcognitive as well as cognitive processes in goal-directed group dynamics.

Fritjof Capra is a physicist by training who over recent years has become not only quite possibly the world's best-known explicator of leading-edge science through his books and lectures worldwide, but also a significant activist in the cause of world betterment. His many books include *The Tao of Physics*, *The Turning Point*, *Uncommon Wisdom*, and most recently, *The Web of Life*, a major synthesis of the systems perspective in terms of new theories of complexity including dissipative structures, autopoiesis, chaos theory and the Gaia hypothesis. As an activist, Capra was the founder of the Elmwood Institute, for a number of years a focal point for leading-edge thinking in many fields. Currently, he is the Director of the Center for Ecoliteracy in Berkeley, California.

Mauro Ceruti is an evolutionary philosopher, a member of the General Evolution Research Group, and the Editor of *Pluriverso*, a new magazine of increasing influence in the current growth of interest in evolution and evolution theory in Italy and in European intellectual circles. Formerly a researcher and professor at the University of Geneva and the Center for the Transdisciplinary Study of Sociology, Anthropology, and Political Science in Paris, Ceruti is presently professor of epistemology at the University of Bergamo in Italy. He is the author of *Constraints and Possibilities: The Evolution of Knowledge and the Knowledge of Evolution* and the forthcoming *The Narrative Universe, Evolution Without Grounds,* and *Solidarity or Barbarism.*

Riane Eisler is a cultural historian best known as the author of *The Chalice and the Blade: Our History, Our Future,* a re-evaluation of 25,000 years of cultural evolution published in 15 languages. Eisler has taught at UCLA and Immaculate Heart College, is a fellow of the World Academy of Art and Science and the World Business Academy, a co-founder of the General Evolution Research Group and honorary member of the Club of Budapest. The cultural transformation theory developed by Eisler in *The Chalice and The Blade, Sacred Pleasure, The Partnership School,* and other publications is influential in fields ranging from sociology, psychology, education, and history to business, peace, women's, and economic development studies. A recent publication by scholars of the Chinese Academy of Social Sciences in Beijing, *The Chalice and the Blade in Chinese Culture,* corroborates for the evolution of Eastern culture the pattern Eisler identified as the interaction of the dominator and partnership models in Western cultural evolution. Dr Eisler was recently named in *Macrohistory and Macrohistorians* as one of 20 major macrohistorians (along with Vico, Hegel, Marx, Adam Smith, and Toynbee).

Hazel Henderson is an independent global futurist, author of *Building a Win–Win World, Paradigms in Progress, The Politics of the Solar Age,* and other books of a rare wit and insight into the foibles of world economics, politics, and technologies and the need for intelligent policies of sustainable global development. Her editorials are syndicated by Interpress Service in Rome to 400 newspapers in 27 languages. She is a fellow of the World Business Academy and the World Futures Studies Federation, an advisor to the Calvert Social Investment Fund, and developer of the Calvert–Henderson Quality-of-Life Indicators. She held the Horace Albright Chair at the University of California, Berkeley, and has served on committees of the National Science Foundation and the US Office of Technology Assessment. Henderson shared the 1996 Global Citizen Award with Nobelist Adolfo Perez Esquivel of Argentina.

Mae-Wan Ho is a biologist whose research focuses on the physics of organisms, in particular the liquid crystal structure of all living organisms—work with wide-ranging implications for holistic health, ecology, and sustainable economic systems. She is a professor at the Open University in England, as well as a scientific adviser to the Third World Network and other nongovernmental organizations on genetic engineering. She is the editor (with Peter Saunders) of *Beyond Neo-Darwinism: An Introduction to the New Evolutionary Paradigm*, and the author of *The Rainbow and the Worm: The Physics of Organisms* and *Genetic Engineering, Dream or Nightmare: The Brave New World of Bad Science and Big Business.*

Ervin Laszlo is a pioneer in the development of systems philosophy and general systems theory and is the founder of the field of general evolution theory. A rare combination of scholar, theorist and activist, Laszlo is a former Programme Director for the United Nations, a director of Planetary Citizens, advisor to the Director-General of UNESCO, author of a major Club of Rome study on goals for humanity, and the founder and president of the new Club of Budapest dedicated to focusing the combined vision of the humanities, art, and spirituality as well as science on global betterment. Laszlo has also taught at Yale, Princeton, Northwestern, Houston, Portland State, and Indiana Universities and at the State University of New York. He is the author of *The Whispering Pond, The Interconnected Universe* articulating his new QVI-field theory of evolution, *Evolution: The General Theory, The Choice: Evolution or Extinction*, and over 30 other books. He is the founder and editor of *World Futures: The Journal of General Evolution* and is founder and director of the General Evolution Research Group.

David Loye is a social psychologist, futurist, and developer of a new theory of moral transformation and a new action-oriented theory of evolution. His many books include *The Healing of a Nation*, which won the Anisfield-Wolfe award for the best scholarly book on race relations in 1971, *The Leadership Passion, The Knowable Future, The Sphinx and the Rainbow*, and (with Riane Eisler) *The Partnership Way*. Currently, he is completing *Darwin's Lost Theory, The Lost Darwin, The Glacier and the Flame*, and *The River and the Star*. A former member of the psychology faculty of Princeton University, Loye for nearly a decade was a professor in the research series and Director of Research for the Program on Psychosocial Adaptation and the Future at the UCLA School of Medicine. He is (with Eisler) a co-founder of the Center for Partnership Studies, a co-founder of the new Society for the Study of Chaos Theory in Psychology, and a co-founder of the General Evolution Research Group.

Alfonso Montuori brings an unusual background as a systems scientist and jazz musician to the study of the impact of creativity on evolution. Montuori is the author of a wide-ranging study of leading-edge thinking, *Evolutionary Competence: Creating the Future*, and an exploration of the application of Eisler's partnership mode in contemporary lives, *From Power to Partnership* (soon to appear in an Italian edition); and is the editor of book series on systems science and social creativity for Hampton Press. He has also been a consultant to many businesses on creativity. Currently on the faculty of the California Institute for Integral Studies, Montuori is a teacher of students throughout the United States and abroad through the CIIS online program. A member of the General Evolution Research Group, he is Associate Editor of *World Futures: The Journal of General Evolution.*

Telmo Pievani is a researcher in the field of evolutive epistemology at the University of Bergamo in Italy, scientific coordinator of the Masters in Intercultural Communication at the University of Bergamo, and Chief of the Editorial Board of the new international journal *Pluriverso*, published by Rizzoli in Italy. He is the author of *La teoria degli equilibri punteggiati e la teoria gerarchica dell' evoluzione: a configurazione di un'epistemologia evolutiva post-darwiniana.* His new book, written with Mauro Ceruti, *Etica della diversita e coscienza planetaria*—which develops themes touched on in his chapter with Ceruti in this book—will be published in 1998.

Karl Pribram is widely considered the foremost neuropsychologist of our time. A neurosurgeon originally by training, gradually over a long span of creative involvement with mid- and late-20th-century shapers of the fields of brain research and psychology, he has come to occupy a unique position in modern science. His books *Language of the Brain, Brain and Perception,* and (with George Miller and Eugene Gallanter) *Plans and the Structure of Behavior* are classics in their fields. He is a former director of the famous Yerkes Laboratories of primate research, research scientist at Yale, an associate of the Center for Advanced Studies in the Behavioral Sciences, and for many years a professor at Stanford. Currently, he is Director of the Center for Brains Research and Informational Sciences at Radford University in Radford, Virginia. A member of the General Evolution Research Group, Pribram's holographic and holonomic brain theory—as well as his holographic universe theory developed in association with physicist David Bohm—are major stimulants in the formulation of advanced brain and evolutionary theory.

Paul H. Ray is the author and developer of the Integral Culture Survey, a series of surveys of 100,000 Americans that in identifying and tracking the development of three major subcultures over the past ten years provides a striking portrait of a society undergoing major cultural evolution. Ray is the Executive Vice-President of American LIVES, Inc., a San Francisco-based market and opinion research polling firm. Previously he was Chief of Policy Research on Energy Conservation, Department of Energy, Mines and Resources of Canada, and earlier an associate professor of urban planning and a faculty associate of the institute for Social Research at the University of Michigan. He is currently completing a new book on the results of the Integral Culture Survey and implications for the 21st century of his findings regarding the "Cultural Creatives" subculture.

Mária Sági is a psychologist and sociologist who has coordinated a number of international research projects as a research associate of the Hungarian Academy of Sciences and of Ervin Laszlo. Currently, she is also research coordinator for the Club of Budapest. She began her career as a classical pianist and received her Ph.D. for a 7-volume work on the experimental investigation of musical creativity. She is the author of 6 books and 30 articles in art and social psychology. For the past decade she has also been a holistic healer, lecturing frequently in Hungary, Germany, and Austria, and is the author of books and articles on this subject. She is a member of the General Evolution Research Group and is Managing Editor of *World Futures: The Journal of General Evolution*.

Contributor Addresses

Ralph Abraham, P.O.Box 7920, Santa Cruz, CA 95061–7920. Ph.: (408) 425–7436. Fax: (408) 425–8612. email: abraham@vismath.org. Visual Math Institute, http://www.vismath.org.

Raymond Trevor Bradley, Institute for Whole Social Science, 25400 Telarama Way, Carmel, CA 93923. Ph.: (408) 626–8057. Fax: (408) 633–9423.

Fritjof Capra, P.O.Box 9066, Berkeley, CA 94709. Ph.: (510) 525–9191. Fax: (510) 525–9192.

Mauro Ceruti, Department of Linguistics and Literature, University of Bergamo, Piazza Vecchia 8, 24129 Bergamo, Italy. Ph. and fax: (39)-35–400895. email: ceruti@cyberg.it.

Riane Eisler, Center for Partnership Studies, P.O.Box 51934, Pacific Grove, CA 92950. Fax: (408) 626–3734. email: eisler@partnershipway.org.

Hazel Henderson, P.O.Box 5190, St. Augustine, FL 32085. Ph.: (904) 829–3140. Fax: (904) 826–0325.

Mae-Wan Ho, Department of Biology, Open University, Walton Hall, Milton Keynes MK7 6AA, England. Fax: (44)-1908–654167.

Ervin Laszlo, Villa Franatoni, 56040 Montescudaio (Pisa), Italy. Fax: (39)-586–658–395. email: elaszlo@mcimail.com.

David Loye, 25700 Shafter Way, Carmel, CA 93923. Ph.: (408) 624–8337. Fax: (408) 626–3734. email: loye@partnershipway.org.

Alfonso Montuori, 865 Vallejo, Apt. 302, San Francisco, CA 94133. Ph. and fax: (415) 398–6964.

Telmo Pievani, Department of Linguistics and Literature, University of Bergamo, Piazza Vecchia 8, 24129 Bergamo, Italy. Fax: (39)-35–235136.

Karl H. Pribram, Center for Brain Research and Informational Sciences, Radford University, Radford, VA 24142. Ph.: (540) 831–6108. Fax: (540) 831–6630. kpribram@runet.edu.

Paul H. Ray, American LIVES, Inc., 2512 Filbert St., San Francisco, CA 94123. Ph.: (415) 921–1946. Fax: (415) 453–1517. email: paulhray@aol.com.

Mária Sági, Managing Editor, *World Futures: The Journal of General Evolution*, Uri u.49, H-1014 Budapest, Hungary. Ph. and fax: (36)-1–156–9457. email: h290las@ella2.sztaki.hu.

Introduction
The Evolutionary Outrider

DAVID LOYE

Like two pieces to a giant puzzle hurtling through space, our world today and evolutionary theory are at an interlocking turning-point.

On one hand is this world of terrorism, overpopulation, environmental degradation, urban decay, sexism, racism, and the consumerism that is eating up our planet alive—all of which must profoundly disturb us if we are concerned about the well-being and destiny of our species. On the other hand is the seemingly remote hothouse of evolutionary theory. How could the two possibly be interconnected?

If we look closely at the matter we see that what we do—or do not do—about the situation of our species depends on what drives our minds. More specifically, whether we feel responsible for, indifferent to, or helpless in relation to our future depends on our vision of who we think we are and what we have the right to expect of ourselves. Are we essentially a form of machine that in "smartness" comes off second best to our computers? Are we little more than naked apes in clothes? Or are we active agents in the making of our destiny? Are we evolution's outriders?

Whether we are to prevail, then, over these problems that assail us depends on the *size* of our vision of ourselves and our future. This vision in turn depends on our beliefs and expectations. Our beliefs and expectations are in turn primarily determined by science—but now comes the critical connection. For ever since Darwin the scientific worldview has been primarily determined by evolutionary theory. And herein lies the crux of perhaps our least generally appreciated but most critical of problems.

For over a century, at all levels of society, in subtle but inescapably powerful ways, the vital vision of who we are and what we can be has been shaped by a theory of evolution developed primarily by natural scientists to fit the *pre*human rather than human-level data base.

That is, on the foundation originally set in place by Darwin in *The Origin of Species*, what we know today as *the* theory of evolution was constructed primarily by biologists to fit prehumans rather than humans. This theory, as Laszlo (1996a) and others note, has been further expanded by astrophysicists, physicists, and other natural scientists to account for the cosmic evolution that underlies biological evolution. The result is a theory based on what has been observed of the nature of the universe and living systems *prior to* the difference that enters life with the radical expansion of brain and cultural capacities that came into being with the emergence of our particular species, the human.

As a consequence, 20th-century mind has chiefly been shaped by the teaching of and debate about evolutionary theory that, in turn, chiefly centers on the question of the Big Bang, yes or no, and other aspects of cosmic evolution, and the three stages for the development of "Darwinian" evolutionary theory that are still everywhere firmly embedded in textbooks, curricula, and the media: neo-Darwinism from the early part of this century; the "synthetic theory" out of the 1930s; and more recently, out of the 1970s, sociobiology (Wilson, 1975; Csanyi, 1989).

But beyond the cosmic and biological foundation, everything we know about our own species—particularly how our radically enlarged brain and mind work, how we come to have imagination, creativity, how our customs come into being, how our belief systems build, how we differentiate right from wrong, how we act to shape the course for ourselves and our species in one direction rather than another —all comes to us from the fields of social science. And for nearly a century now, most of social science has operated "outside" the field of, or "without" an, evolutionary theory.

This disjuncture came about through a monumental quirk of history too involved to go into here.[1] It is the consequences that we are concerned with, for the net effect is that—in lieu of having an evolutionary theory fitted to *our* species to work with—social science has either worked without the grounding of such a vital theoretical base, or it has attempted to fit its findings to an ostensibly Darwinian theory in biology that, as many observers have noted (e.g., Montagu, 1976; Gould, 1980; Lewontin *et al.*, 1984), dangerously distorts them.

Thus, at what many observers agree may well be the most critical of all junctures in the evolution of our species, we lack the kind of evolutionary theory fitted to *our* species that we need to help us face the horrendous challenges of the 21st century with confidence in ourselves and a clear vision of where we are headed. Indeed, so great is this lack that if we go beneath the academic surface to look at the psychological impact of present evolutionary theory, it is apparent that, rather than striding forward with some confidence, psychologically and cognitively ours is a species trying to waddle forward into the future in a straightjacket.

Lest this seem too extreme a view, I should add it is not so much the science involved here that is the problem. It is what is *made* of the science—or the use and abuse of science by overriding social, economic, and political paradigms.[2] Thus, present Darwinian evolutionary theory is used to reinforce the widespread belief, earlier implanted, that we humans, as with all other species, are inexorably shaped by all that goes by the name of environment and by the "blind chance" of random processes—hence we are relatively powerless to do much about our situation. It is further a body of theory that reinforces the belief that there is neither meaning nor direction to our lives, nor to human development, and that at no time do we have much of a say in what happens.

From Kurt Lewin in psychology (1951) to Emile Durkheim in sociology (1951), a large body of studies by their successors in both fields has revealed the disastrous consequences of such a *Weltanschauung* or worldview. Indeed, as noted in Loye (1971), the concerns and insights of Lewin, expressed over half a century ago, foreshadow a major portion of the personal and social breakdown now endemic in global society as we move into the 21st century.

The intention here is not to downgrade the enormous importance of the natural sciences—that is, of astrophysics, physics, chemistry, biology, paleontology, and all the other fields that have established what we know today as evolutionary theory. This foundation, which at least 200 years of science before and over 100 years since Darwin have gone into building, is one of the most inspiring and mighty aspects of humanity's accomplishments. Field after field, the natural sciences provide the scientific grounding for the advance of our species into the future. The intention here is simply to point out that upon this foundation has been raised a super-structure in science and society that is disjointed and imbalanced. The time has come, it seems amply evident, for the development of an evolutionary theory that might wed the natural scientific foundation and the social scientific superstructure in ways that could help restore balance to both the science and society of the 21st century.

To this end, honoring the pioneering articulation of this goal by systems philosopher and evolutionary theorist Ervin Laszlo, the chapters for this book present the latest views of an international group of experts and authorities in a wide range of fields. The need to bridge the gap between natural and social science in the development of new evolutionary theory is reflected by the fact of their cross-disciplinary involvement. The impact of the human agent on evolution is primarily assessed here from the perspectives of psychology, sociology, economics, political science, creativity research, and—woefully neglected in traditional evolutionary theory—brain research and gender-relational theory. Yet at the same time the essential grounding for this human impact is provided by the perspectives of biology and physics, and the essential framework for a larger understanding embracing both social and natural science is reflected by the involvement of mathematics, systems science, systems philosophy, and chaos theory.

The Honoring of Ervin Laszlo, the Activist Perspective, and the Purpose of this Book

In keeping with the larger vision of Darwin himself (Loye, 1994, 1998a, 1998b), the current expansion of evolutionary theory beyond the constraints of neo-Darwinism is very much a multipersonal and often communal endeavor. It has become the product of no one single figure, as is the case with our view now of the 19th century. But if any one person more than others could be singled out as the global leader of what might be called the new *human*-oriented evolutionary movement of the late 20th century, it would be the theorist, activist, and founder of the field of general evolution theory in whose honor the chapters of this book were drawn together, Ervin Laszlo.

Because of the often fiercely entrenched hold of the Darwinian paradigm that has prevailed over the 20th century, shifting focus to the impact and responsibility of the human agent and a general and activist perspective on evolution has not been an easy task. To these ends Laszlo has quietly hammered away with an unusual range of books and activities over the past 20 years. He is the author of 32 books, many of which have been published in a wide range of the world's languages. These include *Evolution: Foundations of a General Theory* (1996a), *The Choice* (1994), *The Systems View of the World* (1996b), *The Interconnected Universe* (1995), and *The Whispering Pond* (1996). He is a former Director of Research for the United Nations, developer of the QVI (quantum-vacuum interactive) field theory of the origin of form in evolution, author of a major Club of Rome report on human goals, founder of the General Evolution Research Group, and founder of the new Club of Budapest. He also founded and has long been the editor of *World Futures: The Journal of General Evolution*—in this capacity, as the leader of the General Evolution Research Group, and in other roles interlinking the world scientific community serving in a unique way to inspire advance in evolutionary theory.

In honoring Laszlo, the main purpose of this book is to provide readers in all fields of science with inspiring new perspectives on evolutionary theory at a pivotal turning-point in both the history and the evolution of our species from the 20th into the 21st century.

In keeping with the statement of the Union of Concerned Scientists and Laszlo's Manifesto for the Club of Budapest this opens this book, as well as the purposes of Scientists for Global Responsibility and the Scientific and Medical Network, this book is a call to scientists in every field to rethink their relationship to evolution theory and more consciously and purposefully become evolution's outriders.

What this book offers is a way for those so impelled in all fields of science to do two things bearing immensely on the shaping of the human future. One is to re-evaluate and re-align themselves to evolution theory as central to the grounding of all science. The other—which the chapters of this book reveal is of great urgency—is to transcend disciplinary differences and cooperate in expanding our understanding to gain both a theory and a story of evolution better fitted to the requirements for survival of ours and all other species in the 21st century and beyond. A special index shaped to serve both needs concludes this book.

It is, further, a goal of this book to provide students who are to become the scientists of the 21st century with the inspirational content, the vision, the sense of mission, and the models for career guidance so often lacking in much of their formal education. Usually this driving personal gestalt—so vital in forging the advancement of science that in turn advances the cause of humanity—must be picked up elsewhere through inspiring personal contact with one particularly beloved or memorable teacher, or through glimpses in books here and there.

Here, in an unusually expressive set of papers, a group of 20th-century scientists and scholars who deeply care about the future for humanity seek to pass on what they have learned to their successors in the 21st century.

Part 1. The Challenge for our Species in the 21st Century

Because of Laszlo's eloquence in outlining, in a series of books over the past decade, the challenge we face, the first section contains two very brief chapters by him to set the stage. It opens with excerpts from an inspiring "manifesto" based on the mission statement written by Laszlo to launch the Club of Budapest. Then in an account of the personal quest seldom expressed, but of vital importance for our understanding of the motivations for social action and the personal challenge that faces scientists today, we are taken behind the scenes of a remarkable career that moved from the stage as a concert pianist to becoming a philosopher, scientist, important evolutionary theorist, and global activist.

This section also contains a brief history of the General Evolution Research Group. Histories of organizations tend to be avoided on the assumption they will inevitably be dull and inbred. I must note, however, that, in keeping with the goal here to provide insight and inspiration rather than only add one more thing to our endless pile-up of information, this particular history differs from most in revealing some of the motivations, beliefs, goals, creative drives, and rough-and-tumble nature of what has gone on into the development of new evolutionary science in the late 20th century. It provides a brief, behind-the-scenes look at the coming into a consciousness of historic mission of one of a large number of similar small research groups at work today throughout the world on the science of the 21st century—in this case, a group, headed by Laszlo, composed of evolutionary theorists from Italy, France, Great Britain, Hungary, Switzerland, and Germany, as well as the United States, Russia, China, and Sri Lanka.

Part 2. The Impact of the Human Agent on Evolution

Here are brief descriptions of the chapters for Parts 2 and 3, in sequence:

Evolution: The Old View and the New View, by Fritjof Capra. Noted for his unusual capacity for making leading-edge science accessible to the general reader as well as across disciplinary boundaries, in a chapter based on his book *The Web of Life*, physicist Capra (*The Tao of Physics, The Turning Point*) takes us from Darwin as currently presented to where we are today. First Capra offers a quick grounding in traditional neo-Darwinian theory. Then he points to some of the problems this theory raises for today's scientists. Last, he provides a taste of some leading-edge theories directed toward updating our understanding of evolution—in this case, the theories of symbiogenesis and symbiosis of Gaia hypothesis cotheorist, biologist Lynn Margulis.

Organism and Psyche in a Participatory Universe, by Mae-Wan Ho. A professor at London's Open University, internationally respected evolutionary biophysicist Mae-Wan Ho writes about her new theory "of the organism and the naturalistic ethic of participation" within the context of Laszlo's QVI-field theory and about her pioneering work in the liquid crystal structure of all living organisms. Moving on from work reported in her book *The Rainbow and the Worm,* Ho eloquently outlines a theory of the organism that runs counter to the mechanistic reductionism of prevailing theory in its vision of the organism as an intercommunicating, coherent whole. Each organism, she contends, participates in the process of creation that at the human level becomes our ability to intervene in evolution, with a voice in choosing our future.

On Brain, Conscious Experience, and Human Agency, by Karl Pribram. One of the most serious problems with present-day evolutionary theory comes from the historical bypassing and ignoring of brain research by its developers. The two foremost brain scientists of this century in establishing the concept of the active brain are Pribram and the late Alexander Luria. Unfortunately, there still prevails a picture of the human brain as only a passive responder to stimulus from our environment. In sharp contrast, the work of Pribram and Luria was decisive in establishing a detailed understanding of the *active,* stimulus-seeking brain and the *self-organizing* nature of the prefrontal executive area functioning that is the core of our new understanding of the human as an active agent in evolution. Here Pribram fills in the gap with a unique review of what 20th-century brain research and psychology from the time of Freud and William James into the 1990s has discovered of how the basic equipment we humans bring to evolution operates.

Toward an Evolutionary Systems Approach to Creativity, by Alfonso Montuori. The thrust of creativity is a fundamental aspect of the impact of the human agent and human agency on evolution. This impact has been mainly studied in terms of historical and psychological studies of great creative individuals (the Beethovens, Einsteins, Da Vincis, etc., as well as political figures such as Napoleon). Within creativity research, a new emphasis is upon the relatively neglected aspect of *social* creativity—or the impact of the creativity of groups, of communities, of organizations as a whole. Editor of a new series of books on this subject published by Hampton Press, a member of the General Evolution Research Group and Associate Editor of the Group's journal, Montuori writes of both aspects of this impact on evolution.

QVI: The Fifth Field of Ervin Laszlo, by David Loye. Over the past decade, in a series of publications in various venues, which eventuated in three books for a widely varying readership, Laszlo has gradually developed a new theory of a fundamental aspect of evolution generating considerable interest among leading-edge thinkers in many fields. Where do the *forms* of evolution come from? Why have we wound up as exactly the kind of creatures we are today in precisely the kind of world we inhabit? Does what we do during our lives here on Earth really make a difference? Is there anything about us that is lasting? And what really holds all of this together? These are some of the questions Laszlo attempts to answer with his new Quantum-Vacuum Interaction (QVI) theory, reviewed here in terms of its differing expressions in *The Creative Cosmos, The Interconnected Universe,* and *The Whispering Pond.*

Healing through the QVI-Field, by Mária Sági. It often seems that science is composed of two kinds of people. On one hand are those made uncomfortable by even the slightest touch of anything that can't be explained by the presently prevailing paradigm, who are strongly motivated to deny the existence of anomalies. On the other hand are those who are intrigued by whatever the presently prevailing paradigm fails to account for, who are—as the evolutionary outriders for science —impelled to find an answer. Social psychologist Mária Sági shows how Laszlo's QVI-Field theory may at last provide a scientific explanation for the mysterious phenomenon, and increasingly widespread practice, of bioenergy healing. A member of the General Evolution Research Group, Sági is Managing Editor of *World Futures: The Journal of General Evolution.*

Quantum-Vacuum Interaction and Psychosocial Organization, by Raymond Trevor Bradley. Sociologist Bradley (*Charisma and Social Structure*) is, with brain scientist Karl Pribram, doing some of the most advanced work in the world today in the study of how our minds work in social settings. Here Bradley brings together into a very large theoretical perspective his own study of the psychosocial dynamics of 55 communes, Laszlo's QVI-field theory, Pribram's holographic and holonomic theory, the holon theory of physicist Dennis Gabor, and the relatively unknown late work of Jean Piaget in the analysis of how we think and reason in situations of cooperation. The result is a new theory of how we both process information and in turn use this information to act upon ourselves and our environment.

Biological Evolution and Cultural Evolution: Toward a Planetary Consciousness, by Mauro Ceruti and Telmo Pievani. Over recent decades a significant change in our consciousness, both generated by and accelerating the activist perspective of the human agent, is a trend for theories of biological evolution and cultural evolution to converge on a vision of our stake in the welfare of the whole planet. Evolutionary systems philosophers Ceruti—a member of the General Evolution Research Group—and Pievani are the editors of a new European intellectual journal highly influential in the new surge of interest in evolution and evolutionary theory, *Pluriverso.* Here they explore the growth of the new planetary consciousness in the work of Ervin Laszlo and other evolutionary theorists and futurists.

Part 3. Human Intervention in Evolutionary Process

Evolutionary Action Theory: A Brief Outline, by David Loye. As a psychologist and co-founding member of the General Evolution Research Group, I have been involved in research over the past ten years into moral as well as general evolutionary process. Out of this research, I have developed a new action-oriented theory of evolution. This theory derives from many sources, among them Freud, Lewin, Rokeach, and many others in psychology, sociology, and other fields of social science. But primarily it evolves from the fact that Charles Darwin developed what, at first glance, appear to be two theories of evolution. The first is Darwinian theory as it is known today, impressively substantiated but used to promote a dangerously truncated and distorted view of human nature and our evolutionary potential. His second theory, still almost wholly unknown, offers the potential for an enormous liberation of mind and action to meet the increasingly critical evolutionary challenge of our time. In articles ("Charles Darwin, Paul MacLean, and the Lost Origins of 'The Moral Sense'") and books underway (*Darwin's Lost Theory* and *The HoloDarwinian Quest*), I tell of the rediscovery and reconstruction of what increasingly appears to be not two theories but the long-ignored, *human*-oriented completion that Darwin intended for his theory of evolution. Evolutionary action theory tries to reconcile the contradictions between Darwin's "first" theory of natural selection and random process and his "second" theory of an active and moral human agency.

Conscious Evolution: Cultural Transformation and Human Agency, by Riane Eisler. Previous chapters have looked at the biology, physics, brain science, psychology, sociology, and thrust of human agency in the shaping of evolution. Now we turn to the overriding and all too generally overlooked and misinterpreted impact of *cultural* evolution. Internationally known for her books *The Chalice and the Blade* and *Sacred Pleasure*, systems scientist and cultural historian Eisler is the developer of a widely influential new gender- and systems-balanced theory of human cultural evolution. Through her books and other writings, Eisler, a co-founding member of the General Evolution Research Group, has been unusually effective in arousing people to the evolutionary challenge facing our species and the critical nature of our choice of futures. Her chapter is based on work in progress for a new book on her theory, in particular outlining a new subtheory of relational dynamics. Probing the role relationships of the human agent, she brings to life the positive impact of a "partnership" model and ethos—in contrast to the negative impact of a "dominator" model and ethos—on our lives today and trends for human evolution.

Social Interventions and the World Wide Web, by Ralph Abraham. A leading chaos theorist and pioneer in the development of computer modeling of evolutionary processes, also a co-founding member of the General Evolution Research Group, mathematician Abraham (*Dynamics: The Geometry of Behavior, Chaos, Gaia, and Eros, The Web Empowerment Book*) reports on a number of ingenious devices for the use of computer modeling and other technologies to provide humanity with new tools for expanding our capacities for greater species' self-realization. In the terse and direct style with the touch of wit for which he is known, Abraham brings together devices he has proposed in a wide variety of journals over the past two decades, including his projection of ways for liberating the human potential through the application of an activist consciousness to expansion and refinement of the World Wide Web.

Economics and Evolution: An Ethos for an Action Researcher, by Hazel Henderson. Though economics may be the least glamorous of the social sciences, because of its bread-and-butter relation to our lives it has long been recognized as one of the most important. Futurist and economist Hazel Henderson (*The Politics of the Solar Age, Building a Win–Win World*) is one of the most perceptive and engaging critics of economics, as well as one of few to perceive this field in terms of its relation to the evolutionary challenge of building a better future for humanity out of the chaos of our time. In her chapter, Henderson proposes a number of striking interventions to this end—including ways of strengthening democracy in the United States and worldwide, and innovations in financing and governance to strengthen the United Nations.

What Might Be the Next Stage in Cultural Evolution, by Paul H. Ray. Sociologist Paul H. Ray recently completed a seven-year study of American values, behavioral patterns, and cultural groups that is rapidly gaining the attention of psychologists, sociologists, and other social scientists as well as leaders in the fields of business and government. Ray finds that we can expand our understanding and potentially our shaping of American society through an understanding of evolutionary dynamics involving three primary cultural groups: the Traditionalists or Heartlanders, numbering 55.6 million; the Modernists, numbering 88 million; and the Trans-Modernists, or "Cultural Creatives." Ray identifies the Cultural Creatives as a long-misperceived alignment, now involving one in four Americans, or 44 million of us, who both resonate to and create the new ideas that seem to drive us in evolutionary optimizing directions. He relates these findings to the cultural evolution theory of Pitirim Sorokin and prospects for our movement toward a new leveling-off for Earth's people at a higher and more stable and satisfying stage of evolution.

Particularly striking in relation to this book's theme of the impact of human agency on evolution is the correspondence between Paul H. Ray's and sociologist Raymond Trevor Bradley's findings shown in the visual pattern for the cover of this book, which I am repeating here in Figure 1.

As noted at greater length in the brief copy on the back of the opening quotes page, to the lower left is the data configuration for the three clusters discovered by Ray in his study of American attitudes and beliefs (see Figure 3, chapter 16). While the first two clusters along the timeline represent orientations to the status quo, or

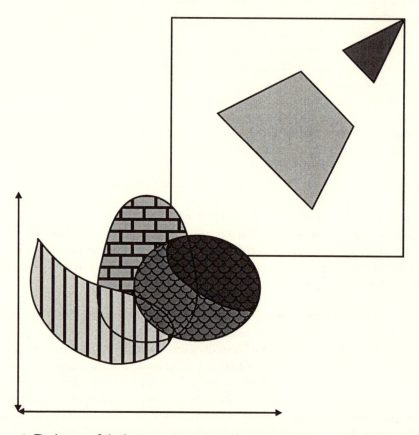

Figure 1. The impact of the human agent on evolution suggested by a configuration of the findings of studies by Paul Ray and Ray Bradley

to what presently exists, the third and farthest along on the rightward time dimension is more attuned to idealism, the future, and social action. To the upper right, then, is the configuration discovered by sociologist Raymond Trevor Bradley in his study of 46 communes (see Figure 4, chapter 10). Here we find what emerges from a study of the pattern to communications and social structure within communes in terms of love and power relationships directed toward purposeful action.

Though there are important differences in variables, what is striking is the similarity for trajectory along the horizontal or *X* axis time line. In both cases, data-point plotting reveals a ascending diagonal thrust for findings that, within context, seem definitely to capture impacts of human agency on evolution.

Notes

1. See Richards, *Darwin and the Emergence of Evolutionary Theories of Mind and Behavior*; Gruber, *Darwin on Man*; and Loye, *Darwin's Lost Theory*, for the story of how the turn-of-the-century efforts of George Romanes, Lloyd Morgan, J.M. Baldwin, and William James in psychology and Lester Ward and George Herbert Mead in sociology to extend Darwinian evolutionary theory into social science were ground under historically. The problem, briefly, was the rise of psychoanalysis, behaviorism, neo-Darwinism, and more generally, the splitting apart, or bureaucratization, of the earlier holism of science into many fields rigidly separated from one another by fierce disciplinary boundaries.
2. The classic case is that of Social Darwinism, as a set of beliefs actually held by Spencer but wrongly attributed to Darwin, used to support racism and wholly unregulated capitalism. See Hofstader, *Social Darwinism in American Thought*.

References

Csanyi, V. (1989). *Evolutionary systems and society*. Durham, NC: Duke University Press.

Gould, S.J. (1980). *Ever since Darwin*. New York: Norton.

Gruber, H. and Barrett, P. (1974). *Darwin on man: A psychological study of scientific creativity*. New York: Dutton.

Laszlo, E. (1994). *The choice: Oblivion or evolution*. Los Angeles: Tarcher.

—— (1995). *The interconnected universe*. London: World Scientific.

—— (1996a). *Evolution: The general theory*. Cresskill Heights, NJ: Hampton Press.

—— (1996b). *The systems view of the world*. Cresskill Heights, NJ: Hampton Press.

—— (1996c). *The whispering pond*. London: Element Books.

Lewin, K. (1951). *Field theory in social science*. New York: Harper and Row.

Lewontin, R.C., Rose, S., and Kamin, L. (1984). *Not in our genes*. New York: Pantheon.

Loye, D. (1971). *The healing of a nation*. New York: Norton.

—— (1994). Charles Darwin, Paul MacLean, and the lost origins of "The moral sense": Some implications for General Evolution Theory. *World Futures: The Journal of General Evolution*, 40, 4, 187–196.

—— (1998a). *Darwin's lost theory*. (Work in progress).

—— (1998b). *The holoDarwinian paradigm*. (Work in progress).

Montagu, A. (1976). *The nature of human aggression*. New York: Oxford University Press.

Richards, R. J. (1987). *Darwin and the emergence of evolutionary theories of mind and behavior*. Chicago: University of Chicago Press.

Wilson, E.O. (1975). *Sociobiology: The new synthesis*. Cambridge, MA: Harvard University Press.

Part 1

The Challenge for our Species in the 21st Century

Part I

1
Manifesto of the Club of Budapest: An Excerpt

ERVIN LASZLO

Abstract
The Club of Budapest, with branches already in many countries of the world, was founded to help focus the attention of cultural (the arts, music, and the humanities) as well as spiritual, business, governmental and scientific leadership on the advancement of human evolution. Founded by Ervin Laszlo in 1994, this is an excerpt from the Club's mission statement.

Key words
social, spiritual, and cultural evolution; problems of poverty, militarism, ecology, population, nuclear warheads, global warming, sustainable development; need for respect for diversity, morality, responsibility, love, compassion, creativity and planetary consciousness and action.

1. In the closing years of the 20th century, we have reached a crucial juncture in our history. We are on the threshold of a new stage of social, spiritual and cultural evolution, a stage that is as different from the stage of the earlier decades of this century as the grasslands were from the caves, and settled villages from life in nomadic tribes. We are evolving out of the nationally based industrial societies that were created at the dawn of the first industrial revolution, and heading toward an interconnected, information-based social, economic and cultural system that straddles the globe. The path of this evolution is not smooth: it is filled with shocks and surprises. This century has witnessed several major shock waves, and others may come our way before long. The way we shall cope with present and future shocks will decide our future, and the future of our children and grandchildren.

2. The challenge we now face is the challenge of choosing our destiny. Our generation, of all the thousands of generations before us, is called upon to decide the fate of life on this planet. The processes we have initiated within our lifetime and the lifetime of our fathers and grandfathers cannot continue in the lifetime of our children and grandchildren. Whatever we do either creates the framework for reaching a peaceful and cooperative global society and thus continuing the grand adventure of life, spirit and consciousness on Earth, or sets the stage for the termination of humanity's tenure on this planet.

3. The patterns of action in today's world are not encouraging. Millions of people

are without work; millions are exploited by poor wages; millions are forced into helplessness and poverty. The gap between rich and poor nations, and between rich and poor people within nations, is great and still growing. Though the world community is relieved of the specter of superpower confrontation and is threatened by ecological collapse, the world's governments still spend a thousand billion dollars a year on arms and the military and only a tiny fraction of this sum on maintaining a livable environment.

4. The militarization problem, the developmental problem, the ecological problem, the population problem, and the many problems of energy and raw materials will not be overcome merely by reducing the number of already useless nuclear warheads, nor by signing politically softened treaties on world trade, global warming, biological diversity, and sustainable development. More is required today than piecemeal action and short-term problem-solving. We need to perceive the problems in their complex totality—and grasp them not only with our reason and intellect, but with all the faculties of our insight and empathy. Beyond the powers of the rational mind, the remarkable faculties of the human spirit embrace the power of love, of compassion, and of solidarity. We must not fail to call upon their remarkable powers when confronting the task of initiating the embracing, multifaceted approaches that alone could enable us to reach the next stage in the evolution of our sophisticated but unstable and vulnerable sociotechnological communities.

5. If we maintain obsolete values and beliefs, a fragmented consciousness and a self-centered spirit, we also maintain outdated goals and behaviors. And such behaviors by a large number of people would block the entire transition to an interdependent yet peaceful and cooperative global society. There is now both a moral and a practical obligation for each of us to look beyond the surface of events, beyond the plots and polemics of practical policies, the sensationalistic headlines of the mass media, and the fads and fashions of changing lifestyles and styles of work—an obligation to feel the ground swell underneath the events and perceive the direction they are taking: to evolve the spirit and the consciousness that could enable us to perceive the problems and the opportunities—and to act on them.

6. A new way of thinking has become the necessary condition for responsible living and acting. Evolving it means fostering creativity in all people, in all parts of the world.

7. Sustained diversity is another requirement of our age. Diversity is basic to all things in nature and in art: a symphony cannot be made of one tone or even played by one instrument; a painting must have many shapes and perhaps many colors; a garden is more beautiful if it contains flowers and plants of many different kinds. And a multicellular organism cannot survive if it is reduced to one kind of cell.

8. The globalized world that is our evolutionary destiny cannot be viable unless it maintains essential elements of the diversity that has hallmarked human communities since our ancestors first emerged from the trees. This means a diversity of cultures, creeds and religions, of economic, social and political orders as well as of ways of life, coexisting in harmony, with mutual respect and unshakable goodwill.

9. In the course of the 20th century, people in many parts of the world have become conscious of their rights as well as of many persistent violations of them. This development is important, but in itself it is not enough. In the remaining years of this century we must also become conscious of the factor without which neither rights nor other values can be effectively safeguarded: our individual and collective *responsibilities*.

10. We human beings need more than food, water, and shelter; more even than remunerated work, self-esteem, social acceptance. We also need something to live for: an ideal to achieve, a responsibility to accept. In today's world all of us, no matter where we live and what we do, have become responsible for our actions:

   a. *As individuals* responsible for seeking our interests in harmony with, and not at the expense of, the interests and well-being of others.
   b. *As citizens of our country*, responsible for demanding that our leaders beat swords into ploughshares and relate to other nations peacefully and in a spirit of cooperation.
   c. *As collaborators in business and actors in the economy*, responsible for ensuring that corporate objectives do not center uniquely on profits and growth, but include a concern that products and services respond to human needs and demands without harming people and impairing nature.
   d. *As members of the human community*, responsibly adopting a culture of non-violence, solidarity, and economic, political and social equality, promoting mutual understanding and respect among people and nations whether they are like us or different.
   e. *And as persons endowed with mind and consciousness*, responsibly encouraging comprehension and appreciation for the excellence of the human spirit in all its manifestations, and for inspiring awe and wonder for a cosmos that brought forth life and consciousness and holds out the possibility of its continued evolution toward ever higher levels of insight, understanding, love, and compassion.

11. In most parts of the world, the real potentials of human beings are sadly underdeveloped. The way children are raised depresses their faculties for learning and creativity; the way young people experience the struggle for material survival results in frustration and resentment. In adults this leads to a variety of compensatory, addictive, and compulsive behaviors. *Evolving human spirit and consciousness is the first vital cause shared by the whole of the human family.*

12. In our world static stability is an illusion, the only permanence is in sustainable change and transformation. There is a constant need to guide the evolution of our species so as to avoid breakdowns and progress toward a world where all people can live in peace, freedom, and dignity. Each of us must start with himself or herself to evolve his or her consciousness to this planetary dimension; only then can we become responsible and effective agents of our society's change and transformation.

Planetary consciousness is the knowing as well as the feeling of the vital interdependence and essential oneness of humankind, and the conscious adoption of the ethics and the ethos that this entails. Its evolution is the new imperative of human survival on this planet. The 21st century shall be a century of planetary consciousness, or it shall not be at all.

2
One Man's Quest: A Brief History

ERVIN LASZLO

Abstract
Systems philosopher and evolutionary theorist
Ervin Laszlo tells of his personal quest through
careers as a concert pianist, philosopher,
teacher, theorist, and global activist in search
of a life of meaningful service to humanity.

Key words
An age of change and transformation; the
challenge for intellect and activism; Yale,
Princeton, the Club of Rome, Goals for
Mankind, the United Nations, systems
philosophy, the new physics, the new biology,
the theory of general evolution, the General
Evolution Research Group, the Club of
Budapest.

This is the brief history of a quest that has engaged me throughout my adult life. This quest was not, of course, all that occupied and preoccupied my mind, for this history is not an autobiography. But it took up a significant portion of my time and energy, and almost all my intellectual interests—and subsequently my moral commitment as well.

I begin with the reasons for my quest, as I have now come to see them. Then I give a brief account of its different phases, and conclude with what it has produced for me in the way of insight and commitment.

What I Have Searched for, and Why

There is little doubt that we live in an age of rapid change and transformation. Not just change itself, also the rate of change is accelerating. Leaders and citizens, producers and consumers, city-people and country-folk in societies "developed" and "developing" are hard put to keep up. The picture that emerges appears ever more vague and confused. The term "chaos" is used increasingly to describe it.

What kind of changes are these? Are they random and haphazard, or do they have a logic of their own? Do they conduce toward anything discernible? Or is it "just one darn thing after another," as the early positivists were wont to say? Merely because human beings and societies triggered the changes does not mean that they necessarily know what these changes are. It could also be a case of the sorcerer's apprentice: launching a process that one can no longer control, much less understand. Understanding calls for an additional effort: information gathering, data analysis, and then synthesis and assessment. For anyone who is capable of these operations the challenge is there: find out what is happening, make sense of it.

Of course, whatever interpretation one comes up with has no guarantee of being the God-given truth—it could be merely a construction one has put on the information one happened to access. But pristine truth is not available to flesh-and-bone humans in any case; even science in the most rigorous mode is but a construction placed on the relevant observations, given the conceptual tools currently available. But already a more modest appraisal argues for a major challenge. Can we find meaning in what is happening, within the limitations of empirical knowledge?

This challenge has a worrisome lemma. What if what is happening leads us toward disaster? One does not need great intellectual insight to appreciate this possibility. The worry and the suspicion are there in daily life. It is there between the lines of newsprint and the reports of TV newscasters. It is there in one's own experience, whether of urban pollution and congestion, or of rural tree-dying and soil-degradation. And in the relentless growth of both population and technological might—an awesome combination that pitches ever more people against each other in ever more competitive marketplaces. Technological might is meant to be constructive, but it can also turn destructive; not only in its military applications but already through the overexploitation of resources and the polarization of societies.

Given that the changes we are living through may not be entirely haphazard but could have an overall direction (even if a deviation- and nonlinearity-filled direction), finding out what they are, and where they are leading us, acquires a dimension beyond intellectual curiosity. The search for meaning shades into the search for a livable future. We may be threatened, but in the absence of understanding we could be blind—or nearly so—to the threat. And the threat could be both individual and collective. It could face entire societies, possibly all of humanity.

Here is where responsibility comes into the picture. Should we not try to find out, so that we could take foresighted preventive or remedial action? Even if a threat to collective survival is but a suspicion, the responsibility to act on it becomes real: it is, after all, better to be safe than sorry.

The above sounds like the stuff of world-redeemers and would-be saviors: idealistic to the point of being utopian. Should we not be wiser to heed Rousseau's advice—*occupez-vous de vos jardins*? Why should it be precisely I who accepts the challenge of discovering meaning and shoulders the responsibility of acting in light of it? Are there not politicians and business executives, engineers and scientists, spiritual gurus and psychiatrists whose job it is to tackle these issues and advise the rest of us? The thought is comforting: it lets us off the hook. More is the pity that it turns out to be a chimera: closer acquaintance with any of these august and otherwise no doubt impressive personalities soon discloses that they are just as much at sea as the rest of us. They may understand the dynamics of their own corner of the woods, but have but rudimentary notions of the rest. And even in their own corner they are exposed to a growing series of shocks and surprises. Things do not work out the way they are expected. "Outside" factors intervene, or hidden dynamics surface from within. It is easy to throw up one's hand and say, *après moi le déluge*—what should I care what comes tomorrow? Enough for me to ensure my interests for today, the best I can.

The reasoning is seductive—another handy way to avoid searching for meaning and accepting responsibility—but it, too, has a fateful lemma. If I do not form some reasonable kind of idea of the nature and direction of the ever-accelerating changes that beset our times, my own interests may be compromised. The commonsense logic of self-interest and self-preservation argues for accepting the challenge. Accepting it, that is, if one possesses the degree of freedom in daily existence to look around oneself and reflect on what one sees. I am fortunate in having had this degree of freedom. I could launch into the search as soon as the need for it matured in my mind.

The Phases of My Search

The predominance and possible threat of change motivates a search for meaning, and the discovery of meaning prompts the acceptance of responsibility. This causal sequence is clear-cut in theory, but far from straightforward in practice. In my own case covering the distance between the recognition of the need for a search for meaning to the acceptance of responsibility for the kind of actions that are constructive in light of that meaning took fully three decades. I began the search in the late 1950s, when I was in my mid-twenties. And it was in the mid-1980s, when I was well into my fifties, that I began to seriously espouse the ways of acting that appeared responsible in the light of my insights.

At first, the search took up all my time and energy; it was all-encompassing. It interfered with my professional career as a pianist—from the age of nine until my early thirties I was active as a concert artist, with frequent appearances in recitals and as soloist with major symphony orchestras in North and South America, Europe, and the Middle East. When I found myself speculating on scientific and philosophical problems even as I was performing on the stage, I became convinced that a decision was in order: either devote the greater part of my time and energy to the career of a concert pianist, or devote my full time to my intensifying quest. As it happened, the choice practically made itself: around this time I received an invitation to spend a year as a Fellow of the Philosophy Department at Yale. Not without trepidation—I had no formal academic background—I accepted.

My tenure at Yale marked the beginning of a second career, in the academic world. Within two years I caught up with the necessary formalities by defending a thesis for the coveted degree of *Docteur ès-Lettres et Sciences Humaines* at the Sorbonne, and after that spent a decade teaching, writing, editing, and doing all the things expected of a full-time philosopher. Then I became involved, unexpectedly but as it turned out irreversibly, in the practical consequences of my ideas. First the Center of International Studies in Princeton asked me to come and present a graduate seminar on the application of my systems-theoretical concepts to international and world-order studies; then the president of the Club of Rome, reading the draft of the book that materialized out of the Princeton seminar, suggested that I prepare a report to the Club focusing not on the outer limits to growth (as did the then much-discussed *Limits to Growth*), but on the inner, human and societal limits. To carry out this challenging task, the executive director of the United Nations Institute for Training and Research kindly offered the institute facilities for worldwide communication and coordination. I moved to the New York headquarters of the United Nations. Though I intended to return to my university after the first year, when my work for the Club of Rome had been completed, the Institute asked me to assume responsibilities for research on questions of international and interregional socioeconomic cooperation. In consequence, my one-year tenure at the UN extended to seven years.

These internationally scaled activities obliged me to apply my theories to the global problems that face all of us, today and in the foreseeable future. Here I came face to face with the question of personal moral responsibility. At first, I managed it in a rather impersonal way: my concern was with how others should behave, not I. I saw my task as coming up with reasoned answers, and communicating them to decisionmakers in the UN and the concerned public through books and articles.

When in 1984 I left the United Nations, I did not return to the State University of New York: the hallowed halls of academe seemed like ivory towers. I began to sense that I should do something more than search for theories and applications and ways to communicate them to others—writing books, articles, and reports was only part of the answer. I should also assume the role of an active and moral human agent, helping to facilitate a movement in the direction indicated by my inquiry into the trends and dynamics of evolution. The phrase I jotted down one night (subsequently published in my 1986 *Evolution: The Grand Synthesis*) began to haunt me: "In a system such as contemporary society, evolution is always a promise and devolution always a threat. No system comes with a guarantee of ongoing evolution. The challenge is real. To ignore it is to play dice with all we have. To accept it is not to play God—it is to become an instrument of whatever divine purpose infuses this universe." I decided to accept the challenge and keep myself free to seize the opportunities that would present themselves. My wife and I moved to our farmhouse (hitherto a vacation abode) on a hilltop in Tuscany.

Life in a setting that was virtually unchanged since the great Florentine painters used it as backdrop for their religious scenes—with hill after hill topped by ancient villages, rows of grapevines rolling down toward the river and the Mediterranean shimmering in the distance—was ideal for immersing myself in a renewed search for meaning. I was soon caught up in the excitement of discovering the latest advances in the new physics and the new biology, and their relevance to the understanding of the evolutionary processes unfolding in society and nature. Though I maintained my commitment to the quarterly journal I inherited as *The Philosophy Forum* (which I renamed *World Futures: The Journal of General Evolution*), I found time to immerse myself in the tasks of reading and reflecting—I did not have the pressures of international civil service and obligation to students and colleagues to contend with. My research could benefit from enduring contacts with the General Evolution Research Group, an informal but dedicated body I founded in the fall of 1986 with close colleagues (many of them contributors to the present volume) at the instigation of Ilya Prigogine and Jonas Salk at a memorable meeting at the San Diego Salk Institute.

Though these activities kept me more than busy, within a year the question of personal responsibility cropped up with great force and demanded to be acted upon. It prompted me to enter on another kind of search, a search for practical pathfinding. When Prince Alfred von Liechtenstein, the founder of the Vienna Academy for the Study of the Future, asked me to join him as founding-rector of this institution, I did not refuse, but undertook to commute between the Tuscan hills and the city of Vienna. Three years later another opportunity came my way: the founding, in Vienna's sister-city of Budapest, of a "club" that would function as the "inner limit" (or, better, "inner opportunity") oriented counterpart to the Club of Rome. As of 1994, I shifted my realworld-related activities to creating, coordinating, and implementing the "planetary consciousness" projects of the Club of Budapest.

What I Have Found

The substance of this process of three—now almost four—decades of search is the meaning that surfaced in the course of it. The first insight came in the form of the concept of organic process, inspired by my reading of Alfred North Whitehead. I came to the view that change in the cosmos, change in nature, and change in the human sphere are not disconnected phenomena. These processes have an internal logic: they bring forth the same kind of entity in the world, an "organism" in the language of Whitehead, or a "coagulate" as a Yale philosophy of science colleague suggested in 1966. To my delight, I discovered that this entity can be, and has in fact been, described as a system. My intellectual home moved from Whitehead's organic metaphysics to Ludwig von Bertalanffy's general system theory.

The question that soon presented itself was how one kind of system can transform into another—seeing that they all had a common origin, either in the Big Bang or in the primeval *ylem*. The answer that crystallized in my mind was couched in the language of evolution; not the evolution of this or that thing or domain, but evolution as the phenomenon of change itself: interdeterministic, nonlinear, yet irreversible and not without overall direction. My intellectual home shifted to Prigogine's nonequilibrium systems theory, the foundation for the theoretical structure I subsequently developed as general evolution theory.

However, the practical question could not be evaded: what do the general laws of complex-system evolution mean for our times? What do they reveal of the paths through the crucial bifurcations and other complexities of our societies, institutions, and enterprises—paths that an informed and moral agent could (and thus should) enter upon and facilitate? If our societies, institutions, and enterprises are complex systems, they are subject to the fundamental regularities of complex-system evolution. Hence we could know something about the nature and direction of today's societal changes and transformations. We could, in principle, act with greater insight and foresight. The search for an answer to these questions expanded my intellectual home to range from the basic premises of general evolution theory to the shared problems of our future.

But where do we find the correct answers? How do we relate the personal quest to the larger world? How do we center ourselves as human beings for the tasks required of us by our times, both on the grand scale and in more intimate, personal ways? In my work at Princeton, and then at the United Nations, a vast variety of projections, scenarios, proposals, and decision-guides had come to my attention, first in regard to the public sector and then in reference to business management and the conduct of personal lives. Then, in Tuscany, my own existence and lifestyle became unexpectedly involved. I developed a hunger for close personal relationships with family and friends, and for direct contact with nature. I began eating simply and with attention to wholeness and biological purity, breathing deeply—both figuratively and literally—and leaving behind unnecessary frills and sophistries. The paramount question became how I should live in accordance with the needs and possibilities of my times.

The insight that dawned on me was that a morally acceptable style of living is one that allows others to live as well. This is not a trivial proposition: as I had ample occasion to note, first as a globe-trotting concert pianist and then as a widely traveling teacher, lecturer, and consultant, the typical lifestyle of Western and Westernized people cannot leave available for long sufficient resources for the rest of the world even to stay alive.

Living in a way that others could live as well implies that all people, regardless of the accidents of birth and the opportunities of life experience, have a basic right to the resources required for a life of basic human dignity. But rights alone are not sufficient: they state claims, but do not imply the responsibility for satisfying the claims. While to live in a way that others could also live allows the possibility that basic resources should be available for the "others," it does not specify the obligation to ensure that such resources become effectively available to them. If I, for example, refrain from eating meat, this does not mean that the grain my behavior liberates from animal feed for human consumption would actually reach the table of the hungry. To the statement of rights we have to add a statement of responsibilities. A lifestyle, I concluded, is moral only if it allows other people effective access to the resources they require for a lifestyle that is qualitatively commensurate with one's own.

A precept such as this may be satisfying in itself, but it is frustrating when one looks for its actual applications in the world. Most people agree with it in principle, but shrug it off in practice. The way to hell, it is said, is paved with good intentions. Our common way, I saw, will doubtless conduce to that damned locale if good intentions are not followed up by good actions. An evolutionary process will not be stopped by public disregard; only its direction will change. The threats will grow, and the cost of remedial action will rise.

How to break through the indifference barrier? The task is to do more than achieve intellectual understanding alone. That is important, but in itself not enough. The objective must be to achieve a change of heart. Only then can we catch up with our changing times, and have a reasonable chance of guiding our evolution along humanly desirable pathways. The crucial issue is the evolution of another system, one that is closest to us yet the most difficult of all to apprehend: our *consciousness*. Consciousness is not a constant; it has been evolving all along our species' history. Yet today it lags behind: the rate of change proves too fast for it. In consequence we are grappling with the problems of a postindustrial age with the mentality of the classical industrial epoch. That is just as hopeless as it would be to try to grapple with the problems of the modern industrial age with the mind-set of the Middle Ages.

The recognition that, when all is said and done, the speed with which our consciousness evolves is the key issue of our times led me to found the Club of Budapest. The Club of Rome, which succeeded in capturing the attention of the world's political and business leaders in the 1970s, was phenomenally effective in calling attention to the limits of continued quantitative growth; to the cancer syndrome of the industrial age. But that realization on the intellectual plane alone proved insufficient: the turnaround impelled by this insight was neither deep nor fast enough. I maintained that the recognition must dawn that our values and priorities need to change; the way we look at ourselves and the world must evolve. We need to evolve our consciousness; evolve it deep enough and fast enough to be of real use.

As I wrote in *Goals for Mankind*, the report I drafted at the UN for the Club of Rome, the evolution of today's consciousness resembles a revolution more than a piecemeal process of evolution. Though it is urgent, this revolution cannot come from above, as Mao had attempted—it must come from below, and from within. The great creators of the culture of our epoch must be mobilized. They are not the political and business leaders of the world, however important they may be in their own right. The great culture-shapers are the writers and the artists, the designers, the spiritual leaders, and the opinion-makers. They must be brought together, their unique creativity informed and focused. That is the *raison d'être* and the ongoing mission of the Club of Budapest, endorsed by its nearly one hundred elected members, who include the Dalai Lama, Yehudi Menuhin, Peter Ustinov, Arthur C. Clarke, Liv Ullman, Václav Havel, Mikhail Gorbachev, Mohammed

Yunus, Riane Eisler, Elie Wiesel, and others of similar stature and commitment. "The Club of Budapest," I wrote in its mission statement, "is dedicated to the proposition that promoting and facilitating the evolution of planetary consciousness is a vital aspect of our sustained well-being and individual as well as social development. *It is an essential mission of our time.*"

Consciousness, my Club of Budapest colleagues believe, is not just feeling, value, and intuition; it is also thinking, insight, and vision. The latter is especially important. But how to develop it? To where can we apply for it?

Developing the correct vision, the same as evolving the right moral criteria, used to be a task for religion. Today, the responsibility is placed squarely in the lap of science. For most people in modern societies a vision is authoritative only if it rests on what they can accept as the scientific understanding of reality. But can science give us a correct vision?

Here the current phase of my intellectual quest became relevant in practice. My theoretical concern has always been the integration of the highly specialized and often mutually isolated branches of the contemporary sciences; and in the course of these efforts I realized that such an integration can provide a meaningful vision of the world and of ourselves. Science, I have come to believe, can give us a vision that is both as true as current knowledge permits, and intensely meaningful. I sought to demonstrate this fact in a series of books: *The Creative Cosmos* (1993), *Science and Reality* (1994), *The Interconnected Universe* (1995), and *The Whispering Pond* (1996). Let me end this brief history with a passage from the last-named book:

The "scientific worldview" [I wrote in the *Introduction*] that dominates many people's minds is not a happy one. In this view the essential features of the human species are the result of a succession of random, accidental events in the history of life on Earth, while the unique features of the human individual derive from the fortuitous combination of genes with which he or she was born. The ongoing struggle for survival in which every individual, every enterprise and every society is ceaselessly engaged has made us into bundles of egotism, separate from all that lies beyond the limits of our body and the compass of our personal and professional interests.

But this is not the view of the world warranted by the concepts and theories of the contemporary empirical sciences. Beyond the accidents of mutation and natural selection in a world dominated by the random concourse of atoms and particles, leading-edge science is discovering a deeper logic. It is not that scientists would appeal to a transcendental mind or spirit that would guide the processes that have led to the human species; rather, it is that they are discovering the integral dynamic of the processes that have brought human beings (as all things in the observable universe) on the scene. In the embracing vision that is now emerging, everything that has evolved in the universe, Mozart and Einstein, you and me, the greatest of galaxies and the humblest of insects, is the result of a stupendous process of open-ended yet non-random self-creation. Nothing that has ever evolved exists separately from all the rest: all things are connected, all are part of an organic totality.

In the "Concluding Thoughts" I posed the following query.

What if nature—the universe itself—is not a passive rock or a lifeless machine? What if people are not complex machines, and not separate from each other and from their environment but profoundly though subtly linked? And what if the entire cosmos throbs with the creative energy of self-organization, constantly evolving, with periodic bursts of explosive innovation? If this is the concept we get from science, and if we assimilate it with all our being, would we still relate to each other and to our environment in quite the same way?

This vision places major responsibilities on the shoulders of informed and responsible moral agents. It is not fantasy, but a concept that the avant-garde branches of the natural sciences are now beginning to project. These sciences are leaving behind the last remnants of the mechanistic view of life and universe. Space and time are united as the dynamic background of the observable universe; matter is vanishing as a fundamental feature of reality, retreating before energy; and continuous fields are replacing discrete particles as the basic elements of an energy-bathed cosmos. And in the light of the new cosmologies we see the final destiny of this world as no longer a lapse into the grayness of a lukewarm, empty, and eternally unchanging nothingness, but as cyclic self-renewal in a self-creating, self-energizing, and self-organizing mega-universe.

The new sciences give us a vision of a universe where all things are linked in a fundamental unity. They confirm William James's image: we are like islands in the sea—separate on the surface but connected in the deep. This image frames the substance of my credo. It is the meaning I have found in my nearly four decades of quest, and the sense of responsibility I have come to feel follows directly from it.

3
The General Evolution Research Group: A Brief History

DAVID LOYE

Abstract
A brief history of the General Evolution
Research Group, the multinational and
multidisciplinary research group founded by
Laszlo and associates in 1986.

Key words
La Jolla, *World Futures: The Journal of General
Evolution*, world *problematique*, chaos theory,
the Cold War, IIASA, Prigogine, Salk, GERG,
Florence, Bologna, the Club of Budapest, World
Futures General Evolution book series.

As with other all other groups, in the case of the General Evolution Research Group there are two histories: one sparse and formal, the other rich, engaging, and informal.

Formally, the General Evolution Research Group was formed in La Jolla, California, in 1986. Its purpose was—and still is—to bring together a small group of scholars from a variety of disciplines and nations to explore possibilities for the development of a *general* (as differentiated from solely biological or paleontological) evolution theory. Following its formation, it has held meetings in Florence, Bologna, Budapest, Potsdam, Vienna, and Turku, Finland. Its primary founder and leader was and is systems philosopher and general evolution theorist Ervin Laszlo. Its journal is *World Futures: The Journal of General Evolution*, with Laszlo as editor and the original co-founding members of the General Evolution Research Group forming the Editorial Board. Currently, in addition to its independent existence, the General Evolution Research Group serves as a consultant scientific research body within the structure of Laszlo's formation of the new Club of Budapest.

Behind this sparse account, however, lies the other history, of the aspirations and frustrations of an unusual group of scholars at a dramatic turning-point in the history of science and humanity. In the account that follows can also be seen at work the dynamics of the very mix of evolution and chaos theory the Group was formed to explore. That is, in how its members met and tenuously, sporadically, but at times in meaningful ways came to work together, can be seen the interplay of the strange attractor, the basins, hypercyles, and most importantly out of the bifurcations of the late 20th century, the glimpses now and then of some vital movement toward the possibilities of the more humanly fulfilling "nucleation" for the future.

A Pivotal Mission and the Early Days

The idea for what eventually became the Group began to form some years before 1986 in Ervin Laszlo's mind. Here had arrived this heady time in human history when, on the one hand, there loom before us the escalating problems of the *world problematique*, which pose the question of whether our species is to fulfill or end itself. On the other hand, out of science had erupted the new theories of nonlinear dynamics and of concepts of self-organizing, complexity, and dissipative structures, all becoming popularly clustered within the general idea of "chaos theory." At the same time the old paradigm for evolution theory had been breaking down under the pressure of the intellectual and social logic for a *general* systems theory—that is, theory asserting the necessity of finding concepts in common across the disciplinary boundaries that too often have stifled creativity within science as well as science's ability to serve society.

What if one could be used to solve the other? That is, what if out of this double-edged explosion within science there might be found a way to apply this new mix of evolutionary theory and "chaos theory" to solutions for the personal, social, and cultural chaos of our time?

This was the idea—as expressed in various books, talks and papers—that originally captivated Laszlo, as the pioneer and organizer for what was bit by bit becoming the new field of general evolution theory. Increasingly, it was also to captivate the handful of scholars that Laszlo began to draw together from many scientific disciplines and countries in attempts to move the idea forward.

As is usual for all ventures, a first attempt in this direction seemingly came to nothing. During the final years of the Cold War, when from both sides scientists sought to transcend politics in a rapprochement to try to solve the mounting problems facing humanity, there had been formed an international organization with an equal representation of Western and Soviet bloc scholars, the International Institute of Applied Systems Analysis (IIASA), based near Vienna. The Director General showed interest in the idea. Hurriedly, a handful of scholars with the requisite activist as well as scientific orientations were invited by Laszlo to meet in Budapest to put together a proposal.

Particularly dramatic in retrospect was the "caravan" that set out from Budapest to drive to IIASA headquarters at the sumptuous Hapsburg hunting palace at Laxenburg, south of Vienna. Still up were the barbed wire corridors separating East from West, along with the guards armed with machine guns, and the grim checking of credentials and passes at each checkpoint for the crossing.

The IIASA project came to naught, but out of it came the mutual admirations, the friendships, and the preliminary working associations that laid the groundwork for what not too long afterward became the General Evolution Research Group. Involved in this critical formative stage, later to join Laszlo in becoming co-founding members of GERG, were biologist Vilmos Csanyi and computer scientist

Georgy Kampis from Budapest; management theorist and futurist Penntti Malaska (with Mika Pantzar joining later) from Finland; and from the United States, astrophysicist Eric Chaisson, psychologist Jonathan Schull, historian Robert Artigiani, cultural evolution theorist Riane Eisler, and myself, a social psychologist and systems theorist.

The Formation of GERG, or a Bit of Order out of Chaos

There also came out of this early attempt a flurry of ongoing contacts steadily advancing the idea. Pivotal in this regard was the meeting between Laszlo, Ilya Prigogine, and Jonas Salk at the "Discoveries 1985" Symposium in October of 1985 in Brussels. Of theorists whose work was most rapidly advancing the formation of a new theory of general evolution, Prigogine was by then the most influential— having received a Nobel Prize for his dissipative structures theory. Salk was of special interest in relation to the activist thrust for the developing project, having attained world stature for applying science to the needs of humanity in the case of the Salk vaccine. Both resonated powerfully to the idea, offering aid in any way possible.

A meeting in Santa Cruz, California, involving Laszlo, Eisler, and myself further enlisted the enthusiasm of mathematician and chaos theorist Ralph Abraham. Then came the invitation from Jonas Salk that led to the Group's formal launching. His offer to provide funds for transportation and housing at last made it possible to draw together from the various parts of Europe and the United States what had become the core group, with the addition now of biologist John Corliss, an American then living in Budapest.

Again the project itself came to naught—the hope had been that Salk and/or the Salk Institute might provide the housing and funding that by now seemed a bed-rock necessity for any further movement of the idea forward. But in the aftermath of this disappointment, meeting in the hotel where we were housed, there erupted the increasingly joyful and devil-may-care brain-storming session out of which GERG came into being.

Based on my observation of the success of the "mom and pop think tanks" then erupting among futurists and other independent scholars, I pointed out that there was nothing that said we couldn't go ahead on our own without funding, without a prestigious institutional attachment, without housing or tenure or infrastructure or all the other formal trappings that were now more often stifling than liberating scientific creativity throughout the world. There was really no good reason why we couldn't simply form our own group to go ahead and do what we wanted to do.

Names were bandied about, out of which "The General Evolution Research Group" emerged. Someone soon remarked this would give us the acronym of GERG—which at first seemed horrible, then to much laughter engaging. But we would need our own journal—mindful of all this would involve, it seemed a hopeless undertaking. But we already have it, Laszlo announced. Leaving the room briefly to call the publishers of his journal *World Futures,* Gordon & Breach, he returned to announce they had blessed going ahead with what now—as of that moment—became *World Futures: The Journal of General Evolution.*

Some Developmental High Points

Thereafter the group met whenever Laszlo found a sponsor for a prestigious event—which in itself was an important accomplishment historically. Contrary to the usual pattern of being unable to move without secure foundation funding or a settled institutional base, driven by his determination to see the purpose of the Group succeed—calling, I have always felt, on his early experience as a concert pianist (see "One Man's Quest" in this volume)—Laszlo now became one of the most skillful and influential "cultural entrepreneurs" of his time.

An early high-point was the meeting in Florence, Italy, which had been selected as the Cultural Capital of Europe for 1986. To provide a suitably important cultural event to commemorate the occasion, along with Italian philosopher (and subsequent GERG member) Mauro Ceruti, Laszlo organized a week-long symposium on the theme Abitare La Terra ("to live on Earth"). Key events included a presentation of papers by scholars from the new General Evolution Research Group, the Club of Rome, and the United Nations University. Another high point was the selection of GERG to provide the cultural event to commemorate the 900th Anniversary of the world's oldest university, the University of Bologna in Bologna, Italy. A third high point was the conference organized in the framework of the International Society for the Systems Sciences by Vilmos Csanyi and Gyorgy Kampis in 1987 in Budapest—which in retrospect emerges as a key original "spiritual" headquarters for what later became GERG as well as the actual headquarters for Laszlo's later formation of the Club of Budapest.

Throughout this period the Group expanded somewhat, with the addition of pioneering chaos theorist Ilya Prigogine from Belgium; the pioneering autopoiesis theorist, Francisco Varela, from Chile and France; historian Ignazio Masulli and philosophers Mauro Ceruti and Gianluca Bocchi from Italy; mathematical biologist Peter Saunders and thermodynamicist Peter Allen from England; philosopher and systems theorist Min Jiayin from China; ecologist and philosopher Eduard Makarjan from Armenia in the Soviet Union; physicist Rudolf Treumann from Germany; management theorist Thomas Bernold from Switzerland; and from the United States, brain scientist Karl Pribram, evolutionary systems theorist Bela Banathy, psychologist Allan Combs, and systems scientist Alfonso Montuori, the Journal's present associate editor. More recently, futurist and evolutionary theorist Duane Elgin and biologist and evolution theorist Stanley Salthe of the United States, and physicist Jurgen Kurths of Germany have become members.

Of particular importance in view of the tendency of 20th-century international scientific groups to be exclusively male was the Group's increasing female membership. Historically, Eisler had been the first woman to be included in the core working membership of a group devoted to evolutionary research as well as the first to contribute an influential new theory of cultural evolution. Over these years psychologist Singa Sandelin Benko from Sweden, political scientist Miriam Campanella, interdisciplinary educator Gerlind Rurik from Germany, social psychologist Mária Sági, the Journal's present managing editor, from Budapest, and evolutionary theorist Sally Goerner, and information theorist Susantha Goonatillake from Sri Lanka and now the United States were also invited by Laszlo to join the Group.

Out of the Past and into the Future

To those who originally aspired to see our world transformed by this venture, it must be admitted that GERG—as well as everything else one can think of—has fallen short. At times, because of the difficulties of the old paradigm for science out of which we come, it seems that we gather together from around the world only to read papers born of separate disciplines, in separate scientific languages, with insufficient cross-disciplinary sharing. But informally, behind scenes, in the chats over breakfast, luncheons, during and after dinners, and afterwards in e-mail and other communications internationally, there has flowed between Group members the creative excitement and the sense of community and camaraderie that historically has been at the making of all attempts at human advancement.

The most promising current development is Laszlo's incorporation of GERG into the structure of the Club of Budapest as its ancillary scientific body. In this capacity GERG will coordinate the research for the main scientific event of the year-long celebration of Weimar as Cultural Capital of Europe in 1999, with the symposium entitled "The Chances of Evolution: Humanity's Prospects in the Next Millennium." Other activities of some Group members as well as experts in other fields are focusing on the exploration of the implications of Laszlo's new QVI (quantum-vacuum interaction) theory, also known as the theory of the Psi-field. This theory, which brings together advanced theory and research in physics, psychology, creativity, and the study of paranormal phenomena, explores the question of how form originates in evolution, the roots of consciousness, and the connection of science to spirituality.

Throughout the history of the General Evolution Research Group its Journal has not only served to hold it together but has also provided one of the most essential things for scientific advancement—a forum where those who resonate to the creation of a more adequate evolutionary theory and a science more adequate to the task of the advancement of humanity can meet across national and disciplinary boundaries and freely exchange new ideas.

Indicative of the Journal's international nature is the fact that its editor, Laszlo, residing in Italy, is former Program Director of the United Nations Institute for Training and Research (UNITAR). Its associate editor for many years, Vilmos Csanyi, is a leading European evolution theorist residing in Budapest. Current associate editor Alfonso Montuori is an Italian residing in the United States. Managing editor Mária Sági is a social psychologist at the Hungarian Academy of Science's Institute of Sociology in Budapest. Published by the international science publisher Gordon & Breach, it is managed out of G&B offices in Newark, New Jersey, with editing and production in Madras, India, and distribution out of Brussels, Belgium.

Some idea of the range of *World Futures: The Journal of General Evolution* can be gathered from the nature of a few special issues. These include: *Evolutionary Consciousness*, edited by Bela H. Banathy (Vol. 38: 2–4). *Theoretical Achievements and Practical Applications of General Evolutionary Theory*, edited by Vilmos Csanyi (Vol. 38: 1–3). *The Presence of the Future: Values, Aptitudes and Behaviors for Life in the 21st Century*, edited by Françoise Parisot-Baratier (Vol. 41: 1–3) *The Path Toward Global Survival: A Social and Economic Study of 162 Countries*, by Hans-Wolff Graf (Vol. 43: 1–4) *The Quantum of Evolution*, edited by Francis Heyligen, Cliff Joslyn and Valentin Turchin (Vol. 45: 1–4). *Unity and Diversity in Contemporary Systems Thinking: Systemic Pictures at an Exhibition*, edited by J.D.R. de Radt and S. Strijbos (Vol. 47: 1). And *The Concept of Collective Consciousness*, edited by Ervin Laszlo (Vol. 48: 1–4).

Additionally, there has been the contribution of the World Futures General Evolution book series. Most representative is the keynote: *The New Evolutionary Paradigm*, 1991, edited by Ervin Laszlo with foreword by Ilya Prigogine. This comprehensive collection brought together papers by the original core group articulating the purpose and horizon for the then new field of general evolution theory. Unusual contributions have been made by: Volume 1, *Nature and History: The Evolutionary Approach for Social Scientists* by Ignazio Masuli; Volume 3, *The Age of Bifurcation: Understanding the Changing World* by Ervin Laszlo; Volume 4, *Cooperation: Beyond the Age of Competition* edited by Allan Combs; Volume 5, *The Evolution of Cognitive Maps: New Paradigms for the 21st Century* edited by Ervin Laszlo and Ignazio Masulli, with Robert Artigiani and Vilmos Csanyi; Volume 6, *The Evolving Mind* by Ben Goertzel. Volume 7, *Chaos and the Evolving Ecological Universe* by Sally Goerner; Volume 8, *Constraints and Possibilities: The Evolution of Knowledge and the Knowledge of Evolution* by Mauro Ceruti.

Also scheduled for 1998 are *Evolutionary Change* by Aron Katsenelinboigen, *The Evolutionary Trajectory* by Richard Coren, *Merged Evolution* by Susantha Goonatilake, *Instinct and Revelation* by Alondra Oubre, and *Science, Education, and Future Generations* edited by Eric Chaisson and Tae Change Kim, and for 1998, *The Mind of Society* by Yvon Provencal, and *The Great Transition* by Crawford Robb.

The publisher of both the journal and the GERG book series is the international science publisher Gordon & Breach (www.gbhap-us.com, for the Web Site with addresses, etc.). So prolific has been the output initiated by Laszlo involving this Group that two other publishers are also now involved. The 21st Century Studies series for British publisher Adamantine Press (www.adamantine.co.uk) and Praeger books in the United States (www.greenwood.com) is the publisher of both this volume and *Changing Visions: Cognitive Maps Past, Present, and Future,* by Ervin Laszlo, Robert Artigiani, Allan Combs, and Vilmos Csanyi. US publisher Hampton Press is also publisher of a series on systems science, of which Montuori is the editor, which includes new editions of Laszlo's key books (*Evolution* and *An Introduction to Systems Philosophy*) and new books by Mauro Ceruti, Edgar Morin, and myself (*Creativity and Prediction in the Dream Factory*).

Information for interested subscribers to the Journal or the book series may be obtained through the above Web site address for Gordon & Breach or by writing to *World Futures: The Journal of General Evolution,* Uri-u.49, 1014 Budapest, Hungary.

Among books independently generated by GERG members that are also more generally available are Laszlo's *The Whispering Pond*—a *Choice* selection for one of the outstanding scholarly books of 1997; Prigogine, *Order and Chaos* and *The End of Certainty;* Eisler, *The Chalice and the Blade* and *Sacred Pleasure;* Pribram, *Brain and Perception;* Salthe, *Development in Evolution;* Csanyi, *Evolutionary Systems and Society;* Varela, *The Tree of Knowledge;* Chaisson, *Cosmic Dawn, The Life Era;* Combs, *The Radiance of Being* and *The Enchanted Loom;* Ceruti, *Constraints and Possibilities;* Bocchi and Ceruti, *The Origin of the Story;* Min Jiayin, *The Chalice and the Blade in Chinese Culture;* Montuori, *Evolutionary Competence* and *From Power to Partnership;* Abraham, *Chaos, Gaia, and Eros;* Saunders, *Beyond Neo-Darwinism;* and Elgin, *Awakening Earth.*

Part 2

The Impact of the Human Agent on Evolution

4
Evolution: The Old View and the New View

FRITJOF CAPRA

Abstract
Physicist Fritjof Capra contrasts the old paradigm with the emerging new paradigm for evolution. In particular, he focuses on the greater scope of the systems perspective and a new understanding of the intimate operations of evolution revealed by the new biology.

Key words
Complexity, living systems, self-organization, systems thinking, natural selection, random mutations, biological evolution, Lamarck, Darwin, Mendel, neo-Darwinism, Monod, reductionism, Lynn Margulis, genetic code, genes, genome, Stuart Kauffman, Ervin Laszlo, grand synthesis, Ilya Prigogine, Maturana and Varela, autopoiesis, Lovelock and Margulis, Gaia hypothesis, coevolution, three avenues of creativity, microbiology, DNA recombination, cooperation, symbiogenesis.

During the past twenty-five years, a new language for understanding the complexity of living systems—that is, of organisms, social systems, and ecosystems—has been developed at the forefront of science. Chaos, fractals, dissipative structures, self-organization, and autopoietic networks are some of the key concepts of this new way of understanding complex systems.

From these recent advances, a new conceptual framework for the scientific understanding of life is now emerging. The intellectual tradition of systems thinking, and the models of living systems developed during the early decades of the century, form the conceptual and historical roots of this new scientific framework. Indeed, what is now emerging at the forefront of science may be seen as a coherent theory of living systems that offers, for the first time, a unified view of mind, matter, and life.

One of the most rewarding features of this emerging theory is the new understanding of evolution it implies. Rather than seeing evolution as the result of random mutations and natural selection, we are beginning to recognize the creative unfolding of life in forms of ever-increasing diversity and complexity as an inherent characteristic of all living systems. Although mutation and natural selection are still acknowledged as important aspects of biological evolution, the central focus is on creativity, on life's constant reaching out into novelty.

To understand the fundamental difference between the old and new views of evolution, it will be useful to briefly review the history of evolutionary thought.

The first theory of evolution was formulated at the beginning of the 19th century by Jean Baptiste Lamarck, a self-taught naturalist who coined the term "biology" and made extensive studies in botany and zoology. Lamarck observed that animals changed under environmental pressure, and he believed that they could pass on these changes to their offspring. This passing-on of acquired characteristics was for him the main mechanism of evolution.

Although it turned out that Lamarck was wrong in that respect, his recognition of the phenomenon of evolution—the emergence of new biological structures in the history of species—was a revolutionary insight that profoundly affected all subsequent scientific thought. In particular, Lamarck had a strong influence on Charles Darwin, who started his scientific career as a geologist but became interested in biology during his famous expedition to the Galapagos Islands. His careful observations of the island fauna stimulated Darwin to speculate about the effect of geographical isolation on the formation of species and led him, eventually, to the formulation of his theory of evolution.

Darwin based his theory on two fundamental ideas—chance variation, later to be called random mutation, and natural selection. At the center of Darwinian thought stands the insight that all living organisms are related by common ancestry. All forms of life have emerged from that ancestry by a continuous process of variations throughout billions of years of geological history. In this evolutionary process many more variations are produced than can possibly survive, and thus many individuals are weeded out by natural selection, as some variants outgrow and out-reproduce others.

These basic ideas are well documented today, supported by vast amounts of evidence from biology, biochemistry, and the fossil record, and all serious scientists are in complete agreement with them. The differences between the classical theory of evolution and the emerging new theory center around the question of the *dynamics* of evolution—the mechanisms through which evolutionary changes take place.

Darwin's own concept of chance variations was based on an assumption that was common to 19th-century views of heredity. It was assumed that the biological characteristics of an individual represented a "blend" of those of its parents, with both parents contributing more or less equal parts to the mixture. This meant that an offspring of a parent with a useful chance variation would inherit only 50 percent of the new characteristic, and would be able to pass on only 25 percent of it to the next generation. Thus the new characteristic would be diluted rapidly, with very little chance of establishing itself through natural selection. Darwin himself recognized that this was a serious flaw in his theory for which he had no remedy.

The solution to Darwin's problem was discovered by Gregor Mendel, an Austrian monk and amateur botanist. From careful experiments with garden peas, Mendel deduced that there were "units of heredity"—later to be called genes—that did not blend in the process of reproduction but were transmitted from generation to generation without changing their identity. With this discovery it could be assumed that random mutations of genes would not disappear within a few generations but would be preserved, to be either reinforced or eliminated by natural selection. Mendel's discovery not only played a decisive role in establishing the Darwinian theory of evolution but also opened up the new field of genetics—the study of heredity through the investigation of the chemical and physical nature of genes.

From Darwinism to Neo-Darwinism

The combination of Darwin's idea of gradual evolutionary changes with Mendel's discovery of genetic stability resulted in the synthesis known as neo-Darwinism, which is taught today as the established theory of evolution in biology departments around the world. According to the neo-Darwinist theory, all evolutionary variation results from random mutation, that is, from random genetic changes, followed by natural selection. For example, if an animal species needs thick fur to survive in a cold climate, it will not respond to this need by growing fur but will instead develop all sorts of random genetic changes, and those animals whose changes happen to result in thick fur will survive to produce more offspring. Thus, in the words of geneticist Jacques Monod, "chance alone is at the source of every innovation, of all creation in the biosphere."[1]

In the view of microbiologist Lynn Margulis, neo-Darwinism is fundamentally flawed, not only because it is based on reductionist concepts that are now outdated, but also because it was formulated in an inappropriate mathematical language. "The language of life is not ordinary arithmetic and algebra," argues Margulis, "the language of life is chemistry. The practicing neo-Darwinists lack relevant knowledge in, for example, microbiology, cell biology, biochemistry . . . and microbial ecology."[2]

One reason why today's leading evolutionists lack the appropriate language to describe evolutionary change, according to Margulis, is that most of them come out of the zoological tradition and thus are used to dealing with only a small, relatively recent part of evolutionary history. Current research in microbiology indicates strongly that the major avenues for evolution's creativity were developed long before animals appeared on the scene.

The central conceptual problem of neo-Darwinism seems to be its reductionist conception of the genome, the collection of an organism's genes. The great achievements of molecular biology, often described as "the cracking of the genetic code," have resulted in the tendency to picture the genome as a linear array of independent genes, each corresponding to a biological trait. Research has shown, however, that a single gene may affect a wide range of traits and that, conversely, many separate genes often combine to produce a single trait. It is thus quite mysterious how complex structures, like an eye or a flower, could have evolved through successive mutations of individual genes. Evidently, the study of the coordinating and integrating activities of the whole genome is of paramount importance, but this has been hampered severely by the mechanistic outlook of conventional biology.

The limitations of the mechanistic model are shown dramatically by the problems of cell development and differentiation. In the very early stages of the development of higher organisms, the number of their cells increases from one to two, to four, etc., doubling at each step as the cells divide repeatedly. Since the genetic instructions remain unchanged in this process of cell division, how can the cells specialize in different ways, becoming muscle cells, blood cells, bone cells, nerve cells, and so on? This basic problem of development, which appears in many variations throughout biology, clearly flies in the face of the mechanistic view of life.

Only very recently have biologists begun to understand the genome of an organism as a highly interwoven network in which genes directly and indirectly regulate each other's activities. These studies have shown that cell types differ from one another not because they contain different genes, but because the genes that are *active* in them differ. In other words, the structure of the genetic network is the same in all cells, but the patterns of genetic activity are different. The evolutionary biologist Stuart Kauffman has used the new mathematics of complexity to model these patterns of genetic activity and was able to derive several known features of cell differentiation and evolution from these models.

Another striking manifestation of genetic wholeness is the now well-documented fact that evolution did not proceed through continuous gradual changes over time, caused by long sequences of successive mutations. The fossil record shows clearly that throughout evolutionary history there have been long periods of stability, or "stasis," without any genetic variation, punctuated by sudden and dramatic transitions. Stable periods of hundreds of thousands of years are quite the norm. Indeed, the human evolutionary adventure began with a million years of stability of the first hominid species, *Australopithecus afarensis*. This new picture, known as "punctuated equilibria," indicates that the sudden transitions were caused by mechanisms quite different from the random mutations of neo-Darwinist theory.

An important aspect of the classical theory of evolution is the idea that in the course of evolutionary change and under the pressure of natural selection, organisms will gradually adapt to their environment until they reach a fit that is good enough for survival and reproduction. In the new systems view, by contrast, evolutionary change is seen as the result of life's inherent tendency to create novelty, which may or may not be accompanied by adaptation to changing environmental conditions.

Accordingly, systems biologists have begun to portray the genome as a self-organizing network capable of spontaneously producing new forms of order. "We must rethink evolutionary biology," writes Stuart Kauffman. "Much of the order we see in organisms may be the direct result not of natural selection but of the natural order selection was privileged to act on ... Evolution is not just a tinkering ... It is emergent order honored and honed by selection."[3]

Toward a New Theory of Evolution

A comprehensive new theory of evolution, based on these insights, has not yet been formulated. But the recently developed models and theories of self-organizing systems provide the elements for formulating such a theory, as Ervin Laszlo showed ten years ago in his brilliant draft of a grand synthesis.[4]

The theory of dissipative structures by Ilya Prigogine, Nobel Laureate and professor of physical chemistry at the Free University of Brussels, shows how complex biochemical systems involve chemical feedback loops that may push the system to a point of instability, called a "bifurcation point," at which new structures of higher order may emerge. Manfred Eigen, Nobel Laureate in chemistry and director of the Max Planck Institute for Physical Chemistry in Göttingen, has suggested that similar chemical cycles may have formed before the emergence of life on Earth, thus initiating a prebiological phase of evolution.

Stuart Kauffman, as mentioned above, has analyzed the spontaneous emergence of order by constructing mathematical models of genetic networks. The neuroscientists Humberto Maturana and Francisco Varela have described the process of evolution in terms of their theory of autopoiesis, in which the basic pattern of organization of all living systems is defined as a "self-making" network of cellular processes. The planetary dimensions of the unfolding of life have been explored extensively by the atmospheric chemist James Lovelock, in collaboration with Lynn Margulis, in the Gaia theory, which is perhaps the most surprising and most beautiful expression of self-organization. At the core of this theory lies the idea that the planet Earth as a whole is a living, self-organizing system.

Gaia theory looks at life in a systemic way, bringing together geology, microbiology, atmospheric chemistry, and other disciplines. It challenges the conventional view that those are separate disciplines, that the forces of geology set the conditions for life on Earth, and that the plants and animals were mere passengers who by chance found just the right conditions for their evolution. According to Gaia theory, life creates the conditions for its own existence.

The resistance of the scientific community to this new view of life was very strong at first. Opponents argued that the theory was unscientific because it was teleological, that is, implying the idea of natural processes being shaped by a purpose. This criticism harks back to the old debate between mechanists and vitalists of the 1920s. While mechanists hold that all biological phenomena will eventually be explained in terms of the laws of physics and chemistry, vitalists postulate the existence of a nonphysical entity, a causal agent directing the life processes that defy mechanistic explanations. Teleology—from the Greek *telos* ("purpose")—asserts that the causal agent postulated by vitalism is purposeful, that there is purpose and design in nature. By strenuously opposing vitalist and teleological arguments, the mechanists still struggle with the Newtonian metaphor of God as a clockmaker.

The new understanding of life has finally overcome the debate between mechanism and teleology. According to the theory of autopoiesis, every living organism "couples structurally" to its environment, that is, it responds to environmental influences with structural changes, which will in turn alter its future behavior. In other words, every living system is a learning system. As long as it remains alive, a living organism will couple structurally to its environment. Its continual structural changes in response to the environment—and consequently its continuing adaptation, learning, and development—are key characteristics of the behavior of living beings. Because of its structural coupling, we call the behavior of an animal intelligent but would not apply that term to the behavior of a rock. Thus the new systems view sees living nature as intelligent without the need to assume any overall design or purpose.

The Gaia theory, as well as the earlier work by Lynn Margulis in microbiology, has exposed the fallacy of the narrow Darwinian concept of adaptation. Throughout the living world evolution cannot be limited to the adaptation of organisms to their environment, because the environment itself is shaped by a network of living systems capable of adaptation and creativity. So, which adapts to which? Each to the other—they *coevolve*. As James Lovelock put it, "So closely coupled is the evolution of living organisms with the evolution of their environment that together they constitute a single evolutionary process."[5] Thus our focus is shifting from evolution to coevolution—an ongoing dance that proceeds through a subtle interplay of competition and cooperation, creation and mutual adaptation.

According to the new systems view of evolution, the basic evolutionary drive is not to be found in the chance events of random mutations but in life's inherent tendency to create novelty, in the spontaneous emergence of increasing complexity and order. Once this fundamental new insight has been understood, we can then ask: What are the avenues in which evolution's creativity expresses itself?

The answer to this question comes not only from molecular biology but also, and even more importantly, from microbiology, from the study of the planetary web of the myriads of microorganisms that were the only forms of life during the first two billion years of evolution. During those two billion years, bacteria continually transformed the Earth's surface and atmosphere and, in so doing, invented all of life's essential biotechnologies, including fermentation, photosynthesis, nitrogen fixation, respiration, and rotary devices for rapid motion.

Three Avenues of Creativity

During the past three decades, extensive research in microbiology has revealed three major avenues of evolution. The first, but least important, is the random mutation of genes, the centerpiece of neo-Darwinian theory. Gene mutation is caused by a chance error in the self-replication of DNA, when the two chains of the

DNA's double helix separate and each of them serves as a template for the construction of a new complementary chain.

It has been estimated that these chance errors occur at a rate of about one per several hundred million cells in each generation. This frequency does not seem to be sufficient to explain the evolution of the great diversity of life-forms, given the well-known fact that most mutations are harmful, and only very few result in useful variations.

In the case of bacteria the situation is different, because bacteria divide so rapidly. Fast bacteria can divide about every twenty minutes, so that in principle several billion individual bacteria can be generated from a single cell in less than a day. Because of this enormous rate of reproduction, a single successful bacterial mutant can spread rapidly through its environment, and mutation is indeed an important evolutionary avenue for bacteria.

However, bacteria have developed a second avenue of evolutionary creativity that is vastly more effective than random mutation. They freely pass hereditary traits from one to another in a global exchange network of incredible power and efficiency. This global trading of genes, technically known as DNA recombination, must rank as one of the most astonishing discoveries of modern biology. "If the genetic properties of the microcosm were applied to larger creatures, we would have a science-fiction world," write Lynn Margulis and Dorion Sagan in their wonderful book *Microcosm,* "in which green plants could share genes for photosynthesis with nearby mushrooms, or where people could exude perfumes or grow ivory by picking up genes from a rose or a walrus."[6]

The speed with which drug resistance spreads among bacterial communities is dramatic proof that the efficiency of their communications network is vastly superior to that of adaptation through mutations. Bacteria are able to adapt to environmental changes in a few years where larger organisms would need thousands of years of evolutionary adaptation. Thus microbiology teaches us the sobering lesson that technologies like genetic engineering and a global communications network, which we consider to be advanced achievements of our modern civilization, have been used by the planetary web of bacteria for billions of years to regulate life on Earth.

Mutation and DNA recombination (the trading of genes) are the two principal avenues for bacterial evolution. But what about the multicellular organisms of all the larger forms of life? If random mutations are not an effective evolutionary mechanism for them, and if they do not trade genes like bacteria, how have the higher forms of life evolved? This question was answered by Lynn Margulis with the discovery of a third, totally unexpected avenue of evolution, now known as "symbiogenesis," which has profound implications for all branches of biology.

Symbiosis, the tendency of different organisms to live in close association with one another and often inside one another (like the bacteria in our intestines), is a widespread and well-known phenomenon. But Margulis went a step further and proposed the hypothesis that long-term symbioses, involving bacteria and other microorganisms living inside larger cells, have led and continue to lead to new forms of life. Margulis published her revolutionary hypothesis first in the mid-1960s and over the years developed it into a full-fledged theory that sees the creation of new forms of life through permanent symbiotic arrangements as the principal avenue of evolution for all higher organisms.

The most striking evidence for evolution through symbiosis is presented by the so-called mitochondria, the "powerhouses" that carry out cellular respiration in all animal and plant cells. The mitochondria contain their own genetic material and reproduce independently and at different times from the rest of the cell. Margulis speculates that their ancestors may have been vicious bacteria that invaded larger cells and reproduced inside them. Many of the invaded cells would have died, taking the invaders with them. But some of the predators did not kill their hosts outright, began to cooperate with them, and eventually natural selection allowed only the cooperators to survive and evolve further.

Over millions of years, the cooperative relationships became ever more coordinated and interwoven, the invading bacteria producing offspring well adapted to living within larger cells, and larger cells becoming ever more dependent on their lodgers. Over time, these bacterial communities became so utterly interdependent that they functioned as single integrated organisms. As Margulis and Sagan put it,

Life had moved another step, beyond the networking of free genetic transfer to the synergy of symbiosis. Separate organisms blended together, creating new wholes that were greater than the sum of their parts.[7]

The recognition of symbiosis as a major evolutionary force has profound philosophical implications. All larger organisms, including ourselves, are living testimonies to the fact that destructive practices do not work in the long run. In the end, the aggressors always destroy themselves, making way for others who know how to cooperate and get along. Life is much less a competitive struggle for survival than a triumph of cooperation and creativity.

While the Social Darwinists of the 19th century saw only competition in nature—"nature, red in tooth and claw," as the poet Tennyson put it—we are now beginning to see continual cooperation and mutual dependence among all life-forms as central aspects of evolution. In the words of Margulis and Sagan, "Life did not take over the globe by combat, but by networking."[8]

Notes

1. Jacques Monod, *Chance and necessity*, New York, Knopf (1971); p. 122.
2. Lynn Margulis, Gaia is a tough bitch, in John Brockman, Ed., *The third culture*, New York, Simon & Schuster (1995).
3. Stuart Kauffman, *The origins of order*, New York, Oxford University Press (1993); pp. 173, 408, 644.

4. Ervin Laszlo, *Evolution*, Boston, Shambhala (1987).

5. James Lovelock, *Healing Gaia*, New York, Harmony Books (1991); p. 99.

6. Lynn Margulis and Dorion Sagan, *Microcosmos,* New York, Summit (1986); p. 89.

7. Ibid. p. 119.

8. Ibid. p. 15.

5
Organism and Psyche in a Participatory Universe

MAE-WAN HO

Abstract

Biophysicist Mae-Wan Ho, with rare passion for a scientist, outlines a scientific vision of the organism as a coherent whole. She shows how the organism is linked to and participates in evolution through a network driven more by love than by brutal struggle.

Key words

Love, Ian Suttie, the whole person, disintegration and re-integration, Jung's theory of the psyche, consciousness, a theory of the organism, individuation, Laszlo's quantum holographic universe, organic wholeness, organic space–time, organism versus mechanism, quantum coherence, thermo-dynamics, the liquid crystalline organism, a participatory universe, brain and body consciousness, wave function, ambient field.

Organism—The Universal Archetype

In the Summer of 1991, I saw something in Mexico City which haunted me for months afterwards. It was a thick round slab of sculpted rock, about 3.25m in diameter. The official guide book says it depicts the Aztec moon goddess, embodying the powers of night, who was killed and gruesomely dismembered by her brother the sungod—an act so terrible that the world itself was torn asunder. Yet, the beautifully executed symmetries of the form evoke a sense of the dismembered parts drawing together again to make a whole, counteracting the violent severance of head and limbs. Mazatl Galindo, who teaches indigenous American cultures and is himself of Aztec Indian descent, has since explained to me that this sculpted disc, which has the same dimensions as the much better known, and widely reproduced calendar stone, is actually also a calendar: the thirteen main joints of her dismembered body representing the thirteen divisions of the year. The alternating disintegration and re-integration it evokes signify the cycles of death and rebirth that mark the passage of time.

I came upon the sculpture while accompanying a group of university undergraduates traveling around the world on an intensive, year-long education program on Global Ecology—Integrating Nature and Culture (of which I was a founding faculty member). In the course of the year and throughout the Third World, we had experienced the same distressing disintegration of the environment and indigenous communities brought on by industrial developments. And yet there remains, everywhere, an indestructible, irrepressible spirit to make things whole again. It was not just a survival instinct, but a genuine lust for life—the psychic energy that created the calendar stone is at work, initiating the healing process even as disintegration is continuing apace. The meaning of that year's journey and the journey of my life as symbolic of life itself came to me like an avalanche. I have died several deaths since my encounter with that symbol. I found myself standing at the gates of the underworld, as Orpheus must have done, torn between the fear of impending hell and the overriding need to recover a lost love. Eventually, it transformed my life, in much the way that Jung (1964) envisaged the transforming power of symbols.

Love rules our lives on many planes. Scottish psychologist Ian Suttie (1924), a critic of Freud, proposed that love, as distinct from sex, is the primary drive for all social organisms. Love comes from the nurturing ministrations of the mother or caretaker during infancy. From this arises a feeling of tenderness that regards all people as possible companions, to be enjoyed and loved, and from whom approval is sought. On another plane, the successful separation of child from mother creates a field of attraction, a "virtual space" of love that we fill with our social and creative activities (Winnicott, 1974).

Love is a desire for wholeness. It is a desire for resonance, for intimacy, a longing to embrace and complete a larger whole. And it is that which motivates our social and creative acts and our knowledge of nature on the most universal plane (Ho, 1994a). At its most personal, love is our affection for specific human beings, it is also one's own process of individuation—of remaking one's "self" out of the fabric of experiences, transcending the well-worn archetypes to become a unique whole person. The whole person is one whose sense of uniqueness is premised on her relationship with all of nature. Thus, the personal and universal are inextricably intertwined. The most intimate knowledge of oneself is, at the same time, the most profound knowledge of nature.

The true love of self is also inextricably the love of humanity and of all nature. That is why we feel obliged to serve, to help, to alleviate suffering and pain just as they were our own. Scientists like David Bohm, Ervin Laszlo, and others are indeed trying to recover that lost love, the universal wholeness and entanglement that enable us to empathize and to be compassionate.

The whole is never static, it is constantly dying and being reborn, decaying and renewing, breaking down to build up again. The same cycles of disintegration and reintegration occur whether one is looking at the energy metabolism of our body or the stream of consciousness out of which we individuate our psyche. During the normal "steady state" of our existence, the multitudes of infinitesimal deaths and rebirths are intricately balanced so that the old changes imperceptibly into the new. However, whenever the attracting center of the new is radically different from the old, a larger, and at times, complete disintegration may be needed before the new can individuate. It is like the caterpillar, which must completely dissolve so that the beautiful butterfly can emerge. That is our hope for the approaching millennium.

The psyche has so much in common with the organism that many of the most perceptive biologists and psychologists have proposed a complete continuity and identity between the two. They were impressed with the "directiveness" of all vital processes, whether developmental, physiological or psychical. In development, the fertilized egg goes through a series of morphogenetic changes directed toward producing the adult organism, and is remarkably resistant to disturbing influences. Similarly, the organism is able to maintain its internal physiology in a constant state despite large changes in the external environment. So it is with the purposiveness of all living things. One has only to try to stop a cat from doing what it wants to do. The mark of a living being is that it always has its own way of doing things, its own directed purpose in life that resists what is imposed on it. It is not at the mercy of its surroundings. It is so even for the simplest unicellular organism. The biologist Jennings (1933) took a lifetime to study the ciliate protozoa *Paramecium*, and became convinced of its purposiveness, it autonomy at the very least. For example, it will swim toward the light, or not, according to whether it is hungry or fully fed.

Geneticist Sinnott (1950) argues in his book *Cell and Psyche* that biological organization, concerned with development and physiology, and psychical activity, concerned with behavior and leading to mind, are fundamentally the same thing.

In some unexplained fashion, there seems to reside in every living thing . . . an inner subjective relation to its bodily organization. This has finally evolved into what is called consciousness . . . through this same inner relationship, the mechanism which guides and controls vital activities towards specific ends, the pattern or tension set up in protoplasm, which so sensitively regulates its growth and behaviour, can also be experienced, and this is the genesis of desire, purpose, and all other mental activities. (p. 48)

To me, the Jungian ideal of the whole person is also one whose cell and psyche, body and mind, inner and outer, are fully integrated, and hence completely in tune with nature. That may be the secret of the golden flower (see Fordham, 1966), the immortal spirit–body created out of the resolution of opposites, the intertwining of darkness and light (moon goddess and sungod) that is the essence of life itself. The encounter with the Aztec calendar stone is the immediate prelude to my work toward a theory of the organism, much of which is in *The Rainbow and The Worm* written almost a year later (Ho, 1993). A recent summary of the main thesis with additional work done since is presented elsewhere (Ho, 1997a).

Jung's ideas on psychical development show many parallels to those relating to living organization, and have since been borrowed back into biology. "Individuation," for example, was used by the embryologist–geneticist Waddington (1956) to describe the process of forming a whole, or a whole organ, such as a limb from the global morphogenetic field. Jung himself was not unaware of these parallels when he presented the psyche as a dynamic, self-regulating system, motivated by psychic energy or *libido*, a general sense of desire or longing, an urge that flows between opposite poles, so that the stronger the opposition the greater the tension (Fordham, 1966). The allusion to the living system and energy flow is unmistakable. Jung's theory of the psyche, drawn largely from his own experiences and imagination, is also a theory of the organism. The organism is the most universal archetype.

Similarly, Laszlo's (1995, 1996) theory of the quantum holographic universe views the universe effectively as a kind of superorganism, constantly becoming, being created through the activities of its constituent organisms at every level. These activities leave traces (quantum interferences) in the universal vacuum field which feed back on the future evolution of the organisms themselves. The universal quantum holographic field is the collective consciousness (including the unconscious) of *all* organisms. My theory of the organism is, in some respects, a microcosm of Laszlo's universe.

The Irrepressible Tendency toward the Whole

What is it to be an organism? It is, at bottom, the irrepressible tendency toward being whole. It is that that underlies both the directiveness of vital activities and the love we express on many planes. In biological development, the most characteristic feature of the embryo is not so much its directiveness toward producing an adult organism or any archetype, rather it is its tendency to maintain and develop into an organized whole, however it is disturbed. Sometimes, this organized whole is so altered that it is no longer recognizable as the same organism, but it is nonetheless an organism in the sense of being an organized whole.

More significantly, there is a special relationship between part and whole in the organism. The egg starts to develop by cell division. At a sufficiently early stage, the cells in the embryo are typically *totipotent*, in that they have the potential to develop into any part of the whole. When they are separated, each cell can develop into a whole organism, albeit a much smaller one than the original. Similarly, if a part of the early embryo is removed, that part can be regenerated from the remaining so that the whole is again recovered. Regeneration can also occur in adult organisms of some species, such as the salamander. It is part and parcel of the healing process that enables all organisms to recover from illnesses and injuries. Whole and part are therefore mutually implicated in the organism. This quality of organic wholeness has eluded mechanistic science right from the beginning, and has been the main sticking-point of the debate between the mechanists and their opponents, the vitalists.

Organic Space–Time versus Mechanical Space and Time

The mechanistic framework broke down at the turn of the present century, giving way to quantum theory at the very small scale of elementary particles and to general relativity at the large scales of planetary motion. In place of the static, eternal universe of absolute space and time, there is a multitude of contingent, observer-dependent space–time frames. Instead of solid objects with simple locations in space and time, one finds delocalized, mutually entangled quantum entities evolving like organisms. The opposition between the mechanistic and the organic worldview hinges on the fundamental nature of space and time.

Mechanical space and time are both linear, homogeneous, separate and local. In other words, both are infinitely divisible, and every bit of space or of time is the same as every other bit. A billiard ball *here* cannot affect another one *there*, unless someone pushes the one here to collide with the one there. Mechanical space–time also happens to be the space and time of the commonest "common-sensible" world in our mundane, everyday existence. It is the space–time of frozen instantaneity abstracted from the fullness of real process, rather like a still frame taken from a bad movie-film, which is itself a flat simulation of life. The passage of time is an accident, having no connection with the change in the configuration of solid matter located in space. Thus, space and time are merely coordinates for locating objects. One can go forwards or backwards in time to locate the precise objects at those particular points. In reality, we know that we can as much retrace our space–time to locate the person that was 30 or 50 years younger as we can undo the wrongs we have committed then. There is no simple location in space and time (Whitehead, 1925).

Psychoanalyst–artist Marion Milner (1957) describes her experience of "not being able to paint" as the fear of losing control, of no longer seeing the mechanical common-sensible separateness of things. It is really a fear of being alive, of entanglement and process in the organic reality that ever eludes mechanistic description. And yet, it is in overcoming the imposed illusion of the separateness of things that the artist/scientist enters into the realm of creativity and real understanding—which is the realm of organic space–time. Mechanical physics has banished organic space–time from our collective public consciousness, though it never ceases to flourish in the subterranean orphic universe of our collective unconscious and our subjective aesthetic experience. In a way, all developments in Western science since Descartes and Newton may be seen as a struggle to reclaim our intuitive, indigenous notions of organic space–time, which, deep within our soul, we feel to be more consonant with authentic experience.

Organism versus Mechanism

The mechanistic worldview indeed officially ended at the beginning of this century. But the profound implications of this decisive break with the intellectual tradition of previous centuries were recognized by a mere handful of visionaries, especially by the French philosopher Henri Bergson (1916), and the English mathematician–philosopher Alfred North Whitehead (1925). Between them, they articulated an organicist philosophy in place of the mechanistic. Table 1 summarizes some of what I see to be the major contrasts between the mechanical universe and the universe of organisms.

Table 1

Mechanical universe	Organic universe
Static, deterministic	Dynamic, evolving
Separate, absolute space and absolute time, universal for all observers	Space-time inseparable, contingent observer (process)-dependent space–time frames
Inert objects with simple locations in space and time	Delocalized organisms with mutually entangled space–times
Linear homogeneous space and time	Nonlinear, heterogeneous, multidimensional space–times
Local causation	Non-local causation
Given, nonparticipatory, and hence, impotent observer	Creative, participatory; entanglement of observer and observed

The contrasts are brought into sharper relief by considering the differences between mechanism and organism, or, more accurately, the opposition between a mechanical system and an organic system. First of all, a mechanical system is an object *in* space and time, whereas an organism is, in essence, *of* space–time. An organism creates its own space–times by its activities, so it has control over its space–time, which is not the same as external clock time. Secondly, a mechanical system has a stability that belongs to a *closed* equilibrium, depending on controllers, buffers and buttresses to return the system to set, or fixed points. It works like a nondemocratic institution, by a hierarchy of control: a boss who sits in his office doing nothing (bosses are still predominantly male) except giving out orders to line managers, who in turn coerce the workers to do whatever needs to be done. An organism, by contrast, has a dynamic stability, which is attained in open systems far away from equilibrium. It has no bosses, no controllers, and no set points. It is radically democratic, everyone participates in making decisions and in working by intercommunication and mutual responsiveness. Finally, a mechanical system is built of isolatable parts, each external and independent of all the others. An organism, however, is an irreducible whole, where part and whole, global and local are mutually implicated.

An even more significant change in worldview is the dissolution of the Cartesian barrier separating the observer from the observed. In the quantum universe, observer and observed are mutually entangled, each act of observation determining the evolution of *both*. Knowledge, therefore, involves the full participation of the knower in the known. As the knower is an organism, she is also an actor who participates in constructing and shaping the universe, and *she does so knowingly*. There is, thus, no escaping from the responsibility of a participatory universe and the moral imperative of one's mutual entanglement, ultimately with all of nature. But let us begin with the central precept of being an organism.

A Theory of the Organism

There are 75 trillion cells in our body, made up of astronomical numbers of molecules of many different kinds. How can this huge conglomerate of disparate cells and molecules function so perfectly as a coherent whole? How can we summon energy at will to do whatever we want? And most of all, how is it possible for there to be a singular "I" that we all feel ourselves to be amid this diverse multiplicity?

To give an idea of the coordination of activities involved, imagine an immensely huge superorchestra playing with instruments spanning an incredible spectrum of sizes from a piccolo of 10^{-9} meter up to a bassoon or a bass viol of a meter or more, and a musical range of *72 octaves*. The amazing thing about this superorchestra is that it never ceases to play out our individual songlines, with a certain recurring rhythm and beat, but in endless variations that never repeat exactly. Always, there is something new, something made up as it goes along. It can change key, change tempo, change tune perfectly, as it feels like it, or as the situation demands, spontaneously and without hesitation. Furthermore, each and every player, however small, can enjoy maximum freedom of expression, improvising from moment to moment, while remaining in step and in tune with the whole.

I have just described a theory of the *quantum coherence* that underlies the radical wholeness of the organism, which involves total participation, maximizing *both* local freedom and global cohesion. It involves the mutual implication of global and local, of part and whole, from moment to moment. It is on that basis that we can have a sense of ourselves as a singular being, despite the diverse multiplicity of parts. That is also how we can perceive the unity of the here and now, in an act of "prehensive unification" (Whitehead, 1925). Artists, like scientists, depend on the same exquisite sense of prehensive unification, to see patterns that connect apparently disparate phenomena.

In order to add corroborative details to the theory, however, I shall give a more scientific narrative beginning with energy relationships.

The Thermodynamics of Organized Complexity

Textbooks tell us that living systems are open systems dependent on energy flow. Energy flows in together with materials, and waste products are exported as well as the *spent* energy that goes to make up *entropy*. And that is how living systems can, in principle, escape from the second law of thermodynamics. The second law, as you may know, encapsulates the fact that all physical systems run down, ultimately decaying to homogeneous disorganization when all useful energy is spent or converted into entropy. But how do living systems manage their antientropic existence?

I have suggested (Ho, 1996a,b; 1997a) that the key to understanding how the organism overcomes the immediate constraints of thermodynamics is in its capacity to store the incoming energy, and in somehow closing the energy loop within to give a reproducing, regenerating life-cycle. The energy, in effect, circulates among complex cascades of coupled cyclic processes within the system before it is allowed to dissipate to the outside. These cascades of cycles span the entire gamut of space–times from slow to fast, from local to global, that all together constitutes the life-cycle. Each cycle is a domain of *coherent* energy storage—coherent energy is simply energy that can do work because it is all coming and going together, as opposed to incoherent energy, which goes in all directions at once and cancels out, and is therefore quite unable to do work.

Coupling between the cycles ensures that the energy is transferred directly from where it is captured or produced to where it is used. In thermodynamic language, those activities going thermodynamically *down*hill, and therefore yielding energy, are coupled to those that require energy and go thermodynamically *up*hill. This coupling also ensures that *positive* entropy generated in some space–time elements is compensated by *negative* entropy in other space–time elements. There is, in effect, an internal energy conservation as well as an internal entropy compensation. The whole system works by reciprocity, a cooperative give-and-take that balances out over the system as a whole, and within a sufficiently long time (Ho, 1997a). The result is that there is always coherent energy available in the system, which can be readily shared throughout the system, from local to global and vice versa, from global to local. That is why, in principle, we can have energy at will, whenever and wherever it is needed. The organism has succeeded in gathering all the necessary vital processes into a unity of coupled nondissipative cycles spanning the entire gamut of space–times up to and including the life-cycle itself, which effectively feeds off the dissipative irreversible energy flow. In thermodynamic terms, the living system can be represented as a superposition of cyclic nondissipative processes, for which entropy production balances out to zero ($\Sigma\Delta S = 0$) and dissipative, irreversible processes, for which net entropy production is positive ($\Sigma\Delta S > 0$).

But how can energy mobilization be so perfectly coordinated? That is a direct consequence of the energy stored, which makes the whole system *excitable*, or highly sensitive to specific weak signals. It does not have to be pushed and dragged into action like a mechanical system. Weak signals originating anywhere within or outside the system will propagate throughout the system and become automatically amplified by the energy stored, often into macroscopic action. Intercommunication can proceed very rapidly, especially because organisms are completely *liquid crystalline*.

The Liquid Crystalline Organism

Several years ago, we discovered an optical technique that enables us to see living organisms in brilliant interference colors generated by the liquid crystallinity of their internal anatomy. We found that all live organisms are completely liquid crystalline—in their cells as well as the extracellular matrix, or connective tissues (see Ho *et al.*, 1996; Ross *et al.*, 1997). Liquid crystals are states of matter between solid crystals and liquids. Like solid crystals, they possess long-range orientation order, and often also varying degrees of translational order (or order of motion). In contrast to solid crystals, however, they are mobile and flexible and highly responsive. They undergo rapid changes in orientation or phase transitions when exposed to weak electric (or magnetic) fields, to subtle changes in pressure, temperature, hydration, acidity or pH, concentrations of inorganic molecules or other small molecules. These properties happen to be ideal for making organisms, as they provide for the rapid intercommunication required for the organism to function as a coherent whole. (Images of live organisms taken from video recordings may be found in Ho, 1997c.)

This imaging technique enables us to literally see the whole organism at once, from its macroscopic activities down to the long-range order of the molecules that make up its tissues. The colors generated depend on the structure of the particular molecules—which differ for each tissue—and their degree of coherent order (see Ross *et al.*, 1997 for the mathematical derivation showing how, for weakly birefringent material, the color intensity is approximately linearly related to both intrinsic birefringence and the order parameter). The principle is exactly the same as that used in detecting mineral crystals in geology; but with the important difference that the living liquid crystals are *dynamic* through and through. The molecules are all moving about, busily transforming energy and material in the meantime, and yet they still appear crystalline.

The reason is because visible light vibrates much faster than the molecules can move, so the tissues will appear indistinguishable from static crystals to the light transmitted, *so long as the movements of the constituent molecules are sufficiently coherent.* In fact, the most actively moving parts of the organism are always the brightest, implying that their molecules are moving all the more coherently. With our optical technique, therefore, one can see that the organism is thick with coherent activities at all levels, which are coordinated in a continuum from the macroscopic to the molecular. That is the essence of the organic whole, where local and global, part and whole are mutually implicated at any time and for all times.

Those images draw attention to the wholeness of the organism in another respect. All organisms—from protozoa to vertebrates without exception—are polarized along the anterior–posterior axis, or the oral–adoral axis, such that all the colors in the different tissues of the body are at a maximum when the axis is appropriately aligned in the optical system, and they change in concert as the axis is rotated from that position.

Knowledge as Intercommunication in a Participatory Universe

The images demonstrate something profound about the nature of knowledge. Are the colors really in the organisms? Yes and no. They are dependent on the particular organism and its physiological state, but no colors would be produced unless we set up the observation in a certain way. Therefore, the observation, and hence the knowledge gained, are always dependent on both the observer and the observed. It is an act of intercommunication, which, in the ideal, is just like that between different parts of the organism (see below). The authenticity of the knowledge gained depends on this delicate balance of obtaining information while respecting the object of one's interrogation. That is why one uses minimally invasive, non-destructive techniques for investigating living organization, which allows organisms to be organisms (Ho, 1993). Crude, destructive methods of interrogation will invariably yield misleading information of the most mechanistic kind, reinforcing a mechanistic view of organisms and of the universe.

In the same way, as we participate in universal wholeness, in Laszlo's quantum holographic field, we do so with the requisite sensitivity and respect. Knowledge is always a gift one accepts with responsiveness and responsibility. Let us look at how intercommunication takes place within the organism.

The Quantum Holographic Body Field of the Organism

There is no doubt that if we could look inside our bodies the same way we have done for the small creatures, we would see our living body as an incredibly colorful, liquid crystalline continuum, with all parts rapidly intercommunicating and colors flashing, so that it can act as a coherent whole. (That may be why we say we are off-color when we don't feel well.) One has been led to believe that intercommunication in large animals like ourselves depends on the nervous system controlled by the brain. However, that may be only half the story, as nerves do not reach all parts of the body, and animals without a nervous system nevertheless have no problems in acting as a coherent whole.

The clue to the other half of the story is in the connective tissues which make up the bulk of most animals including ourselves. These are the skin, the bones, cartilage, tendons, ligaments and other tissues that fill up the spaces between the usual organs. Most people still think that these tissues fulfill mechanical functions of protection and support, like packing material. However, we now know they are all liquid crystalline, and have much more exotic properties.

The connective tissues are further connected to the intracellular matrices of all individual cells, which are also liquid crystalline. There is thus an excitable, liquid crystalline continuum for rapid intercommunication permeating the entire organism, enabling it to function as a coherent whole, as we have directly demonstrated with our noninvasive optical-imaging technique. This continuum constitutes a "body consciousness" that precedes the nervous system in evolution (cf. Ochmann, 1984, 1993); and I suggest, it still works in tandem with, and to some extent independently of, the nervous system. This body consciousness is the prerequisite for conscious experience that involves the participation of the intercommunicating whole. *When the body is fully coherent, intercommunication is instantaneous and nonlocal.* By nonlocal, I mean that distant sites, say my left hand and my right hand, take no time at all to reach agreement as to what to do next, so it is impossible to know where the "signal" originated. This is the *quantum* coherent state.

The quantum coherent state is a very special state of being whole, which maximizes *both* local freedom and global cohesion (see Ho, 1993). This is due to the *factorizability* of the quantum coherent state (Glauber, 1970) in which the parts are so perfectly coordinated that the correlations between them resolve neatly into products of the self-correlations of the parts, so the parts behave as though they are independent of one another. Remember the huge superorchestra I mentioned earlier? Factorizability of the quantum coherent state explains why the body can be performing all sorts of different but coordinated functions simultaneously. As I am writing this paper, my metabolism is working in all the cells of my body, my trunk and leg muscles are keeping in tone so I don't collapse into a heap, while the muscles in my arms and fingers are working together in just the right way to make the appropriate taps on the keyboard, and my eyes are tracking the words on the monitor screen; and hopefully, the nerve cells in my brain are firing coherently. All that is possible also because noiseless and instantaneous intercommunication can occur throughout the system when the system is coherent. In practice, quantum coherence occurs to different degrees, and factorizability is never perfect except in the ideal. Nevertheless, our body approaches that ideal, which also tends to be restored after decohering interactions (see Ho, 1997a,b).

The Coherence of Brain and Body Consciousness

From the perspective of the whole organism, the brain's primary function may be to mediate coherent coupling of all subsystems, so the more highly differentiated or complex the system, the bigger the brain required. Substantial parts of the brain are indeed involved in integrating inputs from all over the body, and over long time-scales. But not all the coordination required is provided by the brain, for this coordination seems instantaneous by all accounts.

Thus, during an olfactory experience, slow oscillations in the olfactory bulb (in the brain) are in phase with the movement of the lungs (Freeman and Barrie, 1994). Similarly, the coordinated movement of the four limbs (or all the hundreds of limbs in the millipede) in locomotion is accompanied by patterns of activity in the motor centers of the brain, which are in phase with those of the limbs (Collins and Stewart, 1992; Kelso, 1991). That is a remarkable achievement, which physiologists and neuroscientists alike have taken too much for granted. The reason macroscopic organs such as the four limbs can be coordinated is that each is individually a coherent whole, so that a definite phase relationship can be maintained among them. The hand–eye coordination required for the accomplished pianist is extremely impressive, but depends on the same inherent coherence of the subsystems that, I suggest, enables instantaneous intercommunication to occur. There simply isn't time enough, from one musical phrase to the next, for inputs to be sent to the brain, there to be integrated, and coordinated outputs to be sent back to the hands (see Hebb, 1958).

I raised the possibility that a "body consciousness" works in tandem with the "brain consciousness" of the nervous system. I suggest that instantaneous coordination of body functions is mediated, not so much by the nervous system, but by the body consciousness inhering in the liquid crystalline continuum of the body. (The nervous system is also liquid crystalline; however, the known activities of the nervous system are not based directly on their liquid crystalline properties.) Ho and Knight (1997), following Oschman (1984, 1993), review evidence suggesting that this liquid crystalline continuum is responsible for the direct current (DC) electric field permeating the entire body of all animals that Becker (1990) and others have detected. Furthermore, this liquid crystalline continuum possesses all the properties required for a body consciousness that can register tissue memory of previous experiences.

Becker (1990) has demonstrated that the DC field has a mode of semiconduction that is much faster than nervous conduction. During a perceptive event, local changes in the DC field can be measured half a second before sensory signals arrive in the brain, suggesting that the activities in the brain may be preconditioned by the local body field. Becker located the DC body field to "perineural" tissues such as the glial cells. But we believe it is located in the liquid crystalline continuum of the connective tissues (Ho and Knight, 1997).

Up to 70 percent of the proteins in the connective tissues consist of collagens that exhibit constant patterns of alignment, as characteristic of liquid crystals (Knight and Feng, 1992). Collagens have distinctive mechanical and dielectric properties that make them very sensitive to mechanical pressures, changes in pH, inorganic ions and electromagnetic fields. In particular, a cylinder of water surrounds the collagen molecule, giving rise to an ordered array of bound water on the surface of the collagen network that supports rapid "jump conduction" of protons, or positive electric charges. Proteins in liquid crystals have coherent motions, and will readily transmit weak signals by proton conduction, or as coherent electric waves. Thus, extremely weak electromagnetic signals or mechanical disturbances will be sufficient to set off a flow of protons that will propagate throughout the body, making it ideal for intercommunication.

The liquid crystalline nature of the continuum also enables it to function as a distributed memory store. The water bound on the surfaces of proteins is known to be altered when the proteins change their shape. Proteins undergo a hierarchy of shape changes over a range of time-scales and different energies. The shapes are clustered in groups that have nearly the same energies, with very low energetic barriers between them. Thus, global shape changes in a liquid crystalline network can easily be triggered, which will, in turn, alter the structure of bound water. As the bound water forms a global network in association with the collagen, it will have a certain degree of stability, or resistance to change. By the same token, it will also retain tissue memory of previous experiences. Additional chemical modifications of the collagen network may also contribute to this memory. The memory may consist partly of dynamic circuits, the sum total of which constitutes the DC body field.

A yet more interesting possibility is that the liquid crystalline continuum may function as a quantum holographic medium, recording the interference patterns arising from interactions between local activities and a globally coherent field. This is exactly analogous to Laszlo's (1995) suggestion that the "zero-point field" of the universe functions as a universal holographic medium, recording the experiences of all the particles, each of which is subject to influences from the rest of the universe as well as feedback from the particle's own activities on the universal medium. If the organism is coherent as I have suggested, then the conditions are there for a quantum holographic memory store in the liquid crystalline continuum of the body itself. Holographic memory is unique in that it is distributed globally, and yet can be accessed and recovered locally. It captures an aspect of the organic whole in developmental biology that has completely eluded mechanistic understanding. It is that that can give rise to the subjective self, or psyche, that guides and regulates all vital activities toward a specific end. It is possible that biological development is based on the same holographic memory, so that the entire organism can be engendered locally in a germ cell, from which the organism is, in turn, recoverable.

Thus, consciousness is distributed throughout the entire body; "brain consciousness," associated with the nervous system, being embedded in "body consciousness." Brain and body consciousness mutually inform and condition each other. The singularity of purpose of the individual is based on a complete coherence of brain and body. The implications for holistic and psychic health are clear. A stressful situation will affect body consciousness through subtle ways in which mechanical pressures build up in the body to block intercommunication. That acts on the nervous system to give a diminished self-image of the body, which feeds back on the body in a vicious cycle that further undermines the individual's physical well-being. By contrast, a supple body is a responsive body that moves and responds with the greatest of ease. It leads to a buoyant self-image that again feeds back to further enhance all bodily functions.

Quantum Coherence and Brain Consciousness

Many recent studies of brain activities are revealing impressive large-scale spatio-temporal coherence that suggests the brain also functions with a high degree of quantum coherence (see Ho 1997b and references therein). These findings come from measurements carried out with the ultrasensitive, noninvasive SQUID magnetometer, also referred to as magnetoencephalography (MEG) (see Iaonnides, 1994) as well as conventional electroencephalography (EEG) (Gray *et al.*, 1989; Singer, 1995; Freeman and Barrie, 1994). Multichannel MEG, in particular, provides high-speed, high-resolution information of spatiotemporal coherence in brain activities. Studies conducted over the past five years have revealed 40 Hz activities that are coherent at both deep and superficial layers of the brain. Similarly, Freeman (1995) and his coworkers, recording simultaneously with an array of 64 electrodes from the rabbit cortex, found oscillations that are coherent over the entire array, for which no obvious "sources" could be identified.

Computer scientist Marcer (1992, 1995) proposes a quantum holographic model of consciousness in which perception involves the conversion of an interference pattern (presumably between a coherent wave-field generated by the perceiver and the wave-field reflected off the perceived) to an object image that is coincident with the object itself. This is accomplished by a process known as phase conjugation, whereby the wave reflected from the object is returned (by the perceiver) along its path to form an image where the object is situated. In the act of perceiving, the organism also perceives itself situated in the environment and, through active phase conjugation directed throughout its body, forms an image of the self coincident with the organism itself, so "self" and "other" are simultaneously defined (Ho, 1997b). What is the source of the coherent wave-field generated by the perceiver? Could it be the body field itself? On the body field as modulated by the nervous system? This could be subject to empirical investigation.

In the same way that body consciousness associated with the liquid crystalline continuum registers memory of its experience, brain consciousness registers memory of sensory images. The idea that brain memory is distributed and holographic has been suggested by a number of neurobiologists over the past 40 years (see Ho, 1997b for more details and references). Holographic memory storage is orders of magnitude more efficient than any model that makes use of "representations," because holographic memory employs actual physical simulations of processes (Marcer, 1992, 1995) and does not require lengthy sequences of arbitrary coding and decoding of isolated bits. Marcer suggests that the brain stores experienced holographic spatiotemporal patterns and compares stored with new patterns directly, recognition and learning being reinforced in "adaptive resonance," thus also making for much faster processing.

As mentioned before, the liquid crystalline continuum supporting the body field may also take part in memory storage, although this possibility has never been seriously considered. Laszlo (1995) goes even further to suggest that much of memory may be stored in an ambient, collective holographic memory field delocalized from the individual; and that memories are only accessed by the brain from the ambient field. This ambient field may well be our collective unconscious. One can begin to see the organism with its own local quantum holographic field as a microcosm of the universal field in which it participates.

The Organism's Macroscopic
Wave Function and Universal Entanglement

If quantum coherence is characteristic of organism and psyche, as I have argued here, then the organism will possess something like a macroscopic wave function. This wave function is ever evolving, entangling its environment, transforming and creating itself anew. There is no "collapse of the wave function" as required by conventional quantum theory (cf. Bohm and Hiley, 1993; see also Ho, 1993, 1997b). When quantum systems interact, they become mutually entangled, and there may be no resolution of their respective wave functions afterwards. So one may remain entangled, and indeed delocalized, over past experiences (i.e., in Laszlo's ambient field). Some interactions may have time-scales that are extremely long, so that the wave function of interacting parties may take a correspondingly long time to become resolved, and large-scale nonlocal connectivity may be maintained, possibly accounting for synchronicities, as Laszlo (1995) suggests.

The "whole" organism is thus a domain of coherent activities, constituting an autonomous, free entity (see Ho, 1996a), *not* because it is separate and isolated from its environment, but precisely *by virtue of its unique entanglement of other organisms* in its environment. In this way, one can see that organic wholes are nested as well as entangled individualities. Each can be part of a larger whole, depending on the extent over which coherence can be established. So, when many individuals in a society have a certain rapport with one another, they may constitute a coherent whole, and ideas and feelings can indeed spread like wildfire within that community. In the same way, an ecological community, and by extension the global ecology, may also be envisaged as a superorganism within which coherence can be established in ecological relationships over global, geological space–times (see Ho, 1993, 1997d). What of the global community of human beings who can potentially intercommunicate in a matter of seconds, given the marvels of informational technology? Could they also be envisaged as a superorganism?

There is an important debate going on in the global arena concerning "globalization"—the idea that the greater part of our life is determined by global processes in which national or local cultures, economies and borders are dissolving. While some are questioning the reality of globalization (e.g., Hirst and Thompson, 1996), others see the globalized economy as the greatest threat to the survival of the global community (Korten, 1995). The problem with the globalized economy under the current terms is that it does not respect the autonomy of individual persons, local communities or nation states, nor does it enable universal participation of all the parties concerned. Local autonomy and universal participation are some of the prerequisites for a coherent, sustainable global society (see Ho, 1996c, 1997c), in which the players must also be sensitive and responsive, or responsible and accountable. Instead, "unaccountable corporate powers" (Korten, 1997) effectively rule the world, depleting the Earth's natural resources with impunity, degrading the environment and creating poverty on a massive scale. The challenge of globalization is, indeed, to create a fully participatory global society, served by an appropriate global economy, that maximizes *both* local autonomy and global cohesion, as consistent with the quantum coherence of a truly organic system.

Note

Parts of this chapter were first delivered as a lecture at the Assisi Conference, "The Confluence of Matter and Spirit: Patterning in the Psyche and in Archetypal Fields," Assisi, Aug. 11–17, 1996. I thank Ervin Laszlo, Walter Freeman, and David Korten for stimulating discussions and relevant reprints.

References

Becker, R.O. (1990). *Cross currents: The promise of electromedicine, the perils of electropollution.* Los Angeles: Tarcher.

Bergson, H. (1916). *Time and free will: An essay on the immediate data of consciousness.* New York: Allen & Unwin.

Bohm, D. and Hiley, B.J. (1993). *The undivided universe.* London: Routledge.

Collins, J.J. and Stewart, I.N. (1992). Symmetry-breaking bifurcation: a possible mechanism for 2:1 frequency-locking in animal locomotion. *J. Math. Biol.* 30, 827–838.

Fordham, F. (1996). *An introduction to Jung's psychology.* Harmondsworth: Pelican.

Freeman, W.J. (1995). *Societies and brains: A study in the neuroscience of love and hate.* Hove: Erlbaum.

Freeman, W.J. and Barrie, J.M. (1994). Chaotic oscillations and the genesis of meaning in cerebral cortex. In G. Bizsaki, Ed., *Temporal coding in the brain* (pp. 13–37). Berlin: Springer-Verlag.

Gibson, J.J. (1966). *The ecological approach to visual perception.* Cambridge, MA: MIT Press.

Glauber, R.J. (1970). Coherence and quantum detection. In R.J. Glauber, Ed., *Quantum optics.* New York: Academic Press.

Gray, C.M., Konig, P., Engel, A.K. and Singer, W. (1989). Oscillatory responses in cat visual cortex exhibit inter-columnar synchronization which reflects global stimulus properties. *Nature* 33, 334–337.

Hebb, D.O. (1958). *A textbook of psychology.* Philadelphia: W.B. Saunders.

Hirst, P. and Thompson, G. (1996). *Globalization in question.* Cambridge: Polity Press.

Ho, M.W. (1993). *The rainbow and the worm: the physics of organisms.* Singapore: World Scientific.

—— (1994a). In search of the sublime. *Metanoia* (Introductory issue) Spring, 9–16.

—— (1996a). The biology of free will. *J. Consciousness Studies*, 231–244.

—— (1996b). Bioenergetics and biocommunication. In R. Cuthbertson, M. Holcombe, and R. Paton, Eds., *Computation in cellular and molecular biological systems* (pp. 251–262). Singapore: World Scientific.

—— (1996c). Natural being and coherent society. In P. Bunyard, Ed., *Gaia in action, science of the living earth* (pp. 286–307). Edinburgh: Floris Press.

—— (1997a). Towards a theory of the organism. *Integrative Physiological and Behavioral Science* (in press).

—— (1997b). Quantum coherence and conscious experience. *Kybernetes* 26, 265–276.

—— (1997c). The new age of the organism. *Architectural Review* (in press).

—— (1997d). *Genetic engineering dreams or nightmares: The brave new world of bad science and big business*. Penang: Third World Network.

Ho, M.W. and Knight, D. (1997). Collagen liquid crystalline phase alignment and the DC body field of consciousness (in preparation).

Ho, M.W., Haffegee, J., Newton, R., Zhou, Y.M., Bolton, J.S. and Ross, S. (1996). Organisms are polyphasic liquid crystals. *Bioelectrochemistry and Bioenergetics* 41, 81–91.

Jennings, H.S. (1933). *The universe and life*. New Haven: Yale University Press.

Jung, C.G. (1964). *Man and his symbols*. London: Aldus Books.

Kelso, J.A.S. (1991). Behavioral and neural pattern generation: The concept of neurobehavioral dynamical systems. In H.P. Koepchen and T. Huopaniemi, Eds., *Cardiorespiratory and motor coordination* (pp. 224–234). Berlin: Springer-Verlag.

Knight, D. and Feng, D. (1993). Collagens as liquid crystals. British Association for the Advancement of Science, Chemistry Session: "Molecular Self-Assembly in Science and Life," Sept. 1, Keele.

Korten, D.C. (1995). *When corporations rule the world*. West Hartford, CT: Kumarian Press.

—— (1997). The responsibility of business to the whole. A People-Centred Development Forum Paper.

Laszlo, E. (1995). *The interconnected universe*. Singapore: World Scientific.

—— (1996). *The whispering pond*. Rockport, MA: Element.

Marcer, P.J. (1992). Designing new intelligent machines—the Huygens' machine. *CC-AI Journal* 9, 373–394.

Marcer, P.J. (1995). The need to define consciousness—a quantum mechanical model. In P.J. Marcer and A.M. Fedorec, Eds., Symposium on Consciouness, University of Greenwich (pp. 23–45).

Needham, J. (1936). *Order and life*. Cambridge, MA: MIT Press.

Oschman, J.L. (1984). Structure and properties of ground substances. *Am. Zool.* 24, 199–215.

—— (1993). A biophysical basis for acupuncture. Private manuscript.

Prigogine, I. (1967). *Introduction to thermodynamics of irreversible processes*. New York: Wiley.

Ross, S., Newton, R., Zhou, Y.M., Haffegee, J., Ho, M.W., Bolton, J.P. and Knight, D. (1997). Quantitative image analysis of birefringent biological material. *J. Microscopy* (in press).

Schrödinger, E. (1944). *What is life?* Cambridge: Cambridge University Press.

Singer, W. (1995). Organizing principles of cortical function. Third Annual BRA Decade of the Brain Lecture Report, *Brain Research Association Newsletter* 22, 3–5.

Sinnott, E.W. (1950). *Cell and psyche: The biology of purpose*. Chapel Hill: University of North Carolina Press.

Suttie, I. (1924/1989). *The origins of love and hate*. Harmondsworth: Penguin.

Waddington, C.H. (1956). *Principles of embryology*. London: Allen & Unwin.

Whitehead, A.N. (1925). *Science and the modern world*. Harmondsworth: Penguin.

Winnicott, D.W. (1974). *Playing and reality*. Harmondsworth: Pelican.

6
On Brain, Conscious Experience, and Human Agency

KARL PRIBRAM

Abstract
Neuropsychologist Karl Pribram tells of what 20th-century brain research and psychology from the time of Freud and William James into the 1990s has discovered about the basic equipment for the active mind we humans bring to evolution.

Key words
Brain, brain and behavior, plans, *Plans and the Structure of Behavior*, cognitive science, feedback, feedforward, Freud, excitation, neural inhibition, images, holographic processes, consciousness, unconsciousness, William James, intentionality, attention, volition, feelings, emotion, motivation, perception, frontolimbic forebrain, transcendental consciousness and spirituality, Laszlo's quantum-vacuum field theory.

Western thought has alternated between two views of humanity's relation to the Universe: One view holds the human organism to be passively shaped by the environment. The other emphasizes an active role, manipulative and selective not only of artifacts but of sense data as well. Recent neuropsychological contributions to behavioral science point to a resurgence of the latter view, emphasizing once again the dignity of the human as a scientific as well as a political and humanistic tenet.
(Paraphrased from Pribram, 1963, pp. 101–111)

The Issue. Over the past two centuries, since the pioneering observations of Frances Gall (1809–1969), it has become common knowledge that there is a special relation between brain tissue and the variety of conscious experiences. Gall initiated the procedure of comparing the locus of brain pathology with aberrations of behaviors of the patients whose brains he examined—a procedure which is continued today in the active field of clinical neuropsychology. Gall inaugurated the view that the faculties of mind are based in brain function. When Gall applied for admission to the French Academy of Science, his view was countered by Napoleon, who felt that evil would be stamped out by appropriate social innovation (see Pribram, 1969).

Though on the whole we today accept the special relation between brain and conscious experience, we are not at all agreed upon the basic nature of the relationship nor, any more than in 1800, upon the consequences our understanding of this nature might have for our understanding of ourselves as agents in our relation to our physical environment and in our relation to others.

Despite such apparent disagreements, brain research *has* shown that physical and social environments become enmeshed by sensory and neural processes to make up our conscious experiences. This chapter reviews some of this research as *I* have experienced it. The dictionary definition of experience is "to try." The research findings reported here have certainly "tried me," and I am seriously "trying" to collate and communicate them so others can also experience them. Perhaps the most trying of these collations is to bring them into harmony with those presented by Laszlo regarding quantum-vacuum field theory and its impact on the human condition. Section 5 of this chapter does at least take a step in this direction.

Section 1 traces my journey of a half-century of research, with special emphasis on the concept of *plans as guides to action* and *images (especially images of achievement) as the origins of the guides*. Section 2 grounds this research as it entails *states of mind* as these were described in the works of William James, Franz Brentano and Sigmund Freud. Section 3 organizes my research results regarding the topics *attention and volition*, which relate states to content and contents to states. Section 4 deals with research in perception—the *contents of consciousness*, especially with the distinction between an allo- and egocentric appreciation of a corporeal "me" versus a narrative "I" composed of episodes and events. Section 5 provides a transcendental synthesis.

1. Sources of a Model of Brain Functions in Consciousness

Some Case Histories

A patient has a tumor removed from the occipital lobe on one side of his brain. The surgery leaves him unable to report the sight of objects presented to him on the side opposite the removal, yet he can correctly point to the location of the objects and even correctly respond to differences in their shape (Weiskrantz, Warrington *et al.*, 1974; Weiskrantz, 1986). Even when repeatedly told that he is responding well, he insists that he is not aware of seeing anything and is only guessing. This is called blind-sight.

A similar occurrence follows a stroke or other injury to the parietal lobe. Now the arm and hand on the side of the body opposite to the injury perform automatically without the conscious participation of the person. One such patient called her absent-from-conscious arm "Alice," and noted that "Alice doesn't live here anymore" (Pribram and Bradley, 1997).

Another patient has the medial structures of the temporal lobes of his brain removed on both sides. He performs well on tests of immediate memory such as recalling a telephone number just read out loud to him, but a few minutes later is not only unable to recall the number but the fact that he had heard a number or even that he had been examined. Even after 20 years of regular exposure to an examiner, the patient fails to recognize her as familiar (Scoville and Milner, 1957). Yet, this same patient, when trained to respond skillfully to a complex task or to discriminate between objects, etc., can be shown to maintain such performances over years despite the disclaimer on his part that he was ever exposed to such a tasks (Sidman *et al.*, 1969).

Still another patient with a similar but more restricted bilateral lesion of her temporal lobe has gained over a hundred pounds of weight since surgery. She is a voracious eater, but when asked whether she is hungry or has any special appetites, she denies this, even when apprehended in the midst of grabbing food from other patients (Pribram, 1965).

This is not all. A patient may have the major tracts connecting his cerebral hemispheres severed with the result that his responses to stimuli presented to him on opposite sides are treated independently of one another. His right side is unaware of what his left side is doing and vice versa. The splitting of the brain has produced a split in awareness (Sperry, 1980; Gazaniga, 1985).

More common in the clinic are patients who are paralyzed on one side due to a lesion of the brain's motor system. But the paralysis is manifest especially when the patient attempts to follow instructions given to him or which he himself initiates. When highly motivated to perform well-ingrained responses, as when a fire breaks out or as part of a more general action, the paralysis disappears. Only intentional, volitional control is influenced by the lesion.

Observations such as these have set the problems that brain scientists need to answer. Not only do they demonstrate the intimate association that exists between brain and human experienced consciousness, they also make it necessary to take into account the dissociation between conscious awareness, feelings, and intentions on the one hand and unconscious, automatic behavioral performances on the other.

Perhaps it is not too surprising therefore that a division in approach to the mind–brain problem has recently occurred. While behavioral scientists and neuroscientists have, for the most part, eschewed a Cartesian dualism in an attempt at rigorous operational and scientific understanding, some thoughtful brain scientists and philosophers have inveterately maintained a dualistic stance (Popper and Eccles, 1977). A brief review of my own struggles with the problem may be helpful in posing some of the issues involved.

Plans

The struggle began modestly with a recounting in the late 1950s and early 1960s of case histories such as those used above. These were presented as an antidote to the radical behaviorism that then pervaded experimental psychology (Pribram, 1959/1962). The formal properties of a more encompassing view were presented in terms of a computer programming analogy in *Plans and the Structure of Behavior* (Miller *et al.*, 1960) under the rubric of a "Subjective Behaviorism." The analogy has since become a fruitful model or set of models known as "Cognitive Science," which, in contrast to radical behaviorism, has taken verbal reports of subjective conscious experience seriously into account as problem areas to be investigated and data to be utilized.

Computer programming has proved an excellent guide to understanding and experimental analysis. Further, a host of control engineering devices have been known to serve as models for the brain scientist. Of special interest here is the distinction that can be made among such models between feedback and feedforward operations, a distinction that is critical to our understanding of the difference between automatic and voluntary control of behavior.

Feedback organizations operate like thermostats—for example, Cannon's (1927) familiar homeostatic brain processes that control the physiology of the organism. More recently it has become established that sensory processes also involve such feedback organizations (see Miller *et al.*, 1960 and Pribram, 1971, chs. 3, 4, and 11, 1990 for review). Thus, feedback control is one fundamental of brain organization.

But another fundamental has emerged in the analyses of brain function. This fundamental goes by the name of feedforward, or information processing (see, e.g., McFarland, 1971, ch. 1). I have elsewhere (Pribram, 1971, ch. 5, 1981; Pribram and Gill, 1976, ch. 1) detailed my own understanding of feedforward mechanisms and their relation to the feedback control. Briefly, I suggest that feedbacks are akin to the processes described in the first law of thermodynamics (the law of conservation of energy) in that they are error processing, reactive to magnitudes of change in the constraints that describe a system. They operate to restore the system to the state of equilibrium. By contrast, feedforward organizations process "information" that increases the degrees of freedom of the system.

The manner by which feedforward is accomplished is often portrayed in terms of Maxwell's demon and Szilard's solution to the problem posed by these "demons," that is, how energy can be conserved across a boundary (a system of constraints), a boundary that "recognizes" certain energy configurations and lets them pass while denying passage to others (see Brillouin, 1962, for review). In such a system the energy consumed in the recognition process must be continually enhanced or the "demon" in fact tends to disintegrate from the impact of random energy. Feedforward operations are thus akin to processes described by the second law of thermodynamics, which deals with the amount of organization of energy, not its conservation. Information has often been called neg-entropy (see, e.g., Brillouin, 1962; Pribram, 1991, Lecture 2), entropy being the measure of the amount of disorganization or randomness in a system. In the section on volition we will return to these concepts and apply them to the issues at hand.

19th-century psychophysicists and psychophysiology dealt directly with feedforward operations. Thus Helmholtz (1924) describes the mechanism of voluntary control of eye movements in terms of a parallel innervation of the muscles of the eye and a "screen" upon which the retinal input falls so that voluntary eye movements are accompanied by a corollary corrective innervation of the cerebral input systems. When the eyeball is pushed by a finger, this corrective innervation is lacking, and the visual world jumps about. Brindley and Merton (1960) performed the critical experiment: When the eye muscles are paralyzed and a voluntary eye movement is undertaken, the visual world rushed by even though the eye remains stationary.

Of especial interest is the fact that Freud (1895/1966) anticipated this distinction between feedback and feedforward in his delineation of primary and secondary processes (Pribram and Gill, 1976). Freud distinguished three types of neural mechanisms that constitute primary processes. One is muscular discharge; a second is discharge into the blood stream of chemical substances; and a third is discharge of a neuron onto its neighbors. All three of these neural mechanisms entail potential or actual feedback. Muscular discharge elicits a reaction from the environment and a sensory report of the discharge (kinesthetic) to the brain. The neurochemical discharge results, by way of stimulation of other body chemicals to which the brain is sensitive, in a positive feedback, which Freud labels "the generation of unpleasure." (This is the origin of the unpleasure—later the pleasure—principle.) Discharge of a neuron onto its neighbors is the basis of associative processes that lead to a reciprocal increase in neural excitation (cathexis) between neurons (a feedback), which is the basis for facilitation (a lowering of resistance) of their synapses (learning).

By contrast, secondary or cognitive processes are based on a host of hierarchically arranged neural mechanisms that delay discharge through neural inhibition. These delays convert wishes (the sum of excitatory facilitations) to willed voluntary acts by allowing attention (a double feedback that matches the wish to external input—a double comparison process that allows control to be exercised as in setting a thermostat by hand) to operate a reality-testing mechanism. Thus, an attentional conscious comparison process is an essential mechanism allowing voluntary cognitive operations to occur.

For Freud and 19th-century Viennese neurology in general, consciousness and the resultant voluntary behavior was a function of the cerebral cortex. Thus the greater portion of brain, which is noncortical, regulates behavior of which we are not aware—behavior that is automatic and unconscious. What then do we know about cortical function and conscious awareness?

Images

Thus plans are not enough. As indicated by the case histories described earlier, today's neuroscientist shares with 19th-century neurology the necessity to understand the special role of the brain cortex in the constructions that constitute consciousness. Freud tackles that problem by distinguishing the "qualitative imaging" properties of sensations from the more quantitative properties of association, memory, and motivation. The distinction remains a valid one today: In *Plans and the Structure of Behavior* the sums of these tests, the comparisons between input and report of the consequences of operations, are called "images." How then are "images" constructed by the brain cortex?

Images are produced by a brain process characterized by a precisely arranged anatomical array that maintains a topographic isomorphism between receptor and cortex but that can be seriously damaged or destroyed (up to 90 percent) without impairing the capacity of the remainder to function in lieu of the whole. These characteristics led me to suggest in the mid-1960s (Pribram, 1966) that in addition to the digital computer, brain models need to take into account the type of processing performed by optical systems. Such optical information processing is called holography, and holograms display exactly the same sort of imaging properties observed for brain; namely, a precisely aligned process that distributes information. In the brain the anatomical array serves the function of paths of light in optical systems and horizontal networks of lateral inhibition perpendicular to the array serve the function of lenses (Pribram, 1971; Pribram *et al.*, 1974).

I have proposed specific brain functions to be responsible for the organization of neural holographic-like processes (Pribram, 1971, chs. 1 and 2). This proposal involves the graded electrical potential changes—changes in polarizations—that occur at junctions between neurons and in their dendrites. Inhibitory interactions (by hyperpolarizations) in horizontal networks of neurons that do not generate any nerve impulses are the critical elements. Such inhibitory networks are becoming more and more the focus of investigation in the neurosciences. For instance, in the retina, they are responsible for the organization of visual processes— in fact, nerve impulses do not occur at all in the initial stages of retinal processing (for review see Pribram 1971, chs. 1 and 3). The proposal that image construction in man takes place by means of a neural holographic-like process is thus spelled out in considerable detail, and departs from classical neurophysiology only in its emphasis on the importance of computations achieved by a web of reciprocal influences among graded, local polarizations, which are well-established neuro-psychological entities. No new neurophysiological principles need be considered.

For the mind–brain issue, the holographic model is of special interest because the image that results from the holographic process is projected away from the hologram that produces it. We need therefore to be less puzzled by the fact that our own images are not referred to eye or brain, but are projected into space beyond. Von Bekesy (1967) has performed an elegant series of experiments that detail the process (lateral inhibition—the analogue of lenses in optical systems) by which such projection comes about. Essentially the process is similar to the one that characterizes the placement of auditory images between two speakers in a stereophonic music system.

From this fact, it can be seen how absurd it is to ask questions concerning the "locus" of conscious experience. The brain processes organize our experience—

but that experience is not of the brain process per se but of the resultant of its function. One would no more find "consciousness" by dissecting the brain than one would find "gravity" by digging into the Earth.

Over the past decades important advances have occurred in our understanding of brain holographic-like processing. Research results have shown that the best mathematical description of the process is holonomic rather than purely holographic—that is, the analogy with a patch or strip hologram serves better than that of an undivided, unlimited hologram. In a patch hologram the holographic surface is made up of patches of hologram spatially ordered with respect to one another. Each patch is bounded and is thus described by what Denis Gabor (1946), the inventor of the hologram, described as a "quantum" of information. The brain process can therefore be conceived as an information process in which the units are quanta of information (Pribram and Carlton, 1986; Pribram, 1990).

Another development has been a system of programming that derives from holography and simulates the properties of neural processing. These "neural networks" implement parallel distributed processing (PDP) in currently available computers (Rumelhart and McClelland, 1986). Computer programming and optical holography thus provide metaphors, analogies, and models of processes that, when tested against the actual functions of the primate brain, go a long way toward explaining how human voluntary and imaging capabilities can become differentiated from unconscious automatic processes by the human brain.

2. Dimensions of Conscious States

States of Mind

What we mean by conscious experience is most readily illustrated by asking the following question: would you say that your pet dog is conscious? Why, you answer, of course he is. We all attribute awareness to organisms when they mind their environment, when they appear to pay attention. The behaviorist philosopher Gilbert Ryle (1949) made note of this when he pointed out that the English term "mind" is derived from minding—and William James in his *Principles of Psychology* (1901/1950) asks whether in fact we need the term "consciousness" since what we mean by it is so intimately interwoven with attention and its limited span. We ordinarily distinguish consciousness from unconsciousness much as do the physician and surgeon: when someone responds to prodding (e.g., by grumbling "Oh leave me alone! Can't you see I'm trying to get some sleep!") we attribute to him a conscious state. When, on the other hand, his response is an incoherent thrashing about, we say he is stuporous, and if there is no response at all, we declare him comatose.

Note that we are now distinguishing between various nervous system *states* that for the most part are subcortical and that are coordinate with such states of consciousness as sleep and wakefulness and states of unconsciousness–unresponsiveness (such as stupor and coma). The interesting thing about such states is their mutual exclusiveness regarding experience: what is experienced in one state is not available to experience in another. Such state exclusiveness emerges in all sorts of observations: state-dependent learning in animal and human experiments; the fact that salmon spawning pay no attention to food, while when they are in their feeding state sexual stimuli are ignored; the observation in hypnosis that a person can be made unaware post-hypnotically of suggestions made during hypnosis (although he carries out these suggestions) and the dissociation between experiences (and behavior) taking place during "automatisms" in temporal lobe epileptics and what is experienced in their ordinary state. I would add to these the mutual exclusiveness of natural language systems that make translation so difficult.

The evidence obtained in all of these situations suggests that the same basic neural substrate becomes variously organized to produce one or another state. Hilgard (1977) and I (Pribram and Gill, 1976) have conceptualized this substrate as being subject to rearrangements similar to those that take place in a kaleidoscope: a slight rotation and an entirely new configuration presents itself. Slight changes in relative concentrations of chemicals and/or in neural depolarizations and hyperpolarizations in specific neural locations could, in similar fashion, result in totally different states.

Intentionality as Characteristic of the Human Condition

William James distinguishes consciousness from self-consciousness and suggests that self-consciousness occurs when we become aware of states of bodily functions. James sees no special problem here, but his contemporary Brentano (Freud's teacher) identifies the issue of self-consciousness as central to what makes man human.

The emphasis by Brentano is on intentional consciousness, which arises from the distinction between the contents of awareness and the person who is aware; the duality between subjective mind and objective matter (brain), which also holds in the writings of Ernst Mach (1914) and of René Descartes (1927). Although Cartesian dualism is perhaps the first overt nontrivial expression of the issue, the duality between subject and object and some causal connection between them is inherent in language once it emerges from simple naming to predication. Neumann (1954) and Jaynes (1977) have suggested that a change in consciousness occurs somewhere between the time of the Iliad and the Odyssey. My interpretation of this occurrence links it to the invention and promulgation of phonemically based writing. Prehistory was transmitted orally/aurally. Written history is visual/verbal. In an oral/aural culture a greater share of reality is carried in memory and is thus personal; once writing becomes a ready means of recording events they become a part of extrapersonal objective reality. The shift described is especially manifest in a clearer externalization of the sources of conscience—the gods no longer speak within the person to guide individual man and woman.

Ever clearer distinctions between personal and extrapersonal objective realities culminates in Cartesian dualism and Brentano's "intentional inexistence," which was shortened by Husserl to "intentionality." It is this reading of the subject–object distinction that philosophers ordinarily mean when they speak of the difference between conscious and unconscious processes.

Brentano derives his analysis from the scholastics and uses intentionality—the "aboutness" of perceptions, that experience is about something—as the key concept to distinguish observed from observer, the subjective from the objective. I have elsewhere (Pribram, 1976) somewhat simplified the argument by tracing the steps from the distinction between intentions and their realization in action, to perceptions and their realization as the objective world.

How is Brentano's distinction between subject and object related to the dualism of Descartes? Brain must always be a part of the objective world even if it is the organ critically responsible for the subjective—from which in turn the objective is constructed. Brentano is perfectly clear on this point and suggests that the study of intentional consciousness is the province of the philosopher–psychologist, not the brain physiologist. However, clinical neuropsychological experience amply demonstrates that brain physiology does in fact have something to say even about intentional consciousness. The case histories presented at the outset of this paper make Brentano's general point perhaps more strongly than any philosophical argument: minding is of two sorts, instrumental and intentional. However, as these and other case histories show, neuroscience has a great deal to say about *both* instrumental *and* intentional consciousness, more in line with James's formulation than with Brentano's. Of special interest is the fact that a pupil of Brentano's, Sigmund Freud, as an outstanding neurologist, also became in his psychoanalytical investigation the champion of the distinction between conscious and unconsciousness processes in determining everyday and pathological behavior, but did not follow Brentano's dictum that intentional conscious experience be left to philosophical investigation. Instead, he opted for an investigation in psychological *science* (Pribram and Gill, 1976).

Consciousness and Unconscious States

Instrumental determinants of consciousness are *not* what Freud or most philosophers have meant by the term. Freud had training both in medical practice and in philosophy. When he emphasized the importance of unconscious states, was he applying the medical definition or the philosophical? Did he mean instrumental consciousness to be "the unconscious"? Most interpretations of Freud suggest that unconscious states operate without awareness in the sense that they operate automatically, much as do respiratory and gastrointestinal processes in someone who is stuporous or comatose. Freud himself seems to have promulgated this view by suggesting a "horizontal" split between conscious, preconscious and unconscious states with "repression" operating to push memory-motive structures into deeper layers where they no longer access awareness. Still in Freud's *Project for a Scientific Psychology* memory-motive structures are neural programs—located in the core portions of the brain that access awareness by their connections to cortex. When the neural program becomes a secondary process, it comes under voluntary control, which involves reality testing and thus consciousness. To use language as an example, one might well know two languages but at any one time "connect only one to cortex," and thus the other remains "unconscious" and unexpressed.

The linking of intentional consciousness to cortex is not as naive as it first appears. As the recently reported cases of Weiskrantz *et al.* (1974; Weiskrantz, 1986) that introduced this chapter have shown, "blind-sight" results when patients are subjected to unilateral removal of the visual cortex. As noted, these patients insist they cannot see anything in the field contralateral to their lesion, but when tested they can locate and identify large objects in their blind hemifield with remarkable accuracy. Furthermore, there are patients with unilateral neglect following parietal lobe lesions (see Pribram and Bradley, 1997; Heilman and Valenstein, 1972, for review). Neglect patients often can get around using their neglected limbs appropriately. Thus, blind-sight indicates that a cortical system is involved in determining an *allocentric*, objective world while somatosensory neglect indicates, as William James suggested, that an *egocentric* subjective aspect to consciousness is also organized by a brain system. H.M., the patient described in the introduction who sustained an amygdala-hippocampal resection, has been trained in operant tasks and the effects of training have persisted without decrement for years, despite protestations from the patient that he doesn't recognize the situation and that he remembers nothing of the training (Sidman *et al.*, 1969). In monkeys with such lesions we have shown almost perfect retention of training after a two-year period, retention that is better than that shown by unoperated control subjects. These monkeys and H.M., the blind-sight and neglect patients, are clearly conscious in the medical instrumental sense. What has gone wrong is their ability to reflect on their behavior and experience, an inability within the impaired sphere of clearly distinguishing personal from extra-personal reality. This leaves them with impaired consciousness in the philosopher's sense: behavior and experience are no longer intentional.

The thrust of contemporary psychoanalytical thinking, as well as that of experimentalists such as Hilgard (noted above), is in the direction of interpreting the conscious–unconscious distinction in the philosophical sense. For instance, Matte Blanco (1975) proposes that consciousness be defined by the ability to make clear distinctions, to identify alternatives. Making clear distinctions would include being able to tell personal from extrapersonal reality. By contrast, unconscious processes would, according to Matte Blanco, be composed of infinite sets "where paradox reigns and opposites merge into sameness." When infinities are being computed the ordinary rules of logic do not hold. Thus, dividing a line of infinite length results in two lines of infinite length, that is, one equals two. Being deeply involved allows love and ecstasy but also suffering and anger to occur. In keeping with this, Carl Jung (1960) defined unconscious processes as those involving feelings.

My interpretation of this conscious–unconscious distinction as it relates to *human* behavior and experience is in line with Matte Blanco's and others that are closely related to the philosophical distinction, and not to the medical. Thus, bringing the wellsprings of behavior and experience to consciousness means the making of distinctions, to provide alternatives, to make choices, to become informed in the Shannon (Shannon and Weaver, 1949) sense of reduction of uncertainty. One of these distinctions distinguishes episodes of *feeling* states and relates them to one another.

An important change in views becomes necessary when these interpretations are considered seriously: unconscious states as defined by psychoanalysis are not completely "submerged" and unavailable to experience. Rather, they produce feelings that are difficult to localize in time or in space and difficult to identify correctly. The unconscious states provide the emotional dispositions and motivational context within which extrapersonal and personal realities are constructed. As the classical experiments of Schachter and Singer (1962) showed, feelings are to a large extent undifferentiated, and we tend to cognize and label them according to the circumstances in which the feelings become manifested. (For a recent review of other experiments that have led to such a view see Hermans *et al.*, 1992.)

It is in this sense that behavior comes under the control of the unconscious states. When I have burst out in anger, I am certainly aware that I have done so and of the effects of the anger on others. I may or may not have monitored the build-up of feeling prior to the blow-up. And I may have projected the build-up onto others or introjected it from them. But I could have been aware of all this (with the guidance of a friend or therapist) and still found myself in uncontrolled anger. Only when the events leading to the anger become clearly separated into alternative or harmoniously related distinctions is unconscious control converted into conscious control. It is ridiculous to think that a person with an obsession or compulsion is unaware, in the instrumental sense, of his experience or behavior. The patient is very aware and feels awful. But he cannot, without aid, differentiate controls on the behavior generated by his feelings.[1]

3. Attention and Volition as Conscious Processes

Consciousness and Attention

Just as did Freud, William James (1901/1950) emphasized that most of the issues involved in delineating "consciousness" from unconscious states devolve on the process of attention. James, however, took the problem one step further by pointing out that attention sets limits on competence—the limits of attention span. As noted, Gilbert Ryle (1949) has reminded us that in fact the term "mind" is derived from "minding," that is, attending.

For a half a century my laboratory (as well as many others) has been investigating the neural mechanisms involved in attention. A comprehensive review of these data (Pribram and McGuinness, 1975, 1992) discerned three such controlling processes: one deals with short phasic response to an input (arousal and familiarization); a second relates to tonic readiness of the organism to respond selectively (activation and selection); and a third (effort and comfort) acts to coordinate the phasic (arousal) and tonic (activation) mechanisms. Separate neural and neurochemical systems (Pribram, 1977a, 1990; Pribram and McGuinness, 1992) are involved in the phasic (arousal) and tonic (activation) processes: the phasic centers on the amygdala; the tonic, on the basal ganglia of the forebrain. The coordinating system (effort) critically involves the hippocampus, a phylogenetically ancient part of the neural apparatus.

Evidence (reviewed by Pribram and McGuinness, 1992) from the analysis of changes in the electrical activity of the brain evoked by brief sensory stimulation has shown that the arousal and activation systems operate on some more basic process centered on the dorsal thalamus, the way-station of sensory input to the cerebral cortex. Brain electrical activity evoked by sensory stimulation can be analyzed into components. Early components reflect processing via systems that directly (via the thalamus) connect sensory surfaces with cortical surfaces. Later components reflect processes initiated in the thalamocortical and related basal ganglia systems that operate downward onto the brain stem (tectal region), in turn, influencing a thalamic "gate" that modulates activity in the direct sensory pathways. It is the activity reflected in these later components of the brain electrical activity that constitutes "activation."

The thalamic "gate" is, however, also regulated by input from the system centered on the amygdala—the arousal system. This system, when stimulated, produces an effect on the "gate" opposite to that of the activation system.

The evidence also indicates that the coordination of phasic (arousal) and tonic (activation) attentional processes often demands "effort." When attention must be "paid," the hippocampal system becomes involved and influences the arousal system rostrally through frontal connections with the amygdala system and influences the activation system caudally via connections in the brain stem. Paying attention becomes conscious in the intentional sense. Thus at this juncture the relation of attention to intention as used in the ordinary sense—that is, volition and will—comes into focus. Again, William James had already pointed out that a good deal of what we call voluntary effort is the maintaining of attention or the repeated returning of attention to a problem until it yields solution.

Consciousness and Volition

William James had apposed will to emotion and motivation (which he called "instinct"). Here, once again, brain scientists have had a great deal to say. Beginning with Walter Cannon's (1927) experimentally based critique of James, followed by Lashley's critique of Cannon (1960), to the anatomically based suggestions of Papez (1937) and their more current versions by MacLean (1949), brain scientists have been deeply concerned with the processes that organize emotional and motivational experience and expression. Two major discoveries have accelerated our ability to cope with the issues and placed the earlier more speculative accounts into better perspective. One of the discoveries has been the role of the reticular formation of the brain stem (Magoun, 1950) and its chemical systems of brain amines (see, e.g., review by Barchas *et al.*, 1982; Pribram and McGuinness, 1992) that regulate states of alertness and mood. Lindsley (1951) proposed an activation mechanism of emotion and motivation on the basis of the initial discovery and has more recently (Lindsley and Wilson, 1976) detailed the pathways by which such activation can exert control over brain processes. The other discovery, by Olds and Milner (1954), is of the system of brain tracts that, when electrically excited, results in reinforcement (increase in probability of recurrence of the behavior that has produced the electrical brain stimulation) or deterrence (decrease in probability that such behavior will recur).

In my attempts to organize these discoveries and other data that relate brain mechanisms to emotion, I found it necessary (as had Darwin, 1872) to distinguish clearly between those data that referred to experience (feelings) and those that referred to expression, and further to distinguish emotion from motivation (reviewed by Pribram, 1971). Thus feelings were found to encompass both emotional and motivational experience—emotional as affective (arousal and familiarization) and motivation as centered on a readiness (activation and selection).

The wealth of new data and these insights obtained from them made it fruitful to reexamine the Jamesian positions with regard to consciousness and unconscious processes (Pribram, 1981). I found James in error (a) in his overemphasis on the visceral determination of emotional experience (attitudinal factors depending on sensory feedback from the somatic musculature were included by James but not emphasized) and (b) in his failure to take into consideration the role of expectations (the representational role of the organization of familiarity and, therefore, novelty) in the organization of emotions. On the other hand, James had rightly emphasized that emotional processes take place primarily within the organism while motivation and volition will reach beyond into the organism's environment. Further, I found that James was almost universally misinterpreted as holding a peripheral theory of emotion and mind. Throughout his writings he emphasizes the effect that peripheral stimuli (including those of visceral origin) exert on brain processes. The confusion comes about because of James's insistence that emotions concern bodily processes, that they stop short at the skin. Nowhere, however, does he identify emotions with these bodily processes. Emotions are always the resultant of their effect on the brain. James is in fact explicit on this point when he discusses the nature of the input to the brain from the viscera. He points out two possibilities: emotions are processed by a separate brain system, or they are processed by the same systems as are perceptions. Today, we know that both possibilities are realized: parts of the frontolimbic forebrain (especially the amygdala and related systems) process visceroautonomic bodily inputs, and the results of processing become distributed via brain stem systems that diffusely influence the perceptual systems (Pribram 1961, 1991).

The distinction between the brain mechanisms of motivation and will are less clearly enunciated by James. He grapples with the problem and sets the questions that must be answered. Clarity did not come until the 1960s, when several theorists (e.g., MacKay, 1966; Mittlestaedt, 1968; Waddington, 1957; R. Ashby, personal communication, 1970; McFarland, 1971; Pribram 1971) began to point out the difference between feedback, homeostatic processes on the one hand and programs, which are feedforward, homeorhetic processes, on the other. Feedback processes depend on error processing and are therefore sensitive to perturbations. Feedforwards, by contrast, process information.

Clinical neurology had classically distinguished the mechanisms involved in voluntary from those involved in involuntary behavior. The distinction rests on the observation that lesions of the cerebellar hemispheres impair intentional (voluntary) behavior, while basal ganglia lesions result in disturbances of involuntary movements. Damage to the cerebellar circuits is involved in a feedforward rather than a feedback mechanism (as already described by Ruch in the 1951 Stevens *Handbook of Experimental Psychology*, although Ruch did not have the term "feedforward" available to him). I have extended this conclusion (Pribram, 1971) on the basis of microelectrode analyses by Eccles *et al.* (1967) to suggest that the cerebellar hemispheres perform calculations in fast-time; that is, they extrapolate where a particular movement would end were it to be continued and send the results of such a calculation to the cerebral motor cortex, where they can be compared with the target to which the movement is directed. Experimental analysis of the functions of the motor cortex had shown that such targets are composed of "Images of Achievement" constructed in part on the basis of past experience (Pribram, 1971, chs. 13, 14 and 16, 1991, Lecture 6; Pribram *et al.*, 1955/1956, 1984).

Just as the cerebellar circuit has been shown to serve intentional behavior, the basal ganglia have been shown to be important to involuntary processes. We have already noted the involvement of these structures in the control of activation, the readiness of organisms to respond. Lesions in the basal ganglia grossly amplify tremors at rest and markedly restrict expressions of motivational feelings. Neurological theory has long held (see, e.g., Bucy, 1944) that these disturbances are due to interference by the lesion of the normal feedback relationships between basal ganglia and cerebral cortex. In fact, surgical removals of motor cortex have been performed on patients with basal ganglia lesions in order to redress the imbalance produced by the initial lesions. Such resections have proved remarkably successful in alleviating the often distressing continuing disturbances of involuntary movement that characterize these basal ganglia diseases.

So far we have noted that experience can be classified as instrumental or intentional to differentiate conscious from unconscious states. We have also explored intentionality in terms of the attentional and volitional processes that activate intentional states to heed certain contents. We now proceed to review the organizations of conscious content initiated and achieved by these states and processes.

4. Perception—The Contents of Consciousness

Objective Consciousness—The Posterior Cerebral Convexity

Surrounding the major fissures of the primate brain lie the terminations of the sensory and motor projection systems. Rose and Woolsey (1949) and Pribram (1960) have labeled these systems "extrinsic" because of their close ties (by way of a few synapses) with peripheral structures. The sensory surface and muscle arrangements are mapped more or less isomorphically onto the perifissural cortical surface by way of discrete, practically parallel lines of connecting fiber tracts. When a local injury occurs within these systems a sensory scotoma, or a scotoma of action, ensues. A scotoma is a spatially circumscribed hole in the "field" of interaction of organism and environment: a blind spot, a hearing defect limited to a frequency range, a location of the skin where tactile stimuli fail to be responded to. These are the systems where what Henry Head (1920) called "epicritic processing" takes place. These extrinsic sensory-motor projection systems are so organized that movement allows the organism to map an "objective" experience and project the results of processing away from the sensory (and muscular) surfaces.

In between the perifissural extrinsic regions of cortex lie other regions of cortex variously named "association cortex" (Fleschig, 1900), "uncommitted cortex" (Penfield, 1969), or "intrinsic cortex" (Pribram, 1960). These names reflect the fact that there is no apparent direct connection between peripheral structures and these regions of cortex that make up most of the convexity of the cerebrum.

Corporeal and Extracorporeal Reality

Lesions of the intrinsic cortex of the posterior cerebral convexity result in sensory-specific agnosias in both monkey and man. Research on monkeys has shown that these agnosias are not due to failure to distinguish cues from one another, but due to *making use* of those distinctions in making choices among alternatives (Pribram and Mishkin, 1955; Pribram, 1969). This ability is the essence of information processing in the sense of uncertainty reduction (Shannon and Weaver, 1949), and the posterior intrinsic cortex determines the range of alternatives, the sample size that a particular informative element must address. A patient with agnosia can tell the difference between two objects but does not know what the difference means. As Charles Peirce (1934) once noted, what we mean by something and what we mean to do with it are synonymous. In short, alternatives, sample size, choice, cognition, information in the Shannon sense, and meaning are closely interwoven concepts. Finally, when agnosia is severe it is often accompanied by what is termed "neglect." The patient appears not only not to know that he doesn't know but to actively deny the agnosia. Typical is a patient I once had who repeatedly had difficulty in sitting up in bed. I pointed out to her that her arm had become entangled in the bedclothes—she would acknowledge this momentarily, only to "lose" that arm once more in a tangled environment. Part of the perception of her body, her corporeal consciousness seems to have become extinguished.

In monkeys the disturbances produced by restricted lesions of the convexal intrinsic cortex are also produced by lesions of the parts of the basal ganglia (implicated in activation, readiness) to which those parts of the cortex project. Further, recent experiments have shown that the neglect syndrome can be produced in monkeys by lesions of the dopaminergic nigrostriatal system (Wright, 1980). This special connection between intrinsic (recall that this is also called "association") cortex and the basal ganglia further supports the conception that these systems make possible, on the basis of use, the distinction between an egocentric objective corporeal self (the "me") and an extracorporeal allocentric experience (see Pribram, 1991, Lecture 6 for detailed exposition of how this process operates). However, this objectively experienced "me" can be sharply distinguished from a subjectively experienced "I." An excellent review of the history of differentiating this corporeal objective "me" from a subjective "I" can be found in Hermans *et al.*, (1992). The next section develops the relation between brain processing and the "I."

Narrative Consciousness—The Frontolimbic Forebrain

As is well known, frontal lesions were produced for a period of time in order to relieve intractable suffering, compulsions, obsessions, and endogenous depressions. When effective in the relief of suffering and depression, these psychosurgical procedures revealed in humans the now well-established functional relationship between frontal intrinsic cortex and the limbic forebrain. This relationship was established by research undertaken in nonhuman primates as a result of clinical experience (Pribram 1950, 1954, 1958). Further, frontal lesions can lead either to perseverative, compulsive behavior or to distractibility in monkeys, and this is also true of humans (Pribram *et al.*, 1964; Oscar-Berman, 1975). Thus, a failure to be guided by the outcomes or the consequences of a patient's behavior can be accounted for—as well as its opposite: the alleviation of obsessive–compulsive behavior. Extreme forms of distractibility and obsession are due to a lack of "sensitivity" of a selective readiness process to feedback from consequences. Both the results of experiments with monkeys (Pribram, 1959/1962) and clinical observations attest to the fact that subjects with frontal lesions, whether surgical, traumatic, or neoplastic, fail to be guided by consequences (Luria *et al.*, 1964; Konow and Pribram, 1970).

Consequences are the outcomes of behavior. In the tradition of the experimental analysis of behavior, consequences are reinforcers that influence the recurrence of the behavior. Consequences are thus a series of events (Latin *ex-venire*, out-come), outcomes that guide action and thereby attain predictive value (confidence estimates). Such consequences—that is, sequences of events that form their own confidential context—become in humans, envisioned eventualities (Pribram, 1964, 1971, 1991, Lecture 10 and Appendix G).

Confidence implies familiarity. Experiments with monkeys (Pribram *et al.*, 1979) and humans (Luria *et al.*, 1964) have shown that repeated arousal to an orienting stimulus habituates; that is, the orienting reaction gives way to familiarization. Familiarization is disrupted by limbic (amygdala) and frontal lesions (Pribram *et al.*, 1979; Luria *et al.*, 1964). Ordinarily orienting leads to repeated distraction and thus a failure to allow consequences to form. When the process of familiarization is disrupted, the outcomes-of-behaviors, or events, become inconsequential. When intact, the familiarization process is segmented by orienting reactions into episodes within which confidence values can become established.

In such an episodic process the development of confidence is a function of coherences and correlations among the events being processed. When coherence and correlation span multiple episodes, the organism becomes *committed* to a course of action (a prior intention, a strategy), which then guides further action and is resistant to perturbation by particular orienting reactions (arousals). The organism is now *competent* to carry out the action (intention-in-action, or tactic). Particular outcomes now guide competent performance; they no longer produce orienting reactions (Brooks, 1986; Pribram, 1980).

This cascade that characterizes episodic processing leads ultimately to considerable autonomy, or confidence in, the committed competence. Envisioned events are woven into coherent subjectivity, a story, a narrative, the myth by which "I" live. This narrative composes and is composed of an intention, a strategy that works for the individual in practice, a practical guide to action in achieving stability in the face of a staggering range of variations of events (Pribram, 1991, 1992).

Consciousness is manifest (by verbal report) when familiarization is perturbed; an episode is updated and incorporated into a larger contextual scheme (the narrative) that includes both the familiar and novel episodes (Pribram, 1991, Appendices C and D). Consciousness becomes attenuated when actions and their guides cohere—the actions become skilled, graceful and automatic (Miller *et al.*, 1960).

5. Transcendental Consciousness—
The Spiritual Nature of Humankind

Transcending conscious and especially unconscious determinants of experience was *the* central concern of philosophers and psychologists in the late 19th century. Freud is famous for his formulations of the import of unconscious processes and their emergence in mythology (e.g., the Oedipus Syndrome); Jung was devoted to exploring the collective unconscious; and James published an essay on religious experience. The esoteric tradition in Western culture and the mystical traditions of the Far East are replete with instances of uncommon states that produce uncommon contents. These states are achieved by a variety of techniques such as meditation, Yoga, or Zen. The contents of processing in such states appear to differ from ordinary feelings or perceptions. Among others, experiences such as the following are described (see Morse *et al.*, 1989 and Stevenson, 1970, for review). One type of experience is known as the "oceanic," namely, a merging of corporeal and extracorporeal reality. Another is known as "out-of-body"; namely, corporeal and extracorporeal realities continue to be clearly distinguished but are experienced by still another reality: "a meta-me." In still another type of experience the "I" becomes a transparent experiencing of everything everywhere and there is no longer the segmentation into episodes, nor do events become enmeshed in a narrative structure. All of these experiences have in common a transcendental relationship between ordinary experience and some more encompassing organizing principle.

It is this relationship that is ordinarily termed "spiritual." As will be developed below, the spiritual contents of consciousness can be accounted for by the effect of excitation of the frontolimbic forebrain (involved in narrative construction) on the dendritic microprocess, which characterizes cortical receptive fields in the sensory extrinsic systems (involved in the construction of objective reality).

In addition to the gross correspondence between dendritic receptive fields in the brain cortex and the organization of sensory surfaces that gives rise to the overall characteristics of processing in the extrinsic systems, a microprocess that depends on the internal organization of each dendritic field comes into play. This internal organization of dendritic fields embodies, among other characteristics, a spectral domain: dendritic fields of neurons in the extrinsic cortex are tuned to limited bandwidths of frequencies of radiant energy (vision), sound, and tactile vibration. I have reviewed this evidence extensively on a number of occasions (Pribram, 1966, 1971, 1982, 1991; Pribram *et al.*, 1974).

Perhaps the most dramatic of these data are those which pertain to vision. The cortical neurons of the visual system are arranged as are the other sensory systems so as to reflect more or less isomorphically the arrangement of the receptor surfaces to which they are connected (thus, the "homunculi" that Wilder Penfield (e.g., 1969) and others have mapped onto the cortical surface of the extrinsic projection systems). However, within this gross arrangement lie the receptive fields of each of the neurons—a receptive field being determined by the functional dendritic arborization of that neuron that makes contact with the more peripheral parts of the system. Thus the receptive field of a neuron is that part of the environment that is processed by the parts of the system to which the neuron is connected. Each receptive field is sensitive to approximately an octave (range from one-half to one-and-a-half octaves) of spatial frequency. It is this frequency-selective microprocess that operates in a holographic-like manner.

Processing can thus be conceived as operating somewhat like the production of music by means of a piano. The sensory surface is analogous to a keyboard. Keyboard and strings are spatially related to provide the organization of the process. When individual strings are activated they resonate over a limited bandwidth of frequency. It is the combination of the spatial arrangement and the frequency-specific resonance of the strings that makes the production of music possible.

The gross and micro-organization of the cortical neurons in the extrinsic systems resembles the organization of a multiplex or patch hologram. A patch hologram is characterized by a Gabor elementary function, which Gabor called a "quantum of information" (Gabor, 1946; Pribram, 1991, Lectures 2 and 4). Technically, what is known as a "Gaussian envelope" constrains the otherwise unlimited sinusoid described by what is known as a "Fourier transform" to make up the Gabor function. Experiments in my laboratory (Spinelli and Pribram, 1967; Pribram *et al.*, 1981) have shown that electrical excitation of frontal and limbic structures relaxes these Gaussian constraints, which inhibit reception. When this occurs during ordinary excitation of the frontolimbic systems of the forebrain, processing leads to narrative construction (for details see Pribram, 1991, Lecture 10). When frontolimbic excitation becomes overwhelming, experience is determined by an unconstrained holographic process.

Holograms of the type involved in brain processing are composed by converting (e.g., via Fourier transformation) successive sensory images (e.g., frames of a movie film) into their spectral representations and patching these microrepresentations into orderly spatial arrangements that represent the original temporal order of successive images (see Bracewell, 1989, for an excellent brief review). When such conversions are linear (as, e.g., when they employ the Fourier transform) they can readily be reconverted (e.g., by the inverse Fourier transform) into moving sensory images. The spectral domain is peculiar in that information in the Gabor sense becomes both distributed over the extent of each receptive field (each quantum) and enfolded within it. Thus sensory-image reconstruction can occur from any part of the total aggregate of receptive fields. This is what gives the aggregate its holographic, holistic aspect. All input becomes distributed and enfolded, including the dimensions of space and time and therefore causality.

This timeless/spaceless/causeless aspect of processing is instigated by frontolimbic excitation that practically eliminates the inhibitory surrounds of receptive fields in the sensory systems (Spinelli and Pribram 1967; Pribram *et al.*, 1981), allowing these systems to function holistically. It is this holistic type of processing that is responsible for the apparent extrasensory dimensions of experience that characterize the esoteric traditions: because of their enfolded property these processes tend to swamp the ordinary distinctions such as the difference between corporeal and extracorporeal reality.

The ordinary distinctions result from an enhancement of the inhibitory surrounds of the receptive fields when the systems of the posterior cortical convexity become activated (Pribram *et al.*, 1981). As a consequence, the sensory system becomes an information-processing system in Shannon's sense: choices among alternatives become possible. This is comparable to the process called the "collapse of the wave function" in quantum physics. By contrast, in the esoteric traditions, consciousness is not limited to choices among alternatives.

Instead, this type of conscious experience shares with unconscious states the attribute of infinity suggested by Matte Blanco (1975). An intriguing and related development (because it deals with the specification of a more encompassing, "cosmic" order) has occurred in quantum physics. Over the past 50 years it has become evident that there is a limit to the accuracy with which certain measurements can be made when others are being taken. This limit is expressed as an indeterminacy. Gabor, in his description of a quantum of information, showed that a similar indeterminacy describes communication. This leads to a unit of minimum uncertainty, a maximum amount of information that can be packed for processing. Thus there is a convergence of our understanding of the microstructure of communication—and therefore of observation—and the microstructure of matter. The necessity of specifying the observations that lead to inferring these minute properties of matter has led noted physicists to write a representation of the observer into this description. Some of these physicists have noted the similarity of this specification to the esoteric transcendental descriptions of consciousness. Books with such titles as *The Tao of Physics* (Capra, 1975) and *The Dance of the Wu Li Masters* (Zukav, 1971) have resulted.

Laszlo's Quantum-Vacuum Field theory (1995, 1996) fits into this tradition. As with physicists, he acknowledges the critical role of observation in all scientific investigation. Observation is a *conscious* "trying" at understanding, as indicated in the introduction to this chapter. Thus many physicists, as well as Laszlo, have embraced a broader definition of "consciousness" than just our experience of "it." These scientists, therefore, take our transformative, holographic-like experience that transcends the space–time coordinates of ordinary appearances as further evidence for such a cosmic unifying field.

There is, therefore, in the making a real revolution in Western thought. The scientific and esoteric traditions have been clearly at odds since the time of Galileo. Each new scientific discovery and the theory developed from it has, up until now, resulted in the widening of the rift between objective science and the spiritual aspects of human nature. The rift reached a maximum toward the end of the 19th century. We were asked to choose between God and Darwin, and heaven and hell were shown by Freud to reside within us and not in our relationship to the natural universe. The discoveries of 20th-century science briefly noted here, but reviewed extensively elsewhere (Pribram, 1986, 1991), do not fit this mold. For once the recent findings of science and the spiritual experiences of humankind are consonant. This augurs well for the upcoming new millennium—a science that comes to terms with the spiritual nature of humankind may well outstrip the technological science of the immediate past in its contribution to human welfare.

Note

1. There is thus a large element of behavior in animals as well as humans that falls under this definition of unconscious. Only to the degree to which nonhumans show intentionality, thus the ability to discriminate themselves from their environment, would we infer that they are "conscious." In addition, as I have claimed, there is a "cuddliness criterion" to be applied (Pribram 1976), by which, as more elegantly stated by Searle (1992), we mean to take into consideration the form of the embodiment of the creature to whom we attribute "consciousness."

References

Barchas, J.E., Ciaranello, R.D., Stolk, J.M., and Hamburg, D.A. (1982). Biogenic amines and behavior. In S. Levine, Ed., *Hormones and behavior* (pp. 235–329). New York: Academic Press.

Bekesy Von., G. (1967). *Sensory inhibition*. Princeton, NJ: Princeton University Press.

Bracewell, R. N. (1989). The Fourier Transform. *Scientific American*, 86–95.

Brillouin, L. (1962). *Science and information theory*, 2nd edn. New York: Academic Press.

Brindley, G.S. and Merton, P.A. (1960). The absence of position sense in the human eye. *Journal of Physiology*, 153, 127–130.

Brody, B.A. and Pribram, K.H. (1978). The role of frontal and parietal cortex in cognitive processing: Tests of spatial and sequence functions. *Brain*, 101, 607–633.

Brooks, C.V. (1986). How does the limbic system assist motor learning? A limbic comparator hypothesis. *Brain and Behavioral Evolution*, 29, 29–53.

Bucy, P.C. (1944). *The precentral motor cortex*. Chicago, IL: University of Illinois Press.

Cannon, W.B. (1927). The James–Lange theory of emotions: a critical examination and an alternative theory. *American Journal of Psychology*, 39, 106–124.

Capra, F. (1975). *The Tao of physics*. Boulder, CO: Shambhala.

Darwin, C. (1872). *The expression of the emotions in man and animals*. London: John Murray.

Descartes, R. (1927). *Selections*. New York: Scribner.

Eccles, J., Ito, M., and Szentagothai, J. (1967). *The cerebellum as a neuronal machine*. New York: Springer-Verlag.

Fleschig, P. (1900). Les centres de projection et d'association de cerveau humain. *XIII Congress International de Medecine (Sect. Neurologie)*, 115–121. Paris.

Freud, S. (1895/1966). *Project for a scientific psychology*, Standard edn., vol. 1. London: Hogarth Press.

Gabor, D. (1946). Theory of communication. *Journal of the Institute of Electrical Engineers*, 93, 429–441.

Gall, F.J. and Spurtzheim, G. (1809/1969). Research on the nervous system in general and on that of the brain in particular. In K.H. Pribram, Ed., *Brain and Behavior* (pp. 20–26). Harmondsworth: Penguin.

Gazaniga, M.S. (1985). *The social brain: Discovering the network of the mind*. New York: Basic Books.

Head, H. (1920). *Studies in neurology*. London: Oxford University Press.

Heilman, K.M. and Valenstein, E. (1972). Frontal lobe neglect in man. *Neurology*, 22, 660–664.

Helmholtz, H. von (1924). *Treatis on physiological optics*, vol. I. Menasha: Optical Society of America.

Hermans, H.J.M., Kempen, H.J.G. and van Loon, R.J.P. (1992). The dialogical self: Beyond individualism and rationalism. *American Psychologist*, 47(1), 23–33.

Hersh, N.A. (1980). Spatial disorientation in brain injured patients. Unpublished dissertation, Department of Psychology, Stanford University.

Hilgard, E. R. (1977). *Divided consciousness: Multiple controls in human thought and action*. New York: Wiley.

James, W. (1901/1950). *The principles of psychology*, vols. 1 and 2. London: Macmillan. New York: Dover Publications.

Jaynes, J. (1977). *The origin of consciousness in the breakdown of the bicameral mind*. Boston, MA: Houghton-Mifflin.

Jung, C.G. (1960). *Collected works*, 2nd edn. Bollingen Series #20. Princeton, NJ: Princeton University Press.

Konow, A. and Pribram, K.H. (1970). Error recognition and utilization produced by injury to the frontal cortex in man. *Neuropsychologia*, 8, 489–491.

Lashley, D. (1960). The thalamus and emotion. In F.A. Beach, D.O. Hebb, C.T. Morgan, and H.W. Nissen, Eds., *The neuropsychology of Lashley* (pp. 345–360). New York: McGraw-Hill.

Laszlo, E. (1995). *The interconnected universe*. Singapore: World Books.

—— (1996). *The whispering pond*. London: Element Books.

Lindsley, D.B. (1951). Emotion. In S.S. Stevens, Ed., *Handbook of experimental psychology* (pp. 473–516). New York: Wiley.

Lindsley D.B. and Wilson, C.L. (1976). Brainstem-hypothalamic systems influencing hippo-campal activity and behavior. In R.L. Isaacson and K.H. Pribram, Eds., *The Hippocampus*, Part 4 (pp. 247–274). New York: Plenum.

Luria, A.R., Pribram, K.H. and Homskaya, E.D. (1964). An experimental analysis of the behavioral disturbance produced by a left frontal arachnoidal endothelioma (meningioma). *Neuropsychologia*, 2, 257–280.

McCarthy, R.A. and Warrington, E.K. (1990). *Cognitive neuropsychology: A clinical introduction*. London: Academic Press.

McFarland, D.J. (1971). *Feedback mechanisms in animal behavior*. London: Academic Press.

Mach, E. (1914). *The analysis of sensations and the relation of the physical to the psychical*. Chicago, IL: Open Court Publishing Company.

Mackay, D.M. (1966). Cerebral organization and the conscious control of action. In J.C. Eccles, Ed., *Brain and conscious experience* (pp. 422–445). New York: Springer-Verlag.

Maclean, P.D. (1949). Psychosomatic disease and the "visceral brain": recent developments bearing on the Papez theory of emotion. *Psychomatic Medicine*, 11, 338–353.

Magoun, H.W. (1950). Caudal and cephalic influences of the brain reticular formation. *Physiological Review*, 30, 459–474.

Matte Blanco, I. (1975). *The Unconscious as Infinite Sets: An Essay in bi-logic*. London: Duckworth.

Miller, G.A., Galanter, A. and Pribram, K.H. (1960). *Plans and the structure of behavior*. New York: Henry Holt & Company.

Mittelstaedt, H. (1968). Discussion. In D.P. Kimble, Ed., *Experience and capacity* (pp. 46–49). New York: New York Academy of Sciences, Interdisciplinary Communications Program.

Morse, M., Venecia, D. and Milstein, J. (1989). Near-death experiences: A neurophysiological explanatory model. *Journal of Near-Death Studies*, 8, 45–53.

Mountcastle, V.B., Lynch, J.C., Georgopoulos, A., Sakata, H. and Acuna, C. (1975). Posterior parietal association cortex of the monkey: Command functions for operations within extrapersonal space. *Journal of Neurophysiology*, 38, 871–908.

Neumann, E. (1954). *The origins and history of consciousness*. Princeton, NJ: Princeton University Press.

Olds, J. and Milner, P. (1954). Positive reinforcement produced by electrical stimulation of septal area and other regions of rat brain. *Journal of Comparative Physiology and Psychology*, 47, 419–427.

Oscar-Berman, M. (1975). The effects of dorso-lateral-frontal and ventrolateral-orbito-frontal lesions on spatial discrimination learning and delayed response in two modalities. *Neuropsychologia*, 13, 237–246.

Papez, J.W. (1937). A proposed mechanism of emotion. *Archives of Neurological Psychiatry*, 38, 725–743.

Peirce, C.S. (1934). *Collected papers.* Cambridge, MA: Harvard University Press.

Penfield, W. (1969). Consciousness, memory and man's conditioned reflexes. In K.H. Pribram (Ed.), *On the biology of learning* (pp. 127–168). New York: Harcourt, Brace & World.

Pohl, W.G. (1973). Dissociation of spatial and discrimination deficits following frontal and parietal lesions in monkeys. *Journal of Comparative Physiological Psychology*, 82, 227–239.

Popper, K.R. and Eccles, J. (1977) *The Self and its brain.* New York: Springer-Verlag.

Pribram, K.H. (1950). Psychosurgery in midcentury. *Surgery, Gynecology and Obstetrics*, 91, 364–367.

—— (1954). Toward a science of neuropsychology (method and data). In R.A. Patton, Ed., *Current trends in psychology and the behavior sciences* (pp. 115–142). Pittsburgh, PA: University of Pittsburgh Press.

—— (1958). Comparative neurology and the evolution of behavior. In G.G. Simpson, Ed., *Evolution and behavior* (pp. 140–164). New Haven, CT: Yale University Press.

—— (1959/1962). Interrelations of psychology and the neurological disciplines. In S. Koch, Ed., *Psychology: A study of a science* (pp. 119–157). New York: McGraw-Hill.

—— (1960). The intrinsic systems of the forebrain. In J. Field, H.W. Magoun, and V.E. Hall, Eds., *Handbook of physiology, neurophysiology*, vol. 2 (pp. 1323–1344). Washington, DC: American Psychological Society.

—— (1961). Limbic system. In D.E. Sheer, Ed., *Electrical stimulation of the brain* (pp. 563–574). Austin, TX: University of Texas Press.

—— (1964) Commitment to dreams. In S. Farber and R. Wilson, Eds., *Man and civilization: The family's search for survival* (pp. 167–172). New York: McGraw-Hill.

—— (1965). Proposal for a structural pragmatism: some neuropsychological considerations of problems in philosophy. In B. Wolman and E. Nagle, Eds., *Scientific psychology: Principles and approaches* (pp. 426–459). New York: Basic Books.

—— (1966). Some dimensions of remembering: Steps toward a neuropsychological model of memory. In J. Gaito, Ed., *Macromolecules and behavior* (pp. 165–187). New York: Academic Press.

—— (Ed.) (1969a). *Brain and behavior*, vols. 1–4. London: Penguin.

—— (1969b). On the neurology of thinking. *Behavioral Science*, 4, 265–287.

—— (1971). *Languages of the brain: Experimental paradoxes and principles in neuropsychology.* Englewood Cliffs, NJ: Prentice-Hall; Monterey, CA: Brooks/Cole, 1977; New York: Brandon House, 1982. (Translations in Russian, Japanese, Italian, Spanish)

—— (1976a) Problems concerning the structure of consciousness. In G. Globus, G. Maxwell, and I. Savodnik, Eds., *Consciousness and brain: A scientific and philosophical inquiry* (pp. 297–313). New York: Plenum.

—— (1976b). Self-consciousness and intentionality. In G.E. Schwartz and D. Shapiro, Eds., *Consciousness and self-regulation: Advances in research* (pp. 51–100). New York: Plenum.

—— (1977). Peptides and protocritic processes. In L.H. Miller, C.A. Sadman, and A.J. Kastin, Eds., *Neuropeptide influences on the brain and behavior* (pp. 213–232). New York: Raven Press.

—— (1980). The orienting reaction: Key to brain representational mechanisms. In H.D.

Kimmel, Ed., *The orienting reflex in humans* (pp. 3–20). Hillsdale, NJ: Lawrence Erlbaum Associates.

Pribram, K.H. (1981). Emotions. In S.B. Filskov and T.J. Boll (Eds.), *Handbook of clinical neuropsychology* (pp. 201–234). New York: Wiley.

—— (1982). Localization and distribution of function in the brain. In J. Orbach, Ed., *Neuropsychology after Lashley* (pp. 273–296). New York: Lawrence Erlbaum Associates.

—— (1986). The cognitive revolution and the mind/brain issue. *American Psychologist*, 41, 507–520.

—— (1990). Frontal cortex—Luria/Pribram rapprochement. In E. Goldberg, Ed., *Contemporary neuropsychology and the legacy of Luria* (pp. 77–97). Hillsdale, NJ: Lawrence Erlbaum Associates.

—— (1991). *Brain and perception: holonomy and structure in figural processing.* Hillsdale, NJ: Lawrence Erlbaum Associates.

—— (1992). Explorations in experimental neuropsychology. In Samson and Adelman, Eds., *The neurosciences: paths of discovery*, vol. 2 (pp. 307–325). Cambridge, MA: Birkhäuser Boston Inc.

Pribram, K.H., and Carlton, E.H. (1986). Holonomic brain theory in imaging and object perception. *Acta Psychologica*, 63, 175–210.

Pribram, K.H. and Gill, M. (1976). *Freud's "Project" reassessed.* New York: Basic Books.

Pribram, K.H. and McGuinness, D. (1975). Arousal, activation and effort in the control of attention. *Psychological Review*, 82(2), 116–149.

—— (1992). Brain systems involved in attention and para-attentional processing. *New York Academy of Science.*

Pribram, K.H. and Mishkin, M. (1955). Simultaneous and successive visual discrimination by monkeys with inferotemporal lesions. *Journal of Comparative Physiology and Psychology*, 48, 198–202.

Pribram, K.H., Kruger, L., Robinson, F. and Berman, A.J. (1955/56). The effects of precentral lesions of the behavior of monkeys. *Yale Journal of Biology and Medicine*, 28, 428–443.

Pribram, K.H., Ahumada, A., Hartog, J. and Roos, L. (1964). A progress report on the neurological process disturbed by frontal lesions in primates. In S.M. Warren and K. Akart, Eds., *The frontal granular cortex and behavior* (pp. 28–55). New York: McGraw Hill.

Pribram K.H., Nuwer, M. and Baron, R. (1974). The holographic hypothesis of memory structure in brain function and perception. In R.C. Atkinson, D.H. Krantz, R.C. Luce, and P. Suppes, Eds., *Contemporary developments in mathematical psychology* (pp. 416–467). San Francisco: W. H. Freeman.

Pribram, K.H., Reitz, S., McNeil, M. and Spevack, A.A. (1979). The effect of amygdalectomy on orienting and classical conditioning in monkeys. *Pavlovian Journal*, 14(4), 203–21

Pribram, K.H., Lassonde, M.C. and Ptito, M. (1981). Classification of receptive field properties, *Experimental Brain Research*, 43, 119–130.

Pribram, K.H., Sharafat, A. and Beekman, G.J. (1984). Frequency encoding motor systems. In H.T.A. Whiting, Ed., *Human motor actions—Bernstein reassessed* (pp. 121–156). Amsterdam: Elsevier.

Rose, J.E. and Woolsey, C.N. (1949). Organization of the mammalian thalamus and its relationship to the cerebral cortex. *EEG Clinical Neurophysiology*, 1, 391–404.

Ruch, T.C. (1951). Motor systems. In S.S. Stevens, Ed., *Handbook of experimental psychology* (pp. 154–208). New York: Wiley.

Ruff, R.M., Hersh, N.A. and Pribram, K.H. (1981). Auditory spatial deficits in the personal and extrapersonal frames of reference due to cortical lesions. *Neuropsychologia*, 19(3), 435–443.

Rumelhart, D.E., McClelland, J.L. and the PDP Research Group (1986). *Parallel distributed processing*, vols. 1–2. Cambridge, MA: MIT Press.

Ryle, G. (1949). *The concept of mind.* New York: Barnes & Noble.

Schachter, S. and Singer, T.E. (1962). Cognitive, social and physiological determinants of emotional state. *Psychological Review,* 69, 379–397.

Scoville, W.B. and Milner, B. (1957). Loss of recent memory after bilateral hippocampal lesions. *Journal of Neurology, Neurosurgery, and Psychiatry,* 20, 11–21.

Searle, J.R. (1992) *The rediscovery of mind.* Cambridge, MA: MIT Press.

Shannon, C.E. and Weaver, W. (1949). *The mathematical theory of communications.* Urbana, IL: University of Illinois Press.

Sidman, M., Stoddard, L.T. and Mohr, J.P. (1968). Some additional quantitative observations of immediate memory in a patient with bilateral hippocampal lesions. *Neuropsychologia,* 6, 245–254.

Sperry, R.W. (1980). Mind/brain interaction: Mentalism, yes—dualism, no. *Neuroscience,* 2, 195–206.

Spinelli, D.N. and Pribram, K.H. (1967). Changes in visual recovery function and unit activity produced by frontal cortex stimulation. *Electroencepholography and Clinical Neurophysiology,* 22, 143–149.

Stevenson, I. (1970). *Telepathic impressions: A review and report of thirty-five new cases.* Charlottesville, VA: University Press of Virginia.

Waddington, C.H. (1957). *The strategy of genes.* London: Allen & Unwin.

Weiskrantz, L. (1986). *Blindsight: A case study and implications.* Oxford: Clarendon Press.

Weiskrantz, L., Warrington, E.K., Sanders, M.D. and Marshall, J. (1974). Visual capacity in the hemianopic field following a restricted occipital ablation. *Brain,* 97(4), 709–728.

Willshaw, D. (1981). Holography, associative memory and inductive generalization. In G.E. Hinton and J.A. Anderson, Eds., *Parallel models of associative memory* (pp. 83–102). Hillsdale, NJ: Lawrence Erlbaum Associates.

Wright, J.J. (1980). Visual evoked response in lateral hypothalamic neglect. *Experimental Neurology.*

Zeigarnik, B.V. (1972). *Experimental abnormal psychology.* New York: Plenum.

Zukav, G. (1971). *The dancing Wu Li masters.* New York: Morrow.

7

Toward an Evolutionary Systems Approach to Creativity: The Contribution of Ervin Laszlo

ALFONSO MONTUORI

Abstract
Systems scientist Alfonso Montuori explores what both the traditional emphasis on individual creativity and the new research perspective on social creativity reveal of the impact of this vital thrust of the human agent on evolution.

Key words
Social creativity, systems perspective, Laszlo's evolutionary systems perspective, context, feedback loop, novelty, disequilibrium, bifurcations, Frank Barron, the creative individual, impact of human agency, risk-taking, complexity, diversity, interdependence, evolutionary action theory, ego-strength, self-replication, self-transcendence, coevolution, Bateson, constraints and possibilities, dominator system, partnership creativity, norm-changing, norm-maintaining, an ethos of partnership.

Introduction

The work of Ervin Laszlo spans an enormous wealth of knowledge pertaining to evolution and change in social and natural systems. Indeed, Laszlo is the pre-eminent systems philosopher of our time, having probably done more to link systems theory with the natural sciences and philosophy than any other thinker in the English-speaking world.

In particular here, Ervin Laszlo's evolutionary synthesis provides the foundations for a new understanding of creativity as an evolutionary, interactive, social phenomenon. An evolutionary approach raises important questions about the nature of creativity and the methodological approaches used to study it, while at the same time presenting a new, pluralist perspective that stresses the need to differentiate between partnership and dominator social systems and their implications for creativity.

In a recent publication, Laszlo (1994) has stressed the importance of "social creativity," a subject I have been interested in for many years (Montuori, 1989; Montuori and Purser, 1995, 1998). In this chapter I will explore social creativity in terms of the evolutionary vision outlined most clearly and succinctly in Laszlo's

(1996a) work *Evolution*. In this regard, I will also focus on the role of creativity in accounting for the human agent in evolution. Elsewhere, I have argued the need to view creativity from a systemic perspective in order to be able to adequately conceptualize *social* creativity. Social creativity has not received much attention in North America and the English-speaking world, I believe, because the present methodologies, philosophies, and indeed our very way of thinking have largely been reductionistic. It has sought to isolate the single variable perceived as most important at the exclusion of "exogenous factors." These exogenous factors have, in the main, been social factors, this exclusion leading to a restricted and constricted view of creativity as a fundamentally intrapersonal phenomenon, discounting social forces, relationships, and the like, in favor of strictly cognitive or personality-oriented approaches. But as Laszlo (1996a, p. 145) has written,

No phenomenon can be adequately known apart from the overall system of natural—and sometimes also social—realities in which it is embedded. Although individual researchers cannot cover all aspects of nature and society within the scope of their special competence, they can frame their research problems and assess their findings in light of general theories of wide multidisciplinary scope. A general evolution theory allows specialized investigators to divest themselves of the blindfolds that normally accompany specialty vision and permits them to situate their particular segment of the empirical world within a larger context.

Although systems approaches have recently become popular in the study of creativity, evolutionary systems approaches still lag behind, with notable exceptions such as Howard Gruber (1989) and Mihaly Csikszentmihalyi (1988). In this essay, I will explore what some of the characteristics of such an approach might be like, and how they might link up to existing findings in creativity research.

Context and Creativity

In order to conceive of social creativity, we must view creativity contextually and relationally (Montuori and Purser, 1995, 1998). For Laszlo (1996b), natural systems are coordinating interfaces in Nature's holarchy. From an evolutionary systems perspective, therefore, creative systems as holons must be studied contextually, within the larger systems or holons of the holarchy in which they exist. This of course also opens up the issue of system definition: what, exactly, is the "creative system"? As Ceruti (1994) points out, it is the *observer* who makes a choice about the system/environment definition. And from a systemic perspective, the environment plays a constitutive role in the existence of any open system, and must therefore be taken into account in any description of the system in question. To say that creativity "occurs" only between an individual's ears, as the typical intrapsychic approach suggests, is to make a system definition that, as Purser and I have shown (Montuori and Purser, 1998), is based very much on cultural and historical grounds, and differs from culture to culture and in different historical periods.

Let us begin with a broad definition. Creativity is generally defined very broadly as the capacity to bring something new into existence: it is the capacity to respond adaptively to the world around us, not just reactively but proactively. Given this definition, it is not surprising to learn that an evolutionary approach suggests that creativity is an intrinsic principle of all human systems in their relation to their environment. Laszlo (1996b, p. 39) states that one of the main organizational invariances of natural systems is that they "create themselves in response to self-creativity in other systems." Laszlo (1996b, p. 36) writes that

The state maintained in and by organisms is the steady-state. This is a dynamic balance of energies and substances, always poised for action. It is never a plain equilibrium, such as the state a watch reaches when it has run down.

Laszlo (1996b, p. 40) writes that individual systems are

capable not merely of repeating certain types of behavior, but of inventing new ones. We get a progressive modification of behaviors: one invention poses challenges as its effects reach other systems, and these respond by their own matching inventions.

Creativity can be viewed therefore as something inherent in the larger feedback loop of system and environment, part of the autopoietic (self-creating) tendency of life (Maturana and Varela, 1987) where novelty appears as an emergent property. Creative systems are continuously and, in the case of human systems, *willfully* creating disequilibria and bifurcations, shattering consistencies and established orders, both "internally," in terms of their own cognitive maps, and "externally," in terms of their at times even revolutionary behaviors/actions.

In human beings, these self-generated interruptions of consistencies bring internal (psychological) diversity and heterogeneity. Barron (1972, p. 111) writes that one may conceive of a human being as "a dynamical natural system, bounded yet open, that is in a continual state of disequilibrium." In light of the recent work in evolutionary theory, and most prominently in Laszlo's evolutionary synthesis, such a system would now be referred to as a "self-organizing dissipative structure," an open system that can survive only through a constant exchange of matter/energy and information with its environment. Such an open system is stabilized by its flowing, but is only relatively stable. The stability is relative to the constant matter/energy and information flow. Without the constant change a system would die; too much change can overwhelm the system and potentially damage it (Laszlo, 1996a).

In mental ecologies there is a considerable amount of complexity arising out of the self-reflective capacity that biological systems such as cells presumably do not share. The capacity for self-reflection allows human systems to consciously operate upon themselves and upon their understanding of the world. Creative individuals allow themselves to become disorganized by constantly challenging the assumptions of their understanding of themselves and the world. They disturb their mental equilibrium—and consequently tend to score higher on some measures of psychopathology, since they may be periodically unbalanced—and yet can return to a dynamic stable state, scoring unusually high on ego-strength (Montuori, 1991).

Creative individuals constantly renew themselves by remaining open to experiences that may force them to reconsider set ways of doing and thinking. They express a preference for disorder, which they then try to integrate into a pluralistic, heterogeneous ecology of mind. Increased autonomy and differentiation go hand in hand with greater instability and openness, and a loosening of the boundaries between what is inside and what is outside. Indeed, in a process worldview (such as evolutionary systems theory) there is really no "inside" or "outside."

Accordingly, in accounting for the impact of human agency and other living systems on evolution, Laszlo (1969, p. 21) writes that

We must do away with the subject–object distinction in analyzing experience. This does not mean that we reject the concepts of organism and environment, as handed down to us by natural science. It only means that we conceive of experience as linking organism and environment in a continuous chain of events, from which we cannot, without arbitrariness, abstract an entity called "organism" and another called "environment." The organism is continuous with its environment, and its experience refers to a series of transactions constituting the organism–environment continuum.

From such a perspective growth is viewed not as a separation or abstraction from the environment, but as a greater awareness of systemic embeddedness and openness to process, paradoxically coupled with greater differentiation, in an ongoing dialectical process of differentiation–integration. This openness and flexibility plays a crucial part in the development of an 'interior ecology', which proves fertile and rich and thus capable of generating new ideas and making new connections. A closed, rigid system inevitably has fewer connections and provides a less fertile psychomass.

According to Laszlo (1996a, p. 90),

The benefit of evolutionary convergence towards high organizational levels is the dynamism and autonomy available to multilevel systems. While the benefit of evolutionary convergence is increased dynamisms and autonomy, the cost is increasing vulnerability. Convergent evolution to higher and higher organizational levels involves a gamble: the exchange of relatively simple and reliable catalytic cycles for complex, hierarchically organized sequences of dynamic individual- and species-maintaining hypercycles.

The evolutionary process therefore involves a degree of risk-taking, whereby simplicity and relative isolation are exchanged for complexity, diversity, and far greater interdependence with the environment. The crucial factor therefore is that the greater the complexity of any system, the greater its interdependence with its environment. As Bateson (1972, p. 483) illustrates, this is a profoundly counter-intuitive notion for the individualist West:

Now we begin to see some of the epistemological fallacies of Occidental civilization. In accordance with the general climate of thinking in mid-nineteenth-century England, Darwin proposed a theory of natural selection and evolution in which the unit of survival was either the family line or the species or subspecies or something of the sort. But today it is quite obvious that this is not the unit of survival in the real biological world. The unit of survival is *organism* plus *environment*. We are learning by bitter experience that the organism which destroys its environment destroys itself. If, now, we correct the Darwinian unit of survival to include the environment and the interaction between organism and environment, a very strange and surprising identity emerges: *the unit of evolutionary survival turns out to be identical with the unit of mind.*

Here Bateson's insight seems to intersect both with the long-ignored Darwin of human impact theory, whom Loye writes of elsewhere in this volume, and Loye's own creativity-driven evolutionary action theory (Loye 1998). This elevation of the impact of mind to higher evolutionary status suggests that in some profound ways, all human creativity is indeed social creativity, that it cannot be de-contextualized, and that creativity viewed from an atomistic perspective that does not take the environment into account may prove profoundly counteradaptive. Phenomena such as industrial pollution are but one example of such a de-contextualized creativity.

Given the greater interdependence that comes along with greater complexity, we must also take into account the greater vulnerability we all experience as we become ever more interconnected in a world where all our actions have wide-ranging effects—effects that we may not at all be aware of, and that a systemic/evolutionary consciousness may be able to envision, but also predict.

The concept of "Ego-strength" (Barron, 1990) reflects an understanding of the healthy individual as someone who is secure enough to be open, fundamentally organized enough to become temporarily disorganized, sure enough in him or herself to have beliefs and identity shaken and indeed profoundly questioned and changed. Creative individuals thrive on this process, this dialectic of deconstruction and (re)creation. Identity and psychological growth involve not a hardening of boundaries, a rigid, unyielding ego, but an ability to immerse oneself in the world, even lose oneself in it, and then come back. The dichotomy between individual and society, self and system, is the product of a static, either/or viewpoint: it is replaced by a process where an ongoing dialog leads to alternating periods of innocence and experience, self-dissolution and self-(re)creation.

By remaining open to new experience, and actively seeking out complex phenomena that cannot be explained, creative persons allow for periodic moments of disequilibrium in order to transform the complex input they are faced with. Complexity, in this sense, is any information that does not easily fit into a preexisting order. It is not intrinsic to the phenomenon being observed, but in the observing system (Bocchi and Ceruti, 1987).

Along with a preference for complexity, creative persons have a preference for asymmetrical forms over symmetrical ones. They seek to create elegant perceptual schemata and they favor disorder and complexity, but only because they wish to integrate it into a higher-order—yet simple—synthesis. Their goal is analogous to the achievement of mathematical elegance, allowing into the perceptual system the greatest possible richness of experience, while at the same time finding in this complexity some overall gestalts, or patterns that are aesthetically pleasing. This constant quest leads to a dynamic, evolutionary process orientation in open systems, as opposed to the static orientation in closed systems.

Finding the simple overall pattern in complexity is a means to bring meaning to disorder, and it is fundamentally an act of *creation*. In this respect creative persons are very much like dissipative structures, reaching out beyond their own boundaries to impact evolution through self-transcendence, integrating complexity and achieving higher levels of organization and heterogeneity (Laszlo, 1996b).

Discussing an analogous process in natural systems, Laszlo (1996a, p. 25) writes: "The emergence of a higher-level system is not a complexification but a *simplification* of system function." He goes on to write that

Less complex systems on a higher level of organization can effectively control more complex systems on lower levels in virtue of the selective disregard, on the higher, controlling level, of the detailed dynamics of the lower-level units, the selective neglect of irrelevant details is a universal property of hierarchical control systems. (p. 25)

Living systems are self-replicating; in other words they can replicate the parts that they are made of, as, for instance, human cells do (Csanyi and Kampis, 1991). Living systems do not just maintain equilibrium through self-replication (or habit formation in mental ecologies), they are also self-transcending, as Jantsch (1980, p. 184) points out:

Evolution is basically open. It determines its own dynamics and direction. This dynamic unfolds in a systemic web which, in particular, is characterized by the co-evolution of macro- and micro-systems. By way of this dynamic interconnectedness, evolution also determines its own *meaning*.

The evolutionary process of self-transcendence is fueled by the ongoing dialectic of complexity–simplicity–complexity that is the hallmark of creative problem formation and problem resolution. Creative persons create order in disorder and disorder in order: in Kuhnian terms, they look for the anomalies on the edges of the existing paradigm in order to build a new one. In the process of developing understandings in areas that were previously thought to be out of the bounds of human knowledge (e.g., far-from-equilibrium systems, dynamic systems, or chaos theory), creativity is also the creation of meaning, and of a cosmos.

The entire human project, the evolutionary journey, can be seen in this light as the creation of a multiplicity of worlds in space and time, each unfolding through our lives and in our attempts to give meaning to life. A question vital to an evolutionary systems approach is how an environment can be created with the capacity to allow for the emergence and coexistence of a plurality of worlds, and a plurality of cosmological motives, not just quantitatively (variety) but qualitatively (diversity).

A conception of creativity based on such a systemic, coevolutionary understanding of self-and-system will also have markedly different implications from those of an excessively individualistic understanding of creativity, which often sees the individual as locked in a struggle for dominion with the environment (Montuori, 1989). An evolutionary approach draws our attention to the fundamental nature of the relationship between any system and its environment. And the decontextualized, atomistic view translates not just into a blindness about the environment and the impact of individual action. At another level of analysis, one finds an adversarial stance, or, in Eisler's (1987) formulation, a *dominator* approach toward what is considered outside the boundaries of the system in question. In other words, an atomistic conception of self, or of a specific system, is almost always accompanied by a perception of the need to dominate and control what is "outside."

Creative Dynamics and the Evolutionary Ecology of Social Systems

A social system that encourages the development of the characteristics associated with creative individuals, such as independence of judgment, tolerance for ambiguity, preference for complexity, and so on is not simply educating for creativity: implicit in these traits are also certain relations to authority, and a willingness to question the status quo that will almost inevitably bring about change. The psychological characteristics of creative individuals therefore have considerable sociopolitical implications, and societies (and social systems in general) influence creative development to the extent that these characteristics are encouraged or not.

Suppression of anxiety may be a strong factor in the perceptual decision not to pay attention to unusual or disturbing experiences, not tolerate ambiguity and complexity or exercise independence of judgment, and thus reduce the potential for creativity. The kind of psychological characteristics closed, totalitarian systems (whether at the individual, group, or societal level) have to enforce clearly include conformity as opposed to independence of judgment, intolerance as opposed to tolerance of ambiguity, and simplicity as opposed to complexity (Montuori, 1989). Closed systems strive for simplicity, homogeneity, and equilibrium—characteristics that are the opposites of those found in creative systems, whether biological, psychological, or sociopolitical (Loye and Eisler, 1987).

Barron (1963) has discussed the importance of originality and creativity, stating that originality is "measured as to be equivalent to the capacity for producing adaptive responses which are unusual" (p. 150). Statistically unusual or infrequent responses, he goes on to write, can also be considered a function of "the objective freedom of an organism, where this is defined as the range of possible adaptive responses available in all situations" (p. 150).

In order to represent the increasing complexity creative individuals choose to encounter and integrate, they have to think systemically and have flexibility as a "coding" or interpretive system. Wilden (1987) has elaborated Ashby's principle of requisite variety into a principle of requisite *diversity*. Ashby's principle states that if a system encounters greater variety in its environment than it can process, the system's stability is threatened since it will be unable to "reduce, absorb, suppress, or transform the uncoded variety (the noise) that threatens it" (Wilden, 1987,

p. 190). Wilden's principle of requisite diversity holds that a system has to be able to represent the basic codings of the *types* of variety in its environment, in other words, *qualitative* and not just *quantitative* differences.

Bateson's Rule: In proportion as the structural diversity of a natural or social ecosystem is reduced, so also is its flexibility to survive future environmental uncertainties. Reductions of diversity deplete the ecosystem's resources of uncommitted potential for change. (Wilden, 1987, p. 194)

The uncommitted potential for future change in any system, which Bateson (1972) equated largely with *flexibility,* can, in human systems, be considered to some extent as the degree of creativity inherent in an individual's or social system's ecology. The characteristics of a creative ecology include diversity, complexity, and heterogeneity. A creative system therefore incorporates diversity and redundancy, and allows for the constitutive role of disorder. Whereas in closed social systems disorder is eliminated at all costs, in creative systems disorder is not perceived necessarily as a deviation from the necessary order, but as the emergence of possibility (Bocchi and Ceruti, 1993; Morin, 1994). Disorder is therefore actually courted, to some extent, with the creative system functioning "at the edge of chaos," to use a term that has gained increasing popularity today.

Evolutionary Systems: Constraints and Possibilities

The Neo-Darwinian view saw evolution as a product of genetic mutation, with the environment acting as a source of natural selection of the fittest, weeding out the unfit mutations. Post-Darwinian views of evolution, particularly as developed by Stephen J. Gould and Niles Eldredge (1986), shift from evolution as seen in Monod's classical formulation of *chance* (random mutations) and *necessity* (adaptation to the biological and physical environment), to evolution as the interaction between *constraints* and *possibilities* (Bocchi and Ceruti, 1993; Ceruti, 1994; Laszlo, 1996a). Complex systems show degrees of spontaneous order and self-ordering properties that cannot be interpreted solely as the product of natural selection. Adaptation is beginning to be seen not as the result of a cause in the environment determining a change in the organism, but rather as the organism's active answer to *perceived* constraints in the environment (Ceruti, 1994).

Laszlo (1996a, p. 84) states that

Evolution occurs when the dominant population within a "clade" (a set of species sharing a similar adaptive plan) is destabilized in its milieu and other species or subspecies that emerged haphazardly on the periphery break through the cycles of dominance. At that point, the stasis of the epoch is broken, and there is an evolutionary leap from the formerly dominant species, threatened with extinction, to the peripheral species or subspecies.

What we are beginning to see is the proliferation of a large number of *viable* (as opposed to adapted) systems, and a form of evolutionary pluralism that recognizes the *constructive*, creative nature of each system's evolutionary process (Bocchi and Ceruti, 1993). In humans our 'cosmological motives' express themselves in myriad interpretations of the world, as we adapt not to *the* environment, but to our interpretation of the environment.

Change depends on the variability of organisms and species, and the infinite possible ways in which this variety is coupled with environmental constraints. Natural history is a history of the reciprocal production of new constraints and new possibilities through the drift of structural couplings between autonomous living systems and their environments, and between differing autonomous living systems within particular ecologies. (Ceruti, 1994, p. 155)

This view leads to a different, more ecological, understanding of constraints and the boundaries of human knowledge and experience. Here constraints are not seen as antithetical to freedom, complexity, and diversity, but as essential aspects of them. This relates back to the new understanding of autonomy as, paradoxically, greater systemic embeddedness. The focus is on the primacy of relationships, as opposed to the stereotypical individualist/reductionist Western view of autonomous atoms that, when put in relationship, typically have to battle for their autonomy. The systemic view, with its clear focus on the primacy of relationship, shows distinct affinities to the work emerging in feminist scholarship (Eisler, 1987; Montuori, 1989). Complexity and diversity are in fact the result of constraints— creative systems such as human agents are complexifying and diversifying entities, and in turn seek out more complexity and diversity, in order to create ever more heterogeneous simplicity and requisite diversity.

The pluralist approach also dismisses attempts at establishing an "optimal" adaptation, a pinnacle of adjustment all should strive for (Ceruti, 1994). A cybernetic epistemology proposes that we simply cannot *know* a best or "optimal" state, but we can know our *desired* state(s). From a social and philosophical perspective, a unitary approach positing an "optimal" (objectively best) and univocal goal is very much associated with what Eisler (1987) calls a "dominator" system, precisely because it is fundamentally "determinist" and actually eliminates the possibility of free human agency, since it leaves only one choice, and one that is determined, at that.

A pluralist approach, on the contrary, holds that the greater the diversity of adaptive systems, the richer and more flexible the ecosystem as a whole becomes, and the greater the freedom of choice and human agency. The freedom of human agency lies precisely in the capacity to explore and create new worlds and new possibilities, while at the same time ensuring that the context for this freedom is constantly supported. The issue then becomes not seeking the "fittest" form of adaptation, a spurious "survival of the fittest," but developing the kind of ecology that can support the greatest amount of complexity, diversity, and heterogeneity created in and by that process of creation. In pluralist social systems, there is an ongoing dialectic between freedom and equality: the freedom to express oneself and to explore possibilities, and the responsibility to ensure that the conditions that allow this expression are constantly nurtured by and through individual and collective freedom.

The real question then becomes: what is the underlying social system, the ecology that supports the emergence of a plurality of creative voices without disintegrating into domination and war? In Eisler's (1987) terms, it is a "partnership" system, one that stresses the capacity to provide what Loye (1988) has called the nurturing, feminine matrix of creativity, the ground of support and sustainability for a plurality of viable systems, and rejects domination in favor of mutual benefit celebrating diversity and difference rather than suppressing them (Montuori, 1989).

Loye's (1977) differentiation between norm-changing and norm-maintaining is useful here. In a pluralist, open system, the creative function of norm-changing is constantly *supported* by a "conservative" function of "maintaining" what is—but in this case maintaining the condition of partnership that allows for the norm-changing to occur in such a way that the integrity of the system is not threatened and the pluralism and diversity of its ecology are not compromised. In traditional political discourse, the conservative function acts in antagonistic opposition to change, and focuses on the maintenance of "power over." In the evolutionary social system I am proposing here, the conservative function is viewed as maintaining the overall system's "power to."

In this sense, politically we are speaking of a radical, pluralist equalitarianism, which allows the greatest possible freedom for individual and collective human agency while at the same time ensuring that this freedom is safeguarded against the imposition and indeed domination of one "correct" view.

These different manifestations of creativity are also expressed therefore in a plurality of fit social systems. This pluralism distinguishes itself from relativism—which recognizes no criteria for judgment—inasmuch as a criterion for fitness may be the capacity for generating a plurality of discourses within the system itself while at the same time maintaining an ethos of partnership. The emphasis is not so much on content as on capacity—the latter being specifically the capacity to "maintain," in Loye's sense, an ethos of partnership underlying the emergence of different and at times antagonistic voices. Whereas in dominator systems antagonism and difference have to be eliminated through homogenization, partnership systems need precisely the capacity to sustain a plurality of views, without necessarily assuming that some higher "synthesis" will emerge. Indeed, it is precisely the creative tension that emerges through the coexistence of differences that is both the greatest achievement and the greatest challenge for any partnership system.

A partnership approach, recognizing that the evolutionary unit of survival is organism *plus* environment, ensures that the generative, supportive capacity of the environment is not depleted: this would be the sociological equivalent of the ecological notion of sustainability. This would combine the Western view of creativity as self-expression with, for instance, the African view of creativity as *Kuumba,* or "leaving the world a better and more beautiful place that we found it."

Such an approach would also stress the inherently dialogical relationship between figure and ground, between creativity and the ground of sympathy, between the rose and the soil from which it emerges.

Whereas the modern Western concept of creativity has typically pitted the individual genius against his environment, and stressed the role of creativity in standing out from, and controlling (dominating) the environment, a perspective drawing from evolutionary systems theory would stress the mutually co-creative, dialogical interrelationship between system and environment. One of the main challenges for human agency in the evolutionary journey is therefore the development of the capacity to envision alternative futures that tackle the challenge of creating sustainable social and natural ecologies.

Conclusion

An evolutionary approach to creativity has many implications, but perhaps the most interesting, in the light of a specifically social focus on creativity, emerges as we begin to appreciate the need to explore the generative context from which creativity springs forth, the requisite diversity for the development of a system sufficiently flexible, permitting sufficient freedom, arising through an awareness and appreciation of evolutionary pluralism. In the human sphere, this suggests the need to foster not just the capacities described by creativity researchers, such as tolerance for ambiguity, preference for complexity, independence of judgment, and so forth, but also the kind of collaborative spirit of partnership and conviviality that permits such a generative social context to flourish. An evolutionary approach to creativity can help us develop social creativity through a recognition of the coevolutionary process, where, in Bateson's terms, we speak of the evolutionary unit of survival as organism plus environment. Ervin Laszlo's extensive elaboration of the evolutionary paradigm provides a powerful starting-point for this process.

References

Barron, F. (1963). The needs for order and disorder as motives in creative action. In C.W. Taylor and F. Barron, Eds., *Scientific creativity: Its recognition and development* (pp. 153–160). New York: Wiley.

—— (1990). *Creativity and psychological health.* Buffalo, NY: Creative Education Foundation. (Original work published 1963.)

Bateson, G. (1972). *Steps to an ecology of mind.* New York: Ballantine.

Bocchi, G. and Ceruti, M. (Eds.) (1985). *La sfida della complessità* [The challenge of complexity]. Milan: Feltrinelli.

—— (1994). *Origini di storie* [The origins of stories]. Milan: Feltrinelli.

Ceruti, M. (1994). *Il vincolo e la possibilità* [Constraint and possibility]. Milan: Feltrinelli;

published in English as *Constraints and possibilities: The evolution of knowledge and knowledge of evolution*. New York: Gordon & Breach.

Csanyi, V. and Kampis, G. (1991). Modeling biological and social change: Dynamical replicative network theory. In E. Laszlo, Ed., *The new evolutionary paradigm*. New York: Gordon & Breach.

Csikszentmihalyi, M. (1988). Society, culture, and person. In R.J. Sternberg, Ed., *The nature of creativity*. New York: Cambridge University Press.

Eldredge, N. (1986). *Time frames: The rethinking of Darwinian evolution and the theory of punctuated equilibria*. London: Heinemann.

Gruber, H. (1989). The evolving systems approach to creative work. In D.B. Wallace and H. Gruber, Eds., *Creative people at work*. New York: Oxford University Press.

Jantsch, E. (1976). Evolution: Self-realization through self-transcendence. In E. Jantsch and C.H. Waddington, Eds., *Evolution and consciousness: Human systems in transition* (pp. 37–70). Reading, MA: Addison-Wesley.

—— (1980). *The self-organizing universe*. New York: Pergamon.

Laszlo, E. (1969). *System, structure, and experience*. New York: Gordon & Breach.

—— (1992). *The age of bifurcation: Understanding the changing world*. New York: Gordon & Breach.

—— (1994). *The choice: Evolution or extinction*. Los Angeles: Tarcher.

—— (1996a). *Evolution: The grand theory*. Cresskill, NJ: Hampton Press.

—— (1996b). *The systems view of the world*. Cresskill, NJ: Hampton Press.

Loye, D. (1977). *The leadership passion*. San Francisco: Jossey Bass.

—— (1988). Hemisphericity and creativity. Group process in the dream factory. *Psychiatric Clinics of North America*, 11, 415–426.

—— (1990). Moral sensitivity and the evolution of higher mind. *World Futures*, 30, 41–52.

Loye, D. and Eisler, R. (1987). Chaos and transformation: implications of nonequilibrium theory for social science and society. *Behavioral Science*, 32, 53–65.

Maturana, H., and Varela, F. (1987). *The tree of knowledge*. Boston: New Science Library

Montuori, A. (1989). *Evolutionary competence. Creating the future*. Amsterdam: J.C. Gieben.

—— (1992). Creativity, chaos, and self-renewal in human systems. *World Futures*, 35, 193–209.

Montuori, A. and Purser, R. (Eds.) (1998). *Social Creativity*, vol. 1: *Prospects and possibilities*. Creskill, NJ: Hampton Press.

Wilden, A. (1986). *The rules are no game*. New York: Routledge.

8
QVI: The Fifth Field of Ervin Laszlo

DAVID LOYE

Abstract

Social psychologist David Loye provides a guide for the lay person and generalist to the quantum-vacuum interactive, or QVI-field theory of Ervin Laszlo. This would add a fifth primary field to the four already identified by physics to account for the existence of the universe and our lives within it.

Key words

Quantum-Vacuum Interaction, QVI-field, physics, biology, cosmology, Big Bang scenario, cognitive science, nonlocality, psi phenomena, Bohm, Pribram, Sheldrake, field concept, gravitation, electromagnetism, weak and strong nuclear interactions, fifth field.

Over the past decade, a provocative manuscript circulated by Ervin Laszlo among leading-edge thinkers in science has been forcing new thought into some fundamental cracks in the prevailing scientific paradigm. More recently, out of his dialogue with many of these scientists, a small family of books has been emerging to advance new thinking about the fundamentals of existence.

The fundamental question these books ask is: where do the *forms* of evolution come from? But also: why have we wound up as exactly the kind of creatures we are today in precisely the kind of world we inhabit? Does what we do during our lives here on Earth really make a difference? Is there anything about us that is lasting? And what really holds all of what we experience during our lives together?

The answers to such questions, Laszlo contends, may be found in what he calls Quantum-Vacuum Interaction, or the QVI-field. Dependent for its understanding on a broad knowledge of advanced physics and biology as well as a range of other fields across the span of social as well as natural science, QVI-field theory is not easy even for experts in these areas to understand. In order to cross the barriers between advanced science and a useful general comprehension, Laszlo has resorted to the unusual step of writing not one but three books for widely varying readerships to express it. This chapter will focus on the commonalities underlying the differences of all three books to reveal something of the facets and significance for this new theory that seeks to define the nature of a new mind-involving and mind-evolving fifth field in addition to the four fields of forces already defined by science.

The Interconnected Universe, published by World Scientific of Singapore, New Jersey, London, and Hong Kong in 1995, is the sparse scientific statement for those equipped to handle the physics and the other sciences without attention to the needs of the nontechnical reader. At the other extreme, drawing on Laszlo's capacity for graceful and engaging writing, *The Whispering Pond*, published in 1996 by Element Books of London with distribution by Penguin Books in the United States, is written to reach the general reader. Of the three books it also develops something that unfortunately very few scientific thinkers do. As indicated by the quotes with which this chapter closes, Laszlo inspires the reader to recognize his or her own personal involvement and to act on the potential for and help bring about the better world that his findings reveal. *The Creative Cosmos*, published by Floris Books of Edinburgh, Scotland, in 1993, is in the middle in offering both scientific depth and detail with attention also to the general reader's needs.

And what are these books about? A track that runs through them is roughly this. Despite the fact that both scientists and the rest of us tend to think of evolution as something reasonably polished off by now as far as theory goes, the fact is that our understanding of it is riddled with holes. Field by field, Laszlo lists these holes or anomalies. In microphysics, cosmology, and biology, one runs into the fact that the universe and we ourselves could never have fallen into place, as we have, if it had all been left up to traditional Darwinian theory—that is, to the natural selection of things emerging through mutations and random processes. Laszlo brings together the calculations of several scientists to show that additionally some nonrandom factor is at work that shapes what comes to be.

Here quite arresting is the picture he develops of the hole in the Big Bang scenario for the origin of our universe. What came before the Big Bang has been a question. What did this hypothetical great formative explosion rise out of? The technical problem that has yet to be answered is how, considering all that would already have had to be in place *before* the Big Bang, our universe could have evolved so rapidly thereafter. Laszlo makes a compelling case for evolution not as something that only got started with the one Big Bang our attention has been focused on, but more reasonably as something that has had to involve a series of giant pulses (or Big Bangs) out of an underlying matrix that both records all the information and generates all the forms of existence.

In the cognitive sciences—e.g., psychology and brain research—the unexplained holes in our present understanding of how everything is put together are revealed by so-called psi phenomena. On the old paradigmatic level that is rapidly passing scientists still question the existence of telepathy, precognition, etc. But among leading-edge thinkers in many fields there is now a quiet acceptance of the data. The question has shifted to asking: what do these phenomena mean?

What does it mean if people can pick up the feelings and thoughts of others at long distance without a telephone? What does it mean if occasionally some of us see into the future with uncanny accuracy? This may violate the requirements of traditional scientific theory, but it does not violate the findings of the new physics regarding nonlocality of event formation or connection, as well as in many other regards. Indeed, these phenomena seem to indicate the dimensions of an enormous and truly unprecedented revolution in scientific thinking that may now lie not too far ahead.

In his careful exploration Laszlo pursues the idea that psi phenomena also seem to indicate some kind of underlying matrix that provides the unseen connections, but what is it? He considers the well-known theories of physicist David Bohm and brain scientist Karl Pribram regarding the idea of a multilevel matrix operating as a kind of giant hologram. Here Bohm's ideas of the interlinking of the known and the unknown worlds of existence through the interaction and dynamics of the implicate and explicate orders are arresting. He considers biologist Rupert Sheldrake's ideas of a morphogenetic field that stores all the memories of existence at all levels as another candidate for the matrix. But in both of these as well as other instances, while Laszlo finds ideas in common with his own in seeking to define what he is looking for, he also finds problems and inadequacies. What then might be the solution?

Throughout his exploration, Laszlo stresses the power of the concept of the "field" in physics and thereafter its use elsewhere. Indeed, seldom is this central but all too often rather fuzzy concept so well articulated. "If an event A at one point in space is connected with an event B at a different point, we must assume that A and B are interconnected by a continuous . . . matrix that has physical reality much like A and B. A physically real connecting matrix of this kind is best conceptualized as a field," he writes in *The Interconnected Universe* (p. 10).

So if a field is what we are looking for, what kind of field? Something is needed besides the four force fields (gravitation, electromagnetism, and the weak and strong nuclear interactions) that seem to hold everything together already established by physics. A new fifth field is needed to account for all the holes and the anomalies, Laszlo says. The best candidate seems to be the "Dirac sea of the quantum vacuum."

In other words, what we see as empty space all around us—and which we know separates quark from quark, etc., even on the subatomic level—now appears to be anything but empty. According to Bohm and many others it is filled with an almost inconceivably enormous energy, and this sea of energy seems to swirl in to fill in and interconnect everything.

What seems to give form to evolution then—what both stores everything that has happened and in turn helps gives birth to everything that comes to be, *including the thrust of human agency in all its many forms*—is what Laszlo calls the "quantum-vacuum interaction," which in turn produces "a self-referentially randomness-mitigating evolutionary process" (*The Interconnected Universe*, p. 25).

It is, as Professor Ignazio Masulli of the University of Bologna says, "one of the boldest scientific theories of recent years." Hungarian evolutionary theorist Vilmos Csanyi sees a potential for launching "a scientific revolution."

"In the embracing vision that is now emerging everything that has evolved in the universe, Mozart and Einstein, you and me, the greatest of galaxies and the humblest of insects, is the result of a stupendous process of open-ended yet non-random self-creation," Laszlo writes in explaining to the nonphysicist the potential significance of this fifth field of the quantum-vacuum interaction he makes the case for. "Nothing that has ever evolved exists separately from all the rest: all things are connected, all are part of an organic totality."

"In the emerging 'total vision' reality is a seamless whole composed of its parts. More than that, it is a whole in which all parts are constantly in touch with each other," he writes of this QVI-field. "There is constant and intimate contact among the things that coexist and coevolve in the universe, a sharing of bonds and messages that makes reality into a stupendous network of interaction and communication: a subtle but ever-present whispering pond."

At a time when we and our societies transit into an interacting and interdependent web of technology, finance, production, consumption, and even leisure and culture, it is vital that our consciousness be infused with this new vision, rather than the old. For enduring connections among humans, and between humans and nature, is a highly useful, in addition to an intensely meaningful, concept. It is the kind of insight that could re-establish harmony and balance in a world of vulnerable interdependence and growing chaos. (*The Whispering Pond*, pp. 4–5).

Earlier, in Chapter 5 of this book, we glimpsed this basic interconnection in biologist Mae-Wan Ho's vision of a QVI-field theory relevance to the operation of an organic force of love universally. Next, in Chapter 9 by social psychologist Mária Sági, we are to further explore the QVI-field potential for explaining the hitherto inexplicable success of methods of bioenergy healing, and then in Chapter 10, how social groups form and intercommunicate in sociologist Raymond Trevor Bradley's probe of its relation to theories of Pribram, Gabor, and Piaget. We will then briefly return to it in Chapter 12 in considering its hypothetical operation within the potential for completion of Darwinian evolution theory with a new articulation of the interface between the human agent and evolution.

References

Laszlo, E. (1993). *The creative cosmos: A unified science of matter, life and mind*. Edinburgh: Floris Books.

—— (1995). *The interconnected universe: Conceptual foundations of transdisciplinary unified theory*. Singapore, New Jersey, London, and Hong Kong: World Scientific.

—— (1996). *The whispering pond: A personal vision of the emerging vision of science*. London and New York: Element Books.

9
Healing through the QVI-Field

MÁRIA SÁGI

Abstract
Social psychologist Mária Sági explores the
potential of Ervin Laszlo's QVI-field theory not
only for explaining many anomalies of science
but also in providing a first rigorously scientific
explanation of the mysteries of bioenergetic
healing.

Key words
Holistic medicine, energy fields, bioenergies,
Wilhelm Reich, scalar-mediated zero-point
field of quantum vacuum, holofield, wave
patterns, morphodynamic patterns, species-
specific pattern, physiological health,
consciousness, self-healing processes,
information medicine, "clairvoyant" healer,
holistic healer, bioenergy medicine.

The new scientific concept of the physical, biological, and human world presented
in Ervin Laszlo's *The Whispering Pond* sheds light not only on a number of
persistent anomalies in the contemporary scientific world picture, but also on a
number of new and surprising methods of preserving and restoring our bodily
health (Laszlo, 1996). Prior to the publication of this book, many of these methods
could not be explained with sufficient scientific rigor.

Holistic Medicine

Holistic (or "alternative") medicine is a generic term covering the types of
diagnostic and healing methods that extend beyond the biochemical and surgical
approaches of Western medicine and yet prove effective. This kind of medicine
does not attempt to cure the symptoms of disease but looks for its causes. It does
not treat the organism by external and unnatural means but enhances the capacities of the organism to cure itself. It treats the living organism as a self-preserving
and self-repairing whole capable of curing many, if not all, of the ills that befall it.

Holistic medicine justifies its name by its approach: in addition to taking into
consideration the patient's body as a whole, it also considers his or her emotional
state and disposition, and his or her ways of thinking, social relations, and intellectual endowments. Also the energy fields relevant to health and disease are
taken into account. Treatment endeavors to influence the body's nonconventional
energy system, which is presumed to maintain its biochemical order. The existence
of nonconventional or "subtle" energies in living organisms was accepted by

almost all classical cultures: in their healing practices they made use of the energies that they believed would permeate the body, as well as the energies that would link the organism to the world at large. But at the dawn of the modern age such factors were dismissed as superstition or fantasy: only the manifest material world was considered real, and within that only what is measurable was seen as relevant to science.

In the course of the 20th century interest in subtler energy factors awakened again: subtle energy research is now pursued in laboratories in many parts of the world. The new sciences have instruments for describing and observing field phenomena that are beyond the ken of the concepts and methods of classical physics. For example, the properties of the electromagnetic field created in the quantum communication of cells can now be understood, measured, and in part influenced. As Laszlo's recent works—*The Whispering Pond, The Creative Cosmos,* as well as *The Interconnected Universe*—demonstrate, holistic medicine and the new sciences are finding meaningful common ground (Laszlo, 1993, 1994, 1996).

Relevance of the QVI–Field

What does the rapprochement between physics and the holistic practices of alternative healers mean for contemporary medical science? How can we interpret the human organism and its various states on the basis of the concepts regarding nature, cosmos, and the human being currently emerging at the leading edge of the sciences?

Laszlo shows that the biochemical processes of the living body are not only governed by systems of interactions linked to the ambient electromagnetic field but are also influenced by a particular field: the scalar-mediated zero-point field of the quantum vacuum. Physicists know that the vacuum, the basic state of the universe, is energetically extremely dense. Laszlo, like David Bohm and a growing number of cutting-edge investigators, suggests that on its tremendous virtual energies a holographic field is superimposed (cf., e.g., Bohm, 1980). This field is in nonlinear interaction with quanta and the intricate matter–energy structures built of quanta. Laszlo calls it the "Quantum-Vacuum Interaction (QVI) field."

Living organisms are embedded in the QVI-field and are in constant interaction with it. Its subtle energies inform all the cells, tissues, and organs of the human body, as well as the dynamic processes that shape the human and natural environment.

In Laszlo's theory, the scalar wave-interference patterns of the zero-point field are not evanescent but enduring: the holofield of the vacuum has "memory." Patterns encoded in, and in turn decoded from, the vacuum account for the various phenomena of healing over finite distances, as well as for numerous phenomena of transpersonal information flows and communication (cf. Laszlo, 1994, 1996).

How the QVI-field links material bodies in space and time can be understood through the analogy of vessels in the sea. Researchers have found that the surface of bodies of water—seas or lakes—is rich in information. The wave patterns yield information on the path of vessels, on the direction of the winds, on the impact of the shore lines and on various other factors that had earlier disturbed the surface. The wave patterns are often preserved for hours or for days after the disappearance of the vessels themselves. The natives of Polynesia, for instance, navigate by following the water patterns produced by islands in their region. Such patterns can be seen even with the naked eye when the surface is quiet and when viewed from a high cliff or an aircraft. Of course, in the sea the patterns eventually disappear since the waves are effaced by gravitation, winds, and interaction with shore lines. But as long as they exist, they yield information on the events that generated them.

The wave patterns yield more than passive information about events in a given part of the sea: they also exert influence on whatever is occurring there. Waves produced by a vessel usually have little influence on the movement of other vessels: when on a large ship, one hardly senses the gentle motions induced by a small boat. The situation, however, can be more dramatic, as anyone can testify who has crossed the wake of an ocean liner in a small motor boat or sailboat.

Whether the meeting of wavefronts carries much energy or not, it always produces information about the events that caused the waves. This information is conserved and communicated for a time by the surface wave patterns of the sea. This is analogous to the encoding of wave-interference patterns on a film. From such holographic patterns the original 3D image can be reconstructed. In the sea, the same as in the scalar component of the quantum vacuum, the holographically coded information produces subtle effects. It influences the motion and behavior of the material bodies—whether they are vessels or quanta—that are embedded in the given region of the field.

After a given time the surface of the sea loses its interference patterns: the surface is sooner or later smoothed out or restructured. Even patterns recorded on a holographic film disappear when the emulsion decays. The holographic field of the universe, however, is not exposed to dissipating forces: as Laszlo points out the "memory" of nature may last indefinitely. In the vacuum's multidimensional holofield the wave-interference patterns are superposed; hence the QVI-field records and preserves wavefronts in space and time without attenuation and the consequent loss of information. Hence the field's memory is complex and, in principle, complete.

Consequences for Human Health

Let us next consider what the content of the enduring memory of the field means for the health and healing of the human organism.

The first thing to note is that the living organism is not only a biochemical machine, but a complex energy field. It is through this field that the organism enters into contact and is continually in interaction, with the QVI-field. The latter cannot be perceived by normal human sense organs, but is capable of being estimated, or measured with refined instruments. The subtle energy field of the body, however, is capable of being sensed, even "seen" by specially endowed individuals. Healers and other sensitives see or otherwise sense the body's energy field as its "aura"; they can also obtain information from the wave-interference patterns in the QVI-field.

As the long-standing practice of natural healers testifies, pathological changes appear in the body's energy field before the corresponding changes would be observable in its biochemistry. The equilibrium and harmony of this field are delicate: in the human being it is strongly affected by the person's consciousness. Negative feelings, for instance a sudden fit of anger, produce an immediate effect on the field; the subject's aura changes color, or can develop a weakness that appears as a hole.

As just noted, according to Laszlo the energy field of the individual is in constant interaction with the scalar-mediated holofield of the quantum vacuum. The organism, like all quantal and multiquantal systems, is embedded in that field, similarly to vessels in the sea. The $3n$-dimensional wavefunctions of organisms are translated (through Fourier or, more exactly, Gabor transforms) into the cosmic "Dirac-sea" and are preserved there in the spectral domain of interfering waveforms. The nodes of these interference patterns constitute the cosmic hologram. Information from it can be re-translated, through the inverse Gabor transforms, to quantal and multiquantal systems with a matching $3n$-dimensional space–time configuration. (See Chapter 10 by Raymond Bradley in this volume for definitions of Fourier and Gabor transforms.)

In this analysis, the unique interference pattern translated from the organism to the QVI-field constitutes the individual's "morphodynamic pattern." This pattern is inclusive: it encodes all events in the organism, including the behavior of the neural nets that underlie consciousness. It also codes the organism's inherited weaknesses, expressed as tendencies to organic malfunctions and disease. This pattern encodes the characteristics of the physical body on the one hand, and the features of the individual's mind and consciousness on the other.

The morphodynamic pattern in the QVI-field is subject to interaction with other patterns in that field. These intra-field interactions are required to account for the healing processes encountered in the various branches of holistic medicine. The relevant intra-field interaction constitutes a "dance" of the individual's unique morphodynamic pattern with the broad-band pattern resulting from the sum of human morphodynamic patterns in the field. The summed pattern is not specific to a given individual, but is generic for all individuals within the species. It is the "species-specific pattern."

Since the species-specific pattern results from the generalized features of all the individuals of the given species who now live or have ever lived, individual difference (e.g., deviations due to individual abnormalities such as genetic or acquired diseases) are canceled out. The species-specific pattern only codes the generic norms of a species. This is important, for in regard to a species such as *Homo sapiens*, they constitute the universal norms of physiological functioning, that is, health.

The health of the individual is thus affected by the intra-field communication of his or her morphodynamic pattern with the species-specific pattern. A well-integrated communication, through mutually resonant frequencies, enhances the effectiveness of the immune system; an impaired communication, due to incoherence and reduced resonance, reduces the system's effectiveness.

The individual is capable of maintaining the organism in a state of health as long as his or her morphodynamic pattern matches the physiological norms encoded in the species-specific pattern. Within these limits the information corresponding to the organic norms of the human species is diffused throughout the atoms, molecules, tissues, cells, and organs of the body; beyond these limits diseases appear. Every deviation of the individual's morphodynamic pattern from the pattern coding the species norms affects his or her energy field and hence the biochemical processes of his or her organism.

Consciousness plays an important role in maintaining the "dance" between the two patterns in the QVI-field. It influences the coherence of the individual's morphodynamic pattern: a sound consciousness ensures an optimal "dance" of the two patterns. A flawed consciousness, on the other hand, sets limits as to the extent that this unique pattern, and hence the corresponding energy field, can benefit from the dance. As a result functional disturbances can spread in the organism. Energy malfunctions may degenerate into physiological malfunctions, while the ability of the immune system to initiate a self-healing process—a process that calls for integral communication with the species-specific pattern—is impaired.

Healing through the QVI-Field

Holistic medicine is basically information medicine. In standard medicine, the information required for diagnosis and therapy is obtained through the familiar methods based on the body's biochemistry. In holistic medicine, however, information is accessed trough the patterns coded in the QVI-field. Access to the latter is possible, since whether we know it or not our brain is constantly "reading" certain patterns in the QVI-field—those, namely, that match the $3n$-dimensional configuration of its neural nets with the spectral transforms in the field.

In modern Western civilization the state of normal waking consciousness is left-hemisphere dominated, and it tends to suppress the seemingly anomalous information resulting from contact with the field. However, in altered states of consciousness the censorship of the left-hemisphere is largely lifted: consciousness opens to the QVI-field. It is as if one attached a parabolic antenna to a television receiver, enabling it to receive additional waves of a specific frequency—those, namely, that are broadcast from a suitably located satellite. Such waves reach the set through the electromagnetic field even in the absence of an antenna; however, without the antenna the set is not capable of transforming them into a manifest image. For the human brain, the functional analogue of a parabolic antenna is the altered state of consciousness (ASC). As hundreds of controlled experiments testify, in ASCs the brain allows a wider range of information to penetrate to the level of ordinary awareness.

There are individuals with highly sensitive "antennas"—evolved abilities to access QVI-field-based information. They appear "clairvoyant" since they seem to "see" things not visible to ordinary persons. It appears that the clairvoyant healer is able tune his or her brain to specific information in the QVI-field. This information includes data from the generic species-specific pattern, as well as from a unique morphodynamic pattern.

In particular, the clairvoyant healer seems able to sense the patient's morphodynamic pattern and to match it against the species-specific pattern. Deviations in the former appear as critical points in the healer's perception—some speak of bright spots lighting up like tiny lamps, marking the points of malfunction in the organism. In this manner the clairvoyant healer identifies the weak or malfunctioning regions of the patient's morphodynamic pattern. In these regions the energy field is blocked or unbalanced. If not opened up or rebalanced, the patient is likely to develop biochemical malfunctions producing the familiar symptoms and manifestations of disease.

Nonclairvoyant healers resort to the use of appropriate instruments. These are the energy-oriented devices of natural medicine. Reports of success indicate that practice can enable the nonclairvoyant healer to reach the diagnostic skills of the clairvoyant. He or she seems also to match the morphodynamic pattern of the patient against the species-specific pattern, but uses an instrument—such as a pendulum or a radionic device—as a vehicle for "sensing" the regions of pathological deviation.

Holistic healers make use of the same method for prescribing a treatment as they use for achieving a diagnosis. In both cases they access information about the state of their patient's morphodynamic pattern. This can occur either directly, through personal contact, or indirectly, through the morphodynamic pattern.

The goal of treatment (whether the healers themselves know it or not) is to restore the communication of the patient's morphodynamic pattern with the species-specific pattern. This can be achieved in several ways. The healer may work on the body of the patient directly, producing inputs in order to alter his or her energy field (for example, by means of acupuncture treatment, acumassage, homeopathic remedies, geometric forms to alter the polarity of the ambient radiation, or by sending energies of specific frequency). Thanks to the continuous interaction between the fields, the rebalanced or unblocked energy field corrects the individual's morphodynamic pattern; in the optimum case it brings it into tune with the species-specific pattern. Once the mutually resonant condition of the intra-field dance is attained, the feedback processes that enable the immune system to maintain bodily health are given fresh scope to operate. Thanks to the resumed communication of the morphodynamic with the species-specific pattern, the organism can again maintain itself in a condition of health.

In indirect healing, as it appears over any finite distance, the healer "directs energy" to the field of the patient. This seems to occur by means of an interaction between the healer's own morphodynamic pattern (the QVI-field-based imprint of his energy field) and that of the patient. The two patterns, as all other patterns, are in potential communication as spectral transforms within the holographic QVI-field. The energy of the healer's own morphodynamic pattern creates a closer match between the patient's morphodynamic pattern and the species-specific pattern. The process appears as if the healer would direct energy flows, or vibrations of appropriate frequency, to the body of the distant patient. A positive modification in the patient's morphodynamic pattern creates a better match with the species-specific pattern. Hence the patient's immune system can again maintain his or her body within the limits of functional normalcy.

The healing methods cited above have been tested and confirmed in this writer's decade-long healing practice.[1] They work, whether or not one provides a scientific explanation for them. Such explanation, however, can give them legitimacy and thus lead to a wider acceptance. This would be beneficial for all concerned, since through the informational methods of holistic medicine a larger number of people could be treated with methods that are less invasive and less inherently risky than those of standard biochemical medicine.

Conclusions

The processes of healing have been constant for the past several thousand years, only the methods and means of activating them have differed. Activating them was the objective of the medicine men of primitive peoples, of the initiation ceremonies of the classical cultures, and constituted the core of the public or secret teachings of religious and esoteric sects. Today, the nature of these processes is becoming clarified. Modern medicine is progressing, in the words of physician Larry Dossey (1989, 1993), from Era I, standard biochemical medicine, through Era II, mind–body medicine, to Era III, nonlocal medicine, including the methods of holistic medicine outlined here. Holistic, nonlocal medicine does not rely on metaphysical or supranatural phenomena, but constitutes processes, such as the subtle communication of information through the QVI-field, that are accessible to scientific investigation. The medicine of the future promises to be information-based energy medicine, with diagnostic and curative methods relying on purposively modified information flows through the QVI-field.

Note

1. cf. Mária Sági, Holistic healing as fresh evidence for collective consciousness, *World Futures* 48, 1–4 (1977); Holistic healing of the third kind (mimeo); Utószó: Gyógyitás az ötödik mezö révén (Afterword: healing through the Psi-field), in Ervin Laszlo, *Kozmikus Kapcsolatok* (Cosmic connections), Budapest: Hungarian Bookclub (1996); Mária Sági and István Sági, Zur Wissenschaftstheorie der neuen Homeopathie: Das Psi-feld nach Ervin Laszlo, *Raum und Zeit* 22, 7–8 (1996).

References

Bohm, David (1980). *Wholeness and the implicate order*. London: Routledge & Kegan Paul.

Dossey, Larry (1989). *Recovering the soul: A scientific and spiritual search*. New York: Bantam.

—— (1993). *Healing words: The power of prayer and the practice of medicine*. San Francisco: Harper.

Laszlo, Ervin (1993). *The creative cosmos*. Edinburgh: Floris Books.

—— (1995). *The interconnected universe*. Singapore and London: World Scientific.

—— (1996). *The whispering pond*. Rockport, Shaftesbury, and Brisbane: Element Books.

10
Quantum–Vacuum Interaction and Psychosocial Organization

RAYMOND TREVOR BRADLEY

Abstract
Sociologist Raymond Trevor Bradley outlines a new theory of how we process information to act upon ourselves and our environment. Involved are the psychosocial dynamics of 57 communes, Laszlo's QVI-field theory, Pribram's holographic and holonomic theory, the quantum-holographic theory of communication of physicist Dennis Gabor, and the relatively unknown late work of Jean Piaget.

Key words
Transdisciplinary unified theory (TUT), quantum-vacuum interaction, QVI-field theory, holography, holofield, Bohm, implicate order, Fourier transformation, Poincaré systems, Gabor, logon, holonomy, social collective, human agency, hololeap, flux and control, urban communes, communication, action paths, active human agent, Piaget, cooperation, *groupement.*

1. Introduction

In his recent, highly acclaimed book *The Interconnected Universe*, Ervin Laszlo (1995) sets himself a daunting, awe-inspiring task: to outline the basic conceptual foundation upon which a "fully elaborated" transdisciplinary unified theory (TUT) would rest. A TUT aims to describe the basic processes "whereby the universe evolves in an unbroken (though not necessarily linear) sweep from basic physical entities to the complex open systems that are physicochemical, biophysical, biochemical, biological, ecological, and even psychological in nature." It therefore "encompasses physics and biology, and ultimately the human and the social sciences, as special aspects within a general scheme" (Laszlo, 1995, p. xiv).[1] A successful TUT, in short, would be the "grandmother" of all scientific theories.

The transdisciplinary unified theory that Laszlo develops, his theory of "quantum-vacuum interaction" (QVI), is impressive. Characterizing the work as "a brilliant testimony of how conceptual imagination—deductively related to careful observation—can make us see the cosmos, and our place within the cosmos, in new ways that are of great inspirational value," distinguished philosopher Arne Naess finds that Laszlo's theories "have a remarkable simplicity in relation to their great power of explanation—in regard to the new, formidable range of phenomena covered by their conceptual framework" ("Foreword," p. v). Karl Pribram, the renowned neuropsychologist, describes the work as "a superb example of post-modern deconstruction at its very best. It demonstrates the anomalies and lacunae in the current narrative we call science and develops a new narrative that aims to carry our comprehension beyond these limitations" ("Afterword," p. 144).

The theory of QVI conceptualizes the universe as a holographic order in which information from all physical, biological, and psychosocial interaction is enfolded into the energy wave-forms of the "empty" space of the quantum vacuum. The quantum vacuum, therefore, is the medium for constant universal interconnection—a "holofield" of potential energy interrelating all orders and scales of organization in the universe. Action in the material world is guided by a holographically generated "prompt." The holographic prompt contains information about a system's past states as well as information about its position within a hierarchy of systems. The prompt is the means by which novelty and change are generated so that self-organizing evolution results.

Laszlo demonstrates the theory's utility by showing how it provides a unified description of order at the physical and the biological levels. As a social scientist, though, my main interest is in how QVI accounts for order at the psychosocial level. Although Laszlo shows how he believes QVI explains such extraordinary psychic and socio-cultural interaction at-a-distance phenomena as extra-sensory perception and collective mind, he leaves unanswered the critical question: what is the role of an active (willful) human agent in the generation of psychosocial organization?

In relation to this question, there are some fundamental scientific difficulties with Laszlo's scheme. In addition to the nonmaterialist basis of QVI and the determinism resulting from the use of classical (or *image* processing) holography, there is also the view of the brain as merely a passive processor of information. Given these elements, how can interaction between the quantum vacuum's holofield and the psychosocial order involve an active human agent? And how is purposeful collective organization generated? In short, as the scheme is presently conceived it appears to preclude human agency.

Following a review of the theory of QVI in Section 2, my goal in this chapter is to show how some of these difficulties can be resolved by proposing a "friendly" alternative to Laszlo's scheme. To do this, in Section 3, I draw on the theory of communication developed by Karl Pribram and I to explain the endogenous processes that generate order in collaborative social collectives (Bradley and Pribram, 1996a,b, 1997). Our theory is a "friendly" alternative to Laszlo's because it, too, is a field theory that uses holographic principles and incorporates the action dynamics of chaos theory.[2] However, in departure from Laszlo's approach, we base our theory on a concept of information, the *logon,* defined by quantum (or *information* processing) holography (Gabor, 1946). Virtually unknown in the social and psychological sciences, the logon is an energy-based elementary unit or quantum of information—essentially a space–time constrained hologram. How a quantum holographic approach opens the system to the indeterminacy of new input and, hence, allows the potential for an active agent in communication is discussed in Section 3.1.

In Sections 3.2–3.4, I show how two patterns of social organization can be translated into the terms of quantum holography and understood as a system for endogenous communication. By analyzing how a field of relations of socio-affective energy (flux) interacts with a system of hierarchical constraints (control) to produce holographic-like units of information, we set the stage for examining how this communicative system in-forms the collective's internal function (Section 3.5).

In the final sections (Sections 3.6 and 3.7) we shift our focus to action and intentionality, to the question of how the collective structures action to be effective in its environment. I argue that while the selection of action paths in natural systems can be described by the dynamics of energy conservation and chaos theory, in human collectives, composed of active brains, rational selection of action must be considered. Here I draw on Piaget's recently translated analysis of the genesis of thought and reason in cooperative systems (Piaget, 1965/1995a,b) to show how the logic of collaborative interaction produces a rational actor in social life, and how this logic, therefore, is the basis of purposeful forms of collective organization.

2. The Theory of Quantum–Vacuum Interaction

2.1. *Conceptual Basis*

The basic axiom upon which the theory of QVI rests is the "reasonable assumption" that "*preferential interconnections* must exist in nature":

When a set of parts or elements are constantly and systematically interconnected, the set generates order spontaneously.... Connections must be selective, though not exclusive of other connections; they must be of the kind where each event is preferentially correlated with a specific set of other events. [If] The system's preferential correlations ... are specific yet sufficiently broad-ranging, the order that evolves does not merely repeat the order that has already emerged, but creates possibilities for attaining genuine novelty within the range of possibility. (pp. 4–5)

To elaborate this precept into the "simplest possible scheme of thought capable of uniting the *prima facie* disparate domains of physical and of living nature" (p. 25), Laszlo develops three concepts: constant universal interconnection among all elements, information storage and retrieval according to holographic principles, and action directed by the probabilistic dynamics of chaotic-state large-scale Poincaré systems.

QVI's fundamental concept is the postulate of *constant universal interconnection*: that everything in the universe—every entity and every event—is fundamentally and inseparably interconnected in a constant state of interaction. Like Bohm's concept of the implicate order (Bohm, 1980), the physical basis for universal interconnection resides in the quantum vacuum, a nonmaterial subquantum field filled with zero-point energies that define the ground state of the universe. A basic property of the quantum vacuum is its enormous energy density, which, based on Wheeler's calculations, is equivalent to 10^{94}g/cm^3, and, according to Bohm, exceeds the energy in all known matter by a factor of 10^{40}. Another property is the complex nature of quantum interactions, which Laszlo attributes to the electromagnetic field in which quanta are embedded.[3] The interaction between electrically charged quanta and the zero-point electromagnetic field (ZPF) produces secondary electromagnetic fields within the vacuum that "must be universally extended" (p. 30). The vacuum's enormous energy density and the production of universal secondary electromagnetic fields enable it to be conceptualized as a cosmically extended field, a medium with virtually unlimited information-storage capacity. This field is the "memory" into which and from which information about *all* interactions in the universe is stored and retrieved.

To describe the physical processes by which the vacuum processes information, Laszlo conceptualizes it as a "universal field with holographic properties" (p. 13). Holographic organization is an order in which information about the features of an object is encoded in the interference patterns created by intersecting waveforms of energy bouncing off the object. Since information about the organization of the whole object is distributed and stored (enfolded) throughout the holographic field, an image of the entire object can be reconstructed from any location. Thus as a field "endowed with memory," the "hologram provides the kind of memory that can connect phenomena at a universal scale" (p. 12). Envisaging the structure of the ZPF to be mediated by secondary scalar fields created by the motion of quanta, Laszlo postulates that the scalars approximate Schrödinger waves. Produced throughout an entire medium, Schrödinger-wave holograms store vast amounts of information. They also allow for storage and retrieval of time-varying information.

2.2. QVI and the Organization of Matter

At this point it would be well to acknowledge the technical difficulties this material poses for the reader not acquainted with the physics and mathematics involved. Thus, while this and the next section (2.3) provide vital information for the technically versed, at this point other readers may want to move ahead to Section 2.4, "A Restatement of the Difficulty."

To produce an effect on "observable phenomena" of the material world, the scalar-mediated ZPF of the vacuum must interact with quanta. This interaction between scalars and quanta approximates a two-way Fourier transformation in that "the vacuum encodes the coefficients of the interfering scalarwave fronts produced by the motion of quanta. In doing so the vacuum carries out the equivalent of the forward Fourier transform: it translates a pattern from the spatiotemporal domain to the spectral domain. In the inverse transform—from the spectral to the spatiotemporal domain—the interference patterns encoded in the vacuum 'inform' the motion of quanta in space and in time" (p. 33).

For the vacuum to effect the action pathways of matter beyond the quantum level, Laszlo employs the macrostatistical dynamics of large-scale Poincaré systems.[4] Because large-scale Poincaré systems are in constant interaction with their environments, the selection of the action path is influenced by a "subtle but statistically significant [contextual] constraint" (p. 9; my addition). At the level of microscale systems—of ensembles of quanta—the constraints on action paths appear in the form of probabilistic irreversabilities, as minute but significant biases in direction generated, thus, by the statistical dynamics of populations of systems. At the level of macroscale systems, the interaction effects from fluctuations in the vacuum, when amplified by chaos dynamics, appear as Poincaré resonances in ensembles of quanta. Because "these interactions involve . . . the $3n$-dimensional configuration-space of the whole multiquantal system . . . in dynamically indeterminate ('chaotic') states macroscale systems can be 'in-formed' with the ZPF-conveyed Fourier-transform of their $3n$-dimensional configuration-space" (p. 36).

It is through the wave-generating properties of large-scale Poincaré systems (viz., continuous spectra and resonance) that the evolutionary direction of action in the material world is selected. Because holographic information can be stored as superposed wave-patterns in multiple dimensions, a holographically generated "prompt" can therefore connect each system to its own evolutionary history and also connect entire hierarchies of multilevel systems to one another. This constant holographic exchange of information between parts and levels within a given system, and between individual systems and the complex multilevel structure in which they are embedded, results in self-generated evolution of increasingly more complex yet coherent forms of order (pp. 13–15).

2.3. QVI and Biological and Psychosocial Organization

In applying the scheme to living systems, Laszlo draws on his concept of the quantum vacuum as an information-rich holofield and on his concept of chaotic-state large-scale Poincaré systems. Living organisms are viewed as far-from-thermodynamic equilibrium systems whose form is holographically encoded into the ZPF of the subquantum domain so that the vacuum's holofield operates as a multidimensional morphogenetic field. The morphogenetic field not only connects the individual organism (via a species-specific frequency resonance) to the evolutionary morphology of its own species, but connects it, as well, to the space–time structure and dynamics of its environment. As a complex multilevel ensemble of populations of macroscale systems, the organism is inherently unstable and ultrasensitive; it is affected by "unmeasurably fine fluctuations" in the form of minute internal and external variations that, when amplified by chaos dynamics, produce "measurable—in fact, decisive—effects" on the organism's evolution (pp. 81–82):

The scalar-mediated vacuum holofield encodes the species-specific imprints of all organisms, and those that 'match' these imprints are constantly affected by them. . . . Whenever the ultrasensitive dynamics of chaos come into play, the interaction-effect guides not only processes of [organic] generation, but also processes of regeneration.

. . . the orienting biofield [is] the scalar-mediated ZPF. The Fourier transforms of the state-space of particles and the configuration-space of living systems are encoded and conveyed to systems in isomorphic spaces, in-forming them both with their own prior states, and with that of the larger systems in which they are integrated. (pp. 83 and 84)

At the psychological and sociological levels, QVI plays a "functionally ana-logous" role. First, the quantum vacuum is the medium of transmission for a wide variety of "space-leaping" spontaneous communications among human "brain/ minds": extrasensory perception, anomalous recall of near-death and past-life experiences, altered states of consciousness (ch. 5), creativity, the sharing of sociocultural 'archetypes', and the 'collective unconscious' (pp. 129–136). Second, the vacuum's holofield functions as an extrasomata memory for storing patterns of psychic and also of socio-cultural "transpersonal experience."

Contrary to present understanding of the brain (e.g., Freeman, 1995; Gazzaniga, 1995; Pribram, 1991), these patterns and the other data that make up long-term memory are *not*, according to Laszlo, physically located and stored in the neural structures of the brain. Instead, QVI suggests that the contents of long-term memory are stored *outside* the brain; they are encoded as interference patterns *in* the vacuum's holofield. Thus the brain acts like a radio or a TV receiver in that it operates "*only as the transducer of signals* received from the vacuum holofield" (p. 100; my italics and emphasis). The pattern encoded in the signals is multidimen-sional and includes information on the individual's position in the multilevel ensemble of systems in which s/he is embedded: "in one direction the pattern would include the Fourier transform of the configuration of cells and molecules that constitute the human body; while in the other it would include the dynamic $3n$-dimensional configuration-space of the social and ecological milieu of the individual" (p. 134).

Retrieval from the vacuum's holofield follows holographic principles: the brain accesses the holofield and, by performing a reverse Fourier transformation, it converts the interference pattern into an image of the original object or event that recorded the pattern. Thus recall of the contents of psychic experience, or of the interactional schemas that in-form socio-cultural life, is a "holographic process occurring in an interaction between the brain of the subject and an ambient holographic field" (p.101).

2.4. A Restatement of the Difficulty

Laszlo's insistence that the brain is merely a *passive* processor of information seems opposed to any concept of a willful human agent and creates a basic difficulty for two aspects of his account of psychosocial organization. It creates a problem for his hypothesis of "interactive creativity" (pp. 129–132). This he defines as "the *elabora-tion* of an idea or a pattern in two or more minds in interaction" by way of interconnection through the vacuum's holofield (p. 130; my emphasis). By its very definition, 'elaboration' connotes an active, purposeful brain—a brain able 'to produce by labor' or 'work out in detail' (Fowler and Fowler, 1964, p. 391). Such a brain is at odds with Laszlo's passive processor of throughput.

The same difficulty arises in Laszlo's account of the collective level. Focusing on the sharing of collective experiences (e.g., "feelings of oneness," "the collective unconscious," or *communion*), Laszlo views QVI-brain/mind interaction as the means by which individuals are integrated into the sociocultural order. But this focus on communion leaves aside the most important aspect of human social experience—the phenomenon of purposeful organization. Purposeful organization is an order of social *communication* that requires an *active*—thinking, reasoning, willful—brain.

As noted at the outset, these difficulties have their roots in the kind of holographic organization that Laszlo uses in his theory, namely the holographic principles of image processing (classical holography). And it is clear from his reference to Gabor's paper in *Nature*, "A New Microscopic Principle" (Gabor, 1948), that this is the kind of holographic organization Laszlo has in mind for the theory of QVI.

3. A Quantum-Holographic Approach

In what follows, I want to show that there may be a way around some of these difficulties by using Gabor's (1946) energy-based concept of *information*, the *logon*, to describe information processing in biological and psychosocial systems. Gabor's concept of information is the basis of a second kind of holographic organization known as *holonomy* or a *quantum-holographic* process, in that logons are quantized (space–time constrained) holographic units (see Pribram, 1991, ch. 2). To illustrate how this concept may be applied to psychosocial interaction, I draw on the theory of communication that Karl Pribram and I have developed to describe the endogenous processes by which order is generated in social collectives (Bradley and Pribram, 1996, 1997; Bradley, 1996). A *social collective* is defined as a durable arrangement of individuals that is distinguished by shared membership (a boundary) and collaborative interaction relative to a common purpose or goal.

Very briefly, this theory shows how two orders of social interconnection, *flux* and *control* (defined below), activate the potential energy of the collective's members—that is, their biological capacity for physical work and social behavior—and direct the expenditure of this energy toward collective ends. The interaction between flux and control operates as a communication system. It generates logon-like units of information and transmits them throughout the collective. Because each unit contains an image of the collective's internal organization, the communicative system *in-forms* (gives shape to) the *inter*-action among members and produces a stable organization.

I begin by distinguishing between classical and quantum holography.

3.1. *Conceptual Foundations*

3.1.1. *Classical holography: image processing and predetermined order.* Classical holography was developed to understand the physics of *image processing* (Gabor, 1948). It is based on a field concept of order in which information about the organization of an object as a whole is encoded as an interference pattern in energy waveforms distributed throughout the field. This makes it possible to retrieve an image of the whole object from any location within the field.

To construct a hologram, two or more Fourier transformed records must be linearly superposed. Mathematically, encoding the features of an object onto a holographic record and retrieving an image is achieved by an invertible linear process involving a Fourier transformation (FT). A forward FT enfolds an image of the object from the spatiotemporal domain into the spectral domain. It does this by decomposing the image into a set of waveform components, the elements of which are completely regular sine and cosine waves. The waveform components are thus the interference pattern of these waveforms, and it is these that are stored in the medium of the holographic field. By representing the entire interference pattern, each location in the field contains information about the whole image.

An inverse FT unfolds the encoded image from the spectral domain back into its form as a three-dimensional image of the object in the spatiotemporal domain. It is important to note that there are *no* degrees of freedom in the transformation relations here; chance and probability are not involved. Both in terms of object identity and structural integrity, the image that is retrieved from the spectral domain is the same as the object's form in space–time.

Classical holography, thus, is a principle of system organization in which constituent parts are enfolded into, and whose behavior is in-formed and, therefore, *determined* by the global organization of the system as a whole. According to this principle, then, the generation of all order would be, as Leibnitz suggested in his *Monadology*, the product of the predetermined harmony of the universe. If one substitutes lens-less for Leibnitz's windowless structures, his monads become holograms. Spontaneous or purposeful behavior (novelty or intentionality) is *not* possible in classical holography because everything is "encased" in a predetermined order. We all would be communing (both spatially and temporally) in infinity, as Loye eloquently puts it, in "one giant hologram," predestined to behave "like so many witless toys in motion" (Loye, 1983, p. 205). Therefore, in the absence of an exogenous means for breaking the endogenous determinism of this form of holography, *human agency*—be it planned or spontaneous—*within a holographic [imaging] system* simply *cannot occur.* This is true whether we are talking about a hologram or a metaphorical social group.[5]

3.1.2. *Quantum holography: information processing and uncertainty.* To appropriately apply a holographic concept to psychosocial organization, we need a model of *communication*, not communion; we need a model of *information processing* to describe the mechanisms for gathering and transmitting information.

Gabor (1946) provides such a model in his classic "Theory of Communication," where he defines a unit of information as the *minimum uncertainty with which a signal can be encoded as a pattern of energy oscillations across a waveband of frequencies,* as in the encoding and transmission of vocal utterances for telephonic communication. Gabor's concept is radically different from, though related to, the more commonly used measure of information developed by Claude Shannon (1949). Shannon's measure is that of information as a reduction of uncertainty through choice among alternatives. His smallest unit of information is the BIT, the BInary digiT—nowadays corresponding to the smallest standard unit of information in computational information systems. In such systems each unit of information in a sequence contributes to resolution of the signal's message by reducing the probability of alternative meanings. So that while Shannon deals with a *reduction in uncertainty,* Gabor designates the *minimum uncertainty* beyond which a message cannot be compressed.

Gabor determined that there exists a restriction to the efficient processing and communication of a set of telephone signals. The restriction is due to the limit of precision that can be achieved in concurrent measurements of the signal's spectral components (frequency, amplitude, and phase) and its (space)time epoch. This restriction is illustrated in Figure 1a in which time and frequency are treated as orthogonal coordinates. Although the energy frequency of a signal, represented by a dashed vertical line, is exactly defined, its duration in time is totally undefined. Conversely, a sudden surge (a "unit impulse function") or change in the signal, the horizontal line, is sharply defined in time, but its energy is distributed evenly throughout the whole frequency spectrum. Since, at the limit, accurate measurement of the signal can be made only in time or in frequency, *it cannot be simultaneously made in both beyond this point* (Gabor, 1946, pp. 431–432).

Gabor was able to show, mathematically, that this limit could be given formal expression by Heisenberg's uncertainty principle.[6] In its rigorous form the uncertainty relation is given as $\Delta t \Delta f > 0.5$, which states that time (t) and frequency (f) cannot be simultaneously defined in exact terms, but only with a latitude of greater than or equal to one-half in the product of the uncertainties. Since certainty can be obtained only by minimizing uncertainty on both ordinates, the *minimum measurement* of the signal in time **and** frequency is $\Delta t \Delta f = 0.5$, which defines an ***elementary unit of information*** (Gabor, 1946, pp. 431–437). This unit of information both minimizes uncertainty and provides the maximally efficient compression of communication; that is, it provides the minimum space or time of transmission for a signal to maintain fidelity in telecommunication.

Gabor called his unit of information a *logon,* or a *quantum of information,* and showed that the signal that occupies this minimum area "is the modulation product of a harmonic oscillation [of energy] of any frequency with a pulse in the form of a probability function" (Gabor, 1946, p. 435; my addition). Mathematically, the

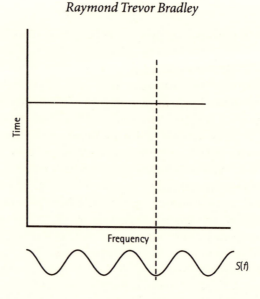

Figure 1a. Limits of concurrent measurement of time and frequency of a signal

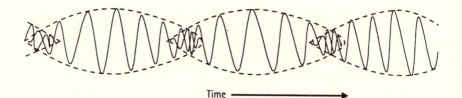

Time ⟶

Figure 1b. Representation of the overlap of logons

logon is a sinusoid variably constrained by space–time coordinates—essentially a *space–time constrained hologram.* This unit differs from Shannon's unit of information, the binary digit, which is the Boolean choice between alternatives.

An important point, which bears directly on the question of determinism, is that logons are *not* discrete units but occur as space–time constrained sinusoids each wrapped in a Gaussian probability envelope; in nontechnical terms, they can be described as a series of overlapping units in which the "heads" and "tails" of adjacent units interpenetrate one another (this is illustrated in Figure 1b). This "overlap" among logons introduces indeterminacy in that the data in each unit are enfolded, to some degree, into the data of adjoining logons. This means, as Gabor puts it, that each logon contains an "*overlap (with) the future*" (Gabor, 1946, p. 437;

emphasis added); in other words, that each unit of information, by virtue of its spectral nature, anticipates the information of the unit that succeeds it.[7]

However, the overlap among logons is not the only feature of this kind of holography that enhances indeterminacy. The degree of overlap itself has been shown to be a function of the contextual properties of the signal-generating apparatus, which affect the energy frequency and the time(space) components of the signal (Xie, 1995). The maintenance of an optimal overlap among logons for efficient information processing requires adjusting the communicative apparatus to set and maintain an optimal relationship between the signal's two components.

In sum, quantum holography is the second kind of holography and it provides a nondeterminist energy-based model of information processing. Quantum holography thus defines two distinct dimensions: an energy dimension (measured in terms of frequency times Planck's constant), and a space–time constraint (either Gaussian or rectangular).

Gabor's concept of information has been found to characterize perceptual processing in the cerebral cortex (see Pribram, 1991, Lectures 1–5, for a review of the evidence). It is, therefore, the unit for biological information processing that allows for indeterminacy.

3.2. Dimensionality of Social Organization

To appropriately apply the principles of quantum holography to the operation of the communicative structure in social collectives, we must first establish that social interaction has a dimensionality that is equivalent to Gabor's energy and space–time ordinates.

Social science has long recognized the importance of two basic patterns of social organization. They were conceptualized by classical social theorists as a distinction between *gemeinschaft* and *gesellschaft* social organization (Toennies, 1957), or between organic and mechanical social solidarity (Durkheim, 1949). Modern observers, however, have found the two patterns in a wide variety of social contexts and have used a number of different terms to describe them, for example, informal versus formal organization (Roethlisberger and Dickson, 1939); socioemotional versus sociotechnical systems (Trist and Bamforth, 1951); communitas versus structure, (Turner, 1969); nominal versus graduated parameters of social structure (Blau, 1977); markets versus hierarchies (Williamson, 1975); and most recently flat structure (networks) versus hierarchical networks (Burt, 1992).

Underlying these conceptualizations is a deeper (often implicit) dimensionality: a distinction between *field-like* and *hierarchical* forms of organization. In field-like organization, the pattern of social relations is fluid and transitory, based on an equivalence among individuals. In hierarchical organization, the pattern is ordered and stratified by relations of authority and social control.

By "field-like" we mean an order of social connection that, like the structure of a market economy, is distributed over the whole region of a social space. Because it is the intermediary for the continuous flow of all interactions and transactions among individuals, it is an order that is in a constant state of fluctuation. Such an order is essentially holographic-like in organization in that each interaction enfolds the operations of the collective as a whole in much the same way that each transaction in a market economy enfolds the activity of the entire marketplace (Pribram, 1982). As we shall see, this type of holistic field-like order is one of the central concepts in this account, the concept we refer to as *flux*. Interestingly enough, flux is defined in *The Concise Oxford Dictionary* as the "flood of talk" and denotes a "continuous succession of changes" (Fowler and Fowler, 1964, p. 469).

My own previous studies of a variety of types of urban communes, community organizations, and small groups have shown that these two patterns of interconnection form the communicative structure in stable collectives.[8] As revealed in my study of 57 communes for stable groups (communes surviving at least 24 months beyond measurement of their social structure), one pattern is a dense web of relations of positive affect (mutual "loving" ties) interconnecting virtually all members (see Figure 2). The web can be interpreted as a social field—that is, a distributed, massively parallel network of reciprocated relations in which individuals are essentially interchangeable. There is an absence of social differentiation so that all individuals are interconnected by an equivalent (*equi-valent*, of equal value) relation. This provides an unrestricted flow of information about virtually all interactions throughout the web.

The second pattern shown in Figure 2 is a densely interlocking order of "power" relations that also extends to interconnect virtually all individuals. This, however, is a hierarchical order—that is, a highly stratified structure of asymmetrical relations. As a system of social constraints, the hierarchy locates each individual in a position that is spatially and temporally localized. In my study of communes, I found that the nature of the relationship between the two patterns was strongly associated with commune survival (see Bradley, 1987, ch. 7).

Following up on these earlier findings that describe *what* the communicative structure was composed of, Pribram and I sought to understand *how* the interaction between field and hierarchy operates as an information-processing system to in-form collective organization. I present a summary of our account in the next two sections, Sections 3.3 and 3.4.

3.3. *Flux and Control*

To develop our understanding, we begin with the premise that collective organization is, first and foremost, a relationship of *collaboration*—of individuals *working together* to achieve a shared end (Roberts and Bradley, 1991). To collaborate entails work, and work requires a supply of energy. It is assumed that, as biological organisms, the members of a social collective are the source of this energy, and that they expend this energy as they work and interact in relation to realizing a shared goal. In addition to the availability of a pool of potential energy, collaboration also

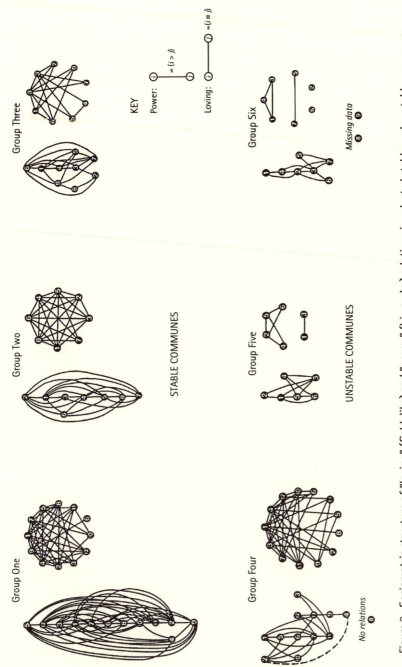

Figure 2. Sociometric structure of "loving" (field-like) and "power" (hierarchy) relations in selected stable and unstable communes

requires that each individual's expenditure of this energy be coordinated and directed toward the collective's objective.

Collaboration, therefore, involves two complementary processes. The first is *flux,* the constant movement of energy throughout the collective as it is activated and expended by the members in physical behavior and social interaction. The second is *control,* the construction of a system of social constraints that directs the expenditure of energy (at specific locations in space and particular moments in time) into collective action. As described below, the interpenetration between flux and control operates as a communication-processing network that *in*-forms the transformation of potential energy into collective work.

Flux, the movement of energy, occurs as a distributed, massively parallel process of *equi*-valent (of equal value) relations interconnecting all members. This field is established by membership in the collective, which creates a sociocultural boundary separating members from nonmembers. Membership thus effects a nominal bond of connection by which members are attuned to one another. As an undifferentiated web of psychic connection extending throughout the collective, this field is the intermediary for *all* interactions among individuals; this includes verbal communication and also nonverbal communication as signaled by bodily position and movement and by the symbolic use of signs, artifacts, and objects. Thus the field is the order through which all movement of the collective's energy is processed.

The collective operates on this field of relations to *activate* individuals to action by *arousing* affective attachments among members. Arousal of affective bonds *excites* emotions, which in turn mobilizes the individual's propensity for action (Pribram and McGuinness, 1975; 1992; Schore, 1994), and thus the potential for expending energy (Pribram and Bradley, 1996). Thus, the *level of aroused affect* reflects the degree to which members are activated to action. It is a *measure of the amount of potential biological energy that has been mobilized and is available for collective or individual use.*

Also at work here, as just noted, is control—the system of social constraints that operates to channel the members' energy toward collective ends and prevents the energy's dissipation in other social activity and physical behavior. The controls influence the movement of energy by constraining the spatial and temporal direction of the paths of flux, thereby in-forming the collaborations among individuals. By differentially constraining the paths by which individuals expend their energy, both with respect to specific locations in space and with respect to particular moments in time, the controls *in-form* (give shape to) the patterning of collective organization.

An example is the interconnected activity of the crew of a river raft. To maintain social and, hence, physical stability while running white water rapids, the crew must know, at each moment, the pattern of their actions and how these are co-ordinated as *co(l)-laborations* in relation to the raft's location in the river. In addition, the crew must also determine which of several alternative paths of action affords them the greatest likelihood of a safe path downriver. Thus, as described below, the coupling of the movement of energy mediating members' interactions (flux) with a system of spatiotemporal constraints (control) creates a communicative structure that *in*-forms collaboration and results in a stable, effective collective.

3.4. *Communication*

We should now be in position to apply Gabor's concept of information and show how the interaction between flux and control operates as a communication system to in-form the collective's expenditure of energy.

The symmetric bonds of the distribution of flux indicate that members are essentially interchangeable and that, among members, the patterning of flux throughout this field is more or less equivalent. As this field is an energy field, it lies within the spectral domain and is related to space and time by way of a transformation (the Fourier transform function). By contrast, because individuals are asymmetrically connected in the hierarchical order, the system of controls operates differentially on the collective's members, both with respect to their energy expenditure in a particular location in space as well as with respect to the their energy expenditure at particular moments in time.

Drawing on Gabor, it is expected, therefore, that the operation of hierarchical controls on the distribution of flux (Figure 3) generates information as a moment-by-moment—*quantized*—description of the collective's internal organization, encoded in terms of both structure (spatial–temporal position) and flux (distribution of energy). The succession of descriptions within space–time and spectral coordinates are logon-like units of information that are constructed and communicated, via a holographic-like process, throughout the collective. Thus the information exchange that characterizes organization, as the collective continuously evolves in an on-going series of interactions, can be described as quantized.

However, whenever there is an imbalance between the amount of distribution of flux and the amount of control, quantization breaks down, resulting in a lowering of information transmission. The reduction in information transmission impairs the efficient operation of the collective, which, in turn, increases the likelihood of instability. This impairment is due to what Ashby (1956) has characterized as the need for "requisite variety" in cybernetic (information and control) systems.

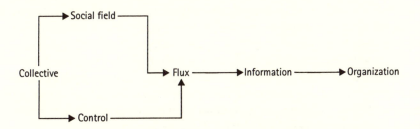

Figure 3. **Logic of the theoretical model**

A point of particular relevance is an important implication of Gabor's concept of information for the role of causality in communication. As described above, logons are not discrete units but, as a result of their spectral nature, occur as overlapping units in which the data in each logon are enfolded into the data of adjoining logons. In addition to the indeterminant order that results, what is of special interest here is that this spectral enfoldment among logons yields an information-processing system in which data about the "future" (potential) order are enfolded into the units that are processed in the "present." In this way, the communicative structure *anticipates*, to some extent, the next moment of collective organization (Bradley, 1996).

However, this anticipation of order requires optimizing the degree of overlap among logons. This entails adjusting the contextual properties of the communicative apparatus that regulate the frequency and time(space) components of the signal. In complex systems, like biological and social collectives, the maintenance of an optimal overlap among logons for efficient information processing requires constant exogenous adjustments to the communicative structure to regulate communication. It is suggested that such constant regulation is a primary function of the cultural order in human social systems. In addition to defining social objectives and prescribing the means for achieving them, the normative order sets and regulates the social parameters that affect the energetic and space–time aspects of communication. This is illustrated in the example that follows.

3.4.1. *An example.* Musical notation is an example of a Gabor-like energic communication system that operates to *in*-form the collaborative interactions of a musical collective such as an orchestra, a band, or a choir. An individual "note" can be viewed as a direct analogue of a logon. It is composed of data "plotted" in a written musical score on the same two orthogonally-related dimensions as a logon: one dimension is *frequency*—the major determinant of pitch—varying oscillations of sound waves (energy vibrations) produced by the operation of a musical instrument; the second dimension is *time*, how long the note is to be played. The second dimension is signified, in part, by the tempo (e.g., *allegro* or *largo*) at which the piece is to be played, and in part by the *not(e)*-tation of the duration of each note (an eighth or a sixteenth, etc.).

The pattern of energy expenditure by which the music is actualized is prescribed on a musical score as a moment-by-moment sequence of operations on the musical instrument, for each musician, specified *both* in frequency and in time. Moreover, the score for all musicians contains a *spatial* component as well: it also specifies which subset of musicians, in relation to the whole orchestra, is to play at each moment. Thus a composer's written musical score represents a description of how the potential energy of a collective of musicians is translated into expenditures of energy, differentiated for each individual on the dimensions of frequency and time–space, to actualize a given composition as "music."[9]

However, our example of musical collectives suggests that there are limits to normative regulation of this kind of information processing. At one extreme is the written musical score—the composer's moment-by-moment prescription for each action by every musician on the two dimensions of frequency and time–space—a formalized embodiment of the ultimate level of normative regulation. Sociologically, this is equivalent to *formal* social organization, like a bureaucracy. At the other extreme, it is clear that certain minimum normative specifications on the two dimensions are also necessary for communication within more *informal* social collectives, such as jazz bands. At minimum, the jazz band must specify—normatively define—the "key" (the progression of harmonic frequencies to be used) and the "time signature" (the number of beats per measure of time) in order to improvise effectively in their construction of "music." As Barrett (1997, p. 20) notes, such "minimal constraints," or what jazz artist Herbie Hancock calls *"controlled freedom"* (Berliner, 1994, p. 341; my emphasis), create a stable collaborative order of constantly evolving *inter*-action.

The example indicates, as noted, that the way that this kind of information processing allows individuals to "anticipate" future collective organization is derived from the harmonic order implied in the oscillation of energy at different frequencies. By defining the progression of musical frequencies that can be played by any member at any given moment, the key defines the set of optional structures within which our jazz band's behavior must be organized to produce coherent order, or "music."

When [jazz] musicians abandon the melody as a model for invention ... they depend on the progression's salient features as signposts for the improvisation's "progress." Moreover, the syntactic implications of harmonic structures assist artists in their endeavor. Once they cultivate a "feeling for form, the form will guide you; it will almost play itself." (Berliner, 1994, p. 173; my addition.)

Thus future action for the individual musician is in-formed by the implicit subset of combinations of musical frequencies that are harmonious when combined with those produced by the other musicians, and that will, when actualized, create coherent sequences of musical *inter*-action.

3.5. *In-formation of Organization*

We have just shown how the interaction between flux and control can be described as a communication system that produces quantized units of information, and have also illustrated this application with an example. To now understand how this kind of communication system in-forms collective organization, it is necessary to show how different states of collective function arise from varying configurations of flux and control. This entails linking levels of the communicative structure's operation to a phase space of potentials for alternative states of collective function (see Figure 4).

The two dimensions shown in Figure 4 represent the communicative structure that is formed by the interpenetration of two networks of internal relations. The values ascribed to the horizontal dimension represent flux, the amount of

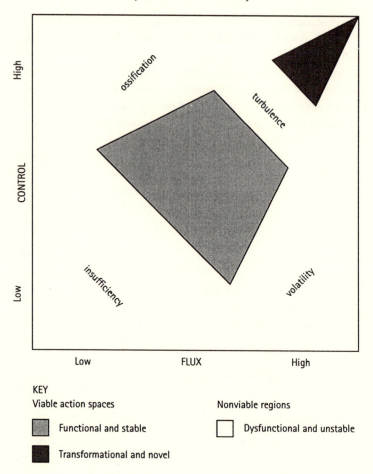

Figure 4. Model of communicative structure and action states of collective organization

potential energy activated in a social collective. The values ascribed to the vertical dimension represent control, the degree to which members are interconnected in a hierarchy. Thus the pair of values allocated in each dimension represents co-ordinates (e.g., high flux and low control) that define points within a social field (Bradley and Roberts, 1989).

Each pair of coordinates represents an amount of information, that is, a quantum of information in Gabor's terms. Each quantum of information characterizes the communicative structure and in-forms the collective's energy expenditure. Therefore, each different configuration of flux and control is associated with a corresponding potential for collaboration among members, and hence with the stability of organization. The varying potentials for collaboration defined by the possible values of flux and control can be termed a "phase space."

Two regions can be distinguished within the phase space. One of these is a *stable region* of organization associated with efficient patterns of communication; it is comprised of two subregions separated by an area of turbulence and instability. The second is an *unstable region* in which the minimum values for efficient communication are not met so that various forms of collective dysfunction result. The regions are separated from each other, marked, in the terms of nonlinear dynamics, by a phase transition from psychosocial instabilities to [far-from-thermodynamic-equilibrium] psychosocial stabilities in collective organization (Jantsch, 1980; Prigogine and Stengers, 1984). The region of stable collective order represents, therefore, a qualitative change in psychosocial organization.

3.5.1. *Unstable organization.* In the unstable region the patterns of potential energy and control are either unable to establish or unable to sustain viable forms of collective organization. Values of low flux and low control (the area labeled as *insufficiency* in Figure 4) fail because, in addition to a certain minimum of energy, stability also requires at least a minimum of direction given to that energy. This direction comes from the interpenetration of flux and control, which *in*-forms the paths by which kinetic energy is expended in social organization. Viable organization—patterns of effective collaboration—thus requires, at minimum, a linkage to each individual on these two relations. Without this a new collective could not be created or founded, and an existing collective would devolve into a loose aggregation of disjointed cliques and isolated individuals unable to communicate and, consequently, also unable to work together as a functional, socially autonomous entity.

Two other combinations are also expected to produce instability. Coordinate values representing high control and low flux (labeled *ossification* in Figure 4) delineate a rigid organization in which insufficient energy is available for social communication. The lack of communication means that the paths to organization are fixed, not adequately informed by the ontological reality of current circumstances, and are therefore unable to adapt as the situation changes.

At the other extreme, combinations of high flux and low control (labeled *volatility* in Figure 4) delineate a turbulent situation in which little of the enormous potential energy is guided by hierarchic controls. Communication is inadequate as insufficient information about the ever-changing situation is distributed.

3.5.2. *Stable organization.* As shown in Figure 4, the region of dysfunction surrounds the region of stable organization which is centered along a main diagonal of the phase space, and which, as noted, embodies a qualitative change in psychosocial organization. The phase transition from dysfunctional to viable collective forms (which includes the area between the two stable subregions labeled turbulence) is described by fluctuations in flux and control that end in a point (the bifurcation point) where the patterns of energy activation and expenditure no longer dissipate or coalesce as merely transitory forms. Instead, the fluctuations in flux and control crystallize into an emergent order of social interdependence signified, normatively, by the creation of a membership boundary.

The lower and upper boundaries of this stable region define the values representing efficient information processing. This region is consistent with the evidence from studies of the interactional dynamics of infant and child development (Schore, 1994, and Hinde, 1992, respectively), and it also is consistent with the thermodynamically inspired connectionist models of neural networks (e.g., Hinton and Sejnowski, 1986; Hopfield, 1982). In such models *efficient pattern matching is found to occur in a region between total randomness and total organization*: in our terms, between rapid flux and rigid control. The relation of flux to control narrows from many degrees of freedom at the low end of the space, to an almost one-to-one correspondence at the high end. There is a progressive narrowing of optional structures for stable collective organization based on the increasingly close articulation between flux and control. Thus the shape of the space of stable collective function is triangular.

To defy the tendency toward entropy (disorder) and sustain a viable, stable order requires minimizing the fluctuations by linking the activation of potential energy to the control operations so that the energy expenditure of *all* members is *in*-formed in relation to the collective's action. Thus, in terms of the data presented in Figure 2, viable organization requires a certain minimum of flux *and* a certain minimum of control. It requires a network of socio-affective relations by which the potential energy of every individual is linked to at least one other member. And it requires the coupling of these relations to a hierarchy of control so that the energy expenditure of each person is linked to that of at least one other member.

Separated by a turbulent gap, at the apex of the optimal region, is a small subregion (shaded as *transformational* in Figure 4) defined by an almost one-to-one relationship between flux and control. To assure stability a tight coupling between the two dimensions must be maintained, taking much effort. Often when such an effortful course is in operation, a sudden organizational spasm occurs. The spasm has two possible outcomes: one is structural transformation in the pattern of information processing, resulting in a totally reorganized, qualitatively different collective; the other is structural devolution, the complete breakdown and collapse of the collective as a viable organization.

In a further investigation of my communes study data, Pribram and I found strong correspondences between these theoretical expectations and the patterns of communication and stability observed in the 46 communes (see Figure 5).[10] Sociometric data mapping all possible dyadic ties among adult members within each commune were used to construct structural measures of flux (triads of mutual ties of positive affect: "loving," or "exciting," or "improving" relations) and control (transitively ordered triads of "power" relations); group stability was measured by survival status 24 months beyond the measurement of sociometric structure (see Bradley and Pribram, 1996, for the details).

Comparing the scatterplot of the observed patterns for the 46 communes in Figure 5 (the measure of control is plotted on the vertical ordinate and flux is plotted on the horizontal ordinate; unstable, nonsurviving, groups are shown as

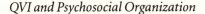

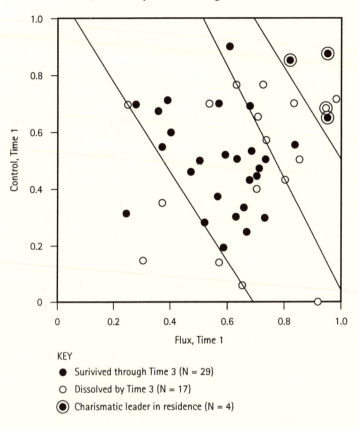

KEY

● Surivived through Time 3 (N = 29)
○ Dissolved by Time 3 (N = 17)
◉ Charismatic leader in residence (N = 4)

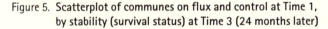

Figure 5. Scatterplot of communes on flux and control at Time 1,
by stability (survival status) at Time 3 (24 months later)

hollow dots) with the model in Figure 4, shows that the communes form a tri-angular pattern, and that those located in the peripheral areas are more likely to be unstable. This triangular region appears to be divided into two stable subregions, separated by a zone of high instability. Beyond the zone of instability, in the apex of the triangle, are five communes of which four had a charismatic leader in residence (shown with a circle in Figure 5) and were intent on achieving a radical restructur-ing of social order.[11] The differences between these four groupings of communes in Figure 5, in terms of their patterns of flux, control, and stability, were found to be statistically significant (Bradley and Pribram, 1996).[12]

3.6. *Selection of Action Paths*

To this point we have focused on developing an understanding of the operation of flux and control as a communicative structure which, by processing data on the collaborative interactions among members, in-forms the collective's internal organization. Now in this and the following section, we shift our focus to the issues of action and intentionality, to the key question of how the collective structures the action of its members to be effective in its environment.

In most physical and biological systems, there is a tendency to minimize work in order to conserve energy. This is known as the *least action principle,* or the system's *Hamiltonian function.* In its general formulation, the principle holds that a system is at equilibrium under conditions that maintain potential energy at a minimum (Considine, 1976, p. 1,454). This means that any departure from equilibrium— any disequiliberating change in the system's structure—creates potential energy. In order to return to equilibrium, the system must expend the potential energy by performing work to use it up. A *least action path* (one that is *optimal* for the system) is determined by piece-wise subtraction of potential by kinetic energy. Thus potential energy is reduced—through a series of successive fluctuations between potential and kinesis—until its minimum level is reached.

Such changes in levels of potential energy have been studied in the natural sciences and have resulted in dynamic systems models—so-called chaos theory (Morrison, 1991; Nicolis and Prigogine, 1977; Strogatz, 1994). These models have enjoyed wide success in accounting for the behavior of far-from-thermodynamic-equilibrium systems in the natural sciences (Kauffman, 1993; Prigogine and Stengers, 1984) and have sparked a growing interest in the social sciences (e.g., Abraham and Gilgen, 1995; Arthur, 1989; Barton, 1994; Dendrinos and Sonis, 1990; Loye, 1995).

In applying these concepts, we assume that the members of the social collective are biologically capable of work, and that this capability is measurable as potential energy. When activated by the collective, the members' potential energy becomes engaged in social interaction. To realize collective action entails work; work is measured as kinetic energy. The tendency to energy conservation leads the collective to strive toward an efficient use of energy. This requires effort to explore alternative paths toward order, patterns of actualization that allow collective work to proceed efficiently—that is, with the least amount of dissipation (Pribram and McGuinness, 1975).

In social collectives, in the absence of other factors, initial conditions such as negative feelings like fear, hatred, or jealousy, will block the efficient conversion of potential energy to kinetic energy; in nonlinear dynamics such systems are characterized by negative Liapunov exponents leading to stasis, to ossification (complete equilibrium), or to regular fluctuations described by relaxation oscillators (Abraham, 1991). On the other hand, initial conditions such as admiration, awe, or love create a kind of harmonic resonance (due to a positive Liapunov exponent) in the relations among members. This will enhance the conversion of potential to kinetic energy—a phenomenon Zablocki (1971, 1980) observed in his studies of communes and called the "cathexis effect." The danger here, if this enhanced kinetic energy is unconstrained, is that undue dissipation of energy will ensue: in the language of nonlinear dynamics, chaos will result (for examples, see Bradley, 1987, ch. 7; Zablocki, 1980, figure 4–5, p. 165).

3.7. *Purpose in Action*

In natural systems, optimal action—that is, action that is both internally efficient and externally effective—results when the principles of least action and self-organization combine to hold the system in an adaptive relationship of coevolution with its environment. In human collectives, however, with the brain as an *active* processor of information, a new alternative is presented: namely, rational choice of action in relation to a purpose or a goal (Miller *et al.*, 1960). This is the issue of intentionality, the question of an *active human agent.*

According to Freud (1895/1966), Piaget (1965/1995a), and Pribram (1991), among others, *thoughts are implicit acts*: they are images of planned or possible sequences of actions—*virtual actions*—that an individual visualizes mentally as objects. As such, the generation of thought is a prerequisite to rational or purposeful action.

In this final section, I want to show how the interactional logic of a collaborative system produces a *purposeful*—thinking, reasoning—social actor in social life. To do this I draw on Piaget's analysis of the genesis of thought and reason in cooperative systems (Piaget, 1965/1995a,b). Piaget's concept of cooperation, a "system of operations carried out in common" (p. 153),[13] is based on reciprocal interactions within the context of a common system of language, values, and social norms, and is analogous to our concept of collaboration as described above and Searle's concept of "collective intentionality" (Searle, 1995, pp. 24–25).

Piaget uses group theory from mathematics to show that the requirements for the development of logic in individual actions are essentially the same as the conditions that characterize cooperation as a system of social exchanges. Piaget demonstrates that stability in both systems (*psychol*ogical action and social cooperation) presupposes certain basic conditions which hold for formal systems composed of logical or qualitative operations.

Mathematically, a stable system of logical operations is a *group* comprised of elements (or classes of elements), operations acting on the elements, and outputs resulting from application of the operations. Four requirements must be met for a system of logical operations to be considered a "group": the system of operations must be composable, invertible, possess substitutional equivalence, and preserve identity. Table 1 defines these requirements and the mathematical logic that meets each requirement, and presents the corresponding "mental function" Piaget equates to that mathematical operation.

Unlike mathematical groups, stable systems of qualitative or simply logical operations are tautological in that an operation composed of elements of itself remains identical (e.g., $A + A = A$). Therefore, for systems composed of *psychol*ogical operations, Piaget adds a fifth requirement: "*groupement.*" This he

Table 1. **Requirements for a group, mathematical functions, and Piaget's "mental function" equivalents**

Requirement for a group	Mathematical function	Mental function equivalent
Composability	A new operation is composable from the application of two operations of the set. $A + \hat{A} = B$	Coordination of two actions by union or serial order, etc.
Invertibility	Each operation has a corresponding inverse operation. $+A, -A$	Psychological reversibility, which allows the reconstitution of a sequence of mental actions.
Substitutional equivalence	Operations that produce equivalent compositions by substitutions of different elements in the set. $(+A + (\hat{A} + \hat{B})) = ((A + \hat{A}) + \hat{B})$	Ability to use different paths to achieve the same result.
General identity	Operation resulting from a direct operation and its inverse. $+A - A = 0$	Assures the identity of the objects of thought.

defines as the final form of logic that generates a stable system of human actions (pp. 141–142). To reason, thus, is "to *effect* on objects, materially or mentally, the most general actions possible while 'grouping' those actions according to a principal of reversible composition" (p. 139; my emphasis).

Piaget begins his analysis by treating the individual as a closed system involving exchanges only with the physical environment:

> . . . it is necessary to conceive the development of logic as a progressive transition from irreversible effective actions [in the child] to reversible virtual actions that are [adult] operations. One can, therefore, interpret logic as the final equilibrated form of actions toward which all sensory-motor and mental evolution tends.
>
> . . . [Thus] considered from the point of their psychological development, logical operations constitute the final equilibrial form of actions when they are grouped into mobile systems that are both indefinitely composable and rigorously reversible. (pp. 142, 145)

Piaget suggests that logic, at this level, is simply the "final equilibrial [stable] form"[14] of a system of actions, of movements or sensory-motor processes that have become completely coordinated with one another and thus constitute a system of reversible compositions. Reversibility enables conservation of the whole system of logic—its identity and structural integrity—for it provides the means for returning to the initial condition by way of an inverse function. Because an operation is never conducted in an isolated state, the evolution of operations involves reworking operations as new situations are confronted, which progressively reconstitutes the whole system of operations. By successive iterations of this restructuring process, a final point is reached where action is stable and the configuration (the *groupement*) of the system of logical operations associated with this condition is the final form of logic that will generate this stability. In essence, the importance of Piaget's concept of *groupement* is that it *provides the means to get from thought—mental images of virtual actions—to effective, purposeful action in the material world.*

Piaget then examines the conditions required for the development of a stable system of intellectual exchange and identifies three requirements: a common system of signs and definitions (language); conservation of valid propositions and obligations; and reciprocity of thought among the individuals involved.

An operatory *groupement* is a system of operations with compositions exempt from contradiction, reversible, and leading to the conservation of the totalities envisioned. Now it is clear that thinking jointly with others facilitates noncontradiction. It is much easier to contradict oneself when one thinks only for himself (egocentrism) than when partners are present to recall what one has said previously and what one has agreed upon. Reversibility and conservation are, on the other hand, contrary to how things appear and only become rigorous on the condition of replacing objects by signs, which is to say by a system of collective expressions. In a still more general way, a *groupement* is a system of concepts (classes or relations) implying a coordination of points of view and a pooling of thought. This is even clearer on the formal plane . . . since hypothetico-deductive thought is, more than anything else, thought based on language (common or mathematical) and, therefore, on a collective form of thought (pp. 144–145).

Finally, Piaget examines three different social contexts within which interpersonal interactions occur—egocentrism, where the individuals involved do not succeed in coordinating their points of view; constraint, where unified collective thought is externally imposed by authority or tradition; and cooperation, where the exchange of thought is organized as a system of reciprocal operations. He shows that it is *only* in cooperation that the *socio*-logical organization of thought corresponds to a *groupement*.

cooperation is opposed to both autism and constraint. It progressively eliminates the processes of autistic or egocentric thought. . . . Discussion produces internal reflection; mutual verification produces the need for proof and objectivity. The exchange of thought presupposes the principles of contradiction and identity conceived as regulative of discourse, etc. As for constraint, cooperation destroys it to the extent that there is a differentiation of individuals and free discussion. Hence cooperation provides for the mind the psychological conditions necessary for the attainment of truth.

Only cooperation assures mental equilibrium, which allows one to distinguish the *de facto* state of psychological operations from the *de jure* state of the rational ideal. (Piaget, 1965/1995b, pp. 208, 210)

In short, not only is cooperation generative of thought and reason, but because intentionality presupposes logical thought—that is, in the form of plans, means–ends schemata, etc., (Freeman, 1995; Miller *et al.*, 1960; Searle, 1983)—

cooperation also is the basis for purposeful social action and hence the source of the active agent in psychosocial life.

An example may help to illustrate how least action and intentionality combine to produce optimal collective action. Henry Ford *experimented* with different ways of joining together the energy of his factory workers to find the *maximally efficient* structure of *co(l)-laboration* for manufacturing cars (Lacey, 1986). To do this he implemented a set of social constraints, based on his application of the assembly line and its associated techniques of mass production, that directed and thus optimized the action paths among the collective of workers. (He also stabilized his labor force and enhanced the activation of their potential energy by paying wages at double the going rate.[15]) The result, optimal action: he produced automobiles at minimum cost, which, in turn, proved effective in the marketplace.

A final point concerns a similarity between the dimensionality of Piaget's analytic scheme and ours (see Pribram and Bradley, 1996). Despite a difference in focus—Pribram and I focus primarily on the movements of energy and information in collaborative systems, while Piaget focuses on the "operatory logic" that produces thought and reason in cooperative systems—a basic commonality is apparent. In Piaget's system of cooperation, reciprocity in "inter-individual relations"—the free distribution and movement of information back and forth between individuals—is one of the two conditions for stability. This idea of a free exchange among individuals is analogous to our concept of flux. The second condition is a "common system of signs and references"—that is, common language, values, and social norms. According to Piaget, the system of common signs and references acts as a constraint system, in our terms, control: it functions to "conserve" the operatory logic and outputs (the "propositions") of prior interactions by ensuring logical consistency in the development and evolution of subsequent *co*-operations. Thus, when a field of reciprocal interactions is coupled with a logic-conserving system of common signs and references, "mobile equilibrium" or stable organization results (pp. 145–153).

4. Conclusion

Laszlo's theory of quantum-vacuum interaction is the product of a lifetime's work. His work embraces virtually all branches of science and has aimed at developing a unified description of the evolution of organization across the physical, biological, and psychosocial levels.

Laszlo's theory is organized around two sets of theoretical principles. The first set is derived from a postulate of universal interconnection: that everything in the universe is fundamentally related by a process of constant universal interaction. This process is mediated by the virtually unlimited potential energy of the quantum vacuum. The wave-forms of energy in this field encode information on all interactions, interactions both across and between the physical, biological, and psychosocial levels of organization. The information describing these interactions is stored and retrieved according to the principles of classical holography.

The second set of postulates rests on the axiom that all interactions are guided by preferential correlations. This introduces an order-generating bias in the interactions between ensembles of systems. These interactions occur by way of a holographic prompt which in-forms the pathways of action. Because the holographic prompt encodes information about the specific system and the multilevel hierarchy to which it belongs, the order-generating process results in self-organized evolution of increasingly complex forms of organization.

However, in considering this framework as an account for interaction at the psychosocial level, we found two basic difficulties, each of which appears to rule out any possibility of an active human agent in social life. One is Laszlo's use of classical holography, the holography of image processing. Based on the linear mathematics of a two-way Fourier transformation, this type of holography renders a predetermined order, which, by definition, precludes chance and choice, and, therefore, agency. The second difficulty is Laszlo's view of the human brain as merely a passive receiver of information. This view makes it virtually impossible to account for purposeful forms of social organization within the quantum-vacuum interaction framework. Thus, as the scheme is presently conceived, it is insufficient: it leaves the key question of an active human agent unaddressed.

This is the basic difference with the alternative understanding of psychosocial organization that I have outlined here and have developed further elsewhere (see Bradley, 1998). Human agency is provided for in two respects. First, I take a quantum-holographic approach and describe psychosocial interaction in terms of Gabor's concept of information, the logon. As energy-based units of information, logons are space–time constrained holograms that require constant exogenous regulation of the signal-producing device to ensure fidelity in communication. This necessity for regulation opens the system to new input (indeterminacy). The introduction of indeterminacy creates the potential for chance and choice and, thus, for an active agent in social life. By using this approach, the determinism of classical holography is broken without losing the benefits of an understanding of the distribution of energy, which is still provided by the principles of quantum holography.

The second basis for agency stems from my assumption that the human brain *is* an active processor of information; this seems the most reasonable interpretation of the evidence (Freeman, 1995; Gazzaniga, 1995; Pribram, 1991; Searle, 1983). Our description of social collaboration, following Piaget's analysis, as generative of a purposeful human agent, rests upon this neurological assumption. Piaget shows that *only* in cooperative interaction is the exchange of thought structured as a system of reciprocal operations and therefore capable of generating *groupements*, stable systems of psychological and sociological actions. Thus cooperation is the basis for purposeful forms of social organization.

Moving beyond this summary, to what degree might Laszlo's scheme be translated into a quantum holographic approach so as to offer a nondeterminist description of the evolution of biosocial organization? There is space only for the very briefest sketch.

As a description of the distribution of potential energy in the quantum vacuum, Laszlo's first order, the holofield, maps directly to Gabor's frequency ordinate. And as a description of the spatiotemporal organization of the actualization of energy, his second order, the multilevel hierarchy of material systems, maps to Gabor's space–time ordinate. Conceived as a quantum-holographic information-processing system, the interpenetration between the vacuum's holofield and a given multilevel ensemble of material systems produces logon-like units of information. Each unit of information enfolds a description (a space–time constrained hologram) of the ensemble's internal organization, both in terms of energy distribution and also in terms of spatiotemporal organization. The ongoing movement, or interaction, between the two orders generates a moment-by-moment quantized description within spectral and spatiotemporal coordinates that is distributed throughout the ensemble. In this way, a constant succession of space–time constrained holograms, reflecting the ensemble's evolving organization, is generated and in-forms the ensemble's path of action in space and also in time.

A final point concerns a tantalizing question of connection between Laszlo's scheme and ours: namely, the relation between his concept of quantum-vacuum interaction and our concept of flux. Could it be that flux, the distribution of energy in psychosocial fields, is actually mediated by the quantum vacuum? The answer, for future research, must await improvements in the measurement of electromagnetic fields.

Notes

I am grateful to Karl Pribram for his suggestions on a earlier draft and for allowing me to draw heavily from our collaborative work (Bradley and Pribram, 1995, 1996a,b, 1997; Pribram and Bradley, 1996). I thank Michele Hardoin, David Loye, and Nancy Roberts for their helpful comments.

1. Unless otherwise indicated, all page references are to Laszlo, 1995.
2. In exploring the QVI scheme and in presenting an alternative, I am obligated to incorporate concepts and formalisms from the natural sciences. I therefore must employ the relevant principles of quantum theory, holography, control engineering, and chaos theory, and must refer to such concepts as energy, space–time, uncertainty, and least action. In the same spirit as Laszlo, it is my sincere hope that readers without background in these technical areas will see the thrust of this essay as part of a larger effort to go beyond metaphorical description to an account of psychosocial organization in terms of rigorous scientific concepts. For readers who seek to achieve greater familiarity with these concepts, so as to better understand the contents of this essay, see Briggs and Peat (1984), Gleick (1987), and Morgan (1986) for readable introductions. More advanced treatments are offered by Bohm (1980), Cherry (1966), Kaiser (1994), Kauffman (1993), Penrose (1989), Pribram (1991), Prigogine (1997), and Prigogine and Stengers (1984).

3. This is a significant point of difference with Bohm, who, in his theory of the quantum potential Q, views quanta as complex systems capable of responding to a pilot wave of "active information" (see Bohm and Hiley, 1993).

4. He argues against Prigogine's dissipative system dynamics (Nicolis and Prigogine, 1977; Prigogine and Stengers, 1984) on the grounds that the individual system is treated as if it is separated from its environment during the bifurcation process, so that, in Prigogine's scheme, chance determines the system's evolutionary trajectory.

5. This problem of holographic determinism also confounds the use of holographic analogies in social science. For examples, see El Sawy, 1985; Hutchins, 1991; MacKenzie, 1991; Morgan and Ramierez, 1984; Ravn, 1985.

6. Heisenberg had developed his mathematical formulation of uncertainty to define the discrete units of energy, *quanta*, emitted by subatomic radiation.

7. This concept of an overlap (of information) with the future is analogous to a concept of communication, the *hololeap*, that David Loye developed in an effort to unravel the puzzle of precognition. He describes the transmission of information over time or across the space between organisms as a "leap" of information between amoeba-like "holographic entities" interacting in a "celestial pond" of energy (Loye, 1983, pp. 201–206; see Bradley, 1996, for a discussion of the parallels between Loye's metaphor and Gabor's concept of the logon).

8. See Bradley, 1987; Bradley and Roberts, 1989a,b; Roberts and Bradley, 1988, 1991; see also the studies by Carlton-Ford (1993), Roberts and King (1996), and Zablocki (1971, 1980).

9. A similar dimensionality has also been used in the performing arts. Starting from the premise that "there are three elements in all [human] movement—space, time, and energy" (Sabatine, 1995, p. 127; my addition), a systematic symbolic language, *Labanotation*, was developed by Rudolf Laban (1967) for recording the minute combinations of energy, space, and time that comprise all of the movements in a dance (see also Hutchinson, 1970).

10. Although data were collected from 57 communes in the original study, only 46 communes had sociometric data of high enough measurement quality to provide reliable mappings of social organization (see Bradley, 1987).

11. The fifth group is a noncharismatic commune whose members expressed a strong desire for charismatic leadership as a means to facilitate their efforts at social change.

12. The three lines shown marking the boundaries of the regions in Figure 5 were established by dividing the full sample of 46 communes into stable and unstable sets such that the probability of survival for the former was maximized while being minimized for the latter. Discriminant analysis, comparing the four grouping of communes separated by the lines, provided a strong statistical confirmation of these results as 45 (98 percent) of the 46 communes were correctly classified by two canonical discriminant functions constructed from the measures of flux and control. It is worth noting that *none* of the other nine sociological variables (measuring aspects of normative and structural organization) investigated in this analysis met the statistical criteria for inclusion in the multivariate stepwise procedure (Bradley and Pribram, 1996b).

13. Unless otherwise indicated, the page references in this section are to Piaget (1965/1995).

14. It should be noted that in a personal communication to Pribram (see Pribram and Bradley, 1996), Inhelder stated that Piaget, after becoming acquainted with the ideas proposed by Prigogine (Prigogine and Stengers, 1984), agreed completely with a change in terminology for his (Piaget's) concepts from "equilibrium" to stability far-from-thermodynamic-equilibrium.

15. Michele Hardoin drew this to my attention.

References

Abraham, F.D. (1991). *A visual introduction to dynamical systems theory for psychology*. Santa Cruz, CA: Aerial Press.

Abraham, F.D. and Gilgen, A. (1995). *Chaos theory and psychology*. Westport, CT: Greenwood Press.

Arthur, W.B. (1989). The economy and complexity. In D.L. Stein, Ed., *Lectures in the sciences of complexity* (pp. 713–740). Redwood City, CA: Addison-Wesley.

Ashby, W.R. (1956). *An introduction to cybernetics*. London: Chapman & Hall.

Atkin, R.H. (1977). *Combinatorial connectivities in social systems*. Basel: Birkhauser.

Barrett, Frank J. (1997; in press). Jazz improvisation and organizational innovation: Implications for organizational learning. *Organization Science*.

Barton, S. (1994). Chaos, self-organization, and psychology. *American Psychologist*, 49(1), 5–14.

Berliner, Paul F. (1994) *Thinking in jazz: The infinite art of improvisation*. Chicago, IL and London: University of Chicago Press.

Blau, Peter M. (1977). *Inequality and heterogeneity: A primitive theory of social structure*. New York: Free Press.

Bohm, D. (1980). *Wholeness and the implicate order*. London: Routledge.

Bohm, D. and Hiley, B.J. (1993). *The undivided universe*. London: Routledge.

Bradley, R.T. (1987). *Charisma and social structure: a study of love and power, wholeness and transformation*. New York: Paragon House.

—— (1996). The anticipation of order in biosocial collectives. *World Futures: The Journal of General Evolution*, 49, 93–116.

—— (1998; in press). Values, agency, and the theory of quantum vacuum interaction. In K.H. Pribram, Ed., *Brain and Values*. Mahwah, NJ: Lawrence Erlbaum Associates.

Bradley, R.T. and Pribram, K.H. (1995). Communication and stability in social collectives. Unpublished manuscript. Carmel, CA: Institute for Whole Social Science.

—— (1996a). Optimality in biosocial collectives. In D.S. Levine and W.R. Elsberry, Eds., *Optimality in biological and artificial networks* (pp. 449–488). Hillsdale, NJ: Lawrence Erlbaum Associates.

—— (1996b). Self-organization and the social collective. In K.H. Pribram and J. King, Eds., *Learning as self-organization* (pp. 478–506). Mahwah, NJ: Lawrence Erlbaum Associates.

—— (1997; in press). Generation of collective order. In A.A. Montuori and R.E. Purser, Eds., *The social dimensions of creativity*, vol. 3. New York: Hampton Press.

Bradley, R.T. and Roberts, N.C. (1989a). Relational dynamics of charismatic organization: The complementarity of love and power. *World Futures: The Journal of General Evolution*, 27, 87–123.

—— (1989b). Network structure from relational data: Measurement and inference in four operational models. *Social Networks*, 11, 89–134.

Briggs, J.P. and Peat, F.D. (1984). *Looking-glass universe: The emerging science of wholeness*. New York: Simon & Schuster, Inc.

Burt, R.S. (1992). *Structural holes: The social structure of competition*. Cambridge, MA and London: Harvard University Press.

Carlton-Ford, S. (1993). *The Effects of Ritual and Charisma*. New York: Garland.

Cherry, C. (1966). *On human communication: A review, a survey, and a criticism*. Cambridge, MA: MIT Press.

Considine, D.M. (Ed.) (1976). *Van Nostrand's scientific encyclopedia*, 5th edn. New York: Van Nostrand Reinhold Company.

Dendrinos, D. and Sonis, M. (1990). *Chaos and socio-spatial dynamics.* New York: Springer-Verlag.

Doreian, Patrick (1986). On the evolution of group and network structure II: Structures within structure. *Social Networks,* 8(1), 33–64.

Durkheim, E. (1949). *The division of labor in society* (transl. George Simpson). Glencoe, IL: Free Press.

El Sawy, O.A. (1985). From separatism to holographic unfolding: the evolution of the techno-structure of organizations. Unpublished paper, ORSA/TIM Conference, Boston.

Fowler, H. and Fowler, F.G. (eds.) (1964). *The concise Oxford dictionary,* 5th edn. Oxford: Oxford University Press.

Freeman, W.J. (1995). *Societies of brains: A study in the neuroscience of love and hate.* Hillsdale, NJ: Lawrence Erlbaum Associates.

Freud, S. (1895/1966). *Project for a scientific psychology,* Standard edn., vol. 1. London: Hogarth.

Gabor, D. (1946). Theory of communication. *Journal of the Institute of Electrical Engineers,* 93, 429–457.

—— (1948). A new microscopic principle. *Nature,* 161, 777–778.

Gazzaniga, M.S. (Ed.) (1995). *The cognitive neurosciences.* Cambridge, MA and London: MIT Press.

Gleick, J. (1987). *Chaos: Making a new science.* New York: Viking.

Granovetter, Mark S. (1973). The strength of weak ties. *American Journal of Sociology,* 78, 1360–1380.

Hinde, R.A. (1992). Developmental psychology in the context of other behavioral sciences. *Developmental Psychology,* 28(6), 1018–1029.

Hinton, G.E. and Sejnowski, T.J. (1986). Learning and relearning in Boltzmann machines. In D.E. Rumelhart and J.L. McClelland, Eds., *Parallel distributed processing: Explorations in the microstructure of cognition,* vol. 1 (pp. 282–317). Cambridge, MA: MIT Press.

Hopfield, J.J. (1982). Neural networks and physical systems with emergent collective computational abilities. *Proceedings of the National Academy of Sciences,* 79, 2554–2558.

Hutchins, E. (1991). The social organization of distributed cognition. In Lauren B. Resnick, John M. Levine, and Stephanie D. Teasley, Eds., *Perspectives on socially shared cognition.* Washington, DC: American Psychological Association.

Hutchinson, A. (1970). *Labanotation: The system of analyzing and recording movement.* London: Routledge, Chapman and Hall.

Jantsch, E. (1980). *The self-organizing universe: Scientific and human implications of the emerging paradigm of evolution.* Oxford: Pergamon Press.

Kaiser, Gerald (1994). *A friendly guide to wavelets.* Boston: Birkhauser.

Kauffman, S.A. (1993). *The origins of order: Self-organization and selection in evolution.* New York: Oxford University Press.

King, J.S., Xie, M., Zheng, B. and Pribram, K.H. (1994). Spectral density maps of receptive fields in the rat's somatosensory cortex. In *Proceedings of the second Appalachian conference on behavioral neurodynamics* (pp. 557–571). Hillsdale, NJ: Lawrence Erlbaum Associates.

Laban, Rudolf (1967). *The mastery of movement.* 2nd end., rev. Lisa Ullmann. New York: Drama Book Specialists.

Lacey, R. (1986). *Ford: The man and the machine.* Boston and Toronto: Little, Brown.

Laszlo, E. (1995). *The interconnected universe: Conceptual foundations of transdisciplinary unified theory.* Singapore: World Scientific.

Loye, D. (1983). *The sphinx and the rainbow: Brain, mind and future vision.* New York: Bantam Books.

—— (1995). How predictable is the future? The conflict between traditional chaos theory and the psychology of prediction, and the challenge for chaos psychology. In R. Robertson and A. Combs, Eds., *Chaos theory in psychology and the life sciences* (pp. 345–358). Mahwah, NJ: Lawrence Erlbaum Associates.

MacKenzie, Kenneth D. (1991). *The organizational hologram: The effective management of organizational change.* Norwell, MA: Kluwer Academic Publishers.

Miller, G.A., Galanter, E.H. and Pribram, K.H. (1960). *Plans and the structure of behavior.* New York: Holt, Rinehart & Winston.

Morgan, G. (1986). *Images of organization.* Beverly Hills, CA: Sage.

Morgan, G., and Ramirez, R. (1984). Action learning: a holographic metaphor for guiding social change. *Human Relations,* 37, 101–106.

Morrison, F. (1991). *The art of modeling dynamic systems: Forecasting for chaos, randomness, and determinism.* New York: John Wiley and Sons.

Nicolis, G., and Prigogine, I. (1977). *Self-organization in nonequilibrium systems: From dissi-pative structures to order through fluctuation.* New York: Wiley-Interscience.

Penrose, R. (1989). *The emperor's new mind: Concerning computers, minds, and the laws of physics.* Oxford and New York: Oxford University Press.

Piaget, J. (1965/1995a). Logical operations and social life. In Leslie Smith, Ed., *Sociological studies* (pp. 134–157). London and New York: Routledge.

—— (1965/1995b). Genetic logic and sociology. In Leslie Smith, Ed., *Sociological studies* (pp. 184–214). London and New York: Routledge.

Pribram, K.H. (1982). The place of brain in the ecology of mind. In Walter Weimer and David Palermo, Eds., *Cognition and the symbolic process,* vol. 2. Hillsdale, NJ: Lawrence Erlbaum Associates.

—— (1991). *Brain and perception: Holonomy and structure in figural processing.* Hillsdale, NJ: Lawrence Erlbaum Associates.

Pribram, K.H. and Bradley, R.T. (1996; in press). The brain, the me and the I. In R. Sternberg and M. Ferrari, Eds., *The development of the self.* New Haven, CT: Yale University Press.

Pribram, K.H. and McGuinness, D. (1975). Arousal, activation and effort in the control of attention. *Psychological Review,* 82, 116–149.

—— (1992). Attention and para-attentional processing: Event related brain potentials as tests of a model. In D. Friedman and G. Bruder, Eds., *Annals of the New York Academy of Sciences,* 658, 65–92. New York: New York Academy of Sciences.

Prigogine, I. (1997). *The end of certainty: Time, chaos, and the new laws of nature.* New York: The Free Press.

Prigogine, I. and Stengers, I. (1984). *Order out of chaos: Man's new dialogue with nature.* New York: Bantam Books.

Ravn, I. (1985). Creating futures, constructing realities. *General Systems Yearbook.*

Roberts, N.C. and Bradley, R.T. (1988). Limits to charisma. In J. Conger and R. Kanungo, Eds., *Charismatic leadership: The elusive factor in organizational effectiveness* (pp. 253–275). San Francisco: Jossey-Bass.

—— (1991). Stakeholder collaboration and innovation: A study of public policy initiation at the state level. *Journal of Applied Behavioral Science,* 27(2), 209–227.

Roberts, N.C. and King, P.J. (1996). *Transforming public policy: Dynamics of policy entrepreneurship and innovation.* San Francisco: Jossey-Bass.

Roethlisberger, F.J. and Dickson, W.J. (1939). *Management and the worker.* Cambridge, MA: Harvard University Press.

Sabatine, Jean (1995). *Movement training for the stage and screen: The organic connection between mind, spirit, and body.* New York: Back Stage Books.

Santa Maria, M., King, J., Xie, M., Zheng, B., Pribram, K. and Doherty, D. (1995). Responses of somatosensory cortical neurons to spatial frequency and orientation: A progress report. In J. King and K.H. Pribram, Eds., *Scale in conscious experience: Is the brain too important to left to specialists to study?* (pp. 157–168). Mahwah, NJ: Lawrence Erlbaum Associates.

Schore, A.N. (1994). *Affect regulation and the origin of the self: The neurobiology of emotional development.* Hillsdale, NJ: Lawrence Erlbaum Associates.

Searle, J.R. (1983). *Intentionality: An essay on the philosophy of mind.* Cambridge: Cambridge University Press.

—— (1995). *The construction of social reality.* New York: Free Press.

Shannon, C.E. (1949). The mathematical theory of communication. In C.E. Shannon and W. Weaver, *The mathematical theory of communication* (pp. 3–91). Urbana, IL: University of Illinois Press.

Sternberg, R.J. (1986). A triangular theory of love. *Psychological Review,* 93(2), 119–135.

Strogatz, Steven H. (1994). *Nonlinear dynamics and chaos: With applications to physics, biology, chemistry, and engineering.* Reading, MA: Addison-Wesley.

Toennies, F. (1957). *Community and Society* (transl. Charles P. Loomis), Book 1. East Lansing, MI: Michigan State University Press.

Trist, E.L. and Bamforth, K.W. (1951). Some social and psychological consequences of the Longwal method of goal setting. *Human Relations,* 4, 3–38.

Turner, V.W. (1969). *The ritual process: Structure and anti-structure.* Chicago, IL: Aldine.

Williamson, Oliver E. (1975). *Markets and hierarchies.* New York: Free Press.

Xie, M. (1995). Signal decomposition for non-stationary processes. Unpublished doctoral dissertation, Virginia Polytechnic and State University.

Zablocki, B.D. (1971). *The joyful community.* New York: Penguin Books.

—— (1980). *Alienation and charisma: A study of contemporary communes.* New York: Free Press.

11
Biological Evolution and Cultural Evolution: Toward a Planetary Consciousness

MAURO CERUTI AND TELMO PIEVANI

Abstract
Evolutionary philosophers Mauro Ceruti and Telmo Pievani outline the challenge of the evolution of an ethically aroused planetary consciousness in terms of Laszlo's vision for a general theory of evolution. In particular, they explore the prospects pro and con in terms of technological action and the implications of the prehistoric data base for Eisler's cultural transformation theory.

Key words
Biological and cultural evolution, planetary consciousness, general evolution theory, human action, responsibility, ethics, technological action, open versus closed system, limits to growth, self-corrective mechanisms, the destiny of humanity, nuclear war, nuclear winter, evolutionary pulsation, genetics, linguistics, unfinished hominization, genetic drift, genetic distance, Neolithic, Marija Gimbutas, Riane Eisler, gylany, planetary civilization.

A feeling of uncertainty pervades the thoughts and practices of many scientists these days. At the center of attention is the complexity of the relationships between the two supposed "dimensions" of human identity, the natural and the cultural. Reflections on the meaning and consequences of the new life technologies in fact find their origin, and a source of serious concern, in the increasing divergence between the biological evolution of the human species and its cultural evolution.

With the appearance of *Homo sapiens* biological evolution has in a certain sense transcended itself. In one respect, the morphology and the organic structure of the human species have altered very little in the last fifteen thousand years (a brief moment in the geological time-scale). But in another respect, cultural and technological evolution have undergone an acceleration unprecedented in natural history.

Can we assert that adequate conscience has developed relative to the use of such extraordinary creative and destructive potential? Does the difference between the relative stability of biological evolution and the great "pulsation" of cultural evolution still render technological paths ecologically sustainable and politically manageable?

Three original directions of research emerge in Ervin Laszlo's work that have profoundly influenced our reflections around these issues. We are referring to the construction of a general theory of evolution integrating the most recent developments of the sciences of complex systems; to the philosophical, ethical, anthropological and political reflection around the issue of a planetary consciousness, and, in more recent times, to the proposal of a unified evolutionary cosmology, which braids together the strands of a common cosmic existence with extreme promise.

In particular, we will outline a few thoughts on the reasons why technological evolution poses a problem for the evolution of a planetary consciousness.

The "Altered Nature of Human Action": A Culture of Responsibility for a Planetary Civilization

The presuppositions of classical ethics are radically shaken by contemporary science. The limits of human ingenuity and of humanity's powers of manipulation are transcended today by biotechnologies, by genetic engineering, and by their Faustian dream of postponing death indefinitely. Modern ethics have been founded on a conception of the relationships between humans, technology and the environment that no longer corresponds to the current state of those relationships. This ethic was:

- centered on the neutrality of technology;
- "infra-human" and anthropocentric;
- based on the concept that the human condition is stable and the goals and consequences of ethical action are "near," in space and time, to the act itself;
- finally, and this is perhaps the determining element, it was based on the distinction between theoretical knowledge (broken down into categories) and "practical reason" (immediate and within reach of any man with willpower).

The "altered nature of human action," as Hans Jonas defined it, diametrically overturns this way of thinking:

- the biosphere is subject to human responsibility, and technology is no longer ethically neutral, with regard either to the environment or to human nature;
- the search for good cannot any longer be confined to the sphere of inter-personal relationships, and the Kantian "end in itself" becomes extended to include nature;
- the technological intervention of the Genome Project alters our conception of human identity and destroys its biological stability; and
- the consequences of human action spread out through space, thus introducing a veritable planetary dimension to ethics, and also spread out through time, projecting the human race's responsibility toward its own destiny and the quality of life for future generations. Even the future becomes part of our responsibility.

It is above all the last modern dichotomy (ethical knowledge versus theoretical knowledge) that becomes the object of profound discussion. The formulation of a new scientific ethic today cannot be kept apart from a reconciliation between the strictly cognitive domain and the domain of ethical responsibility. In such an epistemology, science and ethics find themselves in a heretofore unseen dialogical context.

In the 20th century the sphere of human responsibility was extended in three main directions: (1) toward nature and the planet in its entirety; (2) toward evolutionary destiny and the quality of the survival of the human race as such; (3) toward individual nature, its genetic makeup and its biological identity.

Technological Action as Power to Manipulate Nature

Today the environment, which in Darwinian theory is considered to be the engine of organic transformation by means of natural selection, is substantially transformed, manipulated, and utilized by the human populations. During the last two centuries one can speak of a veritable "adaptive inversion": humans no longer need to adapt to the environment to survive, but rather the environment needs to "adapt itself" incessantly to human activity.

Nature's irruption into the domain of human responsibility touches the heart of contemporary moral philosophy, irreversibly corrodes the very structure of the relationship between humans and the environment, and transforms the concept of human identity that has been reinforced by the developments in modern science.

During the course of modern tradition, the relationships between humans and their environments has been envisioned as an unlimited progress, from both the spatial and temporal perspectives: technological action could have shifted the "boundaries" in all directions indefinitely. The concepts of linearity and optimization had taken shape within the vision of a space and a time that are projectable and tendentially homogeneous, with undetermined boundaries, and infinitely expandable with the increase of tendencies of a quantitative type.

In recent history, this perspective fell short at the moment when humanity found itself coming up against boundaries that were difficult to cross, and faced with irreconcilable discontinuities. The observation of the Earth from outside, in its entirety, has been possible for several decades thanks to artificial satellites. This has resulted in the opening of an extraordinary new frontier of discovery and new adventures in learning. But it has also resulted in the end of a long march of "conquest" of the terrestrial domains; the human race "discovered" the Earth in its beauty and its entirety, but also its faintness and its cosmic isolation. From this moment on, the last frontier of human exploration would be outside the planetary boundaries: first with the technological competition between the two superpowers, from Sputnik to the first man into orbit, from the lunar landing to SDI; then, after 1989, with the uneasy cooperation between Americans, Europeans, Japanese and Russians, and with new challenges to the agenda of planetary exploration (the Alpha base currently under construction, the projected Mars mission).

At this point a series of planetary problems arises. A completely humanized environment is created, within which every local event can, in principle, have a set of consequences that can rapidly become global.

The multiple inquiries into the limits of development characteristic of the 1970s, to whose definition Ervin Laszlo contributed decisively, fall within this perspective. Through these inquiries, the ideas of equilibrium and of a stationary state left the concepts of linear time and constant progress open to question. Modern tradition had placed the quantitative increase of tendencies at the forefront: in the new perspective the establishment of precise stability parameters, around which the system in question would have oscillated, became the central problem. In general, it was held that the global network would have been wracked by substantial shortages.

Within this perspective, the conscientious adoption of the "limits of development" concept and of a more ecological outlook involved the shift from an observational position (with an undefined linear increase) to a different observational position (equilibrium and the preservation of present resources). However, this shift was one-sided: from the limited outlook of an open-system concept to the equally limited idea of a closed system.

The first stage of elaboration of this ecological mind-set thus acquired the slightly prophetic and apocalyptic overtones of the first Report of the Club of Rome. Here it was predicted that with the rates of economic growth of that time the biosphere would have reached a state of crisis within a few years, and that the only possible course of action would be to drastically slow down the economic and demographic growth processes ("zero growth").

The subsequent writings of Ervin Laszlo have quite clearly shown the unilateral nature of such a perspective. The two principal forms of planning strategy that then battled it out are naturally symmetrical and opposite: technology's domination of the environment, present during a great part of the modern era, and the adaptation of the social structure to the environment, which today inspires the majority of environmental theories. Today it is possible and urgent to understand that the dilemma between uncontrolled domination of the environment and passive adaptation to the environment is of an incomplete and limiting nature.

As a result new planning strategies must be outlined in at least three important directions:

1. a direction that questions the traditional distinctions and separations between system and environment. A symbiotic vision is developed in which the concepts of opening and closure would not be in conflict (bioarchitecture, the use of biomasses, intensive use of the solar energy fluxes, etc.);
2. a direction that questions the fixed and definite character of the environmental limits within which human activities are set. We experiment with the evolution and exploration of new opportunities through the extension and transformation of the given environment (a shift therefore from the idea of "limits of development" to one of "development of limits");

3. a direction that questions the inevitability of the internal limits of human society and of the human mind. The radically creative character of technological innovations, information handling systems, and the new criteria for communications organization, are brought to the forefront.

We can therefore pinpoint the fundamental requirement for a new ecology of planning as the amount of attention paid to the plurality of planning strategies and to the anatomy of their interaction. This ecology of planning, on the other hand, requires an analogous paradigm shift in the conception of the scale and time span required for their own realization, thereby becoming drastically simplified. In the implementation of projects in the past, great centralized efforts above established size and energy output levels were given preference. Naturally, centralized operations involve particular time limits related to the completion of the project. In the majority of cases, these time-scales turned out to be on the order of decades and not single years. The consequences are clear: if a project is completed many years after its original conception, it is very probable that this slow and myopic development will incorporate technologies that are already outdated, or at least incompatible with the new social and economic conditions, which by now change significantly in rhythms of years rather than decades.

The often dramatic discrepancy between the estimated timeline of a project, which tends to freeze technological, economic, and social rates of change, and the real rhythms of these changes, as Laszlo has repeatedly emphasized (Laszlo, 1994, pp. 124–127), points us in the directions to explore in order to make our technologies and our projects productive.

A first remedial direction consists of the creation of self-corrective mechanisms within the project, through the implementation of the project itself. The purpose of such mechanisms is so that the project should less and less resemble a pre-established program that would try to anticipate every step of its implementation, and would instead increasingly resemble a strategy able to learn from the events and the circumstances that arise during the implementation process. A planning style is being conceived that would expand, and not reduce, uncertainty; that would aim at amplifying the gamut of possible choices, and render the operation more responsible.

The second direction involves rethinking the nature of global projects, those which deal with "great quantities" (spatial, temporal, or energy-related). Not necessarily the only path toward the realization of this type of project is one that shifts from the inclusion of nothing to the inclusion of everything, so that the time span of its actualization would be nothing more than a "scorched earth" between the moment of its conception and the moment of its initial implementation. These projects can also be actualized through a strategy of accretion, of integration, of interaction, of synergy between localized projects laid out on a more modest scale, but which can be more expediently and effectively organized precisely for this reason. Their implementation would change the essence of the entire system, and would generate new possibilities that were unthinkable at the "zero time" of the main project's evolution. It is not even necessary that a global project should depend on a center: in many instances a net of various localized projects whose heterogeneity (of type or of degree) is not neutralized can become the root cause of the proper functioning of the global system.

Today the science of planning is attempting to redefine an ecology of planning. This is equivalent to taking the complexity of the time spans of human existence and outlining a type of project that would not fight this complexity, but on the contrary would open a creative dialogue with it. This ecology of planning requires, as Ervin Laszlo maintains in his outline of the Club of Budapest project, the adoption of a planetary consciousness and ethos: a consciousness that includes not only the rational faculties but also intuition, empathy, compassion, solidarity for the fate of mankind and its home. In other words, a type of human planning is envisioned that would expand and not diminish uncertainty, widen the spectrum of possible choices, and introduce a dimension of responsibility into the imagination.

Technological Action as a Power to Manipulate the Destiny of Humanity

In 1983 an interdisciplinary team of physicists, meteorologists, chemists, and biologists, led by Carl Sagan, outlined several Earth weather scenarios after a hypothetical conflagration of the superpowers' nuclear arsenals. The study of the direct negative effects of the explosions, of the diverse side-effects, and of the increasing synergisms and interrelationships between these effects, coalesced into the scenario subsequently dubbed "nuclear winter": a terrifying description of the greatest human destruction possible through technology.

In those years it was conceptualized that the biosphere, as an integrated and sophisticated system of physical–chemical relationships, would have been in great danger faced with the ultimate human folly. One of the main sources of inspiration for this research was paleontology, in particular the exogenous model of mass extinction at the K-T boundary proposed by the physicist Luis Alvarez and some of his colleagues at the end of the 1970s. The hypothesis of a comet impact or of a brush with the comet's tail was for many scientists a possible historical example that could be used to describe the nuclear winter scenario: a huge dust cloud rises into the atmosphere, causing a sudden decrease in temperature and the interruption of photosynthesis for months or even years.

The extinction that occurred at the boundary between the Cretaceous and Tertiary periods (65 million years ago) swept the dinosaurs away as well as almost half of all marine animals. This afforded mammals—who had until then been confined to a marginal environmental niche, in an ecosystem dominated by the great reptiles—their great evolutionary opportunity. *Homo sapiens*, lucky inheritor through a sudden planetary crisis, has today developed such powerful techno-logical means that the conditions for a global extinction of the same magnitude are recreated. The inheritor is today the potential agent of his own extinction and of the extinction of most living species.

Interest in the nuclear winter concept, after almost fifteen years and the end of the Cold War, seems greatly reduced. This is undoubtedly a danger, because the collapse of the Soviet bloc seems neither to have induced a reduction in global military spending nor to have eliminated the threat of a nuclear launch. It has only stretched this out over time by relying on the ever more inadequate control systems of the excommunist states, and because of the smuggling of increasingly smaller, more sophisticated, and uncontrollable nuclear materials into Third World coun-tries.

The degree of suffering and destruction that a nuclear war would bring human-ity is not in question (but we can extend this thought to include less dramatic and extensive modes of behavior and environmental change). We can even consider the possibility that a very high percentage of living species would not become extinct, and that *Homo sapiens* would not suffer total extinction. In any event, an atomic war would cause incalculable damage to agriculture, adversely mutate the weather, and give an unforeseen advantage to radiation-resistant species such as cockroaches, rats and crabs. It would constitute an enormous blow to the global ecosystem.

But would this expression of the greatest human destructive ability overwhelm the creative potential of the Earth? The answer would seem to be negative. The extinction caused by humans would be irreversible damage, an unalterable affront to the planet, but it would not mean the end of life, which instead would continue by adopting other forms. The planet would experience a dramatic evolutionary threshold, a discontinuity caused by a single species (paradoxically the only one gifted with an advanced intellect), but over an adequate geological time-scale the event would not bring about a disappearance of life as such.

The destructive potential acquired by the human species therefore appears as a potential for collective suicide. It is precisely from this awareness of mankind's unprecedented ability to end itself that the ecological movement and the concept of a planetary community are simultaneously born: the human race finds itself united by a common journey.

But that's not all: investigating future extinction scenarios, scientists have found that the damaging role of humans has already realized itself abundantly. We are the inheritors, as Niles Eldredge has shown, of an "evolutionary pulsation" without precedent, triggered by the invention and rapid spread of agriculture. For the first time a single species on Earth has been able to bring about an authentic mass extinction, to radically modify surface habitats, and to alter the chemical makeup of the air and water. The shadow of this biosphere upheaval lengthens in the present and is manifested through the multiple crises to which mankind will be subjected by the next "evolutionary wave" (Laszlo, 1991): overpopulation, poverty, wasted resources, deforestation, the greenhouse effect, intensive use of chemicals in monocultures, depletion of traditional energy sources, etc.

The awareness of a new paradigm that would allow us to envision this explosion of the ambivalent potentials of our species is missing, however (Laszlo, 1996; Bocchi and Ceruti, 1993). Today it is more than ever necessary to conceive of natural history as coevolution, and codetermination, between organisms and the environment. Instead of freezing the natural status quo with artificial balances, it is necessary today to imagine a dynamic linking between humanity and the planet, in which technology would be the fragile means (Ceruti, 1994) to alter the rules of coexistence between man and nature on a planetary scale.

The nature of *Homo sapiens*' evolutionary route, and more extensively the loss of centrality that our planet is steadily acquiring in the scientific imagination, are coalesced into a new feeling of belonging: a desire (affective, emotive, aesthetic, and equally economic and rational) to cooperate with nature, of which we are part, within a common "partnership of destiny."

It is necessary to promote a partnership between humans and the environment, so that their interaction should bring about reciprocal satisfaction and not temporary solutions, and their mutual respect produce an ecological "knowledge" and no longer just emergency responses to specific environmental crises. Ecology would then be conceived as a science and ethic of diversity, and as an essential epistemological frame of a renewed educational system.

Technological Action as a Power to Manipulate Human Nature

The dizzy progress of genome-manipulating technologies demonstrates that today we are being carried on a wave of anthropological and spiritual evolution that we can hardly fathom because we are still completely immersed in it, but that urgently requires a qualitative modification of the metaphors of change and of cohabitation. And it is precisely the extension of technological intervention and manipulation of the most intimate biological structures of the human species, at this late stage, that irreversibly transforms the ethical and political horizon of the "responsibility principle."

A critical threshold in human history is probably approaching, where danger and opportunity will be indissolubly linked (Laszlo, 1991). The focus of responsibility is no longer only nature, understood as a context external to human action; nor only humanity either, as a potentially suicidal collective. Today the focus of responsibility is human nature itself, with its modes of function and transmission of genetic information. Biotechnologies, genetic manipulation, new reproductive techniques, new transplant techniques, gene therapies, animal cloning: our very species becomes an object of technology for the first time, forcing us to redefine our conception of human "identity."

Many authors have detected, in this explosion of technological potentials, the narcissistic euphoria of the search for the philosopher's stone (to delay death indefinitely; to finally be "the resemblance and image of God"), a technological utopia, and the thrill of being able to control and direct the evolution of the species. The divergence between the limited intent of human technological intervention and the range of unpredictable and inconceivable consequences that it can have is increasing and at times assumes troubling forms (mainly centered around the risk of an arbitrary "programming" of the tools of genetic engineering).

The boundary between the natural and the artificial seems to grow and become hazier, and the future, placed under the "guardianship" of man, barges roughly into ethical reflection: responsibility is projected well beyond the "immediate future"; it becomes a responsibility toward the subsequent generations, toward the absolute imperative of humanity's survival, toward the same notion of "humanitas" up to now assumed to be well known and immutable.

The philosophical and epistemological paradoxes that derive from this are therefore extremely serious. The extreme boosting of human technological ability occurs precisely when the human species becomes aware of the loss of its centrality in evolution, when the concept of an evolutionary progress toward maximum perfection, represented by *Homo sapiens*, begins to waver. In this context, great help has come in recent years from research in anthropology and comparative genetics.

Genetic and Linguistic Polyphonies: On the Trail of an Unfinished Hominization

In the history of human civilization there hasn't only been linear and cumulative progress: there have also been the fall or shift of central and focal problems in a particular time and place. The entire cognitive experience of the human race, in space as in time, reveals itself to be pertinent for both our present and our future. Instead of believing that the most recent arrivals, the most refined languages, and the new theories surpass or even erase all that human minds have conceived during the course of history, today we find it more sensible to delineate a history that would reconnect and bind problems perceived and experienced in distant times and places.

Human knowledge is becoming planetary, in space as in time. Science itself can no longer pretend to judge other forms of knowledge as if it had the power and the qualities of a neutral and objective tribunal. On the contrary, it can only attempt to initiate an unfinished conversation with them.

The correlations between the mythical narratives, spiritualities, sacred architectures, and the cosmologies of the ancient world challenge the idea of the reduction of the multiple forms of knowledge into a single one, which would be algorithmic, quantitative, formalized, disembodied, and is considered by a large proportion of modern scientists to be the final goal of a linear and cumulative progress in knowledge. It appears clear, with ever mounting evidence, that a huge stock of knowledge has been transmitted in many civilizations with means altogether different from the algorithmic, without sacrificing any precision or effectiveness. The modern Western tradition has seen fit to supersede an age of prescientific knowledge, simply qualitative, with an age of mature science, quantitative and algorithmic. But populations all around the world have developed individual astronomical traditions that don't fit in with either of the succeeding phases of Western civilization.

Until a few decades ago we knew with some precision only the last six thousand years of the history of human civilization. We knew how to reconstruct the roots and origins of Western civilization as far back as the fourth millennium BC, and not much further. Today multiple research approaches have allowed us to dredge the most remote layers of our past, with revolutionary results. These include: the research into the agricultural revolution and the Neolithic age; the comparative study of myths; images and relics from the most diverse sites in the European continent and the Mediterranean basin; the archeological digs over the entire surface of the planet, from Jericho in Palestine to Catal Huyuk in Anatolia, from the ancient cities of Central and South America to the traces of ancient settlements in the Far East; and finally the extraordinary development of genetics and linguistics applied to the study of human population.

By utilizing information generated by reading the genetic makeup of several populations and comparing this with data obtained by other disciplines, such as archeology, linguistics, demographics, and anthropology, a team of geneticists directed by Luigi Cavalli Sforza (Cavalli Sforza *et al.*, 1994) has, in the last few years, provided an extraordinary contribution to the study of the "history of human diversity." This great interdisciplinary research has not only both scientifically and systematically demolished any biological legitimization of racist theories and hypotheses, but also laid out a new interpretative key for the entire evolution of humans on Earth: the branching-out and spreading of populations over the Earth denotes a deep anthropological unity in spite of the substantial diversity of human cultures and morphologies. It belies, in other words, a *unitas multiplex*: a unity within a multiplicity, and a multiplicity within the unity.

In the space of sixty to seventy thousand years *Homo sapiens* colonized every part of the planet, adapted to the most diverse environments and climates, migrated with ease and formed the first organized settlements. We find *Homo sapiens* in China sixty thousand years ago, and a few millennia later it reaches Australia and New Guinea, crossing sea stretches of hundreds of kilometers. *Homo sapiens* arrives in Europe around 40,000 to 35,000 years ago, perhaps driving Neanderthal Man out from the East. During the period of the last ice age (20,000–15,000 years ago) *Homo sapiens* conquers the steppes and tundra of northern Asia, pushes on to the frozen expanses of eastern Siberia and "invades" the American continent, reaching all the way to Tierra del Fuego.

The diversification of populations is quite rapid: the groups no longer communicate with each other because of the enormous distances and this determines a parallel linguistic diversification. A veritable "Tower of Babel" is created, perhaps generated out of a common proto-language whose traits correspond to the research in comparative linguistics and glottochronology by some of the most famous world linguists, such as Joseph Greenberg and his student Merritt Ruhlen.

The divergence caused by the genetic "drift" combines with the divergence produced by different natural selections in different environments. A planetary map of hominization is thus outlined, characterized by an interweaving of analogies and divergences within the same anthropological *unitas multiplex,* in which great anthropometric differences (skin color, eyes, height, pigmentation, etc., for which the "racial" definition is itself controversial) could even correspond to a close genetic relation, and vice versa. Between an African pygmy and an Australian aborigine there is the same genetic distance that could be found between a pygmy and a white European.

From the analysis of the "genetic distance" between the main human groups there emerge two fundamental dates for the great bifurcations on the evolutionary tree of hominization. The model developed by Cavalli Sforza and his team goes all the way back to the migrations that could have shaped the most remote history of a single continent such as Europe. Genetic analysis has allowed us to identify a great migration from the Middle East into Europe (around 12,000 years ago) that corresponds to the colonization of the continent by populations with an agricultural lifestyle, who were sedentary and built the first cities (such as Catal Huyuk in Anatolia, which dates around 9000BC).

The analysis and the geographical distribution of the subsequent genetic gradients (more ephemeral and more recent in time) has produced extraordinary results.

A second (north–south) gradient points to the establishment of a progressive colonization of northern Europe by the Neolithic peoples (with a few "islands" inhabited by preceding Caucasian populations, who will continue to speak a Uralic language, Ugrofinnish).

The third gradient instead shows a massive migration of populations (around 6000–4500BC) from the central steppes of Asia into Europe: this corresponds to the dates that the archeologist Marija Gimbutas has established for the invasion by nomadic herdsmen who spoke an Indo-European language (the Kurgan civilization).

The fourth gradient corresponds to the Greek expansion from the Aegean to the eastern Mediterranean and Italy (around 1000BC).

The fifth gradient, finally, reveals all the niches occupied by populations who resisted the original Neolithic onslaught (such as the Basques).

The connection between the research on the human genetic/linguistic family tree and the archeological hypotheses of Gimbutas denotes a fundamental aspect of these revolutionary studies. Today the background to a history of hominization, and of the cultural and social diversity generated by it, is becoming outlined. A "lost world" has emerged from Gimbutas's findings in all of its facets and peculiarities: Neolithic Europe before the sudden and violent migration of the Indo-European nomads (Eisler, 1987).

Unlike those cultures that later prevailed in the Mediterranean basin (founded on the values of strength and hierarchy), the societies of Neolithic Europe were egalitarian, with a strong middle class of sailors and merchants, with a virtual equality between the sexes: women were entrusted with important social functions, and as priestesses they exercised a particular religious authority connected to the values of fertility and conviviality.

Ancient Europe seems to have been the site of a mind-set totally different from patriarchal thought, which is characterized by the domination of the male sex and the subordination of the female sex. This type of mind-set and social structure has been call "gylanic" by Riane Eisler (1987), a term that is derived from the co-ordination between masculine and feminine prefixes. Gylany (which includes civilizations such as the Minoan and the Mycenaean) has not left behind any decipherable written records, but there are many traces of its material life, art, and spirituality. These express an extraordinary wealth of symbols, signs, images, and myths, united by the concept of a solidarity and an interconnection between the sexes (and not, therefore, by an archaic feminine dominance as in Bachofen's matriarchy theory).

In cultural history paths mix and diverge similarly to the complex interweavings of hominization. Classical civilization, from which Western tradition will originate, always displays a mix of the symbolic gylanic system and the symbolic androcratic system (as in the diversity between male and female deities within the Greek pantheon), thus perpetuating a memory of the great confrontation/clash that was perhaps at the roots of our own history.

With the map of planetary hominization and with Gylany, the rewriting of our civilization's remote past alters the roots and vision of our future as well. The challenge is to build a livable future that would step beyond the rage and the blood of what has seemed to be a necessary history of domination, violence, and barbarism, justified by an alleged human nature reputed to be true to itself (at the root of integralisms and totalitarianisms). The same duality between coevolution and subordination of the sexes is found in other civilizations, such as the Chinese and Indian, thereby indicating a spiritual task of truly planetary scope: to reinvent human history, under the banner of diversity, expansion of possibilities, and joint existence.

Laszlo has wryly noted that: "We live in a tolerant universe: if it is true that we, like all other things, must survive, evolve or perish inside a flux, the way in which we survive, evolve or perish is open to our own choice. Evolution is not fate, but rather opportunity" (Laszlo, 1996, p. 125). The process of hominization appears to be unfinished, open, and still full of unforeseen bifurcations.

An Ocean of Possibilities:
The Knowledge Core of the Planetary Civilization

A feeling of belonging spiritually to the planet and of a common destiny, shared emotively by all its inhabitants, emerged in the 1980s and early 1990s. Western spiritual traditions came into contact with religious and esoteric traditions that had been totally unknown to the West in the past, or at most were the subject of Eurocentric anthropological investigations: Yoga, Tantra, the Tao, Zen, Sufism, the Cabala, Gnosis, Christian mysticism, etc.

We have discovered a common cosmological inspiration behind the diversity and plurality of these traditions: an image of the universe as a fabric (indeed "Tantra" means fabric, the Latin "complexus") of many strands, of forces, processes, polarities, interactive time-scales that contribute to its evolution; and an image of man's life in this universe as a creative dance that continually combines with these strands, and continually generates new worlds (Laszlo, 1996).

Today we discover in our lives not only a profound interconnection between these traditions but also their ability to furnish us with a new horizon for the present problems facing planetary society. We face the huge but stimulating task of transforming our scientific and political notions, which at times have degenerated into intolerant and invasive ideological systems, into complex activities that are respectful of a complex universe (a pluriverse) and participants in it.

In the history of Western tradition, in which we are irreversibly enmeshed, we can discern today one of the many possible paths—neither the only nor a necessary one—that all stem from a common origin. But things could have gone differently. Elsewhere they did go differently: in other traditions we find a unity inside a diversity within an analogous community with a planetary destiny. In accordance with the great hominization scenario portrayed by linguists and geneticists, the other symbolic planetary universes share a good part of the foundation myths, linguistic structures, nostalgias, and memories of our own.

By becoming able to learn from this unity within diversity, and from the diversities within unity, we can both identify the plurality and complexity of our tradition (rediscovering minority events, unnoticed historical perspectives, overlapping derivations; in other words, the diversity inscribed *ab initio* and *in itinere* into Western tradition) and measure ourselves against the common roots of the diverse philosophical universes created on this planet. We thus find, spread over all the Earth, traces of a common archaic cosmology, a cosmology of process and of contingency of forms, that expresses the indivisibility and the links between processes and forms, that life network shared by both natural and cultural history.

Within this cultural ecology and this practice of commonality and coevolution between the terrestrial traditions we find the most radical and fertile concept of the emerging planetary consciousness, the turning-point toward a new humanism awaited by many thinkers: a message no longer simply of tolerance toward diversity, but also of the involvement of each diversity in the pluriverse of the planetary cultures; an invitation to conceive new forms of solidarity between populations and living creatures, also through a renewed religious dimension to human relations, according to the etymological root of *re-ligare*, in other words a religion of solidarity, of planetary compassion, of emotional collective involvement in the planetary destiny.

The traditions of our planet have displayed, in these last decades of study, a multiplicity of internal narratives, small variations, and hidden tensions. Each tradition has discovered the strands of an intricate tapestry of alliances and conflicts, solidarities and differences that form the fabric of planetary hominization. The thought and belief systems of this planet—science, philosophy, the West, the East, Christianity, Buddhism, etc.—can no longer advocate their independence, their supremacy of judgment, their fundamental superiority over other systems. The diverse perspectives transmitted by these great traditions are today found to be strictly interdependent and mutually altering.

The contingency, uniqueness and induplicability of each are the only premises for a constructive dialogue and a new spiritual fertility. Through the incompleteness of every "possible world" we can now implement the spirit of a coevolutionary conception of human history in which, beyond the confusion and the crises that our intellect is navigating, "other worlds" will emerge from the meeting and blending of cultures.

References

Bocchi, G.M. and Ceruti, M. (1993). *Origini di storie* [The narrative universe]. Milan: Feltrinelli.

Cavalli Sforza, L.P., Menozzi, P. and Piazza, A. (1994). *The history and geography of human genes.* Princeton, NJ: Princeton University Press.

Ceruti, M. (1994). *Constraints and possibilities. The evolution of knowledge and knowledge of evolution.* New York: Gordon & Breach.

Eisler, R. (1987). *The chalice and the blade.* San Francisco: HarperCollins.

Laszlo, E. (1991). *The age of bifurcation: Understanding our changing world.* New York: Gordon & Breach.

——(1994). *The choice: evolution or extinction.* Los Angleles: Tarcher.

——(1996). *Evolution.* Cresskill, NJ: Hampton Press.

Part 3

Human Intervention in Evolutionary Process

12
Evolutionary Action Theory: A Brief Outline

DAVID LOYE

Abstract
Social psychologist and systems scientist David Loye shows how the active human agent can much more rapidly advance our evolution at a critical point of challenge. He outlines a new evolutionary action theory based on Darwin's long-ignored theory of the moral sense, and Eisler's and others' works in psychology, brain research, and a wide range of other fields.

Key words
Evolutionary action theory, Darwin's two theories, the moral sense, frontal lobe functioning, active moral agent, direction in evolution, theoria, praxis, action theory, psychosocial selection, cultural selection, organic selection, replicative selection, creativity, creative transcendence, creative transformation, paradigm, paradigm formation, paradigm expansion, paradigm defense, dominator versus partnership systems, moral sensitivity, moral action, activists versus gatekeepers, nurturers versus predators, creators and selectors, changers and maintainers, the human agent as protagonist in the story of evolution.

1. The Case for a New Action-Oriented Theory of Evolution

The main case for an action-oriented theory of evolution is being made today by events rather than by scholars. The development of nuclear bombs, population explosion, environmental disaster, terrorism, and all the other problems now cumulatively raising the question of long-range survival for our species underscore the need for the revival and expansion of the activist perspective in evolution theory. In other words, the presently prevailing perspective for theories of evolution is essentially passive, reactive, and overwhelmingly focused on the past. This is understandable as, with a bare 150 years or so of development, evolutionary theory is essentially still an infant, feeling its way. But the world situation, as in a house afire, requires that we grab up our notes and join the bucket brigade. There must be a shift in focus from learning only of how our planet and our species over the past have come to be, to how we can now—here in the present, fervently attuned to the future—much more rapidly evolve.[1]

2. Perspectives of Evolutionary Action Theory

2.1. *The Perspective of Darwinian Continuity*

Contrary to initial appearances, an action-oriented theory of evolution neither contradicts nor calls for a radical departure from Darwinian theory. It calls only for an expansion beyond what has long been considered Darwinian theory to what, through reconstruction of a long-ignored aspect of his work, we may now see is the *whole* of this theory.

As I develop elsewhere (Loye, 1994, 1998a,b), Darwin had two major theories of evolution, only the first of which, his theory of natural selection, has been seriously pursued by his successors. In brief, the prevailing neo-Darwinian version explains evolution as a process involving the interplay of natural selection and random variation. Grounded on a *pre*human data base, within this process generally there has been detected no direction other than toward greater complexity.[2]

Darwin's other major theory was of the development of the "moral sense." Though long ignored as a 19th-century peculiarity, it has received striking confirmation from modern brain research (Loye, 1994, 1998a,b). The picture that now emerges from both Darwin's original theory and this brain research is of a capacity for moral sensitivity that enters organic evolution with the emergence of sex over 1 billion years ago. This biological basis for the self-transcendence of the caring for another then expands with the emergence of the capacity for parental feeling with reptiles, and then with the capacity for sociability, emotionality, and finally for reasoning that emerges by developmental stages among mammals.

The validity of Darwin's first theory has been massively established by research. But so has the second theory if one takes it seriously and knows where to look—for example, in the sciences of the *human* as well as the prehuman; that is, in social, systems, and brain science as well as biology (Loye, 1998a,b). Most importantly, the two theories together seem to form the completed theory of evolution that Darwin originally visualized as a whole, then severed into the half that became the famous initial statement in his *Origin of Species* and the muffled and indeed even mangled later half long ignored in *The Descent of Man* (Loye, 1998a). Of the greatly amplified aspects of this completed theory, the most important for our purpose here is the role of the *active* (rather than solely reactive) human brain. This is most strikingly exemplified by the vast expansion at the human level of frontal lobe functioning, in which capacities for visualizing and interconnecting future, past, and present, for moral sensitivity, and for decision and action are interlinked.[3]

Unique to the human, along with advanced limbic system capacity, this is the higher brain substratum for the concept of the human as an active moral agent in evolution that is central to evolutionary action theory. *From this physiological fact flows this theory's central rationale:*

IF the human is, as has been massively established, the most advanced general-purpose organism on this Earth.

And if, drawing upon its incredibly advanced mental capacities, this organism is able to visualize, select, and move toward a more moral as well as a more generally favorable future situation.

And if, over the few million years of its development, this organism has managed to create such an advanced level of culture and technology as to have a major impact not only on the evolution of itself but also on the survival of all life on this planet...

THEN there is obviously a direction to evolution beyond mere complexity.
There is the direction that the human, as the culmination of earlier trends, interjects into evolutionary process.

However difficult this may be to visualize or accept within the constraints of the prevailing paradigm, the rediscovery and reconstruction of late Darwinian theory noted earlier further indicates a moral directionality to evolution, emergent at earlier levels, but exemplified at the level of evolution for our species by the human as active and responsible agent for the multibillion year thrust of life on this planet.

If this is true, then a statement of a completed Darwinian theory from the action perspective of this active and responsible moral agent becomes a requirement for both human fulfillment and quite possibly, more generally, for planetary life survival.

2.2. *The Perspective of the Active Agent*

Though long ignored by most formal evolutionary theorists, the requirement for the perspective of the active moral agent has long been perceived by other theorists. Aristotle pointed out the difference between *theoria*, his term for the description of what exists, and *praxis*, the use of this knowledge in an active intervention to change what exists in morally responsible directions. The term "praxis" has since been amplified by action theorists of the Marxist and Frankfurt schools (Jay, 1973) as well as by Piaget (1976) in psychology.

Technically, the basic difference for an *action* theory of anything, including evolution, is this. In social scientific research we talk of everything involved in any situation or process in terms of variables—as, for example, race, gender, and class in sociology, or IQ, ego-strength, or extraversion–introversion in psychology. The interaction of the variability of such variables is known as the variance. Thus, we refer to the degree of our knowledge of what is going on in some situation in terms of the degree to which the variables we focus on seem to explain what is happening, or the degree to which they seem to "account for the variance."[4]

Comparable approaches for factor analysis in statistics focus on the components of the primary factor (Harman, 1967), or in chaos theory, on the components of an attractor (Abraham and Shaw, 1983).

Traditional or prevailing social theory tries to account for a reasonable whole of both the variables involved and their variance, and hence can become so prolix and weighty that lifetimes can be consumed merely in trying to master, refine, or argue about it—for example, the social theories of Weber, Pareto, or, in particular, Parsons (Parsons *et al.*, 1961). As with use of the concept of the static, periodic, or strange attractor to bring complex processes into focus in chaos theory, action theory focuses on that portion of the variance that may affect desirable or un-desirable outcomes in specific targeted areas hence it can be mastered relatively quickly—*and put to use.*

In psychology, the action-research approach coupled with the field theory of Kurt Lewin (1948, 1951; Loye, 1971) remains the most advanced statement of the perspective of action-oriented theory. In evolutionary theory, general evolution theorist Ervin Laszlo (1994, 1996) is the pioneering exponent of this perspective.

2.3. *The Nature of the Human Impact on Evolution*

2.3.1. *Direction in general development.* The idea of direction in evolution is one of the most difficult conceptual departures for this theory. Historically, the difficulty is that evolution theory itself evolved out of an attempt to free science from the shackles of religions committed to the idea of a moral direction for personal and historical development under the guidance of a God. Technically, one difficulty for science is the enormous investment by scientists over the past hundred years in demonstrating the unquestionable operation of random, or nondirectional, pro-cesses at work in cosmic as well as biological evolution. This has led to a relatively rigid belief among neo-Darwinians and others in nondirectionality. Within sys-tems science and general evolution theory, however, there has been steady, albeit tentative and nonconsensual, movement toward the recognition of more and more directionality.[5]

The time has come to transcend the prevailing comfort level for science and face the message of an expanding data base rather than continue to be intimidated by an outmoded paradigm. With the shift from a prehuman data base to the per-spective of the active human agent, it becomes clear that we must go beyond the tentative to drive for consensus, for now the concept of direction in evolution becomes central. It is becoming obvious, for example, that the human agent—for better, as in the case of education, or for worse, as in the case of environmental degradation—interjects *direction* into evolutionary process.

An image that captures the relationship is that of driver and vehicle. Prehuman evolution is the immense and wondrously powerful vehicle. But now, much like a teenager in his or her first attempts to learn how to drive, the human agent has become the multioptional designated driver.

Hundreds, if not by now thousands, of psychological studies have established the fact of this directional thrust for evolution at the human or ontogenetic level. For example, the research and psychotherapies of Erikson (1964), Rogers (1951), and many others show a development along many indicators of growth from immaturity to maturity. Maslow's (1968) work reveals the trend for motivational development from defense, to growth, to meta-motivations. Dabrowski (1964) and many others show the trend over the human lifetime for development from "inauthenticity" to "authenticity" as well as from egocentricity and ethnocentricity toward concern for others.

On the phylogenetic level, or within the larger framework of the species, one of the foremost architects of neo-Darwinian theory, biologist Julian Huxley, in an all-too-easily-forgotten effort to expand the minds and paradigm for his neo-Darwinian colleagues, set forth the crucial difference in this way (Huxley, 1964, p. 34): "Though natural selection is an ordering principle, it operates blindly." It "pushes life onwards from behind." It "brings about improvement automatically, without conscious purpose or any awareness of an aim" at the *pre*human level. But counterposed to natural selection at the human level is "*psychosocial* selection," which also "acts as an ordering principle. But it pulls [us] onwards from in front. For it always involves some awareness of an aim, some element of true purpose." In psychosocial evolution "the selective mechanism itself evolves as well as its products. It is a goal-selecting mechanism, and the goals that it selects will change with the picture of the world and of human nature provided by [our] increasing knowledge."

In other words, however many conceptual obstacles have been put in the path of such "heretical" thinking, an expanded understanding of directionality in evolution seems no longer merely a justifiably tentative speculation, but clearly a *fact* that must be incorporated into an adequate, or completed, evolutionary theory.

2.3.2. *Direction in moral development.* Beyond the above more general trends, a second concept that must be incorporated in an adequate, or completed, theory of evolution is the directional thrust for moral development in humans. Many can accept the idea that human agency can interject direction into evolution, but only as long as this direction is seen as wholly arbitrary, or as a patternless wavering between progression, retrogression, or stasis. But the idea that we may be biased in a prohuman or moral direction bogs down in the semantic pit of a de-moralized culture, in which the connotation for the word "morality" is negatively of right-wing or "old-fashioned" moralism and moralizing, rather than of a positive and indeed essential capacity for self- and societal anchoring and guidance.

Again, however, a large body of studies over a century now reveals certain recurring developmental patterns that confirm Darwin's "new" insights in this regard (Loye, 1998a,b). A general pattern for the studies of Baldwin (1906), Piaget (1965), and Kohlberg (1984), for example, is of movement from selfishness toward altruism. The studies of Gilligan (1982) reveal movement from gender stereo-typing toward gender balancing affecting moral development. Studies by Rokeach

(1973), Loye (1971, 1998b), and many others reveal morally relevant historical, political, and cultural evolutionary trends toward the valuing of freedom and equality out of earlier states of slavery and inequality.

3. Primary Components and the Dialectical Core

Throughout the development of evolution theory there have been many alternatives to what has become fixed in mind as the Darwinian heritage (Salthe, 1993). The approach for evolutionary action theory is to stick with the established Darwinian base for biological evolution, in which there has been a huge and impressive investment. But then—in keeping with the principles of systems science (e.g., Miller, 1978) and general evolution theory (Laszlo, 1996), which look for isomorphy of basic concepts across levels and fields—the approach is to link the human to the prehuman data base and find analogues for key processes for biological evolution at the cultural evolution level.

There is much evidence—including the long-ignored observations of Darwin himself[6]—of the operation of processes other than natural selection and random variation at work on the human level. A logical first step toward joining what appear to be the two halves to Darwin's theory, however, is to look for analogues or isomorphs for what is by now well-established at the first-half or neo-Darwinian level. What then are analogues or isomorphs for natural selection and mutation?

The need for such an analogue has long been recognized. An early flurry in this direction involved psychologists Lloyd Morgan and J.M. Baldwin with the concept of *organic selection* at the end of the 19th and beginning of the 20th century (Richards, 1987; Loye, 1998a). More recently, as earlier noted, Julian Huxley called for the development of the higher-level counterpart process of *psychosocial selection*. Also noteworthy is Campbell's (1960) probe of human-level analogues with the ideas of *blind variation* and *selective retention*. While recognizing the need and pointing the way, in terms of the systems science of today these earlier formulations fell short of what is needed. An important step forward is the new formulation of *replicative selection* of Csanyi (1989, 1993) and Kampis (1993).

This area is both further complicated and at the same time potentially radically simplified by the concept of *organic choice* that I have identified within my reconstruction of late Darwinian theory (Loye, 1998a). That is, *within the context of looking for principles other than natural selection to account for evolution at the human level*, eleven times Darwin identifies a specific dialectical mechanism of the above nature without naming it. Finding a continuity for essentially the same perception ranging from the evolutionary science of the ancient Chinese embodied in *I Ching* through Marx and Engels as well as Darwin into modern cybernetic, chaos, and self-organizing process theory (e.g. Prigogine and Stengers, 1984; Kauffman 1995), for a Darwinian *completion* of theory I have suggested the name *organic choice*.

Within the context of our search for "higher-level" analogues for natural selection and random variation, this concept of the dialectical drive of organic choice may then be visualized as involving two kinds of process. The analogue for natural selection in this formulation of basic concepts and principles for evolutionary action theory might logically be called *cultural selection*.

What then is the analogue for the generation of variability by mutation? Here the seemingly inescapable answer, also to be developed shortly, is the multifaceted force psychology has extensively probed as *creativity*. Two more basic concepts then complete the picture for a dialectical core in keeping with insights ranging, as I have indicated, from ancient Chinese thinking into Aristotle, Hegel, Marx and Engels, to modern systems science and Lewin and Piaget in psychology: *creative transcendence* and *creative transformation* (see Loye, 1998a).

3.1. *Cultural Selection*

It is easy enough to substitute the phrase "cultural selection" for "natural selection," but what does this mean in operational terms? What is the analogue at the Darwinian second-half or human cultural level for the operation of the environmental factors that, according to biological theory, select one variation or species while rejecting another?

A strange and in fact societally dangerous situation presently exists in social theory in that between all the fields of social science and the field of evolutionary theory there is in effect a wide gulf (Loye, 1998a). That is, few social theorists feel compelled to relate their thinking to the requirements for an adequate theory of evolution. Yet within social science a number of concepts bear on an answer to the question of what cultural selection is and how it operates. Particularly original is the analysis of cultural evolution theorist Riane Eisler, whose thinking in this volume and elsewhere (1987, 1995) in many regards parallels or amplifies the following analysis. Most closely approximating what I find is needed is the hard-edged and ubiquitous concept of *paradigm* made well known by philosopher Thomas Kuhn (1970) and recently importantly refined by physicist Fritjof Capra (1996) for social theory.

Though some decry the word as overused—and it is—it is precisely because of wide familiarity with the concept that it can be useful in exploring what to many, other than sociologists and political scientists, might otherwise seem strange and uncomfortable territory. In this paper the concept is being expanded as well as narrowed to incorporate it into evolutionary action theory. A definition of the term as used here would be that paradigms are, in effect, "walled" territories within the mind somewhat akin to the fiefdoms of the Middle Ages—that is, territories each with a specific ruler or rulers, walled and gated, involved in expanding or defensive phases.

Multilayered, continually nudging against one another in our minds, these territories of paradigm not only command our allegiance but also govern much of what we think, feel, and do. Cultural selection is, then, the process through which and by which paradigms form, expand, are attacked, defended, and either continue to expand or are peripheralized or annihilated.[7]

3.1.1. *Paradigm formation.* How does a paradigm form? Though there can be other causes, the classic study is sociologist Max Weber's of the rise and operation of *charisma*.[8] Something about an individual or idea takes hold, gaining fervent adherents, as with the case of Jesus and the rise of Christianity.

3.1.2. *Paradigm expansion.* How does a paradigm grow? Again this happens in many ways, with Weber again outlining the classic wisdom. To the concept of charisma he adds the concept of the *routinizing of the charisma*. The diffuse basic creativity of Jesus gives way to the organizing and promotional genius of St. Paul and the subsequent growth of an enormous bureaucracy that by the Middle Ages rules most of the Western world. The same relation of charisma to its routinizing can also be seen, for example, in the relation of Thomas Edison and Albert Einstein to present-day huge electrical and nuclear power industries.

3.1.3. *Paradigm defense.* Paradigm defense is a process that in varying levels and bits and pieces has been identified by many sociologists, political scientists, and psychologists. But nowhere yet that I know of has the attempt been made to provide the synthesis that could make its power fully comprehensible.[9] It is easiest to comprehend through the similarity of its functioning on the social level to the operation of the famous "defenses" that Freud (1960) theorized we use to protect ourselves against whatever we may perceive as a threat to ourselves or to our basic personality structure.

Repression, projection, fixation, regression, and reaction formation (or the use of "love" to mask hate): these are the psychological defenses we use, according to Freud. On the social level a somewhat different set seems to operate, but two primary characteristics that Freud identified seem to apply at both the level of the individual and the level of society. One is the function of the defenses to deny or falsify reality. The other characteristic is that these defenses operate unconsciously, so that we are not aware of their action or distortion of reality.

3.1.4. *Paradigm formation, expansion, and defense in dominator (or authoritarian) versus partnership (or humanistic, democratic) systems.* A major reason these processes of cultural selection have been so underexplored and arbitrarily identified is because of their confounding by the operation within all of us of "dominator-hybrid mind," or the battle within ourselves as well as our societies of the authoritarian versus democratic, or dominator versus partnership ethos (Loye, 1996, 1998b). To see clearly what is going on here we must be able to abstract the polarity of these models out of the confusion or hybridization of their intermixture in our minds, for paradigm formation, expansion, and defense vary radically according to whether we are dealing with authoritarian or dominator, or humanistic or partnership systems.[10] Specifics will be explored in Sections 4, 5, and 6, after we complete a consideration of the basic components and dialectical core for evolutionary action theory.

3.2. Creativity

Thus far, we have visualized cultural selection as the action of paradigm formation, expansion, and defense at the human level as an analogue for the operation of natural selection in biological evolution. Now let us turn to the other vital partner to this process: the generation of the astounding smorgasbord of variability out of which will be selected the comparatively few ingredients for the meal of evolution for existent paradigms.

It seems overwhelmingly evident that at the human cultural level this function is filled by human creativity in all its forms. Out of the ferment of hundreds of cults before and during Jesus's time, taking a bit from here, another bit from there, emerges the paradigm of Christianity. Out of the proliferation of options for looks, for number of wheels, for devices for starting up and stopping, for fuels ranging from steam and electricity to kerosene and gasoline, emerges the automobile of the 20th century.

Alfonso Montuori captures the relation of this surge of creativity to both generative and paradigm relational dynamics in Chapter 7 of this volume. "The evolutionary process of self-transcendence is fueled by the ongoing dialectic of complexity–simplicity–complexity that is the hallmark of creative problem formation and problem resolution," he writes. "Creative persons create order in disorder and disorder in order: in Kuhnian terms, they look for the anomalies on the edges of the existing paradigm in order to build a new one."

Though the force of creativity as the basic driver for cultural evolution has been shown in hundreds of ways in primarily psychological studies, or in the chaos-theoretical perspective as above, the battle to inject this perspective into evolutionary theory has been uphill all the way. Bergson's *Creative Evolution* (1944) was written off as only philosophy. More recently, Csanyi and Kampis, with the involvement of creativity in replicative selection, in addition to Salthe (1993) and Ho and Saunders (1979) earlier, have forcefully grounded the thrust of creativity within the biology of evolutionary theory.[11] In formulating evolutionary action theory, however, I find it most productive to visualize the action of creativity in terms of concepts more commonly associated in psychology with studies of motivation than of creativity. From this perspective, creativity, as the general evolution theoretical analogue for mutation, seems to involve the factors of:

1. *Urge*—or what impels all life to live, which in turn means to act, to do. This is the *Élan Vital* of Bergson (1944), Eros for Freud (1989), the needs, drives, expectancies, values, ideologies, valences, vectors, constraints, and fields for motivational theory in psychology (see Atkinson, 1964).

2. *Resources*—the basic materials, givens, the wherewithal for the urge to work with. An animal cannot exist, for example, without oxygen to breathe. This is the fundamental problem within evolutionary theory bearing on the question of the origin of form that Laszlo (1995, 1996) is pioneering with his concept of a Quantum-Vacuum Interactive or QVI-field.

3. *Form*—what the urge is to shape out of the available resources. In psychology form is studied as the factor of habit, habit structure, or most extensively in my own work (1977) as norms. In sociology this becomes the study of institutions. Within evolutionary theory, as earlier indicated, this is the focus of Csanyi's study of replication processes.

4. *Goal*—the end destination. Once a specific urge, resources, and form coexist, constituting a forceful gestalt, there rises out of this process, either amorphously or quite specific, the end goal (James, 1890/1950; Miller, Gallanter, and Pribram, 1960).

5. *Will*—the shove to which we are impelled by the active nature of the brain to go beyond urge, resources, form, and goal to actually *act* to bring about what has been set in motion within us (Assagioli, 1973; Pribram, 1971).

3.3. *Creative Transcendence*

First we have *creativity* and the generation of diversity. Then we have *cultural selection* acting through paradigm formation, expansion, and defense as in effect the impresario or editor of this diversity. Now we can begin to visualize the dialectical relationship that lies at the core of the process of *creative transcendence*.

In other words, on one hand there is this vast spewing forth of possibility. On the other hand is this sometimes apt and just, but more generally drastic and even brutal cutting and rearranging of possibility to fit what are perceived to be the requirements of what can or should exist. Underlying this process, what most centrally has been set in motion, for better or worse, is a change, a going beyond, a moving forward from, or the *creative transcendence* of what presently exists.

In evolutionary theory, Eisler (1991) explores this process in terms of the co-creativity of the human interaction with technology. In psychology, in Kurt Lewin's (1951) famous three-stage formulation of change processes, this is the phase embracing the first two stages: the "unfreezing" of what presently exists, and the "movement to new levels."

3.4. *Creative Transformation*

What we have covered so far is, unfortunately, all that the impulse, plans, and theories of most activists cover (e.g., Alinsky, 1971; Millet, 1970). For example, consider the problems of racism and sexism in America or environmental degradation worldwide. In each case, massive attention is focused on the present situation of some undesirable social or personal state that is fixed in place, which is then to be "unfreezed" through media exposure and more general "consciousness raising." There is further recognition that much energy must go into the pressuring of legislatures and all other types of the "powers that be" to effect movement to new levels of awareness and ultimately behavior. But what again and again is overlooked is the tremendous force of what is variously identified as backlash to this movement, as regression, or as just social inertia in its myriad forms (see Eisler, 1978, 1995; Faludi, 1991).

There is the sad wisdom captured by the myth of Prometheus, in which the heart of this archetype for the creative hero is daily torn out by an eagle, or in the myth of Sisyphus, who must endlessly push the stone, which rolls back down overnight, once again daily back up the hill.

In the larger picture of the impact of the active human agent on evolution, creative transcendence is only a way-station that may or may not lead anywhere. It is the tunnel with many dead-ending branches through which we must pass toward the achievement of the firm implanting, grounding, and consolidation of the fruit of struggle that constitutes *creative transformation*.[12]

For Lewin in psychological theory, this is the stage of "refreezing" at whatever new level has, through unfreezing and movement, been tenuously gained. For Prigogine's (1984) dissipative structures view, this is the new "nucleation." For both social theory and now general evolution (Laszlo, 1996) and evolutionary action theory, this is the establishment of the new paradigm.

3.5. *The Nature of Moral Action in Basic Operations and at all Levels*

The completion of Darwinian theory through the revival and expansion of its moral component (Loye, 1994, 1998a) now makes possible a comprehensive visualizing of this aspect of the action of the human agent on evolution.

In *creativity*, as visualized in evolutionary action theory, moral sensitivity enters the process at the *urge* level through biological evolution (the emergence of sex, etc.) as visualized by Darwin and confirmed by modern brain research. It enters again at the *resource* level through the nature of our social milieu (type of family, school, church, peer group, etc.). It enters again at the *form* level through moral and ethical codes (set forth in contexts ranging from religions to businesses to street gangs). It enters again at the *goal* level through the statement of moral models and ideals (set forth in the same range of contexts). And finally, once again, moral sensitivity enters at the level of *will* in moral action (both consciously and unconsciously impelled).

In *cultural selection*, the force of moral sensitivity, and of the pressure to evolve and codify moralities, can be seen throughout the formation, expansion, and defense of all paradigms. This force of the "ought to be" versus "what is" surfaces most dramatically in the avowal of a moral face to whatever is to be done— however reprehensible or heinous it is in actuality. We easily forget, but it is important to remember that, even with the paradigm of the thousand-year Reich for Hitler, the avowed evolutionary purpose was the Nietzschian morality: to create a race of supermen out of supposedly the dregs of the present.

More positively, the force of moral sensitivity and coding can be seen as central to the paradigm formation, expansion, and defense of democracy, feminism, humanism, civil rights, animal rights, environmentalism, the peace movement, etc.

Throughout the processes of *creative transcendence* and *creative transformation* —as Sections 4, 5, and 6 touch on—higher-level complexities of the conflict of moral sensitivity with insensitivity and of morality with immorality and amorality can be similarly tracked.

4. Focus on the Human Agent, not Abstractions

A continuing wonderment is how evolutionary theory—keying either to non-individualized biological organisms at the prehuman level, or to systems scientific configurations (e.g., those of chaos theory) at the transhuman level—so often deals with abstractions that, in a sense, shoot right past the human being without seeing what is there.

It is of the greatest urgency that we get out of our books and references and heads in order to see clearly that both evolution and revolution at the level of cultural evolution take place not in the form of the abstractions of biological or natural science. They take place most fundamentally in the form of the *realities* of individual human beings in their tremendous variability, or at the level of psychology that is easy for most of us to see. But even more powerfully, cultural evolution takes place in terms of the areas parceled out among social sciences that unfortunately command an understanding still limited to only a tiny fraction of the global population, namely, sociology, anthropology, political science, economics, and history.

It is at this self-transcendent level that the abstractions take on living flesh and blood and aspirations, first in terms of the following kinds of *commonalities* among humans of certain roles, ideologies, mind-sets, and political, economic, and spiritual or religious allegiances, and secondly, in terms of the following kinds of central conflicts of, and cooperations among, these allegiances.

4.1. *Activists versus Gatekeepers*

The central dynamics for evolutionary action theory, for example, involve, are built upon observations of, and posit the roles, ideologies, etc., of *activists*, representing the surge of creativity, and *gatekeepers*, acting as the agents of selection for prevailing paradigms, thus differentially encouraging or, contrarily, excluding and repressing creativity.

These roles and identities emerge in answer to the requirements of the conflict model prevailing in the work or life settings of dominator social systems (see Section 5).

4.2. *Creators and Selectors*

In sharp contrast are the role-pairs for the very different situation that is—because our minds presently fit things mainly into the above conflict model—far more prevalent than one would assume. This is the role-pair relationship of *creators* working in cooperation with *selectors*. That is, in this situation both parties are driven by humanistic urges, both draw on humanistic availabilities, both key to humanistic forms, and both are again driven by humanistic will. So embraced and motivated by the same ethos, they tend to collaborate more often than conflict in the movement toward humanistic goals.[13]

These roles emerge in answer to the requirements of both the cooperative models and the kind of competitive models that prevail in the work or life settings of partnership social systems (see Section 5.2 in terms of Eisler's work, as well as Eisler's chapter in this volume for a detailed analysis in terms of her new articulation of relational dynamics).

4.3. *Changers and Maintainers*

A third pair of roles and more fundamental alignments for evolutionary action theory is that of norm changers and norm maintainers, or *changers* and *maintainers*. As a general rule, changers tend to be liberal and maintainers conservative, but these customary ideological alignments can be overridden by factors of history, situation, and/or strategy.

Because of space restraints, I can only indicate here that this is a fundamental aspect of evolutionary action theory under development for articulation elsewhere.[14]

5. The Human Need for and Requirement of the Open-Ended Story: The Case for the Story of Evolution as Our Story, the Human Agent as Protagonist, and the Paths of Domination versus Partnership

For thousands of years, religions and the "humanities" have furnished human beings with stories in which they are given significant roles to play, plots to go by, scripts to follow, and goals or ends to attain. Very significant within this context is the fact that all this is often summed up at the end, or implicit, in the form of what is known as the "moral" to the story.

Rather than recognizing the story as not just a need but in fact a basic requirement for the adequate functioning of our species, science in general has cast out story as being nothing more than mere entertainment. It further writes off as mere superstition whatever surfaces when, in an attempt to make sense of the dimension of the spiritual, the story goes into this area that to billions of humans continues to be deeply meaningful. Thus robbed of story as a method of grounding ourselves on a large scale in space and time and all else that matters, we flounder, ready victims for either the Hitlers, with their fantasies of the thousand-year Reich, or the rightist purveyors of the worst of the old stories that science originally set out to destroy.

In the story of evolution itself, many believe that science can now provide our species with the new grand-scale story that is required for us to regain the old, lost sense of meaningfulness and purpose (e.g., Laszlo, 1996; Swimme and Berry, 1992; Chaisson, 1981; Pagels, 1982; Eisler, 1987, 1995; Loye, 1998a,b). The development of general evolution theory by Laszlo and the members of the General Evolution Research Group and other theorists is an extremely important step in this direction (see the brief history in Part 1 of this volume). But although at times this story is brilliantly rendered by many gifted scientists and writers, in its flash of cosmic explosions, glimpse of dinosaurs grappling with one another, and vast graveyard of fossils, it tends to seem uncomfortably like a Disneyland attraction for the pseudo-intellectual. It tends to be portrayed as this joyride compressing billions of years into a few seconds in which at the end our species—which by now, given the prevailing scientific paradigm, has only a tenuous sense of any connection to or responsibility for the whole—is asked to at last waken from its trance and resonate to the cause of ecology.

Within the context of the present profoundly de-natured and de-moralized story of evolution based on only half a theory of evolution, what is lacking is a sense of the human as active agent—of the ideals that drive, and of the roles for, this agent to play; of the gift and responsibility of choice of direction; of alliances to form, of conflictful alternatives; of the human as a self-organizing creature of moral direction, through choice giving direction to the thrust of evolution as a whole; of the past as something more than dead weight, and of the future as something more than mist; of the human as activist, as protagonist, as heroine or hero in the adventure of this vast open-ended story evolving through our shared journey through space and time.

In short, what is lacking is a sense of the human as the highest evolutionary expression of the basic drive of the "new" Darwinian principle of organic choice (Loye, 1998a), and what, in operational specifics, evolutionary action theory seeks to provide.

5.1. The Hidden Story of Our Evolution

As with so much else in our lives, in bits and scraps this story—*our* story—has long been before us. In part we haven't seen or felt its full dimensions because, as with a child only at an early stage for education, our minds are not yet ready.

So far all we have been able to do is to scratch the incredibly fascinating surface of what physics, biology, paleontology, and the rest of the natural or prehuman sciences have been able to tell us. As for all that beyond this is revealed in rich and compelling detail by sociology, history, psychology, anthropology, political science, and economics, *with only the rare exception this core learning for social scientific knowledge has yet to be put within the context of evolution or evolutionary theory.*

Thus at the core of all these social sciences lies the recurring story of the aspiration toward freedom and equality, of the interaction of the dominated who desire freedom and equality with the dominators who deny it, of the struggle over thousands of years now of the dominated to throw off the yoke of domination. There lies this story, again and again the same, that we are again and again to encounter in our lives conceptualized in terms of class conflict, authoritarianism versus humanism, tyranny versus democracy, slavery versus freedom, male versus female, white versus black, etc. There is this same story that generation after generation is told by Jesus, by Voltaire, Kant, Mary Wollstonecraft, Marx and Engels, John Stuart Mill, Elizabeth Cady Stanton, W.E.B. DuBois, Marija Gimbutas, Ruth Benedict, Erich Fromm, the Adorno–Frankfurt School–Berkeley group, Gunnar Myrdal, Kurt Lewin, etc., etc., etc.

Sidelined into the subspecialties of sociology and political science and thereby radically diminished in range of meaning, this is the story centrally bearing on human evolution to which Darwin—profoundly antislavery, profoundly the humanist—resonated powerfully; but then was cut in half intellectually by his own pioneering (Loye, 1998a,b). That is, we can now see how the success of the Darwin of *The Origin of Species* not only obscured, but also helped bury the pivotal significance of the Darwin of *The Descent of Man*.

This is the story, first reasonably captured by Eisler's cultural transformation theory, that must now be incorporated into both general evolution theory and evolutionary action theory.

5.2. *A Hidden Framework for Evolution*

As I develop at length elsewhere (1998a,b), if we take the completed Darwinian theory (that is, first half plus second half) and add to it the vast new data base bearing on our cultural evolution emerging from a number of fields today, a new large-scale framework or storyline for evolution emerges.

The first half of the story, requiring only the addition of the moral perspective to our long-established understanding of biological evolution, should gradually find acceptance within a sufficient number of scientists to tip the scales in its favor. It is of the emergence of ours as a species uniquely equipped by brain and by the higher mammalian body with simian dexterity to build a self-creating, renewing, and expanding culture that at stress points—many of which the "new" Darwin identifies—drives us to face moral choice, and hence is either positively or negatively moral directional.

For the second half of the story, however, as it must face the still overwhelming bias in both science and society against anything associated with feminism or the women's movement, acceptance will only come after an even more difficult struggle. Supported by a truly huge data base still rigorously being excluded,[15] the picture is of what happened with the shift from the primacy of biological evolution to the primacy of cultural evolution for our species. The picture is of the evolution of a first global culture for humanity of remarkably peaceful, highly creative, Goddess-worshipping societies pivotally grounded in a balancing and harmonizing of forces ultimately deriving from a basic equality of female and male. This earlier culture was then displaced by a violent, conflict-ridden, male-dominant and male-God-worshipping culture featuring rule of the many by the single tyrant, and later, the exploiting elites—thus setting the stage for the basic drama for our species of the past 5,000 years.

Based on hundreds of indicators both then and now, the theoretical framework that Eisler (1987, 1995) poses in her articulation of cultural transformation theory is that of an earlier shift from partnership toward domination now being mirrored in our time by another shift, but this time out of domination toward partnership.

6. The Dynamics of the Human Impact on Evolution

It is important to note that the validity of the evolutionary action theory being formulated here does not depend on whether or not one has read or resonates to Eisler's work. As I have indicated, over at least 2,000 years now, and certainly over the past 200 years of scholarship in many fields, *over and over again it is essentially the same story.* Archeologically, it is the story told in its various parts by Evans, Platon, Mellaart, Gimbutas, the Allchins, Hawkes, Childe, Mallory, and on and on. Sociologically, it is the basic story not only told by Marx and Engels, but that also may be glimpsed in Durkheim, Pareto, and Weber. Anthropologically, it is the story told by Ruth Benedict, with glimpses in Mead, Montagu, and Malinowski. It is further the story told by Erich Fromm, by the forgotten economic historian Alexander Rustow, and by many other male scholars long before the rise of the feminist scholarship of our time.[16]

As I document elsewhere (1998b), the reason we have been continually diverted away from seeing the primacy and deep evolutionary significance of this hidden story is its threat to the prevailing cultural paradigm. That is, as this story fundamentally threatens the prevailing structure for all systems of domination (governmental, economic, religious, educational, etc.), generation after generation the body of insight it has engendered has been relentlessly erased or degraded through the working of paradigm defense.

How does paradigm defense on such an immense scale work? Though the answer can only be briefly sketched here (see Section 6.2.1), identifying this implacable and abiding source of resistance to evolutionary change makes it possible to get a good grasp of the central dynamics for evolutionary action theory.

6.1. *Creativity in the Dominator and the Partnership Mode*

A grounding fact for the operation of creativity in the evolution of our species is that practically everything we consider evidence of our cultural evolution originated before the shift to a prevailing dominator ethos and paradigm, during the earlier Paleolithic and Neolithic partnership culture.

In much the same way, and for the same reasons of paradigm defense, that Darwin's theories of moral agency and a human-level completion for his theory of evolution were buried for over 100 years, this information also has been buried—and in this instance for over 3,000 years. But the fact is that music, art, language both spoken and written, religion, business, education, agriculture, technology in its basic or initiating forms, architecture, city planning, plumbing, all originated during the earlier time. In general, except for the development of advanced weapons and methods of warfare original to the dominator culture that replaced the earlier culture, practically everything else since then essentially has been the elaboration of what was set in motion earlier.

This is not to say—which would be patently absurd—that there has been no basic creativity since then over the span of all we know as recorded history. It is simply to note that what developed thereafter is the complex picture of creativity persisting upward in humanistic directions *against opposition*, creativity diverted into antihuman (e.g., militaristic) ends, and creativity stultified or blocked for the long periods we know as the "dark ages" or the more brief but devastating regressions of modern times—in other words, the familiar patterning for what we know today as recorded history.

Despite the difference in outcomes, it is evident that in the dominator and the partnership modes the creative drive is essentially the same, for aside from the degree to which we are advanced or warped by culture we humans are essentially the same. That is, the same combination of urge, resources, form, goal, will, and all other drives affecting creativity is at work generating the diversity that is the general evolutionary analogue for mutation in biological evolution. *The critical difference—which profoundly affects both the pace and the direction of the evolution of our species—is in the degree to which one or the other of the following two kinds of basic role-type predominates in social situations, and in what is allowed by the following two radically different kinds of cultural selection to filter through.*

6.1.2 *Nurturers versus predators.* With the differentiation of creativity into differences according to whether we are looking at the impact of the partnership or the dominator model, another pair of roles becomes evident. In the partnership mode, we find—for example, in the relation of the good agent to the actor or writer, or the good business leader to employees—that much depends on the prevalence and skills of the *nurturers*, or those who serve through encouragement and other ways to nurture creativity. Typically, in the dominator ethos the foundation of nurturance is considered solely feminine, whereas the physiological actuality is of a human function to which males as well as females resonate. In contrast to this gender-transcendent valuing of the nurturer, in the dominator mode one finds a prevalence of those who recognize their primary function as being to maximally exploit the creativity of others, or the *predators*.[17]

6.2. *Cultural Selection in the Dominator Mode*

In the dominator mode—ranging from the family, school, or work setting to the organization of a region or nation—the creativity–cultural selection relationship primarily operates according to the role relationships of *activist* and *gatekeeper*.

Those with new ideas soon come to know that they must fight for these ideas against varying degrees of opposition, and hence are here designated as "activists." Opposing them are those who find prestige, power, and what seems to be some degree of security in becoming the gatekeepers. In every field and at all levels of society, under a variety of names, as originally visualized by Kuhn solely within the scientific context but in fact socially ubiquitous, these gatekeepers serve to protect the prevailing wisdom from change.

At the same time, the activist is up against the more subtle machinations of the predator, who serves to also disarm the threat of change.[18] The tactic used here— as articulated in Machiavelli's study of the tactics of the predator in dominator systems *The Prince* (1997), and in contemporary detail by Eisler elsewhere in this volume—is to seem to welcome the new idea only to co-opt, or take it over, in a way that not only benefits the predator personally but also presents the appearance of change while in fact maintaining the status quo.

6.2.1. *Paradigm defense in the dominator mode.* Though paradigm formation and expansion also differ in the dominator mode, I will focus here solely on dominator paradigm defense, as much indicates that this is the chief obstacle in the evolution of our species toward fulfillment of its potential.

A first line of defense is the exclusion of whatever seems to threaten dominator systems' stability. Thus, wherever the Gatekeepers have the deciding power, articles or books advocating equality for women or blacks are excluded from publication or review, or facilities are denied to groups advocating environmental protection or nuclear disarmament. Or, as I develop elsewhere (1998a,b), advances are blocked in such a key area for science as evolutionary theory.

If this fails, the gatekeepers fall back to suppression using threats as a second line of defense. Subordinates who express what might be classified as progressive ideas, for example—or who are seen as representing any other kind of threat to the structure in which a gatekeeper clings to power—are denied advancement or relocated.

If this fails, the gatekeepers fall back to annihilation of the threat as the third line of defense. Here we find the use of methods ranging from the character assassination increasingly popular in politics, to the destruction of threatening governmental departments or activities through legislation to end funding, to the actual hiring of the paid killer at the extreme.

This list barely scratches the surface for the devices, tactics, and strategies for dominator paradigm defense, but is enough to indicate a thrust serving to slow down and at times even—as with the Nazis—reverse the direction for human evolution.

6.3. *Cultural Selection in the Partnership Mode*

In sharp contrast, in the partnership mode—again ranging from the family, school, or work setting to the organization of a region or nation—the creativity–cultural selection relationship operates according to the role relationships of *creators*, *nurturers*, and *selectors*.

Those with the facility for creativity are identified as such and encouraged to generate new ideas by nurturers (with protypically the parent or teacher in this role). Thus these gifted people upon whom the human future depends—as is so essential, and at present is so often automatically discouraged—come to identify themselves and be identified by others as creators.

Next we come to those with a facility for helping to fit a new idea to the require- ments of social or personal needs, or for displaying good judgment in the selection of ideas out of many competing possibilities. These people, too seldom appreci- ated or even recognizing the importance of this capacity in themselves, come to identify themselves and be identified by others as selectors.

At all levels of society, then, under a variety of names, we can find these two role- pairs—nurturers and creators, and creators and selectors—working together to develop the triumphs of human advancement in every field.

This is not pie in the sky, but rather what even in the hard-nosed context of the business world by now hundreds of business consultants, writing hundreds of books of counsel, find operating.[19] The problem is that the efforts of creator– selector pairs and teams are not only offset, but with uncanny speed can be swept aside by predators working in tandem with the gatekeepers to keep paradigms and systems of domination in place, as in the case of the escalating corporate takeovers and makeovers of our time.

6.3.1. *Paradigm expansion in the partnership mode.* Though paradigm formation and defense also differ in the partnership mode, I will focus here solely on partner- ship paradigm expansion, as this seems to be the chief hope for the evolution of our species toward fulfillment of its potential.[20]

A first stage for partnership paradigm expansion can be found in the statement of beliefs by advocates of the partnership or humanistic way of life. Thereafter can come the respectful consideration of dominator alternatives, exposing the inad- equacies of dominator alternatives, rationalizing the positives of the partnership or humanistic way, sensitizing others to the advantages of this way—as well as displacement of dominators and dominator or predatory belief systems through a variety of other forceful but peaceful means. In other words, one moves to fill the intellectual, organizational, or geographical territory presently inhabited by dominators and dominator belief systems through persuasion, presentation of benefits to be gained from love and trust rather than hate and distrust, the use of humor and the generation of liberational excitement, the resolution of conflicts, the dispelling of confusion—in general, the replacement of bullying, terrorizing, murder, slaughter and subjugation with friendship, help over the hard places of life, and the benefits of a peaceful sharing of the gifts of life on this planet.

If this fails, one turns to other, more hard-edged tactics and strategies that the advocates for humanity—for example, fighters for this alignment ranging from George Washington and Abraham Lincoln to Elizabeth Cady Stanton and Golda Meier—have been forced to learn, and over the past 300 years to employ with increasing success.

These, of necessity briefly sketched, are the stakes, the nature of the territory, the goals, the tactics, the players, and what seem to be some of the rules of the game for a theory of evolution based on the perspective of the human as active agent in the shaping of our planetary destiny.

Notes

Regarding references in text and notes to my reconstruction of the long-ignored "second half" or "completion" for Darwin's theory of evolution, source documents for *Darwin's Lost Theory* and *The Glacier and the Flame* are Darwin's long-unpublished private notebooks (see Gruber and Barrett, *Darwin on Man*, Dutton, 1974) as well as *The Descent of Man*.

1. This is a condensation of points made by systems philosopher Ervin Laszlo in books such as *Evolution* and *The Choice*, by Riane Eisler in *The Chalice and the Blade* and *Sacred Pleasure*, and by myself in *Darwin's Lost Theory* and *The Glacier and the Flame*.

2. Complexity seems to be the one point upon which there is anything approaching a consensus. See Csanyi, 1989. See note 5, however.

3. See references for Pribram and Luria re frontal lobe futures and managerial sensitivities, MacLean re frontal lobe futures and moral sensitivities. See Loye, 1990, for a preliminary integration of these works into the concept of the Guidance System of Higher Mind.

4. A variety of concepts are used throughout science to convey the basic relationship here, e.g., that of field and subfield, universe and subset, system and subsystem, or population and sample of population, or the relation of attractors to the state space in chaos theory.

5. Jantsch in *The Self-Organizing Universe* and Eisler in *Sacred Pleasure*, for example, boldly "push the envelope" with multiple candidates for directionalty in evolution. Salthe (1993) further extensively documents the factor of directionality in non-Darwinian theory. But consensus among either systems scientists or general evolution theorists is as yet lacking on much beyond complexity. See *Sacred Pleasure*, pp. 36, 46, 49, 52, 162, and 176 for Eisler's case for direction toward greater variability, complexity of structure, integration of function, flexibility of behavior, and "higher consciousness." See Loye, 1998a, ch. 8 for my argument for a moral and multidirectionality in terms of statistics and chaos theory as well as "second half" Darwinian theory.

6. What is now astounding is how for over 100 years his successors have overlooked the fact that in *The Descent of Man*, Darwin admitted that in *Origin* "I probably attributed too much to the action of natural selection or survival of the fittest" (p. 152), indeed remarking of natural selection that he was probably "exaggerating its power" (p. 153). While this mechanism mainly holds for the prehuman level of species, now he tells us—foreshadowing the late-20th-century evolutionary theory focus on the principle of self-organizing processes embodied in Prigogine's autocatalysis, Maturana and Varela's autopoiesis, and Csanyi's autogenesis—that he will explore other processes that, among other things, "relate much

more closely to the constitution of the varying organism, than to the nature of the conditions to which it has been subjected" (p. 154). Then within two paragraphs of the end of the book—where it seems that surely this would have been inescapable—we find this: "Important as the struggle for existence has been, yet as far as the highest part of man's nature is concerned there are other agencies more important. For the moral qualities are advanced either directly or indirectly much more through the effects of habit, by our reasoning powers, by instruction, by religion, etc., than through natural selection" (pp. 403–404).

7. A particularly advanced discussion of the nature of paradigms can be found in Laszlo, Masulli, Artigiani, and Csanyi, *The Evolution of Cognitive Maps: New Paradigms for the Twenty-First Century*. Ralph Abraham, to whom I am indebted for many important suggestions during the writing of this chapter, notes that the concept of paradigm originated with Ludwik Fleck.

8. See Weber, "The Social Psychology of the World's Religions." See Bradley, *Charisma and Social Structure*, for an important updating in terms of modern communes and social activism.

9. Much work on the microtheoretical level has been carried out in psychology in the study of perceptual defense (see references for Beardslee and Wertheimer, *Readings in Perception*) and cognitive consistency, congruity, and dissonance theories of Heider, Newcomb, Osgood, and Festinger (see references for Osgood, *Cognitive Dynamics in the Conduct of Human Affairs*). However, one must wed this with the sociology of Durkheim and Marx and Engels, modern systems science, and much historical data in order to get at the size of what is involved here. My own attempt along these lines, *The Glacier and the Flame*, only scratches the surface of what is needed.

10. For the authoritarian–humanistic differentiation, see Adorno *et al.*, *The Authoritarian Personality* and references here for Erich Fromm and Abraham Maslow. For the dominator–partnership differentiation, see references by Eisler. For related differentiations in Marx and Engels, Pareto, and Nietzsche, see Loye, 1977.

11. General evolution theorists Vilmos Csanyi and Georgy Kampis identify two kinds of natural selection. One is the competitive "survival of the fittest" strain. The other is a cooperative "creative" or "replicative" thrust, allied to the Darwinian concept of mutual aid developed by Peter Kropotkin. This is worked out with considerable ingenuity in terms of Csanyi's probe of the evolutionary implications of the replication process and pioneering concept of replicative selection. See Csanyi, 1989; Csanyi and Kampis, "Modeling biological and social change: Dynamical replicative network theory"; and Kampis, 1993.

12. This is a central point for both the cultural transformation theory of Eisler and my own moral transformation theory. See Eisler, 1978, for an analysis of pragmatic considerations in the case of the attempt to pass the Equal Rights Amendment. See Roberts, *Transforming Public Policy*, for a summary of current action theory in this area and a detailed case study of creative transformation of the Minnesota educational system.

13. I have extensively explored these kinds of role-relationship in an empirical study of creativity and prediction in the movie and television industry, for report in another book underway.

14. Loye, 1977, 1978 for published sources, as well as *Freedom and Equality* and *Creativity and Prediction in the Dream Factory* for works underway.

15. See Loye, 1998b for references for over 100 years of *male* scholarship in this area in addition to the more recent exceptional work of hundreds of women that by and large—in keeping with the dynamics for this time of increasingly pivotal conflict of paradigms—is either being ignored by established or mainstream scholarship or being attacked with holy fervor by small cabals of specialists, female as well as male in composition.

16. See Eisler, 1987, 1995, and Loye, 1998b, for detailed references.

17. These are again relationships empirically explored in my studies of the movie and television industry.
18. See Loye, 1996, 1998b for an analysis of dominator predation in terms of the psychiatric syndrome of what is known as the "borderline personality."
19. See, e.g., the books of Tom Peters, Rosabeth Moss Kantor, Douglas MacGregor, John Naisbitt and Patricia Aburdene, and Gifford Pinchot.
20. The following analysis is based on the study over a decade of the phenomena of partnership paradigm expansion in scores of Centers for Partnership Education and hundreds of partnership discussion groups in the United States and elsewhere inspired by Eisler's *The Chalice and the Blade* and our co-founding of a Center for Partnership Studies in 1987.

References

Abraham, R. and Shaw, C. (1983). *Dynamics.* Part II: *Chaotic behavior.* Santa Cruz, CA: Aerial Press.

Alinsky, S. (1971). *Rules for radicals.* New York: Random House.

Assagioli, R. (1973). *The act of will.* New York: Viking Press.

Atkinson, J.W. (1964). *An introduction to motivation.* New York: Van Nostrand.

Baldwin, J.M. (1906). *Social and ethical implications in mental development.* New York: Macmillan.

Bergson, H. (1912/1944). *Creative evolution.* New York: The Modern Library.

Campbell, D. (1960). Blind variation and selective retention in creative thought as in other knowledge processes. *Psychological Review,* 65, 380–400.

Capra, F. (1996). *The web of life.* New York: Doubleday Anchor.

Chaisson, E. (1981). *Cosmic dawn: The origins of matter and life.* Boston: Atlantic, Little-Brown.

—— (1987). *The life era: Cosmic selection and conscious evolution.* New York: Atlantic Monthly.

Csanyi, V. (1993). Evolution: Unfolding a metaphor. *World Futures: The Journal of General Evolution,* 38, 1–3, 75–87.

—— (1989). *Evolutionary systems and society.* Durham, NC: Duke University Press.

Dabrowski, K. (1964). *Positive disintegration.* Boston: Little Brown.

Darwin, C. (1871/1981). *The descent of man.* Princeton, NJ: Princeton University Press.

Eisler, R. (1978). *The equal rights handbook.* New York: Avon.

—— (1987). *The chalice and the blade: Our history, our future.* San Francisco: Harper & Row.

—— (1991). Cultural evolution: Social shifts and phase changes. In E. Laszlo, Ed., *The new evolutionary paradigm.* New York: Gordon & Breach.

—— (1995). *Sacred pleasure: sex, myth, and the politics of the body.* San Francisco: HarperSanFrancisco.

Erikson, E. (1964). *Insight and responsibility.* New York: Norton.

Faludi, S. (1991). *Backlash: The undeclared war against American women.* New York: Crown.

Freud, A. (1946). *The ego and the mechanisms of defense.* New York: International University Press.

Freud, S. (1989). *Civilization and its discontents.* New York: Norton.

Gilligan, C. (1982). *In a different voice.* Boston: Harvard University Press.

Gruber, H. and Barrett, P. (1974). *Darwin on man: A psychological study of scientific creativity.* New York: Dutton.

Harman, H.W. (1967). *Modern factor analysis.* Chicago, IL: University of Chicago Press.

Ho, M.W. and Saunders, P.T. (Eds.) (1984). *Beyond neo-Darwinism.* London: Academic Press.

Hubbard, B.M. (1998). *Conscious evolution: Awakening our social potential.* Novato, CA: New World Library.

Huxley, J. (1964). *Essays of a humanist.* New York: Harper.

James, W. (1890/1950). *Principles of psychology,* vol. 2. New York: Dover.

Jay, M. (1973). *The dialectical imagination.* Boston: Little-Brown.

Kampis, G. (1993). Creative evolution. *World Futures: The Journal of General Evolution,* 38, 1–3, 131–137.

Kauffman, S. (1995). *At home in the universe: The search for the laws of self-organization and complexity.* New York: Oxford University Press.

Kohlberg, L. (1984). *The psychology of moral development.* New York: Harper & Row.

Kuhn, T. (1970). *The structure of scientific revolution.* Chicago, IL: University of Chicago Press.

Laszlo, E. (1994). *The choice: Oblivion or evolution.* Los Angeles: Tarcher.

—— (1995). *The interconnected universe.* London: World Scientific.

—— (1996a). *Evolution: The general theory.* Cresskill, NJ: Hampton Press.

—— (1996b). *The whispering pond.* London: Element Books.

Lewin, K. (1948). *Resolving social conflicts.* New York: Harper and Row.

—— (1951). *Field theory in social science.* New York: Harper and Row.

Loye, D. (1971). *The healing of a nation.* New York: Norton.

—— (1977). *The leadership passion: A psychology of ideology.* San Francisco, CA.: Jossey-Bass.

—— (1978). *The knowable future: A psychology of forecasting and prophecy.* New York: Wiley-Interscience.

—— (1994). Charles Darwin, Paul MacLean, and the lost origins of "the moral sense": Some implications for general evolution theory. *World Futures: The Journal of General Evolution,* 40, 187–196.

—— (1995). "How predictable is the future: The conflict between traditional chaos theory and the psychology of prediction, and the challenge for chaos psychology." In R. Robertson and A. Combs, Eds., *Chaos theory in psychology and the life sciences.* Mahwah, NJ: Erlbaum.

—— (1996). La psichiatria di Gilania: Moralita del dominio and moralita della partnership [The psychiatric consequences of androcratic and gylanic morality]. *Pluriverso,* 1, 3, 11–118.

—— (1998a). *Darwin's lost theory.* (book in preparation)

—— (1998b). *The glacier and the flame: The rediscovery of goodness.* (book in preparation)

Machiavelli, N. (1997). *The prince.* New Haven: Yale University Press.

Maslow, A. (1968). *Toward a psychology of being.* Princeton, NJ: Van Nostrand.

Miller, G.A., Gallanter, A. and Pribram, K.H. (1960). *Plans and the structure of behavior.* New York: Henry Holt.

Miller, J.G. (1978). *Living systems.* New York: McGraw-Hill.

Millet, K. (1970) *Sexual politics.* New York: Doubleday.

Pagels, H. (1982). *The cosmic code.* New York: Simon and Schuster.

Parsons, T., Shils, E., Naegles, K. and Pitts, J. (Eds.) (1961). *Theories of society.* New York: Free Press.

Piaget, J. (1965). *The moral judgement of the child.* New York: Free Press.

—— (1976). *The child and reality.* New York: Penguin.

Pribram, K. (1971). *Languages of the brain.* Englewood Cliffs, NJ: Prentice-Hall.

Prigogine, I. and Stengers, I. (1984). *Order out of chaos.* New York: Bantam.

Richards, R. (1987). *Darwin and the emergence of evolutionary theories of mind and behavior.* Chicago, IL: University of Chicago Press.

Rogers, C. (1951). *Client-centered therapy.* New York: Houghton-Mifflin.

Rokeach, M. (1973). *The nature of human values.* New York: Free Press.

Salthe, S. N. (1993). *Development and evolution: complexity and change in biology.* Cambridge, MA: MIT Press.

Swimme, B. and Berry, T. (1992). *The universe story.* San Francisco: HarperSanFrancisco.

13
Conscious Evolution: Cultural Transformation and Human Agency

RIANE EISLER

Abstract
Cultural historian Riane Eisler expands her new cultural transformation theory with an exploration of two radically differing kinds of relational dynamics operating in our lives. Shaping personal, social, economic, political, religious, and educational systems are the relational differences between the dominator model and the partnership model of social organization.

Key words
Biological evolution, cultural evolution, human choice, evolutionary path, cultural transformation theory, partnership and dominator models, women and men, social construction of gender, human potentials, relational dynamics, social and economic relations, childrearing, human agency, pain or pleasure, myths and images, templating, replicating, co-opting, cumulating, amplifying, transforming, deconstruction, reconstruction, shift from domination to partnership.

In trying to understand our world and ourselves within it, an obstacle is the fact that most of the theories of evolution we are familiar with, such as the prevailing neo-Darwinian theory, are of biological evolution. Practically everything that raises questions about our lives today and where we as a species may be headed, however, requires a better understanding of our *cultural* evolution. In fact, today human cultural evolution is in critical ways even more important for all life-forms on Earth than biological evolution. We need only look at the massive impact of human technologies on our natural environment to see that we humans are not only co-creators with nature of the course life will take on this planet, but also entering a time of radically expanding responsibility.

In both biological and cultural evolution there is the element of chance. But with cultural evolution, chance increasingly gives way to choice. As Ervin Laszlo notes, "Humans have the ability to act consciously and collectively . . . to choose their own evolutionary path."[1]

Human choices can be constructive or destructive, conscious or unconscious. This is the crux of our evolutionary crisis. For, as we see all around us, many of the policy choices being made today are driving us toward an evolutionary dead-end. But there is also in our time of rapid technological flux and social disequilibrium an opportunity for evolutionary breakthrough rather than breakdown—if adequate attention is given to the fact that most of our choices, including the choices of policymakers, are profoundly, and to a large extent unconsciously, affected by the culture into which we are born.

The cultural transformation theory I have been developing over more than a decade examines our individual and social choices from the new perspective of what I identify as the dominator and partnership models as two basic possibilities for human culture. Based on a study of 25,000 years of the span of human life on this Earth, cultural transformation theory provides a new action-oriented theory of cultural evolution that can be applied to meet the epochal challenges we face (Eisler, 1987, 1995, 1997; Eisler and Loye, 1992).

The departure point for cultural transformation theory is biological evolution: the recognition that humans are part of the continuum of life-forms in nature. But while the neo-Darwinian emphasis in the study of evolution has been on the organism's reaction or adaptation to a changing environment, my focus is on the organism as an active originator of change. Indeed, I argue that our appearance on the evolutionary scene initiates an age of co-creation or coevolution (Eisler 1990, 1995, 1997).

I also emphasize another evolutionary development not generally recognized: that humans are biologically equipped to derive enormous rewards of pleasure from caring connections, without which, because of our uniquely long childhood helplessness, we cannot even survive. Throughout our history we find evidence that we humans have a powerful life-long yearning for love and pleasure, as well as a profound yearning, only in rudimentary evidence with other life-forms, for beauty, truth, and an equitable and peaceful way of living (Eisler 1995).

The basic question that faces us at this critical juncture in our evolution is what kind of socio-economic and cultural structure will support and enhance, rather than inhibit and distort, the expression and actualization of these uniquely human needs and potentials. Equally important, what changes in human consciousness—and thus actions—can help us move toward such a structure.

These are the questions cultural transformation theory asks and seeks to answer.

Earlier works, notably *The Chalice and the Blade: Our History, Our Future* and many journal articles, deal with various aspects of cultural transformation theory (Eisler 1987, 1990, 1995, 1996, 1997). This paper is based on excerpts from my work in progress tentatively called *Cultural Transformation Theory and Applications*.[2] The first section describes some of the differences between cultural transformation theory and earlier theories. The second section briefly outlines the new method of inquiry I call the study of relational dynamics. The third looks at some unconscious mediating dynamics between social structure and human agency. The fourth briefly traces the historical tension between the partnership and dominator models—which in our time is coming to a head.

1. Cultural Transformation Theory

Cultural transformation theory (CTT) differs from previous theories of cultural evolution both in approach and in content. Unlike still popular macrohistorical and structuralist theories that emphasize evolutionary stages, CTT does not posit a linear evolutionary movement from primitive to more complex societies—much less a progression from "barbarism" to "civilization." Instead, it provides a nonlinear and open-ended narrative of human cultural evolution in terms of the underlying tension between the dominator model and the partnership model as two basic "attractors" for social organization.

Cultural transformation theory is thus more congruent with contemporary theories from the life sciences, such as the chaos theorizing of Prigogine and Stengers and the autopoiesis of Maturana and Varela, than with mechanistic Baconian or Newtonian conceptualizations. It focuses on the dynamics of systems self-organization and the possibility during periods of severe systems disequilibrium of systems transformation. It is thus, as its name emphasizes, a theory of cultural *transformation*.

In this regard, cultural transformation theory represents a return to the original Greek meaning of theory. *Theoria* was the reenactment of a sacred story of transformation intended to give participants the opportunity to transform their own lives. But cultural transformation theory radically departs from the classical sacred story of transformation revolving around the life, death, and resurrection of a god as well as from the stories told by most subsequent religious and scientific narratives about our human condition and our human possibilities.

To begin with, most of these stories present our species as so deeply flawed as to require either supernatural redemption (through the sacrificial death and resurrection of a god, a series of our own earthly reincarnations, etc.) or strict human controls (by Plato's philosopher–kings, Freud's super ego, Marx's dictatorship of the proletariat, etc.). Specifically, the prevailing narratives of human cultural evolution claim that we have only gradually, and at best partially, emerged from our original condition of savagery—which still persists in us under our veneer of civilization, accounting for the chronic injustice and violence of most of recorded history. Life for this infancy of our species has been the telling, one after another, of a series of dark fairy tales. So strong has been the grip on our culture of these types of narrative that they have effectively censored out any contradictory information.

There have been other stories presenting humanity as originating more innocently in a "garden" or a "golden age." But these have generally been dismissed as mere fables or utopian fantasies. And even though many scientific narratives reject religious dogmas of "original sin" as well as scientific notions of "killer instincts," "selfish genes," "reptilian brains," "Id monsters," or "the Shadow," the general tenor of "value free" social science and "objective" history has been a dispassionate analysis of what cultural transformation theory identifies as relations oriented to a dominator model as observable truths—rather than as merely one human possibility.

Most of these narratives also contain a subtext of gender stereotypes in which men are active/superior while women are passive/inferior. Accordingly, they describe our human adventure in terms of only one half of our species, with anything pertaining to the female half of humanity only noted in passing, in connection with the family, sex, and love, or as the peripheral "woman question" or "women's issues." Even recent feminist narratives, in an understandable attempt to remedy this imbalance, have generally focused primarily on half of humanity, as have most theoreticians in the emerging field of men's studies.

Cultural transformation theory outlines a very different story of our deep past, more recent past, present, and possibilities for our future. Focusing on the more recent past, it looks at modern movements challenging entrenched traditions of domination. Ranging from the 17th-century "rights of man" and feminist movements to the contemporary civil rights, economic justice, women's and children's rights, and environmental movements, these movements are viewed as components of a larger partnership movement countered by strong dominator resistance and periodic regressions (Eisler 1987, 1995). Unlike other theories, CTT also takes into account archaeological and mythical evidence of more partnership-oriented prehistoric societies. It then examines both prehistory and recorded history in terms of the interaction between major technological phase changes and the degree to which a period orients primarily to the dominator or partnership model (Eisler 1987, 1990, 1997).

In sharp contrast to earlier theories, a central tenet of cultural transformation theory is that how the roles and relations of the two halves of humanity—women and men—are structured is not just a "women's issue" or a "men's issue" but a matter of central significance for all aspects of our lives. It shows how a hidden subtext of gender controls the social construction of all our institutions (from family and religion to politics and economics) as well as our guiding systems of values—thus, in effect, much of our consciousness.

Cultural transformation theory also challenges the notion that the most important aspects of a society are those that can be understood by studying the so-called public sphere of political and economic relations, with scant attention to the so-called private sphere of family, sexual, and other intimate relations. It posits that, on the contrary, it is through these relations that we unconsciously form the basic habits of feeling, thinking, and acting that operate in all our relations, from intimate relations in the so-called private sphere to international relations in the so-called public sphere.

Accordingly, cultural transformation theory probes the hidden dynamics that mediate between individual human agency and social systems maintenance or change. In particular, it probes the hidden dynamics for the maintenance and resurgence of societies orienting primarily to the dominator model—dynamics that operate unconsciously, even though dominator-oriented relations and social organizations foster ways of thinking, being, and relating that diminish, deform, and sometimes destroy human beings.

CTT further argues that the ability to recognize patterns of partnership and domination in our psyches, in our relations, and in our society is a prerequisite to imaging more humane and effective ways of structuring human relations and institutions, and that such a restructuring is crucial for our world today. In short, by identifying patterns and interconnections not visible using earlier theoretical frameworks, it opens up the realistic possibility of fundamental cultural transformation through a shift to societies orienting primarily to the partnership rather than dominator model—and with this, the possibility of more peaceful and equitable relations and the greater realization of our unique human potentials.

2. Relational Dynamics: A New Method of Inquiry

Cultural transformation theory introduces the new approach to inquiry I have called the study of relational dynamics. I developed this approach through a process much like what we do when we test our vision by looking through different refractions of lenses until we see clearly what at first was blurred and diffuse. Through this process, I began to see connections, and thus configurations, that had not been visible. This in turn made it possible not only to see the underlying patterns for the partnership and dominator models; it also made it possible to identify the following basic relational dynamics.

A. The study of relational dynamics distinguishes between two kinds of change:

1. *Change within the systems maintenance requirements of either a partnership or dominator model*—that is, change contained within the parameters of either model.
2. *Transformative change*—or change that results in the shift from one model to the other.

B. The study of relational dynamics focuses on five kinds of relations:

1. *Social and economic relations:* What are our underlying alternatives for social and economic relations? Under what circumstances do these alternatives fall into the configurations characteristic of the dominator or the partnership model?
2. *Systems relations:* How do the key elements of the partnership and dominator models interact in both the so-called private and public spheres?
3. *Technological relations:* What are the interactions between major technological phase changes and social shifts from one model to the other?
4. *Gender and childrearing relations:* How does the social construction of gender roles and relations and childrearing practices relate to individual agency and

either social systems maintenance or transformative change from one model to the other?

5. *Motivational relations:* How do dominator and partnership social structures relate to the primacy of pain or pleasure as levers for human motivation?

C. Relational dynamics identifies an interactive configuration of three core elements characterizing the partnership or dominator model.

1. In the dominator model, the core configuration is composed of:
   a. *Social and economic relations:* Rigid hierarchies of domination based on authoritarian controls prevail.
   b. *Gender roles and relations:* Rigid male dominance, along with the elevation of what in dominator societies are considered masculine characteristics over stereotypically feminine ones, prevails.
   c. *Pain or pleasure:* A high level of institutionalized or built-in violence and abuse prevails. This ranges from child-beating and wife-battering to warfare, along with the idealization—and even sacralization—of the infliction and/or suffering of pain.

2. In the partnership model, the three-way core configuration is composed of:
   a. *Social and economic relations:* The principle of linking rather than ranking prevails. This linking goes along with hierarchies of actualization, based primarily on the empowerment of self and others (power to help and achieve with others) rather than hierarchies of domination, based on disempowerment (power over others, as is characteristic of the dominator model).
   b. *Gender roles and relations:* An equal partnership between the female and male halves of humanity prevails, as well as a high valuing of empathy, nurturance, caring, and other characteristics that in the dominator model are stereotypically considered feminine.
   c. *Pain or pleasure:* Bonds between people are largely forged through mutuality of pleasurable benefits. This is accompanied by a low level of institutionalized or built-in social violence and abuse, as fear of pain is not needed to maintain rigid rankings of domination.

D. Relational dynamics identifies three core areas for the molding of consciousness that determine whether we and our societies are to be predominantly governed by the partnership or dominator core configuration:

1. *Foundational human relations:* These are the relations between the female and male halves of humanity and the relations between children and their caretakers.
2. *Myths and images:* These are basic shapers of partnership or dominator consciousness through formal education in the home, school, or religious institutions, as well as informal education through the arts, music, and, of particular importance in our time, the mass media.

3. *The economic structure*: In addition to fundamental differences in the production and distribution of resources and the development and uses of technology, a basic difference between partnership and dominator economics is indicated by the economic and social prioritizing of activities. For example, activities such as caring for young children and the health of all members of a family, and maintaining a clean, healthy environment are prioritized in the partnership model but deprioritized as only "women's work" in the dominator model.

E. Relational dynamics identifies six basic processes for maintaining or changing social systems. Here I will begin to provide examples showing how the two models take form in political, economic, gender, childrearing, and all other relations.

1. *Templating*. Every system, whether a person, an organization, or a society, has to go through a process of including some things and excluding others in order to establish its basic identity. I call this self-organizing process "templating." On the individual level, it involves the interaction of a number of cognitive and affective processes. On the social level, there is in addition the interaction of various institutions, cultural narratives, etc. The end result serves to maintain the system's basic template of defining characteristics.

For example, people produced by families with a dominator template—where the normative ideal is for men to rule, women to serve, and children to learn not to question orders, no matter how unjust—tend to carry this templating into all other human relations. They will generally take this dominator templating with them into other institutions (religious, political, educational, etc.) and try to conform relations in these institutions to this template. In turn, institutions templated to conform to the dominator model will self-select individuals whose personal templates will support family, legal, economic, and educational institutions that also conform to, and thereby reinforce and replicate, this dominator template.

Conversely, people who come from partnership-oriented families—where women and men are considered equals and there is such a thing as children's rights—will tend to take this templating outside the family. They will tend to either try to form and maintain institutions that orient more to the partnership than dominator model or make efforts to change dominator institutions in partnership templating directions. Institutions that orient more to the partnership model will in turn self-select individuals who also orient more to the partnership model and will provide incentives rather than disincentives for behaviors conducive to partnership rather than domination/submission in human relations.

2. *Replicating*. Social systems, like all living systems, reproduce themselves over time. As the work of Vilmos Csanyi (1989) articulates over many levels of evolution, in biological systems replication involves the reproduction of cells and organs that conform to the biological template defining a particular species. In social systems, replication is the reproduction of institutions, ideas, images, etc. that conform to the cultural template defining a particular system. This replicating

process is cross-generational, in effect carrying forward through time the basic defining characteristics of the system from generation to generation even in the face of the change that is a constant in living systems. Relational dynamics focuses on how both organization-formation processes and socialization processes operate through institutions such as the family, education, religion, etc., so that the basic character of the system as orienting primarily to a partnership or dominator model is not affected even by major changes.

For example, in Western history the fall of the Roman Empire and the Christianization of Europe did not substantially affect the replication of dominator templating for political relations, whether they were between a feudal lord and his serfs or a king and his subjects. Similarly, gender roles and relations did not substantially change. As for cultural narratives, although substantially different from earlier ones, they continued to replicate stories and images in which their dominator templating was presented as normal and desirable.

Conversely, even though the Bronze Age Minoan civilization of ancient Crete was technologically and culturally very different from the earlier Neolithic culture of Crete, the art of both periods replicated partnership rather than dominator templating. The prominence of plants, flowers, birds, dolphins, and other images from nature and of the sacralization of the female form, along with the absence of scenes of violence and domination, is in sharp contrast to the idealization of conquest and domination characteristic of images and cultural narratives appropriate for the dominator model.

But replicating can also be part of the process of transformative change. Thus, the proliferation of images and stories of heroic male violence in ancient art signaled the shift to the dominator model. While there are in Minoan art no images of powerful rulers looking down on their subjects from elevated pedestals (symbolizing hierarchies of domination), in the art of Bronze Age cultures orienting primarily to the dominator model, we already find the frequent replication of such images.

3. *Co-opting.* This is a process characteristic of societies that orient primarily to the dominator model. It maintains the system by subsuming, exploiting, marginalizing, and otherwise absorbing partnership elements that are essential for human survival in a watered-down and/or distorted fashion.

An example is how stereotypical women's work (caring for children, the sick, the elderly, and other activities essential for human survival) may be idealized in dominator-oriented societies, but women are excluded from social governance and this socially essential work is supposed to be performed by women in male-controlled households for free. Similarly, "effeminate men" (artists, poets, visionaries) are sometimes idealized, but such men are not considered appropriate for positions of social governance.

Co-opting can also function to create a false partnership facade; for example, through the admission of token members of subordinate groups into leadership positions. An "exceptional woman," for instance, can occasionally be admitted to social governance. But she is expected to adopt a stereotypically "masculine" leadership style and/or convince other women not to deviate from stereotypical "feminine" roles (a strategy today successfully used by leaders of the so-called religious right in the United States). Similarly, ideas appropriate for partnership-oriented societies, such as freedom and equality, are co-opted merely as slogans. They are celebrated, but applied only in ways that do not affect the basic dominator template of top-down rankings or in any other way disturb a social structure based on the limiting of freedom and the elevation of *in*equality. (Orwell's *1984* offers a dramatic illustration of how co-option serves to distort and falsify partnership concepts).

4. *Cumulating.* This is the effect built up over time of the replication of partnership or dominator templating. For example, in our time, the cumulating effects of strip mining, the clear-cutting of forests, chemical air, soil, and water pollution, and other forms of dominator templating for the use of technology for the "conquest of nature" are having extremely serious consequences in terms of the depletion of natural resources and damage to the environment. By contrast, the cumulating effect of the replication of partnership templating for ecological consciousness (for instance, of technologies and practices resulting in conservation and renewal of resources such as recycling, organic farming, etc.) will be more conducive to environmental sustainability.

5. *Amplifying.* Amplifying is the magnification in numbers and/or volume of key elements of the basic partnership or dominator template. Characteristically, when a system is severely threatened, key elements of its basic template are amplified. For example, in periods when the movement toward partnership accelerates, societies orienting primarily to the dominator model tend to respond through policies that promote a widening of the gap between those who control resources and those on the bottom of the economic pyramid. The rapidly widening gap between rich and poor in the United States and globally is a striking current example. As has been evident during the Cold War and the subsequent escalation of the global arms trade, the dominator system's investment in weaponry and both the capability and actualizing of violence and destruction are also characteristically amplified. This in turn produces real or perceived scarcities, which further reinforce the misperception that the only alternative in human relations is to dominate or to be dominated.

In other words, in times of disequilibrium the systems-maintenance process of amplification is powerfully mobilized to maintain the system, as is dramatically illustrated in our time of disequilibrium by the media barrage of gender stereotypes of heroic male violence, of women as powerless victims, etc., amplifying this basic template for in-group versus out-group/dominator versus dominated human relations.

However, like replication, amplification can also be a process for transformative change. For example, the amplification of a partnership rather than dominator templating for the relations between the two halves of humanity has been gradually shifting from the periphery into mainstream cultural narratives and images, and is foundational to the shift from a dominator to a partnership model.

6. *Transforming.* A shift from one model to the other as the primary templating for the social system is possible during periods of great systems disequilibrium. Involved here are two basic transformational processes: *deconstruction* and *reconstruction.*

Deconstruction (which we hear a great deal about today) is the conscious dismantling of the old system's foundations, including its most basic cultural narratives and other forms of symbology. The system is increasingly perceived as dysfunctional (another term we hear a great deal about today). *But deconstruction alone is not transformative. Because of the dominator system's power of templating, replicating, subsuming, co-opting, cumulating, and amplifying, deconstruction can, and often does, only result in a reconstitution of (or fall back into) the old system in changed form.*

For example, in the replacement of Czarist Russia by Stalin's Soviet Union we see only the shift from one form of the dominator model to another. Despite massive disequilibrium and consequent deconstruction, the basic templating for domination and submission did not change—either in the macrocosm of the state or the microcosm of the family. For instance, there was for some time a policy to abolish the traditional family in order to bring about fundamental cultural change. But as Trotsky wrote from exile, you cannot abolish the family; you can only change it. And there was no sustained policy to support fundamental changes in traditional gender roles and relations or childrearing practices. Hence, the "traditional family"—in which women were expected to serve men and be responsible for the care of children (now in addition to outside employment) and the infliction or threat of pain was still key to childrearing—reasserted itself, again providing a basic template for dominator relations.

In short, in times of systems disequilibrium—when transformative change becomes a real possibility—the cultural transformation from the dominator to the partnership model can only succeed through *both* deconstruction and reconstruction. This entails a clear understanding of the basic dominator and partnership templating (including their hidden subtext of gender) as the foundation for a process that can only be successful if pursued with attention equally given to:

a. Deconstruction focused only on dominator templating—rather than the tearing apart of the entire social fabric; and
b. Reconstruction focused on the conscious replication, amplification, and eventually cumulation of *partnership* rather than dominator templating.

3. Mediating Dynamics between
Human Agency and Social Organization

As noted in Section 2, Cultural Transformation Theory identifies three major mediating dynamics between individual action and social structure. One is the *templating of the foundational human relations between the two halves of humanity and between children and their caretakers.* The second is the *templating of myths and images through both formal and informal education.* The third is *economic templating.* The three are interactive and play a major role in shaping all aspects of life—from sexuality and spirituality to science and technology.

I will here briefly deal with only the first of these three mediating dynamics, focusing on how it operates to maintain a dominator-oriented social system.

A. *The Social Construction of Gender*

I have already noted the importance for both prediction and intervention of CTT's focus on how the unconscious internalization of particular types of gender roles and relations as natural is a major mediating force between individual agency and social structure.

Children universally form patterns of thinking, feeling, and acting based in large part on how the roles and relations of the two halves of humanity are socially constructed. After all, every child is born either female or male. And dominator gender stereotypes provide the very early social cues for how women and men should feel, think, and behave so that a dominator system is maintained.

This helps explain why social psychologists David Winter and David McClelland both found that the intensified replication and amplification of stereotypes of dominator masculinity characteristically precedes periods of aggressive warfare and/or repression (McClelland 1980; Winter 1973). It also helps explain why during the dominator regression of the last decades of the 20th century we find the massive replication and amplification of stories and images eroticizing domination and violence (Eisler 1995).

The unconscious internalization of a higher valuing of men and the stereotypically "masculine" also helps explain why in times of dominator regression we see a pulling-back from the public funding of activities stereotypically considered "feminine." At the same time that the allocation of funds for caring for children, the elderly, people's health, and the environment (all stereotypical "women's work") are slashed, funds are made available for the stereotypical "men's work" of building and using weapons. A recent example is the allocation of seven billion dollars for aircraft that will be obsolete by the time they are finished during the same session of the United States Congress that justified severe cutbacks in funding for such stereotypical "women's work" on the grounds that the US government deficit must be reduced.

The relationship between teaching dominator gender roles and relations and regressions toward the dominator model also helps explain why a return to the "traditional" family ("traditional" being a code word for male-dominated, procreation-oriented, and authoritarian) is a major priority for the leaders of so-called religious fundamentalism today, be they Muslim or Christian, and why this was also a rallying cry of both Hitler and Stalin. Conversely, in the case of Scandinavian nations, we can see that the higher status of women helps explain why they were able to institute policies giving priority to stereotypical "women's work"—and thus consistently have had high quality-of-life ratings in United Nations *Human Development Reports* and other global measures.

B. *The Social Construction of Childrearing*

As noted earlier, another major hidden mediator between human agency and dominator systems formation and maintenance is the replication of childrearing methods that, as we sometimes hear, make relations not based on hierarchies of domination not "feel right." In its more extreme or "pure" dominator form, this is a process that produces the unconscious state clinicians call "post-traumatic stress syndrome" and I have called the "dominator trance."

Like the institutionalization and replication of dominator gender stereotypes, this institutionalization and replication of trauma through dominator child-rearing functions primarily on an unconscious level. It is embedded in entrenched traditions that—as in the adage "spare the rod and spoil the child"—have long been considered natural, and even moral.

Basically, a pure dominator system can be viewed as a trauma factory, since the way it structures human relations—particularly intimate relations that involve touch to the body beginning in early infancy—tends to produce chronic post-traumatic stress disorder. Indeed, if we look at what we today call trauma, we see that for the last several thousand years what during the Middle Ages was aptly referred to as an "earthly vale of tears" was considered by many people as "just the way things are." Hence, to speak of trauma during the Middle Ages would have been just as incomprehensible as speaking about human rights. Neither concept has meaning in a system orienting closely to a dominator model.

For example, the inquisitions and witch-hunts of the medieval Church, the drawings and quarterings used to punish rebels and other "criminals" by the medieval state, the chopping-off of hands for thefts by medieval law, the extreme economic deprivation of the mass of people who were serfs, the generally un-sanitary and unhealthy living conditions, as well as the accepted brutal treatment of serfs in feudal fiefs—not to speak of women and children in households—are all situations that we today would describe as traumatic and, even beyond this, that clinicians identify as causative factors in chronic post-traumatic stress disorders.

Even as late as the early 1800s, when there began to be some doubts about child-beating as sound pedagogy, there was still a debate among educators about whether, as a substitute for beatings, children should be taught to understand that "the parents' will is supreme" by tying a child to a chair and/or lightly burning its hand with hot tea.[3] That is, the replication of dominator childrearing was still advocated by some "experts." More extreme recent examples are the deforming foot-binding of girls in prerevolutionary China and the genital mutilation that still maims millions of girls in parts of Africa and Asia today—brutal practices replicated as valuable cultural traditions. In sharp contrast, the second half of the 20th century has seen the growing replicating of scientific findings that traumatizing children has extremely adverse life-long effects—representing an important partnership trend.

C. *The Politics of the Body*

Most of us are not used to thinking of intimate relations—relations characterized by touch to the body—as political. But when viewed from the systems perspective proposed by CTT, it becomes evident that they are. I have called this the "politics of the body" (Eisler 1995).

To briefly sum up, the social construction of the two foundational templates for human relations—the relations between parent and child and woman and man—are very different in times and places orienting more to a dominator or a partnership model of society. In societies that orient closely to the dominator model, these two foundational relations are structured in such a way that people learn early on, on the most basic unconscious, bodily, level that what happens to the body of one type of person is legitimately to be decided by someone else.

Dominator politics of the body are unconsciously internalized by children early on through dominator childrearing. This may even be on a cellular, neurological, biochemical level, incorporated into the neural organization of the brain, which we now know to a large extent takes place after birth during the first years of life.

This feeling that dominator relations are natural is then culturally reinforced through dominator beliefs (myths and images) and institutions (educational, economic, etc.). And again on an unconscious bodily level, it is further reinforced through other dominator intimate relations, particularly sexual relations modeled on the dominator template.

In short, if we put together what we are today discovering about how both physical and psychological trauma alter body chemistry and brain development with an understanding of the hidden dynamics of dominator systems maintenance, we can better understand how people unconsciously replicate precisely the kinds of beliefs and institutional forms that cause them misery and pain.

These then are some of the hidden mediating processes between human agency and the maintenance of social systems orienting to a dominator model. Together with the other two mediating processes mentioned earlier, this dominator templating of foundational human relations in large part accounts for what Marx called false consciousness and I call the dominator trance.

What this highlights is that it is not true that we humans have some genetic predisposition to dominator human relations. Neither is it true that testosterone inevitably leads men to express frustration and anger violently. In fact, there are studies indicating that when men who have low testosterone levels are given testosterone they actually become less violent.[4] Most critical here are the social cues we receive in connection with hormonal arousal, which, in the dominator model's "real masculinity" are equated with domination and violence—a lesson constantly taught boys, beginning with war toys when they are children to life-long stories of the hero as killer.

The point is that while dominator relations are entrenched among us, they are only one possibility for human relations. And it is this entrenchment that systemically interferes with both men's and women's profound yearning for caring connections, with our yearning for a more equitable and less violent way of living, and with the formulation and implementation of more humane and rational social and economic policies.

4. The Historical Tension between the Partnership and Dominator Models

It is increasingly evident that our mounting global crises cannot be solved within the system that has given rise to them. From the perspective of cultural transformation theory, the problem is not, as we are sometimes told, one of modern technology, but of the mix of high technology with a dominator social and cultural organization (Eisler 1987, 1990, 1997).

Our once hallowed "conquest of nature," the violent conquest and domination of other humans, the global arms trade, the overbreeding that has led to the population explosion, the inequitable misdistribution of resources—all these could be changed through rational policies and actions. But the issue is not one of reason, but of the hidden dynamics that serve to replicate precisely the kind of social and cultural organization that has led to our global crises.

As we have seen, cultural transformation theory identifies two basic templates as isomorphisms that transcend conventional classifications based on right versus left, religious versus secular, capitalist versus communist, level of technological development, time, and geography: the dominator model and the partnership model. It makes it possible to see that the degree to which a society orients to one or the other of these models is critical to whether a society will be more equitable or inequitable, more authoritarian or democratic, more peaceful or warlike.

Cultural transformation theory also traces the tension throughout our cultural evolution between the partnership and dominator models in terms of what, in the language of nonlinear dynamics, we may call two attractors. While my work has drawn primarily from data on Western prehistory and history, cultural transformation theory was recently tested by Chinese scholars at the Chinese Academy of Social Sciences in Beijing for its application to Asian history, and similar patterns were found (Min, 1995).

The general sequence outlined by cultural transformation theory is as follows:

1. During a period of massive disequilibrium linked to severe climate changes and environmental degradation as well as large-scale population movements in prehistory, a shift from a partnership to a dominator direction in the mainstream of cultural evolution radically altered the course of Western civilization. For example, there is a general lack of fortifications and imagery idealizing warfare in the early Neolithic (and in some places as late as the Bronze Age). Thereafter, massive fortifications and imagery idealizing warfare appear, as well as major changes in all mythical images and stories, with a cumulating idealization, and even sacralization, of the infliction and/or suffering of pain.

2. During most of recorded history, the partnership model has been subsumed by the dominator model. There have been intermittent periods of partnership resurgence (e.g., early Christianity) followed by periods of dominator regression (e.g., the Crusades, Inquisition, and witch-burnings of the rigidly male-dominated, hierarchic, authoritarian, and highly violent subsequent orthodox Church).

3. During modern history, along with the disequilibrium of the industrial revolution, the tension between the partnership and dominator models intensified. A powerful partnership resurgence becomes the major trend for this period. We find the cumulating challenge to entrenched traditions of domination by progressive movements. Sequentially, for example, we find the 17th- and 18th-century challenge to the "divinely ordained" right of kings to rule; the 18th-, 19th-, and 20th-century challenge to the "divinely ordained" right of men to rule over the women and children in the "castles" of their homes; the 19th- and 20th-century challenge to the control of one race by another through the abolitionist, civil rights, and anticolonialist movements; the 19th-century pacifist movement and the 20th-century peace movement; the 19th-century feminist and 20th-century women's liberation and women's rights movements; the 19th- and 20th-century movements for social and economic justice, and most recently, the 20th-century environmental movement.

   This cumulating movement toward partnership general systems guidance, however, has been countered by massive dominator systems resistance and punctuated by periodic regressions (e.g., Hitler's Germany, Stalin's Soviet Union, Khomeini's Iran, the so-called Christian right in the United States, so-called Muslim religious fundamentalism, etc.).

4. Even though this struggle between partnership resurgence and dominator resistance/regression is still obscured by conventional systems of classification such as right versus left, capitalism versus communism, religious versus secular, etc., largely due to ever more rapid technological change, today it is coming to a head.

Simply put, at our level of technological development we are on a collision course between the requirements of dominator systems maintenance and human species maintenance—a critical bifurcation that offers both unprecedented challenges and unprecedented opportunities for fundamental cultural transformation.

The disequilibrium entailed in the move to a new technological phase-change based on nuclear, electronic, and biochemical technological breakthroughs is both a crisis and opportunity. It is a crisis because we are at a point where the mix of a dominator system's guidance of policies and high technology is not sustainable. But it is also an opportunity because it is during periods of great disequilibrium that fundamental change is possible (Eisler 1987, 1990, 1997).

This may or may not occur. In the last analysis, whether the development and use of our powerful technologies is governed by partnership or dominator social guidance is up to us—to whether or not we consciously choose to do everything in our power to accelerate the shift from a dominator to a partnership model.

As cultural transformation theory emphasizes, this will not mean an ideal, or even completely violence-free, society. But it will mean a society in which violence and domination are no longer institutionalized, in which they are not idealized as heroic or manly. It will mean a society in which stereotypically feminine values, such as caring and nonviolence, and stereotypical "women's work," such as caring for children, for a family's health, and ensuring that we have a clean and aesthetic environment, are no longer relegated to a secondary place in the guiding social and economic policies.

What is necessary is appropriate interventive action on both the individual and the social and economic policy levels so that we may consciously, rather than merely unconsciously, co-create our future.[5] This means focusing on hitherto ignored areas such as those briefly outlined in this paper, particularly the three mediating dynamics between dominator systems maintenance and individual and collective human agency.

In keeping with the challenge set forth by Ervin Laszlo in many books and his formation of groups such as the General Evolution Research Group and the Club of Budapest, I believe that evolutionary and systems scientists today have a great opportunity—and responsibility—to play an active part in this process.

Notes

1. E. Laszlo (1985), The crucial epoch, *Futures*, 17, 16.
2. This paper is excerpted from my notes for a work in progress that will provide a full statement of my cultural transformation theory (here sometimes abbreviated as CTT).
3. K. Taylor (1987), Blessing the House, *Journal of Psychohistory* 12, 443–444.

4. Study conducted by Dr. Christina Wang at the University of California, Los Angeles, reported in *Newsweek*, July 3, 1995.
5. The awareness of the need for conscious human intervention in our cultural evolution is beginning to emerge as part of the *zeitgeist* or worldview of our time. For example, Laszlo deals with conscious evolution in *The choice* and *Evolution*, as do Eric Chaisson in *The life era: Cosmic selection and conscious evolution* and Barbara Marx Hubbard in *Conscious evolution: Awakning our social potential*.

References

Abraham, R. and Shaw, C. (1984). *Dynamics*. Santa Cruz, CA: Aerial Press.

Chaisson, E. (1987). *The life era: Cosmic selection and conscious evolution*. New York: Atlantic Monthly.

Csanyi, V. (1989). *Evolutionary systems and society*. Durham, NC: Duke University Press.

Eisler, R. (1987). *The chalice and the blade: Our history, our future*. San Francisco: Harper & Row.

—— (1990). Cultural evolution: Social shifts and phase changes. In E. Laszlo, Ed., *The new evolutionary paradigm*. New York: Gordon & Breach.

—— (1995). *Sacred pleasure: Sex, myth, and the politics of the body*. San Francisco: HarperSanFrancisco.

—— (1997). Cultural transformation theory: A new paradigm for history. In J. Galtung and S. Inayatullah, Eds., *Macrohistory and macrohistorians*. Westport, CT: Praeger.

Eisler, R. and Loye, D. (1990), *The partnership way*. San Francisco: Harper.

Gimbutas, M. (1982). *The goddesses and gods of old Europe*. Berkeley: University of California Press.

—— (1991). *The civilization of the goddess*. San Francisco: Harper.

Hubbard, B.M. (1998). *Conscious evolution: Awakening our social potential*. Novato, CA: New World Library.

Laszlo, E. (1996). *Evolution: The general theory*. Cresskill, NJ: Hampton Press.

Loye, D. (in progress). *The river and the star*.

Maturana, H. and Varela, F. (1980). *The tree of knowledge*. Boston: Shambhala.

McClelland, D. (1980). *Power*. New York: Irvington.

Mellaart, J. (1967). *Çatal Hüyük*. New York: McGraw-Hill.

Min, J. (Ed.) (1995), *The chalice and the blade in Chinese culture*. Beijing: China Social Sciences Publishing House.

Platon (1966). *Crete*. Geneva: Nagel Publishers.

Prigogine, I. and Stengers, I. (1984). *Order out of chaos*. New York: Bantam.

Winter, D. (1973), *The power motive*. New York: Free Press.

Willetts, R.F. (1977), *The civilization of ancient Crete*. Berkeley: University of California Press.

14
Social Interventions and the World Wide Web

RALPH ABRAHAM

Abstract
Mathematician and chaos theorist Ralph Abraham describes the formation of the General Evolution Research Group (GERG) and a range of his own social inventions. These include new ways of applying the World Wide Web to social activism and of applying other aspects of the computer and computer modeling to the advancement of human evolution.

Key words
General Evolution Research Group (GERG), global activism, Santa Cruz, Salk Institute, *World Futures: The Journal of General Evolution*, bifurcation paradigm, electronic intervention, the animated Atlas, RIMS, political weather reports, mathematical hermeneutics, action research, action mechanics, erodynamics, mathematical cooperation, the World Wide Web.

1. Introduction

While it is widely agreed that we now live in the midst of a major social transformation, everyone has a different idea of the outcome. For many, we are in the last stages of a catastrophic disaster. For others, we are on the threshold of a golden age. Either way, according to these theories, it matters little what we do. But for a few visionaries, such as those of the General Evolution Research Group, the future is not yet determined: it is up to us. And according to this view, which we may call the "creative posture," it does matter what we do; it matters enormously. For we are now in the process of creating the future.

2. The Creative Posture

Among the devotees of the creative posture we find, first of all, the systems philosopher Ervin Laszlo. He is the author of several books on this theme. He also founded the General Evolution Research Group (GERG) and the Club of Budapest, which are action groups devoted to the creative posture. To Laszlo, global activism is the key to the future.

Another sharing the creative view is the cultural historian William Irwin

Thompson, author of several books on this theme. He is also the founder of the Lindisfarne Association, another creative posture action group. To Thompson, we are turning from the dynamic mentality to the chaos mentality.

Others of this posture include: Riane Eisler, champion of the partnership society, Hazel Henderson, crusader for social responsibility in economics, Jean Houston, impresario for the possible human, social psychologist David Loye, Fritjof Capra, the advocate of Ecoliteracy, and many others. According to them all, we must work to create the future; paradise will not come by itself.

3. GERG and the Intervention Controversy

The General Evolution Research Group emerged autopoietically from various small groups involving Ervin Laszlo in Budapest, Vienna, and Santa Cruz. It was in Santa Cruz in 1985 that I first met Laszlo, along with David Loye and Riane Eisler, and we shared our ideas to put chaos and evolutionary theory to work on world problems.

Soon after the formation of this group a meeting was organized by Ervin Laszlo and the late Jonas Salk at the Salk Institute in La Jolla, California. Salk, a medical doctor and researcher, had been focused on the population explosion for many years. He told us: "As a doctor, when I see something wrong, my instinct is to fix it."

In the context of the population explosion and other related global and environmental problems of the world *problematique*, "to fix it" means an intervention. That is, something revolutionary, provocative, and probably risky must be done. It takes a lot of hubris to plan and execute an untested social intervention. The working group could not agree on a strategy with Dr. Salk. In our hotel and the cafés of La Jolla after this meeting, the working group named itself the General Evolution Research Group, and turned in the safer direction of academic research and publication.

Soon we acquired an indispensable window for publication. Talks between Laszlo and Gordon & Breach, publishers of the *Journal of World Futures*, resulted in a change of name and scope, and the new journal *World Futures: The Journal of General Evolution* was born, Those of us who had gathered in La Jolla became its editorial board. Since then, this journal has provided us and all others similarly interested in a futures-oriented evolutionary theory with the publication channel so crucial to intellectual advancement. Over the past decade, under Laszlo's leadership, GERG has expanded to include scholars from Russia and China, as well as the European countries and the United States. Many articles and books have been published under the GERG umbrella, and GERG meetings in Bologna, Florence, Vienna, and other European cities have advanced the GERG agenda. At some point an informal pact was agreed to identify some of our individual books, in the front matter, as "A Catalyst Book of the General Evolution Research Group." Two examples are *The Chalice and the Blade* by Riane Eisler, and my *Chaos, Gaia, Eros*.

4. The Bifurcation Paradigm

Among the basic ideas explored by GERG members are dynamic versions of the fundamental tenets of general systems theory, especially those pertaining to evolution of course, such as morphogenesis, pattern formation, self-organization, autopoiesis, autocatalysis, and so on. In this view, culture is in a process of self-organization. This process of social morphogenesis, also known as world cultural history, has smooth phases punctuated by bifurcations, like any dynamic process. According to the dynamic way of thinking we have learned from chaos theory and the new mathematics, these occasional bifurcations are the hinges of history, the special times of social meltdown when small intentional actions may produce major results. This perspective is what we mean by the bifurcation paradigm. In short, we are now in the midst of a major bifurcation of history (Laszlo says it is the greatest), as well as a fabulous window of opportunity. Thus the bifurcation paradigm is equal to the creative posture multiplied by a mathematically informed optimism.

5. Electronic Intervention Schemes

The synergy of GERG and the publication opportunities it provided naturally led to a subset of all the publications devoted to the bifurcation window, and the spirit of intervention did manifest in some of them. In my own case, the articles listed in the References, from 1985 to 1990, were all interventionist efforts of the creative posture, deeply indebted to GERG. Only from 1994 did I perceive the World Wide Web as a vehicle for intervention, and a new opportunity for all my GERGian ideas of the past decade. Here are brief abstracts of these earlier intervention schemes. (These papers may be found on the WWW at http://www.vismath.org/ralph/articles.)

5.1. MS#40, Complex dynamics and the social sciences, June 1, 1985 (dedicated to Erich Jantsch, 1929–1980). Abstract: Complex dynamic systems theory is an evolution of nonlinear dynamics, developed for modeling and simulation of biological systems. Here, we speculate on the potential of this strategy for the emerging theory of social systems, for general evolution theory, and the implications for the future of our own planetary society.

5.2. MS#41, Mathematics and evolution, a manifesto, August 18, 1986 (to Teilhard de Chardin, 1881–1955). Abstract: This paper deals with various possibilities for the role of mathematical modeling and computer simulation in attempting to deal with the crises of evolution. Brief introductions to some concepts of holarchic dynamics are included.

5.3. MS#43, Mathematics and evolution: a proposal. This paper bundled four proposals:

1. The Animated Atlas, September 4, 1986 (to Bucky Fuller, 1895–1984). Abstract: Using optical storage media for digital images, reference works with animated illustrations will soon be available for home computers. The translation of familiar cartographic materials, such as an atlas of world history, will soon follow. In this paper, we discuss the possibility of extrapolating such an atlas of world history into an atlas of world futures, using digital simulation of mathematical models for complex social systems. Potential applications to governance, decisionmaking, and education are considered.

2. RIMS: a proposed institute, September 9, 1986 (to Ludwig von Bertalanffy, 1901–1972). Abstract: A proposal for a novel research institute, the Research Institute for Mathematics and Society and the RIMS Social Exploratorium, capable of supplying a political weather bureau with adequate data in computer-readable form suitable for graphic presentation on video broadcasts, together with a public display center based on the animated atlas.

3. Political Weather Reports, November 29, 1986 (to Lewis Frye Richardson, 1881–1972). Abstract: According to the hermeneutic theory of the evolution of consciousness, the development of a new relationship between our species and the biosphere may be encouraged by monitoring political and ecological variables or indicators, and feeding them back into society through broadcasting media. This possibility was foreseen by Richardson in 1919, as a means for avoiding wars. In this paper we describe a practical implementation of this program, based on the animated atlas technique.

4. Mathematical Hermeneutics, February 24, 1987 (to Kurt Levin, 1890–1947). Abstract: After Descartes and Mersenne, mechanics (the art of making mathematical models for processes) became disenchanted, and fell into disrepute. The advent of the computer revolution has brought a shift of style in mechanics and in applied mathematics in general. This provides an opportunity for the reenchantment of mechanics, by integrating modeling more tightly into the hermeneutic circle of action research. This paper introduces the basic concepts of this reenchanted circle, action mechanics, and suggests its potential importance for postmodern society.

5.4. MS#49, Social and international synergy: a mathematical model, June 1, 1989 (to Ruth Fulton Benedict (Ann Singleton), 1887–1948). Abstract: Lecturing at Barnard College in 1941, Ruth Benedict introduced a unique and important idea of synergy in a human social context. In this paper, striving toward a mathematical anthropology, we develop a complex dynamic model for her concept of social synergy, and discuss its application to international synergy, in the emerging planetary society of nations.

5.5. MS#60, Erodynamics and cognitive maps, July 8, 1990 (to Oskar Morgenstern

1902–). Abstract: We defend the place of mathematics in the cognitive map aspect of the history of consciousness, describe erodynamics, a specific modeling strategy for evolving social structures, and apply it to model habitual behavior and social synergy, Ruth Benedict's measure of harmony between the individual and the tribe.

5.6. MS#62, Mathematical cooperation, December 18, 1990 (to Kenneth Ewart Boulding, 1910–). Abstract: This is an application of Erodynamics: dynamic modeling and computer simulation used as navigational aids, in complex social systems, to enhance the cooperation of the participants.

This sequence of six papers, beginning immediately after my meeting in May 1985 with Ervin Laszlo, Riane Eisler, and Dave Loye, develops a single theme, eventually named erodynamics, developed further in my book *Chaos, Gaia, Eros.*

6. The World Wide Web

According to the bifurcation paradigm, the current world process is the embryo-genesis of a new planetary society. We are now proposing the idea that the World Wide Web is the nervous system of this embryo, and is currently evolving as the neurogenesis of our cultural future. According to this idea, our collective influence on the future evolution of our culture may be extended through this nervous system. The leverage of a new idea, thus extended, may be many times more powerful than its leverage under previous media, such as print media, radio and television broadcasts, and so on. In other words, the Web may be the revolutionary medium of dreams, for those interested in influencing the creation of the future. If so, it may become the cyberfield of the perennial contest between the forces of good and evil. At the very least, the socially evolutionary activities infusing the Web must be of considerable interest to social activists, action researchers, historians, sociologists, historians, and students of pop culture. One interesting trend we have noted is that many traditional culture producers are under the influence of a paranoid, luddite attitude to the Web, and therefore tend to leave the cyberfield open to the cultural mafia. (See Abraham, MS#81, Educational hypermedia and the world-wide web.)

7. Conclusion

Action researchers, environmental activists, educational revolutionaries, spiritual revivalists, old dogs, lend me your mice. A unique and narrow window of opportunity has opened. Think it over. If you have abandoned a program of intervention because the time was not right, the media unresponsive, the funding withdrawn, or whatever: browse the Web, think again, learn new tricks.

Note

It is a pleasure to dedicate this paper to Ervin Laszlo, and to acknowledge the stimulus, support, and companionship of the International Synergy Institute, the General Evolution Research Group, the Lindisfarne Association, and the international community devoted to research on chaos theory and its applications. And a thousand thanks to David Loye for suggesting this topic and following through with critical feedback.

References

Abraham, R. (1987a). MS#40, Complex dynamics and the social sciences. *World Futures, 23,* 1–10.

—— (1987b). MS#43, Mathematics and evolution: A proposal. *IS Journal, 2,* 27–45.

—— (1988a). MS#41, Mathematics and evolution: A manifesto. *World Futures, 23,* 237–262.

—— (1988b). MS#49, Social and international synergy: A mathematical model. *IS Journal, 3,* 18–26.

—— (1990). MS#62, Mathematical cooperation. In Allan Combs, Ed., *Cooperation, Beyond the age of competition* (pp. 68–74). Philadelphia: Gordon & Breach.

—— (1991). MS#60, Erodynamics and cognitive maps. In Ervin Laszlo and Ignazio Masulli, Eds., *New paradigms for the 21st century: The evolution of contemporary cognitive maps* (pp. 255–264). Philadelphia: Gordon & Breach.

—— (1994). *Chaos, Gaia, Eros.* San Francisco: HarperSanFrancisco.

—— (1995). MS#81, Educational hypermedia and the world-wide web. *Syllabus, 8,* 34–36.

Laszlo, E. (1991). *The age of bifurcation: Understanding the changing world.* Philadelphia: Gordon & Breach.

—— (1994). *The choice: Evolution or extinction?* New York, NY: Tarcher/Putnam.

—— (1996). *Evolution: The general theory.* Cresskill, NJ: Hampton Press.

Thompson, W.E. (1981). *The time falling bodies take to light: Mythology, sexuality, and the origins of culture.* New York: St. Martin's Press.

—— (1985). *Pacific shift.* San Francisco: Sierra Club Books.

—— (1989). *Imaginary landscape: Making worlds of myth and science.* New York: St. Martin's Press.

—— (1996). *Coming into being: Artifacts and texts in the evolution of consciousness.* New York: St. Martin's Press.

15
Economics and Evolution:
An Ethos for an Action Researcher

HAZEL HENDERSON

Abstract
Futurist Hazel Henderson tells of the personal experiences and causes that have motivated her in her drive to build a better world. She proposes innovations in economics, social monitoring, democratic governance, gender balancing, and new ways of financing the United Nations.

Key words
Cultural DNA code, economics and human evolution, ecosystems, evolutionary action theory, the love economy, lose–lose vicious circles, virtuous circles, GNP, GDP, creating alternative futures, Country Futures Indicators, Human Development Index, social innovation, technological innovation, World Bank, Wealth Index, US Office of Technology Assessment, domination versus partnership, backlash, action research, global casino, global action, Calvert–Henderson Quality of Life Indicators, UNSIA, ARM-PC, FXE, COPORA.

Over my life I have found evolution to be not as it has been taught to us, as some vast impersonal force, but instead meaningful in terms of the people who have been meaningful to me personally, as activists working generation after generation to advance human evolution. So I will write here of those who have been meaningful in this way to me, and how I have been inspired by them in my own work. In this way I hope to show the limited potential for what has been called "the dismal science"—economics—to more adequately contribute to human evolution.

As a child of the particular cultural DNA code of Western scientific enlightenment, I was inculcated with reductionism, materialism, the stance of scientific objectivity, as well as individualism and self-interested competitiveness to "succeed" in the short term. This paradigm was reaching its zenith in the late 20th century. I was taught that it was "unscientific" to trust my own experience and deepest motivations—based as they were on subjective, unverifiable feelings. Yet I found inescapable the inner drives that steered my life: a fierce sense of injustice, moral indignation, and reflexive championing of underdogs and unpopular causes—common in those who have experienced marginalization as I had as a woman. I became a "deep contrarian"—believing that all reigning assumptions, elites, institutions, and establishments should be examined and challenged by two criteria: Were they life-affirming? Did they serve the age-old, magnificent, bumpy processes of human evolution within the family of living species on "Gaia," the evolving planet Earth itself?

I sought out the works of Ervin Laszlo, David Loye, Pierre Teilhard de Chardin, Buckminster Fuller, Barbara Ward, E.F. Schumacher, Margaret Mead, Kenneth and Elise Boulding, Fritjof Capra, Erich Jantsch, Alice Mary Hilton, Heinz von Foerster, and later, Riane Eisler and joined in the global debate about world dynamics unleashed by Jay Forrester, Donella and Dennis Meadows. Yet more deeply motivating were my original set of inner visions and motivations—still inexplicable by Western science—based on personal experience and the observation of Nature. Key to my moral development, I learned to love, to read, and to grow food from my mother, to revere the cycles and seasons of life from the land, people, flora, and fauna of a small English village on the stormy Atlantic coast. I learned fear of arbitrary power from the nights of aerial bombing of Nazi planes during World War II, while in our home air-raid shelter, and from seeing the rain-filled craters and hearing the news of dead playmates that the morning light revealed. I learned also that to confront arbitrary power one had to use one's wits. I learned what I needed to know largely outside classrooms, outwitting teachers, and often playing truant.

I left high school for the exciting "university of life" to explore the promises of the planet. I became a citizen of the United States of America, whose cultural DNA code suited my sense of autonomy, love of risk-taking, and challenging of sacred cows. I owe much to fellow European Ervin Laszlo, for helping bring integration to my cognitive awareness and experience, as he has for countless others, nudging us all to become "global citizens." Prior to David Loye's reconstruction of Darwin's lost theory of the moral agent, evolutionary action theory and its impressive supporting evidence that individual humans develop a moral sense and can act to make a difference, I often viewed myself as a rebel, an eccentric, and sometimes wondered whether I was neurotic or even crazy. My writings were a hopeful probe to find fellow humans who shared my concerns for the future of the human family, as well as to reflect on my life's purpose. Having been raised as an atheist, I was suspicious of religious explanations for my "evolutionary yearning." Yet, almost surreptitiously, I followed a quest for spiritual guidance and found role models from Omar Khayyam (at least, the Edward Fitzgerald translation!) and Leonardo da Vinci to Mahatma Gandhi, Mother Teresa, and Martin Luther King, Jr. Through the 1960s and 1970s I started civic groups and organized campaigns to combat air pollution and corporate irresponsibility, bringing labor unions together with environmentalists to work for full employment, and to debate technological choices, automation, guaranteed incomes, and new forms of business enterprise. In 1974 I was appointed to the founding Advisory Council of the US Office of Technology assessment (OTA), and began to push my way into the science policy area to challenge the underlying paradigms of Western science and its path of technological development, as well as to challenge the paradigms of conventional economics.

Economics and Human Evolution

I began studying what was wrong with economics because my community organizing experiences had convinced me that this discipline and its trained professionals had a key role in justifying and enforcing the paradigms and policies I actively opposed. Economics, never a science, seemed to be getting in the way of humans talking to each other about what was valuable under rapidly changing conditions. I began to devote myself to understanding where economics had gone astray. Economists often had become a *de facto* "thought police" reinforcing self-interested materialism. This dysfunctional paradigmatic strand of the Western cultural DNA code had resulted in unsustainable forms of technology, industrial development, and wasteful consumer lifestyles. My first articles[1] stated my case against economics. In these and other articles I explored how this powerful but malfunctioning strand of Western cultural DNA was replicating itself worldwide in unsustainable government policies, business activities, and individual behavior patterns that would continue destroying other human cultures, other life-forms, and whole ecosystems.[2]

The missing capstone of my argument—Loye's evolutionary action theory—was not available then. How much more it would have helped to explain! Evolutionary action theory would have helped me and countless other "action-researchers" (to use Kurt Lewin's useful term) to understand the task and tactics of millions of social activists in my generation and down through history, beyond the culturally permissible metaphors of psychology (as neurotic personalities), or religiously interpreted, as "missionaries" for various causes.[3] My full critique of economics from ecological and evolutionary perspectives is documented elsewhere.[4] Among the points I make is that the discipline of economics (even as still taught today) rests on a series of assumptions caricaturing human behavior and preferences as unchanging, motivated by individual self-interest and insatiable desires to consume material goods and later, services. These preferences are revealed in the marketplace by prices. The sum of these behaviors of economic actors bargaining in markets with producers is held to lead to a self-regulating macroeconomic system in general equilibrium.

At least human actors (if not their future generations) have always been recognized in economic theories. But the assumptions of their unchanging behavior and "human nature," as expressed only in markets and prices, has led to the idea that their collective actions are statistically insignificant. This economic model has allowed for no human consumers' role in changing the system's structure or even moving it toward disequilibrium, let alone evolution. Meanwhile, social action depends almost entirely on volunteers, since few social organizations will pay people to "rock the boat." Thus, economics ignored this kind of unpaid work—along with the unpaid work of women in what I have termed "The Love Economy" (see Figure 3). Values and technology were considered parameters and even producers were assumed to be passive pawns in the market. Ubiquitous evidence of growing oligopolies, corporate trusts, and other forms of institutional power and market failures are still taught as "exceptions" to the model. When such assumptions are criticized, the response from economists is that they know these assumptions are unrealistic, but that they continue to employ them so as to make their models work. Or they attack the credibility of the critics—for example in the editorializing of the London-based *The Economist*, a bastion of neo-classical orthodoxy.[5] Traditional economics has also focused on self-interested competition or the win–lose paradigm. But a much wider repertoire of human ways of being and becoming has been discovered by game theorists. They have also described the win–lose games and their outcomes: prisoners' dilemmas and lose–lose "vicious circles." Yet game theorists have also studied the "contrarian" strategies that avoid such herd behaviors and create novel win–win games and "virtuous circles" based on humanity's age-old cooperation, sharing and altruism, such as the gifts and potlaches of tribal societies described by Lewis Hyde, Karl Polanyi, and Marshall Sahlins.[6] Human actions during the Great Depression also clearly refuted classical economic assumptions, as documented after the fact in John Maynard Keynes' *General Theory of Employment, Interest and Money.*[7]

How much of this bears on human evolution is explored in my *Politics of the Solar Age*, where I review 300 years of economic theorizing from the French Physiocrats to Keynes and the so-called "neo-classical synthesis," which tried unsuccessfully to incorporate Keynes's disequilibrium view.[8] An important part of my analyses focused on the 50 percent of all productive work in industrial societies that is unpaid and its counterpart informal, traditional economies in the developing world. Constituting some 60–70 percent of all production, this unpaid and informal economy is still invisible to economists. I also documented economists' belated recognition of technological and ecological disequilibria impinging inevitably on the margins of the placid, reversible Newtonian economics paradigm. Karl Marx seeded, documented, and led in the demonstration of how human action changes economic equilibria and our evolution. He showed that the role of organizations of workers, the poor and the role of capitalists and technological inventions caused revolutionary and sometimes evolutionary changes affecting the structures of whole societies and millions of people. Marx was an evolutionist, as were the early ecological economists—notably Frederick Soddy, a chemist who shared the Nobel Prize with E. Rutherford, for discovering isotopes. Soddy was the first of many natural scientists to challenge and pierce the deductive web of assumptions of economics. Soddy's *Cartesian Economics*, published in 1913 and ridiculed by economists, pointed out that solar energy and ecological cycles drove all the processes underlying combustion, human and agricultural production, and the Industrial Revolution itself.

Nicholas Georgescu-Roegen continued in Soddy's path with his transdisciplinary treatise *The Entropy Law and the Economic Process*, which incorporated much knowledge from the natural and social sciences, including the disequilibrium view of human evolution.[9] Georgescu-Roegen, in his fundamental critique and re-contexting of economics, was arguably one of the greatest economists of this century, but he died unsung in 1994, with only a well-deserved eulogy by his most famous student, Herman Daly.[10] Herman Daly, continued and expanded Georgescu-Roegen's work in *Toward a Steady State Economy* (1973) as did others, including Barbara Ward, Fred Hirsch, E.J. Mishan, Pentti Malaska, Orio Giarini, this author, and many others in Asia and Latin America. With Donella and Dennis Meadows's report to the Club of Rome, *Limits to Growth* (1972), the debate on "the global *problematique*" went public.

Desacralizing the Sacred GNP and GDP

With the generous encouragement of Nicholas Georgescu-Roegen, Kenneth and Elise Boulding, Eric Trist, Aurelio Peccei, Donald Michael, Erich Jantsch, and Heinz von Foerster, and in collaboration with Barbara Ward, E.F. Schumacher, and Fritjof Capra,[11] I embarked on a broader overview of societal organization, human cultures, and ecological dynamics. I was looking for more precise interventions that could serve as "trim-tabs," as another mentor, Buckminster Fuller, advised. The first such exploration was that of publicly calling into question the Gross National Product (GNP) and its narrower domestic version Gross Domestic Product (GDP), enshrined in 1953 by most nations as the United Nations System of National Accounts (UNSNA).[12]

Media amplification and other "chaos effects" had led to the emergence of this type of narrow national economic accounting as the unchallenged scorecard of progress and wealth on a global scale—a use unintended by the measure's early innovators. Building on the work of Frederick Soddy, K.W. Kapp, Kenneth Boulding, and Georgescu-Roegen, my first critiques of the shortcomings of GNP/GDP were summarized in three diagrams (Figures 1–3) that I used in my books, articles, and thousands of lectures. Increasingly I realized that all social interventions in large information-rich societies, such as the United States, must employ mass media as well as precise visual images and linguistic compressions that can humanly engage the society's cultural DNA code: its collective experience, values, and goals. So I further battered away at GNP and GDP in my CBS/TV Sunrise Semester series in 1974, and my 1984 TV series "Creating Alternative Futures," uplinked to PBS stations from the University of Florida's WUFT-TV.[13]

After over a decade, this activity—along with many other efforts worldwide, both documented and undocumented—began to bear fruit. In Rio de Janeiro at the United Nations (UN) Earth Summit in 1992, some 20,000 leaders of civic organizations joined with me and other grassroots spokespeople in calling for the correction of GNP/GDP so as to include unpaid work and account for environmental costs and the value of natural resources.

In 1987 I had developed my own set of multidisciplinary alternatives to GNP/

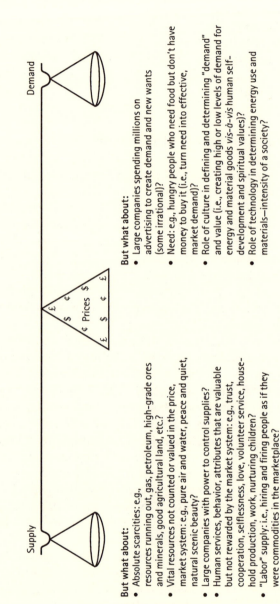

Supply

Prices
$ ¢
£ ¢ $
¢ $ £
£ ¢ £

Demand

But what about:

- Absolute scarcities: e.g., resources running out, gas, petroleum, high-grade ores and minerals, good agricultural land, etc.?
- Vital resources not counted or valued in the price, market system: e.g., pure air and water, peace and quiet, natural scenic beauty?
- Large companies with power to control supplies?
- Human services, behavior, attributes that are valuable but not rewarded by the market system: e.g., trust, cooperation, selflessness, love, volunteer service, household production, work, nurturing children?
- "Labor" supply: i.e., hiring and firing people as if they were commodities in the marketplace?

But what about:

- Large companies spending millions on advertising to create demand and new wants (some irrational)?
- Need: e.g., hungry people who need food but don't have money to buy it (i.e., turn need into effective, market demand)?
- Role of culture in defining and determining "demand" and value (i.e., creating high or low levels of demand for energy and material goods vis-à-vis human self-development and spiritual values)?
- Role of technology in determining energy use and materials—intensity of a society?

Figure 1. The "free market" equilibrium model of supply and demand
(*Economists admit it's only a theory—but they often write, advise, and act as if it were real*)

Source: © Hazel Henderson, 1978

220

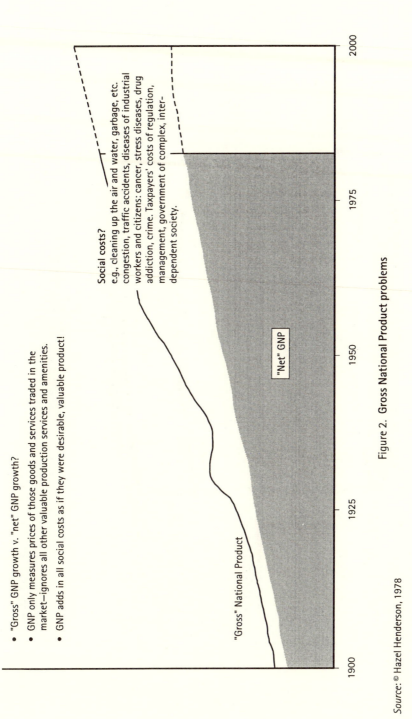

- "Gross" GNP growth *v.* "net" GNP growth?
- GNP only measures prices of those goods and services traded in the market—ignores all other valuable production services and amenities.
- GNP adds in all social costs as if they were desirable, valuable product!

Social costs?
e.g., cleaning up the air and water, garbage, etc. congestion, traffic accidents, diseases of industrial workers and citizens: cancer, stress diseases, drug addiction, crime. Taxpayers' costs of regulation, management, government of complex, inter-dependent society.

"Gross" National Product

"Net" GNP

1900   1925   1950   1975   2000

Figure 2.   Gross National Product problems

Source: © Hazel Henderson, 1978

221

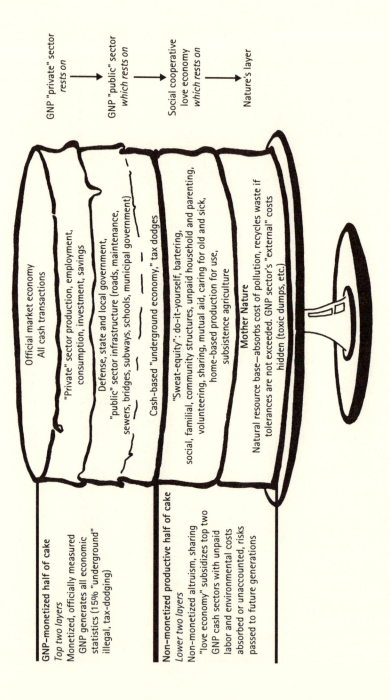

GNP-monetized half of cake
Top two layers
Monetized, officially measured
GNP generates all economic
statistics (15% "underground"
illegal, tax-dodging)

Non-monetized productive half of cake
Lower two layers
Non-monetized altruism, sharing
"love economy" subsidizes top two
GNP cash sectors with unpaid
labor and environmental costs
absorbed or unaccounted, risks
passed to future generations

Official market economy
All cash transactions

"Private" sector production, employment,
consumption, investment, savings

Defense, state and local government,
"public" sector infrastructure (roads, maintenance,
sewers, bridges, subways, schools, municipal government)

Cash-based "underground economy," tax dodges

"Sweat-equity": do-it-yourself, bartering,
social, familial, community structures, unpaid household and parenting,
volunteering, sharing, mutual aid, caring for old and sick,
home-based production for use,
subsistence agriculture

Mother Nature
Natural resource base—absorbs cost of pollution, recycles waste if
tolerances are not exceeded. GNP sector's "external" costs
hidden (toxic dumps, etc.)

GNP "private" sector
rests on
→
GNP "public" sector
which rests on
→
Social cooperative
love economy
which rests on
→
Nature's layer

Figure 3. Total productive system of an industrial society (layer cake with icing)

Source: © Hazel Henderson, 1982

GDP: Country Futures Indicators (CFI) (see Table 1). I continued promoting CFI and also the Index of Sustainable Economic Welfare (ISEW) of Herman Daly and John Cobb in *Toward the Common Good* (1987). This Index, in my view, was very useful but still too highly aggregated and reliant on money-coefficients and

Table 1. **Country Futures Indicators™**
beyond money-denominated, per capita averaged growth of GNP

Reformulated GNP to correct errors and provide more information:	Complementary indicators of progress toward society's goals:
• PURCHASING POWER PARITY (PPP) corrects for currency fluctuations	• POPULATION birth rates, crowding, age distribution
• INCOME DISTRIBUTION is the poverty gap widening or narrowing?	• EDUCATION literacy levels, school dropout and repetition rates
• COMMUNITY-BASED ACCOUNTING to complement current enterprise basis	• HEALTH infant mortality, low birth rate, weight/height/age
• INFORMAL, HOUSEHOLD SECTOR PRODUCTION measures all hours worked (paid and unpaid)	• NUTRITION e.g., calories per day, protein/carbohydrates ratio, etc.
• DEDUCT SOCIAL AND ENVIRONMENTAL COSTS a "net" accounting avoids double counting	• BASIC SERVICES e.g., access to clean water, etc.
• ACCOUNT FOR DEPLETION OF NON-RENEWABLE RESOURCES analogous to a capital-consumption deflator	• SHELTER housing availability/quality, homelessness, etc.
• ENERGY INPUT/GDP RATIO measures energy efficiency, recycling	• PUBLIC SAFETY crime
• MILITARY/CIVILIAN BUDGET RATIO measures effectiveness of governments	• CHILD DEVELOPMENT World Health Organization, UNESCO, etc.
• CAPITAL ASSET ACCOUNT FOR BUILT INFRASTRUCTURE AND PUBLIC RESOURCES (Many economists agree this is needed. Some include environment as a resource.)	• POLITICAL PARTICIPATION AND DEMOCRATIC PROCESS e.g., Amnesty International data, money-influence in elections, electoral participation rates
	• STATUS OF MINORITY AND ETHNIC POPULATIONS AND WOMEN e.g., human rights data
	• AIR AND WATER QUALITY AND ENVIRONMENTAL POLLUTION LEVELS air pollution in urban areas
	• ENVIRONMENTAL RESOURCE DEPLETION hectares of land, forests lost annually
	• BIODIVERSITY AND SPECIES LOSS e.g., Canada's environmental indicators
	• CULTURE, RECREATIONAL RESOURCES e.g., Jacksonville, Florida

Source: © Hazel Henderson, 1989

macroeconomic methods. The Human Development Index (HDI) was launched in 1990 by the UN Development Programme, to the consternation of the UN Statistical Department, whose economists still hewed to the UNSNA, namely, the GNP/GDP approach to human development. HDI broadened the scope of development theory beyond the economic view toward integrating social and environmental factors. HDI is released annually and has made significant strides since its first edition. It has also overcome many efforts to suppress it. The 1995 HDI documented for the first time the US$16 trillion missing from global GDP annually: the unpaid work of women (US$11 trillion) and of men (US$5 trillion). This unpaid contribution to world production amounted in 1995 to almost two-thirds of the official count of some US$24 trillion; that is, a more accurate account of 1995 global GDP would have been closer to US$40 trillion—calling into question much of today's agonizing over deficits and "balancing" national budgets.

Over 170 countries signed *Agenda 21*, the final document of the 1992 Earth Summit, which included the provisions to expand and correct GNP/GDP national accounts so as to include unpaid work, environmental costs, and the value of natural resources.[14] Cognitive dissonance grew among policymakers, professionals, economists, and other social and natural scientists whose charge was to implement these provisions of *Agenda 21* under the guidance of the new UN Commission on Sustainable Development. By 1994, a veritable alphabet soup of new indicators joined the UNDP's HDI. Besides my CFI, several versions of Daly and Cobb's ISEW appeared in Britain, Scandinavia, the Netherlands, Germany, and later the United States. Grassroots and women's organizations, as well as environmentalists, devised their own new "scorecards" and hundreds of cities around the world developed their own "Healthy Cities Indicators." Riane Eisler and David Loye's *Women, Men, and the Global Quality of Life* (1995) used gender-disaggregation of existing data from many countries to show the close correlations between the status of women and overall quality of life for whole populations. These new indicators were often networked by Dr. Ilona Kickbush of the World Health Organization and other scientist/activists, including sociologist Marion Chambers, innovator of the Jacksonville Quality Indicators for Progress, Florida—in continuous use since 1983. Meanwhile, work on the first version of my CFI was initiated in 1994 as a joint venture with the Calvert Social Investment Funds of Washington, DC as the Calvert–Henderson Quality-of-Life Indicators[sm].

Evolutionary Prospects for Social Innovation

It remains to be seen whether this kind of social intervention can help reorient the path of industrialism into healthier, more humane, and equitable forms of ecologically sustainable development. On the hopeful side, the rapidity with which public awareness grew worldwide about the deficiencies of steering economies on the GNP/GDP course offers further evidence supporting both the chaos model of human social evolution and the role that determined action-researchers can play in bringing about rapid change. By late 1995, the World Bank had capitulated to public pressure and released its own new Wealth Index, which classifies 60 percent of the wealth of nations as "human capital" (education, social organization, etc.), 20 percent as "natural capital" (environmental and natural resources), and a mere 20 percent as "human-built capital" (factories, buildings, bridges, finance, etc.). This admission that most of the Bank's policies for 50 years have been overly focused on this latter 20 percent of "human-built capital" represents a revolutionary paradigm shift.

The fact that, as of 1997, the Bank's actual operations still do not incorporate the shifts required by the criteria of its new Wealth Index, however, is another example of both the resistance and inertia the activist must overcome, as well as the stability of social structures and the power of replication.[15] On the biological level, bias in favor of replication over innovation (or mutation) is life-preserving, as in maintaining the stability of DNA, yet can also be life-threatening if organisms, as our society is, resist change required for survival.

My involvement in these social innovations increased my interest in the process of social innovation itself, which I define as an innovation employing human technics (both "hardware" and "software," as in the Greek "techne") that can be imagined and applied systemically to ameliorate life-threatening social or environmental conditions. My intervention in redesigning indicators for evaluating and steering sustainable human development is a case in point. Here my goal was to directly affect the human evolutionary process—an academically outrageous proposition. Yet it did not raise the taboos and resistance that would have greeted a purely intellectual approach. Using the conventional social science approach of my Country Futures Indicators helped make this attempt to intervene in human evolution quite acceptable.

The 22-year experiment at the US Office of Technology Assessment (OTA), itself a social innovation, however, demonstrates how far *technological innovation* has run ahead of human capabilities for foresight and management, as Laszlo, Loye, and others have shown. Indeed, the pace of technological change is still accelerating, as Alvin Toffler warned in Future Shock.[16]

What kind of system-wide *social innovations* are needed to steer prosocial technologies toward the evolution of human societies and cultures, which lag behind by decades and sometimes generations?[17] Here Riane Eisler's *The Chalice and the Blade* (1985) provides a key. For some 5,000 years, technology has evolved within male-dominated social systems. The emphasis has been on ecologically incompatible technologies, weapons, and social domination rather than partnership with women, other humans, and nature. By contrast, social innovation must be a subtle, system-wide process, rooted in holistic, transdisciplinary cultural, social, technical, political, economic research, and policy analyses. Models of general evolution, disequilibrium, systems, chaos, and game theories are necessary—but not sufficient. Social innovations require experimentation by action-researchers, the imaging of alternative futures scenarios, and ethical motivations beyond self-interest and a time perspective considerably beyond any single human life-span. Evolutionary action-researchers must be motivated to accelerate social innovation and cultural evolution in the *short term* to preserve *long-term* societal options and ecosystems for their descendants.

Backlash and what to Do about It

In terms of both history and cultural evolution theory, Eisler also points out the fierce resistance to shifting cultural paradigms and their technical/social systems away from male-dominance toward what she calls the "partnership model." For example, the Office of Technology Assessment was warned at its inception that assessments of military technology were out of bounds. Then as now, the US Congress, the administration, and courts were male dominated, and I, not surprisingly, was the only woman on the 14–person Advisory Council composed of corporate CEOs, university presidents, and Nobel award scientists. OTA's subsequent groundbreaking scientific studies, which I and a few other Council members fought to make transdisciplinary, were continually opposed by neo-classical economists, business groups, and conservatives.

The Republican Congress finally succeeded in shutting down OTA in 1996. In addition to these fundamental currents and struggles in human societies, it must be remembered that change itself is disequilibrium—generating discomfort, fear, and resistance among dominant cohorts. This undoubtedly accounts for the ubiquitous backlash historians have noted.[18]

As I have elaborated elsewhere, on a more surface level the Western scientific/political/economic paradigm reinforces technological innovations driven by free markets, profit motives, and consumer preferences.[19] This seems to account for technology's focus on weapons, powerful, ecologically destructive energy, and resource utilization, as well as the flood of often trivial consumer products. Further, the "free market" economic paradigm masks the role of government subsidies, industrial policies, market power, corporate research and development, as well as advertising and marketing budgets devoted to selling and portraying all such technological innovations as "progress." By contrast, social innovation is excoriated in this paradigm as "social engineering," "planning," or merely as "socialism."

Since the end of the Cold War, markets and privatization have accelerated their global penetration and technological development. Economists often equate these globalizations with the spread of democracy, while urging the further downsizing of governments—already in retreat worldwide. I have documented these global trends elsewhere and how they created the vacuum of governance at all levels that increasingly is being filled by an emerging "third sector" of voluntary, nonprofit organizations and individuals.[20]

For all these reasons, action-research on social innovation is an urgent priority.

At the same time, all social innovations should be introduced in "pilot" projects, or as small, reversible, error-friendly experiments to be carefully evaluated for their unanticipated consequences. Historical evaluation of previous social innovations —for example in the United States, the Reconstruction years following the ending of slavery by the Civil War and the "New Deal" of Franklin D. Roosevelt, both of which generated enormous opposition—require deeper understanding and review.

Another observable pattern is that the social and economic restructuring that inevitably follows human invention and technological innovation in the *private sector* eventually seems to call forth adaptation in the *public sector*. However, as mentioned, such needed social innovations arrive only after long lagtimes. Sometimes they are triggered by industrial accidents, as in the Union Carbide plant's toxic releases, which killed and maimed thousands in Bhopal, India, or after crises like the meltdown of the nuclear reactor at Chernobyl, Ukraine. The crises of World War I and World War II led to the social innovations of the League of Nations in 1918 (doomed by US backlash) and the United Nations, founded in 1945, to protect "We the Peoples" from "the scourge of war."[21]

In the end, however, it is over and over again the story of the mismatch between the "tortoise" of social innovation and the "hare" of technological innovation—a story of ego-states (fear of death and lust for control, power, money), sheer arrogance, and social, spiritual, and environmental crises. Studying this great mismatch can provide a key to reengineering our productive sectors, re-designing our communities and cities, and addressing the great issues of globalization with new global agreements and renewing our societies for the fast-approaching 21st century. Social innovation involves remapping outside conventional "boxes" as well as creative and cooperative responses. Agreements must be devised to complement and coordinate private, competitively driven technological innovations, and to consciously and proactively mesh these two processes.

In the final analysis, social innovation, like technological innovation, is about the power of the human mind. Ever since we humans learned to stand upright, freeing our hands, with their versatile opposing thumbs, our growing forebrains have allowed us to create visions and manifest them on Earth.[22] We have emerged as the only species able to change the face of the Earth, its ozone layer, its flora and fauna, with our technological and architectural structures, some of which, like the Great Wall of China, are visible from the moon. Today's task is, therefore, to shape our mental, moral, and decisionmaking skills to meet the challenges to our very survival that our misguided technological innovations have now created. This requires a flowering of *social* innovation, rethinking our paradigms, reengineering, and redesigning of our social as well as physical architecture.

The brief 300–year period of the industrial era is a page in human history when societies appeared, first in Britain, that were based on and driven by technological innovation. The current stage of industrialism and its competitive technological acceleration involve the globalization of these processes. Futures research methods, technological forecasting and assessment, systems theory, decision sciences, and the growing capabilities of computers themselves have given us earlier warnings. Attempts in this century at the social control of technology, however, have often been too late to prevent irreparable damage and irreversible changes.

Why did policymakers not respond more adequately to these early warnings urged on them by a generation of policy analysts? The problem is that paradigms persist long beyond their usefulness and, as Thomas Kuhn noted in his *Structure of Scientific Revolutions*, changing a paradigm usually involves a new generation of humans.[23] Here the new understanding of the dynamics of paradigm defense and change of Loye's evolutionary action theory offers great promise in spanning the gulf between the "value-free, objective observation" model of Western science and the realities of human intervention and action. An integration of this institutionalized schizophrenia is long overdue.

Global Action: Ups and Downs and Some Specific Proposals

Fortunately there is much we can turn to for important lessons on how to integrate technological and social innovation into broader public policy goals. Social information technologies—telephones, faxes, computers, teleconferences, electronic town meetings, satellites, etc.; small group encounters as developed by Kurt Lewin; the "futures search conferences" of Eric Trist and Fred Emery; "anticipatory democracy" advocated by Alvin and Heidi Toffler; the "public interest polling" pioneered by the Americans Talk Issues Foundation's Alan F. Kay—all can reinforce and accelerate such harmonization processes.[24] We have a large, underutilized repertoire of such methodologies to facilitate conferencing and networking for scientific and policy bodies with businesses and civic groups as well as to enhance participation in democratic policymaking.[25] Information technologies, including radio and television (whose owners can no longer avoid their social responsibility by hiding behind their press freedoms), can be far better used for conflict resolution, norm and standard setting. It is imperative that a design revolution now occur on a planet-wide scale if we are to work *within* Nature's design and enhance our life prospects for the future. Social innovations, from *habeas corpus* and Roberts Rules of order, to the rise of universal suffrage, democracies, social pensions, insurance, and welfare systems, are in place as models to build upon.[26]

Beyond the Calvert–Henderson Quality-of-Life Indicators[sm], described earlier, I have proposed other social innovations based on the need to redesign economic paradigms and monetary systems now severely stressed by 24–hour financial markets and the massive volume and velocity of trading in what I describe elsewhere as the "global casino" in today's "financial cyberspace." I have proposed ways to reframe national security beyond weapons and military approaches as risks that can be insured collectively by nations, and to overhaul the UN—itself perhaps the most important social innovation of the 20th century.

To outline them briefly:

1. The United Nations Security Insurance Agency (UNSIA) and its companion proposal, the Anticipatory Risk-Mitigation Peace-building Contingents (ARM-PC) developed with Alan F. Kay. Similar in structure to INTELSAT and the World Bank, UNSIA would be authorized by the UN General Assembly and report to the Security Council in response to requests from member-nations to provide "insurance policies" to deter potential aggression. This would allow such countries to shift significant percentages of their military budgets to investments in their civilian sectors and reduce their overall national expenditures.

To motivate private sector involvement, the insurance industry would provide risk-assessment services to such countries to determine their overall insurability. This would depend on the extent to which they maintained good relations with neighboring states; eschewed nuclear, biological, chemical, and other weapons of mass destruction; and did not harbor terrorists, practice or teach violence, "ethnic cleansing," or other policies unacceptable under international law. Each "insurance policy" would be individually-negotiated and the pool of premiums would constitute a trust fund available to provide peace-keeping and conflict-resolution contingents—including civic groups already based in the country.

This proposal was debated at the UN Social Summit in Copenhagen in 1995 and has received wide support from Nobel Prize winners Oscar Arias, John Polanyi, and Betty Williams, as well as many other notables. The companion proposal for the civil society component—ARM-PC—was debated in the UN Security Council in April of 1996. In May, 1996, then UN Secretary General Boutros Boutros-Ghali requested the Security Council to explore the possibility of a "rapid-deployment humanitarian force."

The UNSIA and its ARM-PC, if operational, might have helped forestall such tragedies as those in Bosnia, Rwanda, and Somalia, as well as demonstrating that countries today can buy much more deterrence and genuine security at much lower cost by using such preventive and insurance routes to security.[27]

2. A state-of-the-art Foreign Exchange for currencies (FXE) to tame today's computerized financial trading systems in our daily US\$1.3 trillion global casino.[28]

The FXE proposal was based on the concept of Ruben Mendes of Yale University and codeveloped with Alan F. Kay, former founder and CEO of AutEx, the first computerized market for stocks and bonds. The FXE would be operated as a "public utility" by the largest possible group of central banks in cooperation with the UN. The FXE would offer much-needed competition to the virtual monopoly over global currency exchange by large private banks and currency traders.

Since these enormous currency exchange flows are 90 percent speculative, they have increased volatility. This has sharply diminished the power of central banks to stabilize their nations' currencies and reduced domestic sovereignty and macroeconomic control over fiscal and monetary policies as well as employment rates, social "safety-nets," and environmental protection. The proposed "public interest" FXE would help governments control and collect fees on currency transactions and limit speculation, money-laundering, and other criminal activities. Central banks could play against private traders on a level playing-field and governments could use the transaction fees collected (many are mandated already in various countries) to fund multilateral emergency measures.

3. The Congressional Office of Public Opinion, Research and Assessment (COPORA).

This proposal for widespread public interest polling, developed with Alan F. Kay, was introduced by Congressman Ron Klink into the 103rd Congress. COPORA employs electronic "Consensus Location" survey methods to reopen the channels from people to Congress and their government. It was tested in surveys by the Americans Talk Issues Foundation in 1993, 1994, and 1995 and is favored by majorities of between 65–75 percent of the American people. It side-steps the influence of lobbyists and PAC money by re-randomizing the feedback to members of Congress from all the American people and "dampening out" the influence of special interests. Perfecting and redesigning our 18th-century democratic machinery for the 21st Century in such ways is crucial to introducing many other needed social innovations. Survey results would be released immediately to all news media so that Americans could assess the extent to which Congressional actions were representative of their constituents' priorities. No directives would override legislators' prerogatives, but COPORA would vastly augment the anecdotal information and spotty feedback on which Congressional members currently rely. Nevertheless, COPORA encountered a firestorm of criticism and was pronounced "dead on arrival," as described more fully in Alan F. Kay's forthcoming book, *Locating Consensus for Democracy: A Ten-Year U.S. Experiment.*[29] This social innovation may first take hold in other democracies where special interests have less of a stranglehold on their legislators.

Some of these social innovations are more easily understood and may be adopted more quickly. Others are unlikely to make much headway in this country without a social crisis or a wholesale paradigm shift, yet may find more fertile ground in other countries before they are accepted in the United States.

Two Lessons:
The Power of Prevention and the Cooperative Advantage

Two rubrics, "the power of prevention" and "the cooperative advantage," codify many of the lessons learned from these and earlier historical experiences. Win–win and "contrarian" strategies can complement economics' win–lose, competition. Today's narrow globalization of competitive markets is leading to vicious cycles and their lowest common denominator "races-to-the-bottom," locally, regionally, nationally, and globally. By contrast, game theory maps a broader, overlooked repertoire of human behavior, altruism, cooperation, nurturing, and contrarian rather than "herd" behavior—verified by generations of cultural anthropologists and psychologists. These complementary human behaviors in such new movements as those of socially-responsible investors (now accounting for US$1.3 trillion of assets in the United States alone), as well as the promulgation of global codes of conduct, standards, and treaties, can lead to "virtuous cycles."[30]

If we pursue policies such as these, eventually we can raise the ethical floor under today's anarchic global economic playing-field so that the most ethical corporations and countries can win. Today's challenges to create new paths to sustainable forms of development must channel and employ the energies and talents of increasingly more of us, and with a much greater sense of urgency. An expanding effort to steer our technical genius can build more peaceful, prosperous, and conscious paths to human development and continuing evolution of all life on this planet.

If we humans fail to evolve culturally and morally, the planet will survive without us. The choice is ours.

Notes

It is an honor to contribute to this tribute to Ervin Laszlo and his pioneering intellectual and social contribution to human evolutionary processes in the 20th Century.

1. See Should business tackle society's problems, *Harvard Business Review*, 46(4), July–August, 1968; Toward managing social conflict, *Harvard Business Review*, 49(3), May–June, 1971; Ecologists versus economists, *Harvard Business Review*, 51(4), July–August, 1973.

2. H. Henderson, *Business economics*, 1970; *Columbia Review of World Business*, 1972; *Financial Analysts Journal*, 1974.

3. Kurt Lewin, *Resolving social conflicts*, New York: Harper and Rowe, 1948.

4. H. Henderson, *Politics of the solar age*, chs. 8 (Three hundred years of snake oil) and 9 (Workers and environmentalists: The common cause), New York: Doubleday, 1981; reprinted Indianapolis, Indiana: Knowledge Systems, Inc., 1988, and New York: Toes Books, 1989.

5. See, e.g., Palindrome repents, *The Economist*, January 25, 1997 (p. 18), an editorial attacking financier George Soros for debunking economics and free markets.

6. Lewis Hyde, *The gift*, New York: Vintage, 1979; Karl Polanyi, *The great transformation*, Boston: Beacon, 1944; Marshall Sahlins, *Stone age economics*, Hawthorne, NY: Aldine de Gruyter, 1972.

7. John Maynard Keynes, *General theory of employment, interest and money*, New York: Harcourt Brace, 1934.

8. H. Henderson, *Politics of the solar age*, Part II.

9. Nicholas Georgescu-Roegen, *The entropy law and the economic process*, Cambridge, MA: Harvard University Press, 1971.

10. Herman E. Daly, On Nicholas Georgescu-Roegen's contribution to economics, *Ecological Economics*, June, 1995, p. 149.

11. I collaborated with Barbara Ward in preparation for the first UN conference on the environment, Stockholm, 1972; with E.F. Schumacher (who wrote the foreword to my *Creating alternative futures*, Kumarian Press, 1978, 1996) in arranging his first lecture tour in the United States in 1973; and with Fritjof Capra in preparing a research paper on the paradigmatic foundations of economics for his book, *The turning point*, New York: Simon & Schuster, 1981.

12. H. Henderson, What's next in the great debate about measuring wealth and progress?, *Challenge*, May, 1996.

13. H. Henderson, producer, "Creating alternative futures," TV Series, WUFT-TV, Public Broadcasting System, 1984. Video cassettes from Bullfrog Films, Oley, PA 19547. Ph.: 1–800–543–3764.

14. *Agenda 21*, New York: United Nations Commission on Sustainable Development, 1992.

15. H. Henderson, *Building a win–win world*, ch. 10 (pp. 224–225), San Francisco: Berrett-Koehler, 1996.

16. Alvin Toffler, *Future shock*, New York: Random House, 1970.

17. H. Henderson, *Creating alternative futures*, ch. 18 (Awakening from the technological trance), New York: Putnam's Sons, 1978; reprint by Kumarian Press, 1996.

18. Roszak *et al.*, cited in Riane Eisler, Cultural evolution, in Ervin Laszlo, Ed., *The new evolutionary paradigm* (ch. 9), London, Paris, New York: Gordon & Breach, 1991.

19. H. Henderson, Social innovation and citizen movements, *Futures*, 25(3), 322–338 (April, 1993).

20. H. Henderson, *Building a win-win world*, ch. 6 (Grassroots globalism).

21. Charter of the United Nations, New York, 1945.

22. David Loye, *The knowable future: A psychology of forecasting and prophecy*. New York: Wiley-Interscience, 1978.

23. Thomas Kuhn, *Structure of scientific revolutions*, Chicago, IL: University of Chicago Press, 1961.

24. Copies of the Americans Talk Issues surveys can be purchased by addressing requests to Americans Talk Issues, 10 Carrera St., St. Augustine, FL 32084.

25. H. Henderson, *Building a win-win world*, chs. 11 (Perfecting democracy's tools) and 12 (New markets and new commons).

26. Charlotte Waterlow, *The hinge of history*, London: One World Trust, Ltd., 1995.

27. Col. Daniel Smith (Ret.), The United Nations Security Insurance Agency (UNSIA) proposal: A preliminary assessment, *Futures*, March, 1995, pp. 209–213; see also Cleveland, Henderson, and Kaul, Eds., The United Nations: Policy and financing alternatives, *Report of the Global Commission to fund the United Nations*, 1996, 2100 Connecticut Ave., NW, Suite 204, Washington, DC 20008 or fax: 202–639–9459.

28. H. Henderson and Alan F. Kay, Introducing competition to the global currency markets, *Futures*, 28(4), 305–324 (May, 1996).

29. Alan F. Kay, *Locating consensus for democracy: A ten-year U.S. experiment*, forthcoming.

30. H. Henderson, Building a win–win world, contribution to volume on globalization, *Boundless?*, Germany: Wuppertal Institute, forthcoming.

16
What Might Be the Next Stage in Cultural Evolution?

PAUL H. RAY

Abstract
Sociologist Paul H. Ray takes a look at where his seven-year survey of American attitudes and values indicates we are headed in the 21st century. The main movement he finds is away from earlier entrenchment in Traditionalist and Modernist alignments into the new social thrust of the "Cultural Creatives."

Key words
Survival of the wisest, limits to growth, Integral Culture, information economy, Sorokin's theory of cultural dynamics, Cultural Creatives, Heartlanders, Modernists, humanistic psychology, transpersonal psychology, ecology movement, women's movement, ecological sustainability, globalism, feminism, altruism, spirituality, social conscience, civil rights movement, peace movement, environmental movement, alternative health care, vegetarian and natural foods movement, new religions, New Age movement, communitarian movement.

The issue before us is to describe the role of the human in evolution as it affects us directly today—so that we can deal with the emerging global *problematique* that must inform our present decisions. This inevitably means we must deal with the limitations of our data, images, and beliefs about humanity and the global prospect over long periods of time. Our culture's inherited beliefs and values about "man's" place in nature are grotesquely inappropriate to the era we are entering. My own fear is that human extinctions of other species on an accelerating basis are reducing the carrying capacity of the Earth, as is the great likelihood of global warming. Humanity as an evolutionary actor could be well on its way to creating another great evolutionary die-off. Can we reverse course, saving ourselves along with countless other species?

Survival of the Wisest?

Most ecologists and global *problematique* writers observe with alarm that there are limits to growth, first suggested by Malthus, and as nailed down by the research of Meadows *et al.* for the Club of Rome (1972 and 1992). In his evocatively titled

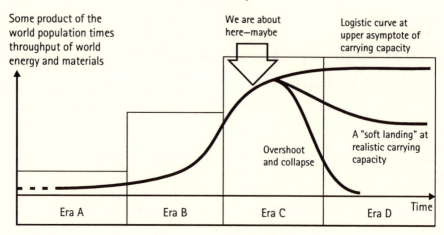

Figure 1. **Variations on the logistic curve**

Survival of the Wisest (1973), famed viral researcher Jonas Salk suggested that at its best the evolutionary envelope of possibilities for humans in relation to our environment might look like a gigantic sigmoid curve of the kind described by biologist Raymond Pearl in the 1920s (see Figure 1). (Though Salk did not specify it, I interpret that curve as population size times throughput of energy and materials per unit time.) It is the image of the equilibrium growth curve of the number of fruit flies in a bottle—which, if you've ever seen a bottle of mashed bananas with a pullulating mass of fruit flies crawling over it and hovering in its fetid air, is actually a nasty image. Salk believed that evolutionary survival in the future requires a new rule, survival of the wisest. The fundamental cultural assumptions and lifeways for humans in the leveled-off, no-growth period after accelerated growth is really the topic of this paper.

Let us step back and look at the whole of a sigmoid curve envelope as applied to our own species' cultural evolution, from past to future. Over a long time span, it would look like four eras: Era A has growth too slow to measure on most timescales, Era B has accelerating growth, Era C has decelerating growth, Era D has growth too slow to measure if we attain a new equilibrium (top line), or if we find a "soft landing" at a realistic carrying capacity (mid line), or if we have an overshoot and collapse (bottom line), which is explained below.

Era C, which is our era, is obviously the time of choice—and danger. Figure 1 could depict many, many curves, as Meadows *et al.* have done. While many can crash, and many can level off at various levels of well-being, none can continue to accelerate. Whatever else is true, we now seem to face extinction or life on a leveled-off curve.

For one or two million years, creatures biologically human have been acquiring the culture that makes them distinctively human. From a human ecology viewpoint, population and total human societal throughputs of energy and materials from the environment were flat, extremely slow growing, and humans had a negligible impact on other species, except for a few large prey animals that we may have hunted to extinction. Humans saw themselves as few and relatively helpless against poorly understood forces in nature. Between 10,000 and 6,000 years ago humans acquired agriculture and early cities in the early surge of human development. The Biblical command "go forth and multiply" came then, and indeed these urban–agrarian civilizations were themselves quite capable of filling up all the lightly populated spaces of the Earth and killing off other most other plant and animal species, given enough time. China, India and Medieval Europe were all well on their way to doing just that by AD1300.

But in Europe the Black Death intervened, and out of that recovery from devastation came not only the discovery and exploitation of the Americas, but industrial modernism and colonialism. For the last 500 years, human exploitation of the Earth has accelerated in step with the accelerating technology and economy of the "modern" world. In that time, we Moderns have lived as if an upward-turning curve of accelerating growth were our birthright, and as if "go forth and multiply" could be unending. Today, however, the *annual* increment of world population is about as great as the *total* world population of early Biblical times, and despite the claims of cornucopians (Simon, 1995), it is self-evidently unsustainable. The massive extinctions of other plant and animal species and global warming guarantee that our modernizing global civilization cannot continue on its current trajectory. Whatever else is true, the world we have grown up with, and are intellectually comfortable with, cannot continue. We stand at the threshold of a new evolutionary era.

In each historical era, humanity's characteristic ways of believing and behaving have been tied to making the most of what it takes to adapt to a given kind of environment. "What adapts best" is "what's good." For most of history, humans were small in numbers and impact relative to the global environment. The traditional church-bound ideology of "man in nature" imagines a relatively empty slow-growth "world of limits" imposed by lack of knowledge and technology. It is an equilibrium-type of ideology that could not imagine change, and modernism rudely overthrew it. Hence, as soon as we found the means, usury, greed, status display, and covetousness could be elevated from sins to social and financial desiderata (not to mention decontrolling sexuality).

Now humanity's numbers, and our use of available energy, plant materials, and technology are all huge relative to our planetary environment. A sociologist of knowledge would predict that our societal definition of success and the good will quickly shift to making a virtue of our necessity. What adapts best now is "survival of the wisest," and if we succeed, that will soon come to define what's good. Global overpopulation and overexploitation of the environment demand overthrowing our modern growth-justifying ideologies, in much the same way that early modernism overthrew medieval scholasticism. The priesthood of economists and financiers is still in deep denial that their own view may be as passé as the medieval one. Today's Modernist economists and financiers may take on the role of the Counter-Reformation's Catholic Church and Inquisition.

A population dynamics argument would say that the sigmoid curve may be too simple and too optimistic, that in fact the real danger is the overshoot and collapse model (bottom line, Figure 1) developed by Meadows *et al.* in *The Limits to Growth* (1972) and in *Beyond the Limits* (1992). Those global simulation models started with the premise that our planet is "one world" for the very first time, and showed that actually it is very difficult for the planet to remain at a large human population at the limits to growth, with simple fluctuations around the limit. All living systems have time lags. Overshoot and collapse results from reaction times and corrective mechanisms that are too slow for the objective conditions. That is, overshoot of the carrying capacity of the globe is almost inevitable in our present system, and it produces serious negative feedbacks in economy and ecology that this class of models says will almost inevitably lead to a massive die-off of human population, quite possibly accompanied by collapse of our ecology, economy, and civilization. It is an ugly prospect. More recent work by Meadows *et al.* (1992) suggests we are already beyond the limits to growth, and that it will take extraordinary efforts to avoid devastating consequences.

Ervin Laszlo (1994) argues that the kinds of breakdown that would come with the end of the modern industrial era could be a veritable cascade of multiple system failures. Systems theory suggests that chaotic developments and waves or cascades of bifurcating changes must accompany great complexity in the kind of multilevel systems we have today, with the real possibility of oscillations around a local limit, and of major departures from a local regime, *either upward or downward in complexity*. Like other great thinkers, Laszlo is concerned about the illusory ideas we have carried forward from the past that especially affect our relations to ecology and economy. These illusions complicate the prospect of a soft landing immensely, and we must quickly become conscious of these major perturbations. Ignorance and illusion is a formula for disaster.

In order for overshoot and collapse not to be inevitable, and for the departure from our local regime to be upward rather than downward, we need to move toward a new kind of social and cultural system. My research says it may be possible to think in those terms.

The Potential for a New Kind of Civilization: Integral Culture

Assuming it may be possible to survive cascades of perturbations of a new and severe kind, what kind of desirable social system should we try to steer ourselves toward?

First of all, a viable social system needs ecological sustainability as a simple criterion of existence. In the least-bad world, we might be able to slow down and reverse human population growth, and reduce its overexploitation of the environment, with significant restoration of lost environments. Our next evolutionary era would be characterized by our accepting a new "world of limits"—with humans living in a finite ecological niche, with total population size of perhaps 2 to 4 billion, and dramatically less throughput of materials and energy.

Secondly, a viable social system probably needs to be an information economy. Most industrial nations are presently in the process of developing a single cross-national information economy, with trade and communications making the globe a single system. An information economy is clearly going to have dramatic miniaturization (reductions of tens of thousands to one in both scale and cost) of many artifacts from our immediate past and present. This will come, not only through microelectronic devices, but also through the emerging industries of biotechnology and nanotechnology, which will alter molecules and even bump individual atoms to make infinitesimal machines, and new kinds of chemistries and materials technologies. In this way it is possible to have a drastic reduction of the throughput of the total energy and materials of a postindustrial society in a kind of "etherealization of product." The same new technologies may make it possible to clean up the environment—or make new disasters on an unprecedented scale.

In the third place, a whole new set of institutions compatible with the above situation will need to emerge. But with rare exceptions (e.g., Eisler, 1987; Loye, 1989) the cultural matrix for the institutions that permit an ecologically sustainable society has never been described by technologists, economists, systems theorists, or ecologists. In fact most seem unaware that this is an issue. Let us look at what is emerging at this level.

Sixty years ago, the largest study of social change ever done started appearing in four volumes. Pitirim Sorokin's (1937–1941) description of the alternation of major forms of culture (based on 3,000 years of data) said that in the late 20th century we would be at the twilight of the "sensate" form of culture (which we would call "modernity" and "materialism" today) that has existed since the 1400s. Sorokin's argument and data boils down to the proposition that whole worldviews, cultural systems, and beliefs about reality oscillate irregularly over 500- to 800-year periods of history, with the two main contenders being a fairly secular materialism and a fairly church-establishment-driven traditionalism/idealism. He showed that the permutations and combinations of cultural forms in our current sensate cultural system were starting to indicate exhaustion as early as the 1920s. He suggested that the theory of ultimate reality adumbrated by even the quantum theory of his day was no support for a materialist ontology.

Sorokin firmly expected that in the 1960s a successor form of culture would begin to arise to replace the prevailing culture of today. It would be one that is idealistic and spiritual rather than materialistic and secular, and eventually there would be a swing toward a stable religious culture characteristic of many of the high civilizations of the past. This transition away from our present type of culture could occur either through a new flowering of creativity in what could legitimately be called a "renaissance," or through a chaotic disintegration, possibly through atomic war (or today we might say, through ecological collapse, with wars) into a new dark age.

In the 1940s and 1950s, Sorokin wrote of the evolutionary importance of a possibility of an "integral culture" emerging, anticipating that it would have the potential to integrate many parts of our lives that have been dis-integrated by sensate culture. Closely related views—actually using the same term "integral"—were independently stated by Sri Aurobindo (1955; see also Chaudhuri, 1974) and by Jean Gebser (1953). A generation later, in *The Turning Point* (1981), Fritjof Capra suggested Sorokin was right, and adduced various qualitative developments, especially in our ideas about reality, to suggest that the time had come for a new kind of civilization. Capra's point is that a spiritual culture is not only what comes next in the natural cycling of cultural forms, but is more compatible with the needs of ecological sustainability than a materialistic market-driven culture. Among many other notable books in the same hopeful pattern of re-visioning who we are, what we believe to be reality, and what that says of the future of our culture, were Riane Eisler's *The Chalice and the Blade* (1987) and Willis Harman's *Global Mind Change* (1988).

I have been doing survey research on subcultures of values and lifestyles for ten years, and have found what seems to be the carrier population for the kind of integral culture that Sorokin expected to emerge. My survey research, plus library research, suggests Sorokin, Capra, Eisler, Harman, and Laszlo are right about the more hopeful developments in our time. I call the carrier population for the values of an emergent culture the "Cultural Creatives," for collectively they show every sign of being at the forefront of most new developments in American culture today (not the technology, however). The kind of culture that their values lead them toward is best described in terms like Sorokin's. It is precisely the kind of culture capable of an upward surge in complexity to fit Laszlo's kind of model, one that is also adequate to the evolutionary challenges of our time. As important, perhaps, it is the kind of culture capable of maintaining an ecologically sustainable society. Most surprising, Cultural Creatives are 24 percent of adult Americans, or 44 million people.

The Cultural Creatives, Bearers of the Potential Integral Culture

Values are part of the deep structure of what people believe and find important in their lives, and are intimately related to their worldviews. Customarily, values are very slow to change, unlike opinions and attitudes. Careful analysis of patterns of values shows that the particular values people believe in are less a matter of individual psychology than of subcultures: they learn and share with others a whole pattern of living and valuing. Values are extremely good predictors of the lifestyles that people lead, and of their complex consumer choices and decisions as citizens.

The research reported here grows out of ten years of research in two stages. In the first eight years my research company did carefully crafted commercial research in dozens of small, tightly focused client studies (classifying over 100,000 respondents) that related the values subcultures of the United States to consumer and voter behavior. From that emerged a reliable portrait of the distinctive values that allow one to reliably cluster Americans into subcultures, people with distinctly different lifestyles and worldviews as well as values. In the second stage, a research project (with a big specially designed national survey) was set up to test the hypothesis that this pattern is there and is related to spiritual and ecological values, and that these predict behaviors. The Fetzer Institute and the Institute of Noetic Sciences commissioned a national mail survey to assess the extent to which a new culture is emerging in the United States. A survey was mailed to a representative national sample of the population by National Family Opinion in November and December of 1994, using their panel of persons who had preagreed to be available for a mail survey, and it yielded 1,036 returns (67 percent return rate). The survey did indeed confirm the pattern of American subcultures of values I had seen over the years.

Technically, the identification of several subcultures of values employs a battery of about 70 questionnaire items. They are analyzed by a combination of factor analysis and multidimensional scaling to create orthogonal values dimensions, and to create dimensions of various other attitudes and reported activities. Ours is further a hierarchical two-stage analysis: first, creating a measurement scale for each value, or other concept; and next using factor analysis to aggregate these scales into orthogonal dimensions (i.e., measures that are uncorrelated with one another and represent all the interesting sources of variation in the values data). The resulting five value and socioeconomic dimensions are treated statistically as a five-dimensional property space in which globular clusters are identified using a variant of a K-Means clustering algorithm, to give optimal clustering of the respondents into subcultures.

The factor analysis of values measurement scales yielded the following orthogonal dimensions, each of which is a distinct and different part of the profile of every respondent. That is each person has a score on each of the following dimensions:

- A "Heartland" dimension that combines values and beliefs of the religious right, traditionalism, and desire for traditional gender relationships.
- A "Winner" dimension that combines values and beliefs of achievement-oriented moderns: materialism, desire for success, hedonism, having money problems (this occurs at all income levels and reflects living beyond one's income, not poverty).
- A "Person-Centered" dimension that combines spiritual and psychological values of the more Transmodern kind: altruism, self-actualization, idealism, relationship-orientation, xenophilism (love of what is exotic, foreign).

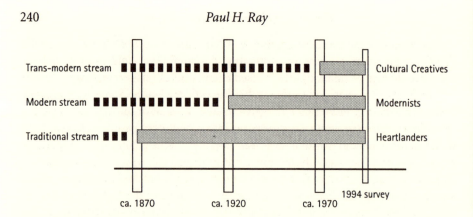

Figure 2. Approximate dates from which today's American world-views, values, and idealized images derive

- A "Greens versus Big Business" dimension that combines all the parts of ecological sustainability orientation ("Green" beliefs, voluntary simplicity, concern for global ecology issues, willingness to pay for major programs to clean up the environment and prevent global warming) with attitudes pro and con toward big business. Values of ecological sustainability and big business conservatism have a strong negative correlation.
- And socioeconomic status (income, occupation, education) is added for the creation of clusters for identifying values subcultures. This social class dimension is statistically independent of the values; that is, it conveys a different and unique kind of information.

As seen in Figure 2, three different streams of cultural meanings and worldviews are evident at this moment in history: Traditional, Modern and Transmodern (i.e., becoming Integral), each comprising distinct subcultures of values. I use the terms "Heartlanders," "Modernists," and "Cultural Creatives" to denote, respectively, the bearers of these three subcultures. Values and worldviews differ systematically according to subculture, depending both on the cultural era in which they were formed and on a stream of meanings and cultural concerns that predates that era.

The cultural stream carried by Heartlanders. The roots of today's Traditional stream can be traced to two origins: (1) Medieval European Catholics and Protestants who objected to secular Modernism, and the antidemocratic Right that persists today; (2) the rural and nativist (racist, antiforeigner) movements of the United States from which 19th-century fundamentalism arose in reaction to Modernism in its American form. Today's Heartlanders believe in a nostalgic image of return to small-town, religious America, corresponding to the period 1890 to 1930. It is a mythical image that defines for its adherents the Good Old American Ways. The Heartlanders, America's cultural conservatives, are 29 percent of the population, or 56 million adults.

The cultural stream carried by Modernists. Modernism emerged 500 years ago in Europe at the end of the Renaissance, and continued to spread beyond Europe to its colonies throughout the period. Modernism may in part be seen as an over-throw of authoritarian political and religious controls. Yet it has important roots in the urban merchant classes and in other creators of the modern economy, in the rise of the modern state and armies, and in the rise of scientists, technologists, and intellectuals. The imagery and worldview of today's American Modernism of the post-1920s is already late Modernism, with 19th-century roots in European in-tellectualism and in American urbanism and industrialism. The dominant values are personal success, consumerism, materialism, and technological rationality. Bearers of Modernism represent about 47 percent of the population, or 88 million adults.

The cultural stream carried by Cultural Creatives. The origins of Transmodernism include the esoteric spiritual movements that grew out of the Renaissance, such as the transcendental movement of the early to mid-19th century. Transmodernism is also informed by today's New Age movement, the humanistic psychology and transpersonal psychology movements, the ecology movement, and the women's movement. The Cultural Creatives are about 24 percent of adults in the United States, or 44 million persons.

Cultural Creatives (CCs) are so called because they are coming up with most new ideas in American culture, operating on the leading edge of cultural change. They tend to be middle to upper middle class. A few more CCs are on the West Coast than elsewhere, but they are in all regions of the country. The overall male:female ratio is 40:60, or 50 percent more women than men.

CCs have two wings: Core Cultural Creatives and Green Cultural Creatives.

- Core CCs (10.6 per cent, or 20 million) have both person-centered and green values. They are seriously concerned with psychology, spiritual life, self-actualization, self-expression, and they like the foreign and exotic (are xeno-philes), enjoy mastering new ideas, are socially concerned, advocate "women's issues," and are strong advocates of ecological sustainability. They tend to be "leading-edge" thinkers and creators. They tend to be upper middle class, and their male:female ratio is 33:67, twice as many women as men.
- Green CCs (13 percent, or 24 million) have values centered on the environ-ment and social concerns from a secular view, with average interest in spirituality, psychology, or person-centered values. They appear to be followers of the Core CCs and tend to be middle class.

For the most part, demographics (e.g., age, race, social class) have very low correlations with values, and have little predictive power for describing these sub-cultures. The Heartlanders are older and have less education, which is typical of an earlier generation, and CCs have more women, and are slightly more educated—but that is about it. Values must be taken on their own terms, though many

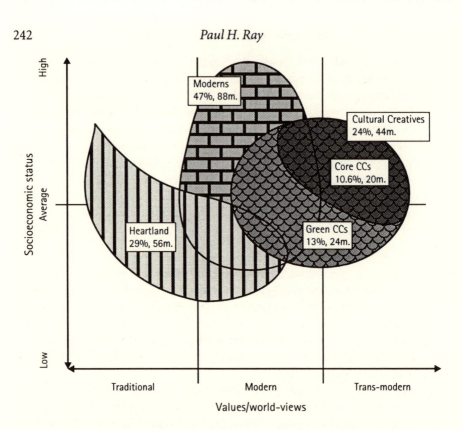

Figure 3. **The dominant subcultures of the United States**

Note: As found in the 1994 Integral Culture Survey sponsored by the Fetzer Institute and Institute of Noetic Sciences. The 1994 US population was 188 million adults

Source: Ray, 1996; © Paul H. Ray, 1995

Modernists often seem to want to reduce them to demographics when they are presented with this data.

Figure 3 shows a scatter plot of the survey respondents by three subcultures on a plane defined by the cultural era each crossed by socio-economic status. Each respondent is a point on the plane. In that plot, there appears to be an overlap of Moderns with Heartlanders and Cultural Creatives, but that is only an appearance. Actually there is another dimension vertical to the plane of the page, and that is the degree to which success and status display is important to those respondents. Imagine that in looking at Figure 3 you are looking into the side of a fish tank: seen from the top, it would be apparent that there is no overlap of the three subcultures. Rather, the Moderns are "behind" the other two subcultures on that depth dimension, because success and status are more important to them than the other two subcultures.

Values of the Cultural Creatives

The comparative values profiles of the three subcultures are shown in Table 1. The underlying belief structure of the CCs suggests what is "Transmodern," that is, what is emerging "beyond Modernism":

- *Ecological sustainability, beyond environmentalism.* If you can name an aspect of ecology and sustainability, CCs are leading the way. They are eager to rebuild neighborhoods and communities, committed to ecological sustainability and limits to growth, see nature as sacred, want to stop corporate polluters, are suspicious of big business, interested in voluntary simplicity, and willing to pay to clean up the environment and to stop global warming, etc.
- *Globalism.* Two of the top values for CCs are xenophilism, love of travel to foreign places, of foreigners and the exotic, and ecological sustainability, which strongly includes concern for the planetary ecology and stewardship, population problems, etc.
- *Feminism, women's issues, relationships, family.* The fact that CCs are 60 percent women versus 40 percent men is a major focus for understanding this subculture. Their focus on women's issues includes concerns about violence and abuse of women and children, a desire to rebuild neighborhoods and community and to improve caring relationships, and concerns about family. (Though they are no more family oriented than most Americans, it is near the top in their list of values).
- *Altruism, self-actualization, alternative health care, spirituality, spiritual psychology.* This is a complex of highly intercorrelated beliefs and values centered on the inner life. In reality, this is a new sense of the sacred that incorporates personal growth psychology and the spiritual and service to others as one. It also includes a stronger orientation to holistic health and alternative health care as part of this complex.
- *Well-developed social conscience and social optimism.* Contrary to the social critics, an emphasis on the personal does not exclude the political nor social conscience, though individuals may do them in sequence. CCs are engaged in the world just as much as in personal and spiritual issues. Rebuilding and healing society is related to healing ourselves, physically and spiritually. With that goes a guarded social optimism.
- *What they reject.* As a whole, the CCs reject the hedonism, materialism and cynicism of modern media, consumer and business culture, the survivor/scarcity/fear orientation of the working class, the antisustainability orientation of ultraconservatives, and the intolerance of the religious right.

All this is developed at more length in Ray (1996).

Table 1. **Differences in values among the three subcultures**

	Heartland	Moderns	CCs	Total
Values where Heartlanders are highest (%)				
Religious right	70	26	31	40
Traditional relationships	55	25	26	34
Religious conservatives	53	21	30	33
Conventional religious beliefs	47	36	15	34
Against feminism in work	46	35	20	35
Values where Modernists are highest (%)				
Financial materialism	61	82	51	68
Not religious right	14	55	46	41
Not self-actualizing	43	51	26	43
Not altruistic	21	49	16	33
Cynicism about politics	29	48	19	35
Not idealistic	33	44	18	35
Secular and nature is sacred	15	42	29	31
Orthodox religion and beliefs	29	40	17	31
Success is high priority	11	36	12	23
Not relationship-oriented	14	32	8	21
Hedonism	5	12	4	8
Values where Cultural Creatives are highest (%)				
Want to rebuild neighborhoods/communities	86	84	92	86
Fear violence against women and children	84	75	87	80
Xenophilism	69	63	85	70
Nature as sacred	65	72	85	73
General Green values	58	59	83	64
Believe in ecological sustainability	52	56	83	61
Believe in voluntary simplicity	65	53	79	63
Relationships important	65	49	76	60
Success is not high priority	61	39	70	53
Pro-feminism in work	45	56	69	56
Not concerned about job	41	50	62	50
Altruism	55	32	58	45
Idealism	36	32	55	39
Believe in religious mysteries	19	25	53	30
Self-actualization	29	32	52	36
Not financial materialism	34	17	48	29
Want to be activist	34	29	45	34
Not financial problems	33	31	44	35
Believe in spiritual psychology	36	24	40	31
Not cynical about politics	24	21	40	27
Optimism about future	26	24	35	27
Want creative time	19	31	33	28
Believe in holistic health	23	21	31	24
Don't want traditional relationships	5	18	22	15

Note: Values are from column percentage tables for each values scale. This shows the percentage who agree with the stated value. Omitted are those who are neutral about or disagree with the stated value.

Source: Ray, 1996, p. 27

Lifestyles of the Cultural Creatives

Cultural Creatives are middle- to upper-middle-class people with a lot of spending power, but much of American business ignores them, so they have developed a number of ways to get what they want anyway. Here are some sweeping generalizations about the CC lifestyle from ten years of surveys. What is shocking to many people is how accurately the values profile predicts to a highly recognizable way of life—often one they thought they had invented themselves:

- *Readers and radio listeners, not TV watchers.* CCs buy more books and magazines, listen to more radio, including classical music and NPR, and watch less television, than any other groups. They are literate and discriminating, and dislike most of what is on TV.
- *Arts and culture.* CCs are aggressive consumers of culture, and are also producers of culture. They are more likely to be involved in the arts as amateurs or pros, and are more likely to write books and articles, and to go to meetings and workshops about them.
- *Stories, whole process, and systems.* CCs appreciate good stories, and demand systems views of the "whole process" of whatever they are reading, from cereal boxes to product descriptions to magazine articles. They want to know where a product came from, how it was made, who made it, and what will happen to it when they are done with it. They hate to read mail or articles that come in bullet points and race to the bottom line (unless they are very time pressed and don't care much about the topic). They also want symbols that go deep, and actively resent advertising and children's TV more than most Americans.
- *Careful consumers.* CCs are the kind of people who buy and use Consumer Reports on most consumer durable goods: appliances, cars, consumer electronics, etc. For the most part, they are the careful, well-informed shoppers who do not buy on impulse, and read up on a purchase first. They are practically the only consumers who regularly read labels.
- *A different kind of car, please.* CCs are far more likely to want safety and fuel economy in a mid-price car. If they could also get an ecologically sound, high-mileage, recyclable car, they'd snap it up. The Volvo speaks to many CCs, but so do well-made Japanese cars. They loathe car dealers even more than most people do. Hence, the Saturn car with a fixed, no haggle price, and top dealer service is designed for CCs.
- *Soft innovation.* CCs tend to be innovators and opinion leaders for some knowledge-intensive products, however, including magazines, fine foods, wines and boutique beers.
- *The foodies.* A high proportion of CCs are "foodies": people who like to talk about food (before *and* after), experiment with new kinds of food, cook food with friends, eat out a lot, do gourmet and ethnic cooking, try natural foods and health foods, etc.

- *Desire for authenticity.* CCs invented the term "authenticity" as consumers understand it, leading the rebellion against things that are "plastic," fake, imitation, poorly made, throwaway, cliché style, high fashion, etc. If they buy something in a traditional style they want authentically traditional; Smith and Hawken garden tools speak to this desire for authenticity, as does much of the natural foods industry.
- *A different kind of new house, please.* CCs tend to buy fewer new houses than most people of their income level, finding that they are not designed with them in mind. So they buy resale houses and fix them up the way they want. They abhor the status display home that shows a lot to the street, preferring to be hidden from the street by fences, trees and shrubbery. They tend to prefer established neighborhoods with a lot of trees and privacy. All this militates against buying the kinds of new home that builders are prone to put out there for the upper middle class. CCs rate builders down there with car dealers.
- *The home as nest.* When CCs buy homes, they like homes that are "nests": not only a lot of privacy externally, but private spaces within, including the buffering of kids' space from adult space, and with lots of interesting nooks and niches. They are more prone to live out of the living room and not bother with a family room. They are far more likely to have an office in the home, and to have converted a bedroom, den, or family room into that office. They also like authentic styling in homes, but collectively their notion of what's included is all-embracing: authentic New England salt box, authentic Georgian, authentic Frank Lloyd Wright, authentic desert adobe, authentic contemporary Californian, etc. Whatever fits into its proper place on the land is what's good. They want access to nature, walking and biking paths, ecological preservation, historical preservation, and to live in master planned communities that show a way to recreate community.
- *Personalization of the home.* Interior decoration for CCs is typically eclectic, with a lot of original art on the walls and crafts pieces around the house. Many Core CCs seem to think a house is not properly decorated without a lot of books. The same house that vanishes from the street should be personalized so that it shows on the inside who they are. Status display happens *inside* the house not outside, though it is not blatant: it is display of personal good taste and creative sense of style. No CC buys a single decorator style that goes through the whole house, and no interior decorators need apply.
- *Experiential consumers.* Core CCs are the prototypical consumers of the experience industry, which tries to sell you a more intense/enlightening/enlivening experience rather than a thing. They are involved with psychotherapy, weekend workshops, spiritual gatherings, personal growth experiences, experiential vacations, vacations-as-spiritual-tours, vacations-as-self-discovery, etc. The providers of these services have to be CCs too, or they can't do it authentically (the kiss of death), and so one sometimes gets the impression that everyone is taking in everyone else's wash—or workshop.

- *The leading edge of vacation travel.* CCs define the leading edge of vacation travel that is exotic, adventuresome-without-(too much)-danger, educational, experiential, authentic, altruistic and/or spiritual. Tours of temples in India, tours of the back country where tourists don't go, eco-tourism, photo-safaris, fantasy baseball camps, save-the-baby-seals vacations, help-rebuild-a-Mayan-village vacations. They don't go for package tours, fancy resorts or cruises—and resent having to take the kids to Disneyland.

- *Holistic everything.* CCs are the prototypical innovators in, and consumers of, personal growth psychotherapy, alternative health care and natural foods. What ties these together is a belief in holistic health: body–mind–spirit are to be unified. They are forever sorting out the weird from the innovative. They may include a high proportion of people whom some physicians describe as "the worried well": those who monitor every twitch and pain and bowel movement, in a minutely detailed attention to the body, which may be why they spend more on alternative health care and regular health care even though most are fairly healthy. They may live longer, because they do at least some kinds of preventive medicine—in contrast to the Modernist executive pattern of treating the body like a machine that you feed, exercise, and vitaminize, and otherwise ignore until it breaks down.

The Important Role of the New Social Movements

One of the first responses by social scientists, is "Why haven't I seen these people before?" and the second is "Where did they all come from?" The answers are two-fold and very simple.

1. If you look at values instead of just at demographics, you'll see them. In particular, these are women's values, coming out of hiding in private, into a more public realm, and they are also the values of other parts of the culture that Modernism has not wanted to recognize.
2. You *have* seen some of these people, marching in demonstrations; and you've seen them where they come from—in the new social movements that have emerged since the 1960s.

CCs have followed the ideas and moral stances of those who have spoken out, and marched and demonstrated, on big issues of the day. There's an essential connection between the emergence of the Cultural Creatives subculture and a little-understood part of our recent history. Over the past generation Americans have experienced wave after wave of a new kind of social movements, different from the political movements of the beginnings of this century. These new movements have been much less concerned with seeking political power than with wanting to uproot some fundamental aspect of society, or to challenge the codes of behavior that stultify us, and the labels that bind our perceptions and thus our minds. They have also been preoccupied with working through new values, new experiences and personal identities, and especially new ways of framing the crises of our age.

It is a long list to name the many *kinds* of movements we have seen: civil rights; peace; environmental; ecological sustainability; feminism; student movement; jobs and social justice; hippie movement; gay and lesbian lib; alternative health care/holistic health; vegetarian and natural foods; human potential; spiritual psychology; new religions; New Age movement; communitarian movement. The list is probably longer than that.

This includes hundreds of good causes and thousands of individual organizations, often sharing the same illusion, "Only we are working to save the world!" They are seriously mistaken. However, the news media coverage frequently gives them—and us—a false impression: by reporting that only a few are there, or that those who marched don't represent anyone but themselves; by refusing to report what they actually are saying on the grounds that it is not news; and by refusing to ask how many people share their values and concerns. The media act as guardians of the official reality that these movements are challenging. Millions *have* acted on their values and concerns, and it *has* made a difference, but slowly.

We live in a time when many conservatives condemn the loosening of social controls over people's behavior. The argument is that it leads to crime and deviance. But the same loosening that leads to some social problems also gives enough latitude for other more creative people to try new social innovations. And that is what can be seen here. What is striking is how these movements have reinterpreted almost every aspect of social life, and have creatively sought for new meanings and worldviews appropriate to our time. The 44 million Cultural Creatives are like an envelope who encompass these movements, because it is they who are their constituencies.

There has been a great deal of ferment in both the United States and in Europe. It is documented in a surprisingly large historical and sociological literature about the new social movements (see, e.g., Melucci, 1996; Laraña *et al.*, 1994; Darnovsky *et al.*, 1995; Johnston *et al.*, 1995; Lyman, 1995; McAdam *et al.*, 1996). These social movements have forced upon the West the kind of cultural learning that has a large cumulative impact on cultural evolution. On balance, that impact seems to have been largely positive:

- The civil rights movement reframed issues of justice for African Americans, introduced Gandhi's nonviolence into our repertoire, and also led more of society to develop more respect for nonwhites. In the spring of 1997, a *New York Times*/CBS poll found that the top three people Americans most admire are Colin Powell, Tiger Woods, and Michael Jordan. Such admiration for *any* nonwhite males would have been unthinkable 50 years ago. Racial issues have changed, at least for high achievers who support the dominant culture.
- The peace movement reframed fundamental issues of the war system, and

may have succeeded at delegitimating major wars. It is very hard to get Americans to want to go to war any more.

- The environmental movement has succeeded at convincing about 85 percent of Americans they are pro-environment, in a variety of areas of life. These were unknown issues before the 1960s. Even though 62 percent tell pollsters they want more environmental regulation, not less, neither government nor industry gives them many opportunities to act on that sentiment.
- The ecology movement has moved well beyond local environmentalism to concerns for the global environment, and limiting economic and population growth to what is ecologically sustainable. Ecological sustainability is favored by 61 percent of Americans (Ray, 1996).
- Feminism and other aspects of the women's movement have reframed fundamental gender issues not only in the workplace, but up close and personal in the home, and the gender gap probably defeated Bob Dole in the 1996 election. Yes, many women are overworked, taking care of a job and the home, and there will be pressures to change.
- The student movement of the 1960s came and went but carried a whole generation into engagement with other movements. Contrary to media stereotypes, most of those who were engaged with such movements retained their interest in progressive issues.
- The jobs and social justice movement worked to reframe the right to income and housing, and while it is at low ebb today, it's likely to come roaring back in the wake of growing income inequality.
- The hippie movement left a permanent legacy of psychedelic use among teens, showed millions that reality was more complex than modernism allowed, opening the door to the new spirituality, and helped popularize the idea of voluntary simplicity.
- Gay and lesbian lib have blurred the boundaries of fundamental issues of sexuality and sexual preference. Gay-bashing is far more difficult now than 50 years ago.
- Alternative health care has become a giant industry rivaling the hospital network in its expenditures, and the ideology of holistic health is reframing what we think medicine should be about. In 1994, 37 percent of Americans used alternative health care, and half of Cultural Creatives used it (Ray, 1996).
- The vegetarian and natural foods movements have refocused a plurality of Americans on the healthfulness of food, and along with the medical findings about the dangers of animal fats, have contributed to a reversal of trends in the consumption of red meat.
- The human potential movement reframed the question of who we are away from materialism and mass culture, and helped millions find their way into personal growth psychology and body work. Today, half of Cultural Creatives and one-third of all Americans see self-actualization as a value that is important to their lives (Ray, 1996).

- The spiritual psychology movement evolved beyond the human potential movement, blurring the boundaries of psychology and religion by pointing to the primacy of spiritual experience in a new synthesis of East and West. Spiritual psychology is important to about one third of all Americans. (Ray, 1996)
- The new religions have worked to redefine spiritual reality on a broad front from new forms of fundamentalism and charismatic religion to importations of ancient Eastern religions into an Americanized context to reformulations of liberal Christianity, in an efflorescence of new possibilities that is un-paralleled since the latter days of the Roman Empire. Again, 30 percent of Americans believe in the religious mysteries (Ray, 1996).
- The New Age movement drew from the above and as it spread, it acted as much as an envelope for commercial exploitation as for the encouragement of various forms of lifestyle, social, psychological, and spiritual experimenta-tion, ranging from the sublime to the foolish. It is only about 5–10 percent of the population, however (Ray, 1996).
- The communitarian movement is a recent arrival that seeks to dissolve the boundaries of left versus right in politics and reinvent workable new com-munities and social responsibilities.

The people who actively participate in such movements are a small portion of the much larger moral constituency who sympathize with them and often give material and moral support to them. There is agreement with most of those movements by a plurality, even a majority, of the general population. However, that agreement is not usually true of the business elite, the media elite, nor cultural conservatives. The general population's sympathy for these movement ideas does not have nearly as strong a voice in the media, nor in political or corporate circles, as those who oppose them. These movements' opponents are not only in the minority, they are actively trying to conceal that fact. Moreover, it is precisely these movements that have had a large cumulative impact on many Americans, especially the Cultural Creatives.

In summary, these are times when evolution becomes a reflexive process, because it contains information about the world, its processes, and the subject of knowledge within itself. The self-awareness of the subject of evolution changes the object. Interestingly enough, what is evidently so today was anticipated by the great biologist and evolutionary theorist, Julian Huxley, who said that while "natural selection is an ordering principle, it operates blindly." It "pushes life onwards from behind" and "brings about improvement automatically, without conscious pur-pose or any awareness of an aim." Yet, he argued, psychosocial evolution also "acts as an ordering principle. But it pulls [us] onwards from in front. For it always involves some awareness of an aim, some element of true purpose." In psychosocial evolution "the selective mechanism itself evolves as well as its products. It is a goal-selecting mechanism, and the goals that it selects will change with the picture of the world and of human nature provided by [our] increasing knowledge" (Huxley, 1964, p. 34). In effect, we are collectively trying to become more self-aware. A larger consciousness of the ecology of the planet, and indeed of the evolution of our species, is now attempting to emerge.

The people who are most influenced by this movement in history seem to be the Cultural Creatives. If we take seriously the description of our times that such thinkers as Sorokin, Aurobindo, Eisler, Harman, and Laszlo have made, this coming to larger awareness is essential to our survival strategy as a species. But lest we celebrate the coming of the Cultural Creatives too soon, we must face the fact that it is a more difficult process than the description so far allows. There is the quintessential problem of increasing our collective awareness. We—meaning people like the author and the reader—must go out there to mobilize the Cultural Creatives. It won't happen by itself.

Many questions then arise: How are we to do this? What do we have going for us? What opposes this? What would be our prospects for success? Out of our 100,000 survey responses, and our hundreds of focus groups and in-depth interviews, there are many strong indications of both the problems and the opportunities for the emergence of a new kind of cultural adaptation led by the Cultural Creatives. The possibilities are very promising, for we are in the process of creating many new institutional forms as well as new kinds of understandings.

Potential Impact of the Cultural Creatives: Problems and Opportunities

When my company does focus groups with CCs, or when I give talks to them about this research, they themselves are first astounded there can be so many people who share their values. Suddenly they are very hopeful. Someone invariably says, "Oh, then it's all right to have hope again." For they are more optimistic than the rest of the population, but usually feel they have to explain that away. This is what many Cultural Creatives have been made to feel: that their values, commitments, and beliefs are more idealistic than can be said at work, or is publicly acceptable these days. They care deeply for the whole complex of CCs' values, but believe they are almost alone, that it's just them and a small circle of friends. With 44 million of them, how could they share such a gigantic illusion? Is the hypnotism of Modernist ideology so strong?

Many Cultural Creatives are particularly susceptible to biased media coverage because they are information junkies. This also relates to the preferred cognitive style that probably led many of them to adopt this new worldview. They are very good at efficiently scanning their information environment, taking in information from a variety of sources, and synthesizing it into their own "big picture." They scan widely, then zero in on something that interests them and explore that topic in depth. But if most of what is in the media ignores them, and the news stories they read ignore CC values, then they will come to a biased conclusion that there are very few people like themselves out there (Ray, 1997).

Each member of this subculture is like a member of an audience at a music concert: all facing in the same direction, sharing the same tastes, attitudes, opinions, and knowledge as other members of that concert-going audience, but not facing one another, not having any real conversations with one another. Yet individually they long for community (Ray, 1996). CCs are consumers of the same informational culture. They read the same things, come to the same kinds of conclusions, worry about the same issues, value the same kind of future, and tend to agree on what is most important in life. But because the opinion-makers of the media reflect the dominant Modernist culture, the CCs conclude there are not many others to talk to. And because any talk of values is normally considered bad taste or illegitimate in the workplace, most do not suspect they may have allies there. They often tell us they are silent in what may be enemy territory.

Though CCs have in common values and dreams and views of what is most important and how the world works, they are lacking in something critical: a shared awareness of ourselves as a subculture, as a collective self. Why is this collective awareness missing? Why do they act as if they're merely an audience unable to speak to each other?

Consider the women's movement. Until women created consciousness-raising groups there was no way of *collectively* grappling with their deepest fears and longings and frustrations. There were no conventional ways to discuss their actual experiences of being a woman. It is hardly that there were, or are, not enough women around, with 52 percent of the population. The problem has been un-certainty whether one's feelings, and fumblings for ideas, would be accepted. There was fear of embarrassment, fear of exposure as somehow deviant. In the traditional culture prior to the 1970s, if women got together, it had to be something trivial—"hen-parties"—or suspicions arose that perhaps there was a hidden lesbianism involved, or a conspiracy against men, etc. There were no words for what women felt within conventional culture. So something new had to be in-vented. These were not only brave women; they were desperate for the company of those who shared their perceptions, their pain, their fears, and their fumblings for the new words.

Another reason CCs may believe "I am almost alone" grows out of the way they became Cultural Creatives in the first place. Nearly all of them came from some other values subculture, and the way they got to where they are now was "one by one by one" (Ray, 1996). Some came with a few friends, but most did not. They left behind the values of the home they grew up in, and probably those of the home town. In order to get where they are in life, many had to be very individualistic. Many also see life through a very psychological filter. While that was once adaptive for one's personal development, individualism is no longer very adaptive, nor for our communities and society. It is more difficult to form communities, for many fear that they'd have to give up a hard-earned individuality and become merged into a community. Many no longer have good habits of making community, and fear to expose their values in casual conversations. It's like dying of thirst on a desert island—only to discover that the island is on a fresh water lake!

It turns out that CCs have both fewer links to groups or institutions that can deeply support their values, and wider networks of impersonal connections. This is too complex a picture to more than touch upon here. Essentially, there is a difference between a well-connected minority of activists, and the large majority who feel more isolated because they lack the support and stability of the kinds of organizations supplied by traditional society. The busy connections among elite activists are often combined with a distinct sense of being an embattled minority, and that one's voice and true values can never be heard in the larger public media. The majority can find no CC analogues to the Rotary Club or Lions Club or the other service clubs. Despite the long-time resonance of minority churches (e.g., Quakers, Unitarians, Unity) to the stream of values and worldviews that CCs took up, there are fewer churches that CCs could easily join that would support new forms of spirituality. (Ray, 1996) Despite a continuing proliferation of weekend workshops, they just do not offer continuity or a permanent institutional connection. New versions of consciousness-raising groups are continually arising on a small scale, but locally and invisibly, and nowhere on the visible and national scale of the big social movements like civil rights, women's rights, and ecology. While CCs volunteer in large numbers out of a sense of civic duty, they often feel co-opted by the Modernist agenda and institutional assumptions of those organizations. In the long term it is alienating. What will be the new events and occasions that will let the Cultural Creatives face one another, realizing their numbers, to declare that "it's old home week, and time to celebrate, because now I can relax among my friends"?

Most people have the experience of coming to new experiences and different friends first, and only then realizing that these new experiences and friends are better than the ones they have had before. But to do that, they seem to have only three options: they have to stumble accidentally onto those new associates, or they have to take the risk of being involved in one of those social movements, or they have something break down in their old lives—illness, divorce, losing a job, and so on. It is very hard to move only from ideas and principles into changing one's life.

Does this matter? If you are true to yourself and are following your own deeply seated values, does it matter whether your old culture spits you out? Does it matter whether the popular media gives no hint that anyone might exist like you and your friends, nor is what you care about reflected in anything written there—or else it is stereotyped and belittled?

It matters. This is a form of psychological pain and suffering. Without others who share our values, who can listen and reflect what we are saying and can express their own concerns and inspirations, we can lose heart. In everyday life, we can forget or submerge what we know. There is a Sufi teaching story called "The day the waters changed" about a man who knows better than to drink the "water of madness" but finally decides to go mad with all the other people in his community because he cannot stand being alone. On the positive side, every spiritual tradition speaks of the need for companions on the path, for a sangha, a community, saying that for the development of the soul, the maturing of the individual, we each need to find our own community.

In terms that are fundamentally important to those who care about what is happening in our country and our planet, those who want to aid the conscious evolution of humanity need first to find others who share their commitment, face to face. It is not enough to write and think about it. Indeed, the writing style of this article is not adequate to the task of reaching those who must act. The Core Cultural Creatives who hold most intensely to CC values do not like to read articles with bullet points marching to the bottom line, and want a wider authenticity than only our standard technical arguments, to include artistry and appeals to the emotions as well as the mind. They believe additional truth is found in stories that show someone's subjective personal experience, but they also want such stories contextualized into "the big picture" of how the world is changing (Ray, 1997). So why do we restrict ourselves to an insufficient Modernist objectivity as if our constituency doesn't exist? It's the power of old cultural forms.

Most technical and scientific writers have been told that this "objective style" is what works and is effective, and indeed that only this is legitimate, separating facts from values, as if values were not implicit in the choice of subject, and in the conclusions that affect humankind. We are too concerned for our image as thoughtful public intellectuals. We know that we must write for our real audience, yet we fear the unnamed critics and editors who will attack our work as not good enough. Not good enough because it fails to follow the old forms, despite the fact that they no longer work for our own constituency, who most care about the subject we are here writing about. We who read and write only in the style of this article's technical prose are engaging in behavior that is necessary, but is also insufficient.

This is what women did for generation after generation. They wrote and spoke to persuade men. And nothing changed, according to Carolyn Heilbrun (1988) and Gerda Lerner (1993), until the women started talking to each other—and telling each other the truth about their lives and what they cared about. Consciousness-raising groups were electrifying, because they were telling the truth about what you had seen and what your dreams were for the future. It matters enormously to the West that the women's movement has been a wave passing through our collective awareness, and now none of the new social movements can dare ignore the implications of consciousness raising. Conservatives who oppose changes to our next evolutionary step know this very well, and save some of their bitterest opposition for consciousness raising.

There is a double conclusion and both parts are ineluctable.

First, concentrating our efforts on just one good cause at a time will fail, because all the shards and splinters of single-issue politics and single-issue social movements taken one at a time will not add up to a coherent vision of the new civilization humankind so desperately needs. The next big task is to evolve an image of an Integral Culture, which will draw all these movements together under the "big tent" of a common vision and philosophy, with enough clout to matter. Single-issue movement organizers must see that they all are working from a common culture defined by values and worldview, not by demographics nor by left–right ideology. They can see themselves as competitors for a limited set of loyalties, or they can grasp the golden opportunity to move under a wider vision toward a new civilization capable of sustainability.

Second, merely writing books and articles to persuade experts of the dominant culture is not enough. There are thousands of well-meaning books out there, as well-meaning as this one, all getting lost in the flood of information. If we students of evolution are ourselves Cultural Creatives, then we ourselves have to evolve in our own communications. Painful as it may feel to intellectuals, we too have to write and propagandize to the rest of our culture, in magazines, radio shows, and cable TV shows designed just for CCs, by CCs.

Most particularly, we must meet face to face, building solidarity as we share our stories, hopes and dreams, and evolving a common banner of who we are, with a realistic hope for the future, and thrashing out together how we want to reinvent this civilization—not just for survival but for our heart's longing. Only if our hearts are engaged with a common vision of what is positive will we know how to avoid the worst negatives, and what to do next: what to organize for; what to plot and scheme for; what and whom to raise money for; to find who will lead us and what churches and communities will serve us, what new kinds of business are suitable, and what new ways of life will suit us.

The role of the human in evolution has become obvious: we too must evolve in our own consciousness, and include ourselves as part of the evolution, not of particular species, but of our planetary biosphere. Evolution is now reflexive, because it includes human knowledge as part of what evolves. It doesn't just happen "out there," but "in here" in our own minds and in our own culture. If we think big about evolution, we must think big about the society that must evolve, and share that knowing. And then we must act big, individually evolving into the elders of our society, and then aiding the collective, or we too will become extinct—from failing to do it. Nothing else will do.

References

Capra, F. (1982). *The turning point: Science, society and the rising culture.* New York: Simon and Schuster.

Chaudhuri, H. (1974). *Being, evolution and immortality: An outline of integral philosophy.* Wheaton, IL: Quest Books.

Darnovsky, M., Epstein, B. and Flacks, R. (Eds.) (1995). *Cultural politics and social movements.* Philadelphia, PA: Temple University Press.

Eisler, R. (1987). *The chalice and the blade.* New York: Harper and Row.

Gebser, J. (1953/1993). *The ever-present origin.* Athens, OH: Ohio University Press (original German, 1953).

Ghose, S. A. (1955). *A practical guide to integral yoga.* Pondicherry, India: Sri Aurobindo Ashram.

—— (1970). *The life divine.* Pondicherry, India: Sri Aurobindo Ashram.

—— (1970). *The human cycle, the ideal of human unity.* Pondicherry, India: Sri Aurobindo Ashram.

Harman, W. (1988). *Global mind change.* Indianapolis, IN: Knowledge Systems, Inc.

Heilbrun, C. (1988). *Writing a woman's life.* New York: Ballantine Books.

Huxley, J. (1964). *Essays of a humanist.* New York: Harper.

Johnston, H. and Klandermans, B. (Eds.) (1995). *Social movements and culture.* Minneapolis, MN: University of Minnesota Press.

Laraña, E., Johnston, H. and Gusfield, J.R. (Eds.) (1994). *New social movements: From ideology to identity.* Philadelphia, PA: Temple University Press.

Laszlo, E. (1994). *The choice: Evolution or extinction?* New York: Tarcher/Putnam.

Lerner, G. (1993). *The creation of feminist consciousness.* New York: Oxford University Press.

Loye, D. (1989). The partnership society: Personal practice. *Futures,* 21, 1 (February), 19–23.

Lyman, S.M. (Ed.) (1995). *Social movements: Critiques, concepts, case-studies.* New York: New York University Press.

McAdam, D., McCarthy, J.D. and Zald, M.N. (Eds.) (1996). *Comparative perspectives on social movements: Political opportunities, mobilizing structures, and cultural framings.* New York: Cambridge University Press.

Meadows, D.H. *et al.* (1972). *The limits to growth.* New York: Universe Books.

—— (1992). *Beyond the limits.* Post Mills, VT: Chelsea Green Publishing.

Melucci, A. (1996). *Challenging codes: Collective action in the information age.* New York: Cambridge University Press.

Polak, F. (1961/1973). *The image of the future.* 2 vols., New York: Oceana Publications; 1 vol. (edited), New York: Jossey-Bass/Elsevier.

Ray, P.H. (1996). *The integral culture survey: A study of the emergence of transformational values in america.* Sausalito, CA: Institute of Noetic Sciences, Research Report 96–A.

—— (1997). The emerging culture. *American Demographics,* February.

Salk, J. (1973). *Survival of the wisest.* New York: HarperCollins.

Simon, J. (Ed.) (1995). *The state of humanity.* Cambridge, MA: Basil Blackwell.

Sorokin, P.A. (1937–41/1962). *Social and cultural dynamics.* 4 vols. New York: Bedminster Press.

Commentary

ERVIN LASZLO

Friend and colleague David Loye and the distinguished contributors to this volume do me great honor in dedicating their work to me. I have read their papers with appreciation, all the more that they reinforced the belief, which on my own I have seriously questioned, that in my intellectual development I have pursued the right path. What this path is the reader can have found out by reading the substance of this volume; yet a brief restatement from my personal point of view may be helpful in disclosing its principal features.

Of the many ideas that crossed my mind in the nearly forty years that I had attempted to work out my thoughts and intuitions in a systematic form, two are the most basic; in a sense they sum up all the rest. The first is that in some ways, not yet clearly understood, all things in this world are linked with all other things. This, of course, is an ancient notion, the counterpart to the notion that all things can be decomposed to their individual parts. Holism and atomism—or organicism and mechanism—have accompanied systematic speculation throughout the last two-and-a-half millennia. But, even if they are not new, I am deeply struck by their contemporary pertinence. How dominant was, at least until recently, the mechanistic-reductionistic mode of thinking—and how vexing were, and still are, its consequences! And how insightful is the holistic-organismic concept, and how very much needed in our times . . . If to nothing else, a dedication to exploring the evidence and the rationale for the latter mode of thinking has always seemed to me a reasonable justification for a lifetime spent in thought about the nature of things.

There is more, however, to the task of thinking out the way things are than the basic holistic-organismic tenet. Account must be taken of the fact that things are not only linked to each other in their current state; they are linked to each other in their joint evolution. With hardly a trace of exaggeration, one can say that there is no evolution in the cosmos but coevolution. Here the prefix "co" applies to the universe in its totality. When we think of all things evolving together, we contemplate the universe evolving as an interlinked whole. This means that there are no relations but internal relations, and that there are no internal relations other than those that map change in the totality of the cosmos.

This, too, is a classic notion: change in the part reflects change in the whole. But it, too, has great pertinence to our times, even if the insight it harbors is independent of our times, as indeed it is independent of any time and any place.

The second intuition that I find fundamental is that this tremendous process of coevolution, though subtle in many of its manifestations, produces critical junctures where the path toward the future branches in various and remarkably underdetermined directions. The whole that evolves is not a deterministic mechanism (it is for this reason that it is not reducible to independent parts), and its evolution is not fated but created—self-created, to be exact. The whole generates its own path of evolution. This is possible in principle: all parts in organismic wholes have that modicum of freedom that translates into influencing, if not entirely creating, their own future together with the future of the whole in which they participate.

In the context of mechanistic thinking, this seems to raise a problem. How can a highly interlinked and interacting whole endow its interlinked and interacting parts with the freedom to make an impact on its own, whole-system evolution? If a whole is determined by its parts, it is not a true whole; and if it is a true whole, it is not determined by its parts.

Phrased in this way we have either/or alternatives that disregard the subtleties of the real world. There is increasing evidence that the whole of this world evolves as the integral coevolution of its parts. Each part, down to the smallest microparticle, charts its way into the future, and the sum total of these charted paths, linked together, makes up the evolution of the whole. The notion may be subtle but it is not metaphysical: a mathematical physicist would point out that a fully coherent ensemble can nevertheless be factorizable to the function of its parts.

The world around us is one, but it is not a monolithic one. Rather, it is a finely tuned one evolving through the interlinkage and interaction of its many individually self-determining parts. This tenet, examined in more detail, has further ramifications. Self-determination in the parts can and indeed is likely to be proportional to their coherence and integration. Parts that more coherently integrate more complex elements are likely to have greater self-determination than simpler and less integrated parts. Autonomy grows with complexity and integration, though it never grows beyond the network of linkages within the larger whole in which it occurs.

The implications for human beings are obvious. We humans, with our complex and integrated brain and organism, are the most complex and integrated chunks of matter–energy, if not in the whole universe, than surely in this biosphere. We are, by that token, also the most autonomous actors in this sphere. But we are not disjoined from the rest of the world. On the contrary, we are linked to our fellow humans and to nature in ever more complex and penetrating ways. For us, as for all coevolving entities, greater freedom does not mean greater independence from our environment but, on the contrary, more varied and far-reaching interactions with it. Through our ever-present linkages and growing autonomy we have a greater impact on the world at large: a greater say in the way the biosphere evolves.

This highlights the facet of our responsibility as a correlate of the facet of our freedom. We have more autonomy than any other system in our planetary habitat, but by that token we also have greater responsibility. While the solar system, the galaxy and the meta-galaxy are likely to continue on their way no matter what we do, our own world, the world of interconnected life with its miraculous adaptations and rise toward complexity and integration, is crucially affected by us. We, minor though real coevolvers in the universe, are major coevolvers on this planet. On the thought- and feeling-processes that dominate our brain and filter through to our behavior depend the fate of our species and of myriad other species, and perhaps of the entire web of planetary life.

The above intuitions—I am now encouraged to think of them as insights—define the leitmotif that has run through my writings for the last several decades. Their elaboration may have been essentially correct or partly flawed. Yet, as long as it constitutes an elaboration of these very insights, it merits being taken seriously. It is with sincere pleasure that I note that the contributors to this volume have taken my insights seriously, and have by and large agreed also with the arguments whereby I attempted to shore them up and spell out their consequences.

A final thought. We are all, especially those of us who have the inclination and the opportunity to reflect on our place and role in the larger scheme of things, evolutionary actors with profound responsibility for our actions. At this critical juncture in human affairs we need to ride out beyond our immediate time and place to chart the branchings ahead, assessing the viability of the paths toward which they open. In the late 20th century AD to be a *Homo* deserving of the name *sapiens* means being an evolutionary outrider. An evolutionary outrider I have tried to be, and try to be still. Evolutionary outriders are also what the contributors to this volume have tried to be—and have succeeded in being splendidly.

EL

December 1997

Introduction to Indexes

As we move out of the 20th into the 21st century, two primary needs for science in relation to evolution theory become increasingly evident. The chapters and perspectives of this book make it evident that: (1) all fields of science need to re-evaluate and re-align themselves to this central source for the grounding of science; and (2) all fields need to cooperate in an expansion of theory that can, in the end, provide both a theory and a story of evolution better fitted to the requirements for the survival of ours and other species in the 21st century and beyond.

The subject index for this book differs considerably from those for 20th-century books on evolution in being specially arranged to serve both of these ends.

A primary consideration in its arrangement has been the question, What kind of evolution theory do the multidisciplinary perspectives of the chapters of this book indicate is needed? What do these chapters indicate are the requirements for the needed expansion of theory?

Most centrally, they indicate the need for a vastly greater incorporation of what is actually of most pressing importance to *our* species, acting on the behalf of *all* species and life itself at the human level. In other words, what do we need in order not only to adequately confront, but also to *solve*, the vast problems that are the responsibility of *our* species at this time?

It seems evident, for example, that there needs to be a new focus on the long-peripheralized data and perspectives on the central evolutionary driver for human agency, the *brain* (as Pribram's chapter articulates). There needs to be more attention to *a theory of cultural evolution* comparable in force and clarity to those prevailing for biological evolution (Eisler, Ceruti and Pievani). The same goes for our bedrock survival activity of economics (Henderson). We need to develop a truly cross-disciplinary and systems-scientific-oriented *general* theory of evolution (Laszlo, GERG members). Other threads for incorporation into an expanding theory of evolution include attention to technology as the extension of the human that can either kill or liberate us (Abraham, Eisler, Henderson, Ceruti and Pievani); the impacts of creativity (Montuori) and values (Ray) as far more important factors in evolution at the human level than the focus on genes that has filled available mind space throughout the 20th century; and the action orientation and the moral orientation so long missing, yet so vital to our species' attainment of its highest potential as well as survival (Laszlo, Loye, Eisler, Henderson, Ceruti and Pievani).

There needs to be both the dedication and the courage to move ahead in one of the most difficult of all areas for both its explorers and its potential users to understand. This is the immensely baffling physics/organism/brain/psychology/sociology/spirituality interface involving the search for answers to questions of anomalies, such as presently controversial psi phenomena, that riddle our current understanding of life and evolution. As explored by Laszlo in QVI-theory and in varying but related ways by Pribram, Bradley, Ho, and Sági, what is the nature of the hidden "holo" fields linking organism to organism across space as well as time? More clear-cut and all-embracing, reflected in chapters by Laszlo, Bradley, Loye, Eisler, Abraham, Montuori, Ray, and Ceruti and Pievani, is the need for the flexibility of systems science and theory (e.g., of chaos and complexity theory as an outgrowth of the systems perspective) to transcend the present prisons of para-digm in the weaving of the adequate evolution theory of the future.

The very word "future," of course, further indicates a crucial and decisive shift of emphasis. During the 20th century, evolution theory—and this understandably, in view of its newness and the prior establishment of natural science—has over-whelmingly involved the data and theories of natural science in focusing on the past. The question has been, How did we get here? While throughout respectful of and committed to retaining the gains of natural science, the chapters and perspect-ives of this book reflect the 21st-century need for a shift of perspective and a new sharing of responsibility to *social science* and a new emphasis upon the *future*. The question becomes, Where is it we should *ideally* be going? And how do we get there?

A Brief Guide to Categories
To serve the above needs of scientists to relate their fields to and help expand evo-lution theory, this subject index groups concepts according to *disciplines*. This should facilitate freer movement across the disciplinary boundaries and between natural and social science, the restrictions on which movement have weakened and blocked advance throughout the 20th century. Thus concepts explored in these chapters are grouped according to identities for the natural sciences (biology, chemistry, paleontology, physics) and social sciences (psychology, sociology, economics, political science, history), as well as the cross-over disciplines (mathematics and systems science).

Also grouped here are observations bearing on some of the major areas for the activities and concerns of life at the human level, which augment the data base for an expansion of evolution theory: e.g., architecture, business, communication, education, family, government, health, religion, spirituality.

A guide to the basic phenomena of evolution itself is provided (see evolution). Here will be found the familiar basics of natural science on which there is wide consensus—e.g., genes and natural selection. But now the reader will also find much that is both new and arresting—and this purposefully to encourage expansion of the creative scientific mind in directions these chapters indicate it must go.

There is another category for *theories* of evolution (see evolution theory). Here again will be found the familiar (neo-Darwinism, sociobiology, the synthetic theory), but also much that is new and mind-expanding in this context (e.g., the three-stage pattern for change of Kurt Lewin's field theory, and the conceptual patterns for Ervin Laszlo's QVI-field theory, Riane Eisler's Cultural Evolution

Theory, and my own Evolutionary Action Theory). Also notable is how the category of *economics* reveals the free-wheeling pattern to the first-rate theorizing of Hazel Henderson in this area, as well as that of Mae-Wan Ho under *organism*.

Throughout, most fundamentally, runs the shift from the 20th-century emphasis on the past and an essentially passive or solely reactive and adaptive organism to a 21st-century emphasis on the future and an essentially active and self-organizing organism driven to self-actualization, as well as driven by both moral and more general goals at the human level.

This becomes particularly dramatic in the case of the explosive spread into the consideration of evolutionary theory for the index categories of *psychology* and *sociology*—currently boxed off within the radical reductionism of sociobiology and an offshoot presently called evolutionary psychology. (Although laden with problems, both subfields arose to address unmet needs. But they hardly figure in these papers, since the purpose for the authors of this book has been to focus on the needs of the future rather than remain bogged down in the controversies of the past.) The reader will further find categories devoted to: the evolutionary thrust of *social movements*; the *world problematique* as a compilation of the enormous problems our species faces at this critical juncture in its development; and *morality* and *ethics* posing the critical factor of personal, social, and cultural guidance. There is also an emphasis on the critical evolutionary involvement, in the categories of *women* and *gender*, of the half of our species so widely neglected in the "old" theory, and on organizations driven by evolutionary ideals, such as the United Nations and its agencies, the Club of Rome, the new Club of Budapest, the Union of Concerned Scientists, and Scientists for Global Responsibility.

The *future* is also a separate category for items of intersecting concern for advanced evolution theorists and futurists, such as projections of the possibilities and probabilities of what lies ahead for our species. In particular, this category includes specific *interventions* for the positive impact of human agency on evolution offered by the authors of this book—or what they variously think and feel we need to do to actualize our potential during, as well as to survive, the 21st century.

DL

Subject Index

Name Index

Abraham, F.D., 146
Abraham, R., 8, 31, 35, 138, 170, 187, 188, 207, 209, 213, 214
Acuna, C., 88
Ahumada, A., 90
Akart, K., 90
Allen, P., 32
Alinsky, S., 176, 188
Alvarez, L., 156
Anderson, J.A., 91
Arias, O., 229
Aristotle, 169, 173
Arthur, W.B., 138, 146
Artigiani, R., 31, 34
Ashby, W.R., 80, 99, 131, 146
Assagioli, R., 176, 188
Atkin, R.H., 146
Atkinson, J.W., 175, 188
Atkinson, R.C., 90
Aurobindo, S.G., 238, 256

Bachofen, J., 162
Baldwin, J.M., 11, 171, 172, 188
Bamforth, K.W., 127, 149
Banathy, B.H., 32, 34
Barchas, J.E., 79, 87
Baron, R., 90
Barrett, F.J., 133, 146
Barrett, P.H., 186, 188
Barrie, J.M., 59, 62, 64
Barron, F., 93, 95, 97, 99, 103
Barton, S., 138, 146
Bateson, G., 93, 96, 97, 100, 103
Beach, F.A., 88
Becker, R.O., 60, 64
Beekman, G.J., 90
Benedict, R., 181, 182, 212
Bergson, H., 53, 64, 175, 188
Berliner, P.F., 133, 146
Berman, A.J., 90
Berry, T., 180, 189
Blau, P.M., 127, 146
Bocchi, G., 35, 97, 100, 103, 101, 158, 164

Bohm, D., 50, 63, 64, 105, 107, 110, 117, 119, 120, 144, 145, 146
Boll, T.J., 90
Bolton, J.S., 65
Boulding, E., 216, 219
Boulding, K., 213, 216, 219
Boutros-Ghali, B., 229
Bracewell, R.N., 85, 87
Bradley, R.T., 7, 9, 10, 68, 76, 112, 117, 118, 123, 128, 130, 132, 134, 136, 137, 139, 142, 143, 144, 145, 146, 148, 187
Brentano, F., 68, 74, 75
Briggs, J.P., 144, 146
Brillouin, L., 78, 87
Brindley, G.S., 71, 87
Brody, B.A., 87
Brooks, C.V., 83, 87
Bucy, P.C., 80, 87
Burt, R.S., 127, 146

Campanella, M., 33
Campbell, D., 172, 188
Cannon, W.B., 70, 79, 87
Capra, F., 5, 39, 86, 87, 173, 188, 210, 216, 219, 232, 238, 255
Carlton, E.H., 73, 90
Carlton-Ford, S., 145, 146
Cavalli Sforza, L., 160, 161
Ceruti, M., 7, 32, 34, 35, 94, 97, 100, 101, 103, 151, 158, 164
Chaisson, E., 31, 34, 35, 180, 188, 207
Chambers, M., 224
Chaudhuri, H., 255
Cherry, C., 144, 146
Childe, V.G., 182
Clarke, A.C., 25
Cobb, J., 223, 224
Collins, J.J., 64
Combs, A., 32, 34, 35, 148, 189
Considine, D.M., 138, 146
Csanyi, V., 2, 11, 30, 32, 34, 35, 98, 104, 107, 172, 175, 176, 186, 187, 197, 207
Csikszentmihalyi, M., 94, 104

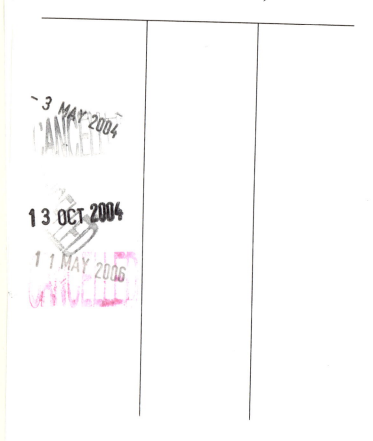
ISBN 0-275-96408-6

90000>

EAN

9 780275 964085

HARDCOVER BAR CODE